MODERN WARPLANES

A technical survey of the world's most significant combat aircraft in service

MODERN WARPLANES

A technical survey of the world's most significant combat aircraft in service

Doug Richardson

CRESCENT BOOKS
New York

A Salamander Book Credits

First English Edition published by Salamander Books Ltd.

This edition is published by Crescent Books, distributed by Crown Publishers, Inc., One Park Avenue, New York, New York 10016, United States of America.

h g f e d c b a

ISBN 0-517-378116

Library of Congress Cataloging in Publication Data

Richardson, Douglas.
    The illustrated encyclopedia of modern warplanes.

    1. Airplanes, Military. I. Title.
UG1240.R53   1902   023.74'0   02-17200

All correspondence concerning the content of this volume should be addressed to Salamander Books Ltd., Salamander House, 27 Old Gloucester Street, London WC1N 3AF, United Kingdom.

Editor: Ray Bonds

Designers: Barry Savage and Mark Holt

Color profiles: © Pilot Press Ltd.; and Terry Hadler, Mike Roffe, Ray Rimell and Steve Archibald, and Tudor Art Studios Ltd. (© Salamander Books Ltd.)

Filmset by Modern Text Typsetting Ltd.

Color reproduction by Bantam Litho Ltd., and Rodney Howe Ltd.

Printed in Belgium by Henri Proost et Cie.

The Author

Doug Richardson is a defense journalist specializing in the fields of aviation, guided missiles and electronics. Editor of *Defence Materiel,* the journal devoted to the British defense industry, he trained initially as an electronics engineer, starting his career as a technician with an R&D team working on avionics for the Buccaneer and the cancelled TSR-2 project.

After an electronics R&D career encompassing such diverse areas as radar, electronic warfare, rocket engine control systems, computers, automatic test equipment and missile trials, he switched to technical journalism and joined the staff of the internationally-respected aerospace journal *Flight International,* where he served as Defense Editor before moving on to become Editor of the international technical defense journal, *Military Technology and Economics.*

He was a co-author of the Salamander book "The Balance of Military Power", and his work has appeared in technical journals such as *International Defense Review, NATO's 15 Nations, Defence, Technologia Militar* and *Wehrtechnik.* In 1981 he edited *Defense Review,* a Chinese-language report on the British defense industry prepared for controlled-circulation in the Chinese Government, industry and armed forces.

Acknowledgements

When a finished book finally appears on the shelves of bookstores, its cover bears only the name of the author, despite the fact that he is only one member of the team whose joint efforts are reflected in the final product.

Working with artist Mike Badrocke is always a pleasure. Few would deny that he is one of the leading aircraft artists; in my opinion he is the best. Without his meticulously researched and executed line drawings illustrating the differences between variants of the same aircraft type, this book would be much less informative.

Bill Gunston's name needs no introduction to most readers, many of his books having become accepted reference works. Having recently tackled volumes on US and Israeli aircraft for Salamander Books, Bill was able to give valuable assistance with the present volume, preparing most of the material on fixed-wing US types as well as the Israeli aircraft.

The publishers and I wish to thank wholeheartedly all the aircraft and weapons systems manufacturers, and the various defense ministry departments for supplying so many dramatic photographs.

Doug Richardson

Contents

Introduction

The modern warplane is one of the most sophisticated machines of late 20th century technology. Advances in aerodynamics, structural engineering, hydraulics, physics, electronics, computing and many other sciences combine to produce an end product often worth more than its weight in gold.

For almost a quarter of a century, military aircraft design had been on a performance plateau. Most of the planned Mach 3 combat types never saw first flight let alone squadron service, while today's F/A-18 Hornet has a lower top speed than the F-4 Phantom it replaces. High agility, advanced avionics and sophisticated weaponry are the important factors in modern combat. Until the 1970s, designers attempting to improve existing aircraft followed the traditional route of adding more powerful engines and better weaponry. Over the last decade, newer avionics and improved data-handling capability have more often been the features added instead of, or at least in addition to, the traditional formula—a process documented in this volume.

Meanwhile new designs continue to appear, while older aircraft are reworked to take advantage of new technology. Most

exotic of these new developments are the US "Stealth" designs, which do not represent a major technological breakthrough in any one field, but embody the results of many projects aimed at reducing or falsifying the radar and infra-red signature of aircraft. Stealth aircraft are likely to feature smooth shapes designed to minimise radar echoing area, materials capable of absorbing rather than reflecting radar energy, devices to suppress the infra-red output of the engines, and advanced ECM systems to confuse tracking radars and missile seeker heads.

Technology-demonstration stealth aircraft have been flying for several years, but new designs are under development—including a Lockheed reconnaissance aircraft probably based on experience obtained during the SR-71 and US lifting-body research and a Northrop strategic bomber.

No evidence of a Soviet equivalent has yet been reported, but a new reconnaissance aircraft (RAM-M) is known to be flying. Similar in concept to the Lockheed TR-1 but with twin vertical tail fins linked with an OV-10-style horizontal boom, this will not attempt to penetrate hostile airspace, but will use sideways-looking

sensors from a patrol line close to the border of the territory under observation.

Other new or improved designs continue to enter Soviet service, including the Foxhound interceptor (formerly known as Super Foxbat) while the Flogger J strike aircraft is the first Soviet type to feature leading-edge extensions.

In Western Europe indecision continues to affect defence planning. Despite many attempts to reconcile national requirements and cost constraints, there seems little chance that the projected British/French/West German "Eurofighter" project will result in even a viable paper design acceptable to all partners, let alone the construction of actual hardware. The European Combat Aircraft (ECA) design proposed in 1980 was a single-seat aircraft with double-delta wings plus canard foreplanes. In parallel with the ECA work, Britain has continued with a series of national design studies such as the twin-RB.199 P.105 tilt-engine ultra-short take-off and landing design, and the P.106 canard-delta, culminating in the P.110 project, which was supported through 1982 by private-venture funding from industry. If a prototype is to be built and flown in a reasonable timescale, Govern-

ment funding will be needed by 1983.

The high cost of aviation fuel has forced economies in all forms of military aviation, including training. Faced with the need to concentrate resources on front-line forces, many operators now require new and fuel-efficient trainers powered by turbofan engines. The USAF has just selected Fairchild to develop the New Generation Trainer, a twin engined design of A-10-like configuration but with side-by-side seating, while Kawasaki is to build its KA-850 design for the JASDF, a twin-turbofan aircraft similar in appearance to Alpha Jet. Even Jugoslavia is turning to turbofan power with its new Super Galeb trainer, an aircraft similar in appearance to the British Aerospace Hawk.

In the field of armed helicopters, the process of experimentation with weaponry continues. There have been few recent sightings of the Soviet AT-6 armed Mil Mi-24 Hind-E but a new version has been observed carrying heavy cannon in fairings on either side of the fuselage. In the UK, Westland has begun work on a new and heavier version of Lynx. Powered by two Rolls-Royce Gem 61 turboshafts, the Lynx 3 will probably be armed with Hellfire missiles, and optional nose-, roof- or mast-mounted locations for sensors and sights are being provided.

Most of the above types may well become the major combat aircraft of the late 1980s, but the purpose of this book is to detail the main combat aircraft in current service or soon to enter service. Propeller-driven trainers have been omitted in order to allow more space for current and future combat types.

Rather than give a detailed description of one variant of each aircraft, this book attempts to follow the development of the types it describes, showing how and sometimes why the design evolved, and highlighting any performance strengths or weaknesses reported by operators. Specifications have been kept to a minimum to allow space for description and the many drawings illustrating the evolution and main features of each design. When converting dimensions or other data from Imperial to metric units or vice versa, the converted figure has been rounded off to the same order of accuracy as that of the original figure. In the case of well-known weapons such as the 7.62mm machine gun or 2.75-inch rocket, no conversion is given since the calibre in mm or inches is for all practical purposes the weapon designation. Although engine thrusts should be expressed in Newtons or kiloNewtons in the metric system, this book uses the better-known kilogram, since the latter will be more familiar to many readers than the Newton. (To convert rating in kg to kN, multiply by 0.00098).

Aircraft are listed in alphabetical order of manufacturers' names, but to avoid such horrors of designation as the Rockwell International F-100 Super Sabre or the British Aerospace Shackleton, the manufacturer's name quoted for types no longer in production is generally that under which they are best known or under which most were built.

Doug Richardson

Aeritalia G.91

Type: light strike fighter.
Specifications: length, 38ft 3in (11.67m); span, 29ft 6in (8.99m); height, 14ft 6in (4.43m); weight (normal take-off), 17,150lb (7,800kg).
Maximum speed: Mach 0.95.
Service ceiling: 41,000ft (12,500m).
Range: 324nm (600km).
Armament: two 30mm DEFA cannon plus up to 4,000lb (1,815kg).
Powerplant: two General Electric J85-13A turbojets, each rated at 2,725lb (1,235kg) dry thrust, 4,080lb (1,850kg) with afterburner.

This lightweight fighter is nearing the end of its operational career with the air arms which originally adopted it. Variants in current service are the R/1, R/3 and R/4 single-seat fighters, the T two-seat trainer, and the twin-engined Y model. The R/1 was the original version which first entered Italian service in 1958. One undoubted weakness of this version was the limited armament of four 0.5in Colt—Browning machine guns and up to 500lb (230kg) of external ordnance, weaponry more suited to the needs of 1938 than 1958. Germany opted for the more advanced R/3 and R/4 models, equipped with two 30mm DEFA cannon plus up to 1,000lb (450kg) of external stores, a strengthened structure and a Doppler radar.

German examples were phased out in the early 1980s as the Alpha Jet entered service, but the Italian fleet will remain operational until the AM-X fighter enters service in the late 1980s.

Although small in number, Portugal's G.91 fleet is still that nation's only useful interceptor, since plans to procure the Northrop F-5E had to be abandoned. In 1976, to keep the force effective, Portugal obtained 14 G.91R/3 and R/4 aircraft plus six G.91T trainers from the West German Luftwaffe to supplement the surviving 14 R/4 fleet. A further 12 followed from the same source in April 1980. All have been fitted with AIM-9 Sidewinders and a computerised weapon-delivery system. So short of aircraft is Portugal that in the late 1970s some G.91s were used as maritime patrol aircraft.

By the early 1960s the aircraft was becoming distinctly dated, so Fiat—later to become part of Aeritalia—began work on the G.91Y version, which substituted two afterburning General Electric J85-GE-13E turbojets for the single Bristol Orpheus used in the earlier variants. Commonality may have suffered, but maximum installed thrust rose from 5,000lb (2,270kg) to 8,160lb (3,700kg), maximum payload was now a useful 4,000lb (1,800kg), while the low-level combat radius increased from 196 miles (315km) to 372 miles (600km). This version was only produced by Italy.

Aeritalia G.222

Type: tactical transport
Specifications: length, 74ft 5in (22.7m); span, 94ft 2in (28.7m); height, 32ft 1in (9.8m); weight (maximum take-off); 61,700lb (28,000kg).
Maximum speed: 291kt (540km/hr).
Range: 1,300nm (2,410km).
Maximum payload: 19,800lb (9,000kg).
Powerplant: two General Electric T64-GE-P4D turboprops each rated at 3,400 shp (2,535kW).

Development of the G.222 twin-engined transport was protracted. The aircraft first flew in 1970, but a production order was not placed until 1974. Service deliveries started in 1975.

Prototype aircraft were unpressurised and powered by two General Electric CT64-820 turbo-prop engines, but production examples were pressurised and fitted with the more powerful T64-P4D driving three-blade propellers.

Conceived as a replacement for the ageing C-119 piston-engined transport, the G.222 can carry up to 19,800lb (9,000kg) of freight, 32 troops, 42 paratroops or 36 stretchers. The main cabin has a large side door on the port side, plus a hydraulically operated tail ramp and upward swing door. Both may be used by parachutists.

This basic aircraft was ordered by the air arms of Italy, Argentina, Dubai and Somalia. Faced with a

Above: T64-powered G.222 transport of the Italian Air Force.

US Government embargo on the supply of General Electric T64 engines to Libya, Aeritalia opted in 1978 to develop a new version powered by a derated version of the Rolls-Royce Tyne. This allowed operation at higher gross weights but involved designing new engine nacelles and wing attachment points and improving the undercarriage to handle the higher weight. One theoretical disadvantage of the British engine is its higher fuel consumption, but in practice this is offset by the ability to save fuel by cruising at 30,000ft (9,150m) rather than the 25,000ft (7,600m) of the standard version. Empty weight of the Tyne-powered aircraft is some 7,500lb

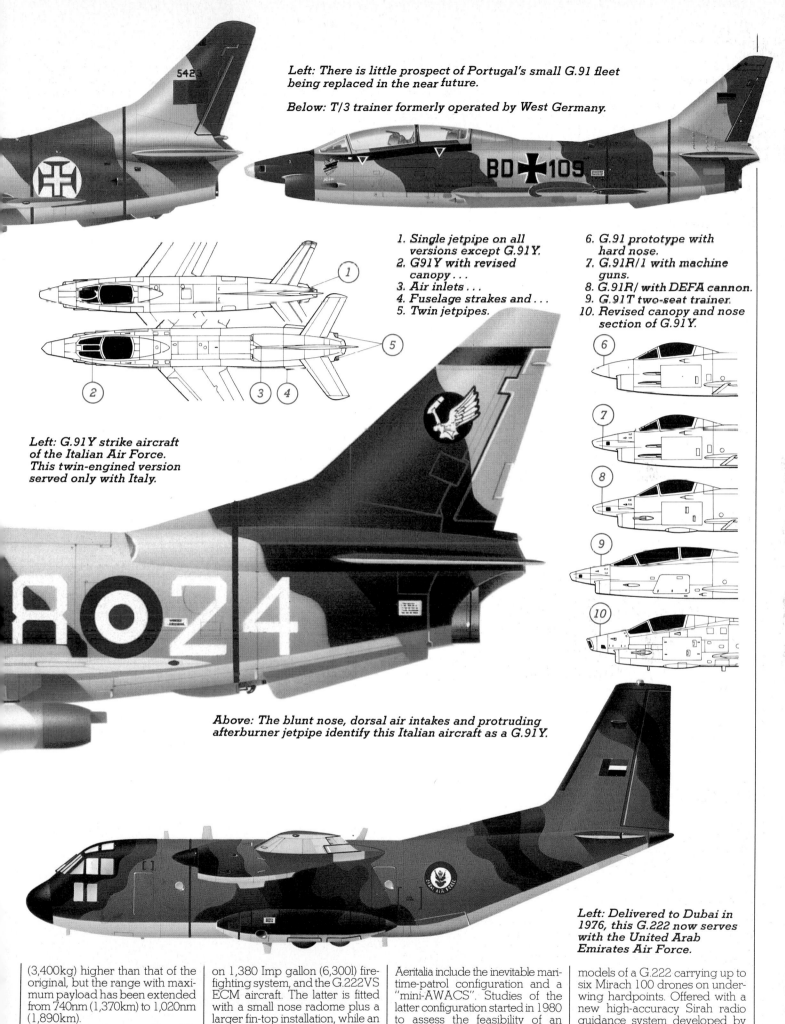

Left: There is little prospect of Portugal's small G.91 fleet being replaced in the near future.

Below: T/3 trainer formerly operated by West Germany.

1. Single jetpipe on all versions except G.91Y.
2. G91Y with revised canopy . . .
3. Air inlets . . .
4. Fuselage strakes and . . .
5. Twin jetpipes.

6. G.91 prototype with hard nose.
7. G.91R/1 with machine guns.
8. G.91R/ with DEFA cannon.
9. G.91T two-seat trainer.
10. Revised canopy and nose section of G.91Y.

Left: G.91Y strike aircraft of the Italian Air Force. This twin-engined version served only with Italy.

Above: The blunt nose, dorsal air intakes and protruding afterburner jetpipe identify this Italian aircraft as a G.91Y.

Left: Delivered to Dubai in 1976, this G.222 now serves with the United Arab Emirates Air Force.

(3,400kg) higher than that of the original, but the range with maximum payload has been extended from 740nm (1,370km) to 1,020nm (1,890km).

Several versions are currently available, including G.222RM for navaid calibration, the G.222 SAMA (Sistema Aeronautico Modulare Antincendio) with a bolt-on 1,380 Imp gallon (6,300l) firefighting system, and the G.222VS ECM aircraft. The latter is fitted with a small nose radome plus a larger fin-top installation, while an upgraded generating system provides the 40kW of electrical power which is needed by the cabin-mounted electronic equipment racks.

Other variants offered by Aeritalia include the inevitable maritime-patrol configuration and a "mini-AWACS". Studies of the latter configuration started in 1980 to assess the feasibility of an airborne early-warning platform for the Italian Air Force.

One other potential role is that of RPV parent aircraft. The Italian company Meteor has displayed models of a G.222 carrying up to six Mirach 100 drones on underwing hardpoints. Offered with a new high-accuracy Sirah radio guidance system developed by Pacific Aerosystem, this combination could prove an attractive and relatively inexpensive reconnaissance system for Third World operators.

Aeritalia/Aermacchi/Embraer AM-X

Type: light strike fighter.
Specifications: length, 44ft 6in (13.57m); span, 29ft 1in (8.88m); height, 15ft 0in (4.58m); weight (maximum take-off), 26,455lb (12,000kg).
Max speed: Mach 0.95?
Range: see text.
Armament: 3,800kg of external stores, two heat-seeking missiles, plus one 20mm Vulcan cannon (Italy) or two 30mm DEFA cannon (Brazil).
Powerplant: turbofan rated at one Rolls-Royce Spey 807 11,030lb (5,010kg) dry thrust.

The AM-X concept dates back to 1977, when Aeritalia began design studies into a potential replacement for the G.91 and G.91Y fighters. By 1979 the Italian Air Force was funding project definition work. A year later the Brazilian aircraft company Embraer joined forces with Aeritalia and Aermacchi to initiate joint development and production. Embraer will develop and manufacture the wing, while the fuselage is split between Aermacchi (cockpit section and nose) and Aeritalia (centre and rear fuselage). Italy requires 187 examples, while the Brazilian air force plans to procure 100. The first of seven prototypes is due to fly by early 1984 and service deliveries are expected to begin in 1987.

Baseline specification calls for an aircraft capable of carrying a 3,000lb (1,350kg) ordnance load over a lo-lo-lo tactical radius of 180nm (330km). The aircraft must be able to fly this sortie at a height of only 200ft (61m) all the way, and have sufficient fuel for a 50nm (93km) dash at Mach 0.8 during the run in to the target Brazil requires a tactical radius of around 500nm (930km), but this will not be flown at low level.

In 1978, after an analysis of several potential powerplants for single and twin-engined AM-X designs, the Italian Air Force selected a non-afterburning version of the Rolls-Royce Spey rather than any of the more modern turbofans. In order to lift the specified warload out of short strips—such as poorly equipped or even damaged runways—without the aid of an afterburner, the wing will be fitted with Fowler-type double slotted flaps and full-span slats. The latter could also be deployed in combat to increase manoeuvrability. Roll control will be by means of ailerons and overwing spoilers, which will also serve both as airbrakes and as lift dumpers. Four underwing pylons will be fitted, the inner pair being plumbed for use with external tanks to meet the Brazilian range requirement. Sidewinder-class heat-seeking missiles may be carried on wingtip launch rails. A fifth hardpoint is to be mounted beneath the fuselage.

Most of the avionics will be located in bays beneath and ahead of the cockpit, locations chosen so that technicians will not require platforms or ladders. A range-only radar will be mounted in the extreme nose for air-to-air and air-to-ground use. The cockpit design would give good downward visibility over the nose, and contain two displays for weapon and navigation data—the main HUD and a second smaller unit. Navigation will be inertial.

The flight control system will use a mixture of mechanical actuation and fly-by-wire. Should the electrically controlled wing spoilers fail, for example, the pilot will still have roll control via the mechanically actuated ailerons. Should one system fail, the other would have sufficient authority to allow the aircraft to be flown safely back to base.

For reconnaissance missions AM-X may be fitted with three types of pallet-mounted camera systems or an external camera pod. ECM systems will be internally mounted, including a RWR. Studies of a two-seat version have been carried out but no formal requirement exists. The extra seat would be housed without stretching the fuselage, and could be used for advanced training or ECM operations.

Aermacchi MB.326

Data for MB.326G
Type: basic and advanced trainer
Specifications: length, 34ft 11in (10.85m); span, 35ft 7in (10.85m); height, 12ft 2in (3.72m); weight (maximum loaded), 10,090lb (4,577kg).
Max speed: (clean) 468kt (867km/hr).
Service ceiling: 47,000ft (14,320m).
Range: 998nm (1850km).
Armament: see text.
Powerplant: one Rolls-Royce Viper 20 turbojet rated at 3,410lb (1,550kg) dry thrust.

One of the most successful jet trainer projects since the veteran T-33 has been the Aermacchi MB.326. Operated by a total of 12 nations and built on four production lines in Italy, Australia, Brazil and South Africa, the MB.326 offered high performance at a reasonable price. For some Third World operators, such as Dubai, Ghana, Paraguay, and Tunisia, the aircraft forms the first-line combat strength of the local air arm. A total of more than 780 had been built as this book was in preparation, with production continuing in Brazil and South Africa.

The maximum external ordnance load of 4,000lb (1,800kg) may seem small by modern standards, but represents some 30 per cent of the maximum take-off weight. An impressive array of stores may be carried, including gun and rocket pods, "iron" bombs, AS.11 or AS.12 wire-guided missiles or even heat-seeking air-to-air missiles such as the R.550 Magic.

The MB.326 handles well in the air, the controls being light and responsive, while the design is both manoeuvrable and vice-free. Its practical internal layout makes for easy maintenance. The view from the rear cockpit is poor by current standards, but this is a criticism which may be levelled at many of its contemporaries too. The basic configuration was developed in the mid-1950s and the prototype first flew in December 1957.

Throughout its development history, the MB.326 has been powered by the Rolls-Royce Viper; progressively more powerful engines have followed since the 2,500lb (1,130kg) Viper 11 was fitted to the original Italian Air Force MB.326s and to such various export versions as the MB.326D and M unarmed trainers and the B, F and H armed variants. South Africa initially took delivery of 40 MB.326M aircraft before setting up a local production line for the type, known as the Impala Mk 1 to the SAAF.

In 1967 the first "second-generation" MB.326G took the air, powered by the 3,410lb (1,550kg) Viper 20, and having minor structural modifications in

Above: The MB.326 flies with jettisonable wingtip fuel tanks.

order to cope with the resulting increase in performance. Most customers bought the GB armed version, and the broadly similar MB.326GC was built in Brazil by Embraer as the AT-26 Xavante.

By switching to the even more powerful Viper 632-43 of 4,000lb (1,800kg) thrust, Aermacchi were able to offer the single-seat MB.326K light-attack aircraft from 1970 onwards. By eliminating the rear cockpit, designers were able to more than double the internal fuel capacity—an extra 189 Imperial gallons (878l)—and add two 30mm DEFA cannon plus 250 rounds of ammunition. The airframe was further strengthened, and the ailerons were servo-assisted to improve low-altitude handling. Experience with this model—built by Atlas in South Africa as the Impala Mk 2—allowed Aermacchi to offer the MB.326L two-seat attack/training version.

Below: Italy will use its AM-X fleet to handle the close-support and interdiction task. It will also be used for strikes against enemy air bases, supplementing the longer-ranged Tornado. Brazilian aircraft will be similar in appearance to the Italian version, changes being largely confined to avionics and weaponry. The canopy gives good rearward visibility, an essential quality for an aircraft which may have to take part in air-to-air combat.

Above: The Embraer AT-26 Xavante is a licence-built MB.326GC with alternative avionics.

Left: The Royal Australian Air Force has used the MB.326H as its advanced trainer since 1968.

Left: The MB.326K light strike aircraft features:
1. Revised cockpit and canopy.
2. Firing port for 30mm DEFA cannon.

Below: Zaire operates 12 MB.326GB two-seater trainers plus six single-seat MB.326K attack aircraft.

Aermacchi MB.339

Data for MB.339A
Type: basic and advanced trainer.
Specifications: length, 36ft 0in (10.97m); span, 35ft 7in (10.86m); height, 11ft 10in (3.6m); weight (clean take-off), 9,700lb (4,400kg).
Max speed: 485kt (898km/hr).
Service ceiling: 48,000ft (14,630m).
Range: (hi-lo-hi with four Mk 82 bombs) 320nm (593km).
Armament: up to 4,000lb (1,820kg) of external ordnance.
Powerplant: one Rolls-Royce Viper Mk 632-43 turbojet rated at 4,000lb (1,820kg) dry thrust.

In creating the MB.339A trainer Aermacchi were able to draw on the experience gained from the MB.326 series, and, wherever possible, components from the earlier design were adopted for the new trainer. The forward fuselage was given a modern "humped" appearance to allow the instructor's seat in the rear cockpit to be raised, while the size of the vertical tail surface was increased to maintain the handling qualities.

After a series of Aermacchi design studies which considered the merits of single and twin-engine configurations with engines such as the Viper, Adour and Larzac, the Italian Air Force decided to stay with the well-tried Viper, selecting the same 632-43 version as was used in the MB.326K and L. This may burn more fuel than a modern turbofan such as the Adour, but Aermacchi were pleased with the Viper's safety record in the earlier MB.326 and by its proven ability to take the roughest handling which students can subject it to.

This retention of commonality with the MB.326 has resulted in a performance penalty, since the resulting performance cannot rival that of all-new designs such as Hawk, but the price-tag for the end product may be much nearer what many operators are prepared to pay for a trainer, both in terms of purchase price and operating costs. At time of writing a basic unit cost of only $3.5 million was quoted.

Although based on the airframe of the MB.326K attack aircraft, a design already toughened to resist the stresses of combat flying, the MB.339 structure is further strengthened and improved. The wing leading-edge box has been stiffened, while the entire airframe has been simplified in detail to facilitate production.

Given the sales success of the single-seat MB.326K, development of a dedicated strike version of the two-seat MB.339A was an obvious move. The MB.339K Veltro 2 (Greyhound) revives the name of one of the Macchi 205V propeller-driven fighters of World War II fame, and was flown in prototype form in May 1980. Armament includes two internal DEFA 30mm cannon plus the six underwing hardpoints which are standard on the two-seater. Despite the revised forward fuselage section, the Veltro has 85 per cent commonality with the two-seat A model. The prototypes used a Marconi Avionics AD-620C radio/dead-reckoning navigation system and a Saab-Scania RGS2/2A lead-computing sight, but production aircraft will have an avionics fit dictated by the customer. Advanced features such as a nav/attack system with a HUD, and internal ECM would be possible.

Aermacchi has already flown the MB.339 with a pod-mounted Elettronica ECM system, and drawn up plans for the installation of an RWR system and dispensers for chaff and flares. Such

Aero L-29 Delfin

Type: basic trainer
Specifications: length, 35ft 5in (10.81m); span, 33ft 9in (10.29m); height, 10ft 3in (3.13m); weight (maximum take-off), 7,230lb (3,280kg).
Max speed: 354kt (655km/hr).
Service ceiling: 36,100ft (11,000m).
Range: 345nm (640km).
Armament: see text.
Powerplant: one Motorlet M 701 or S-50 turbojet rated at 1,960lb (890kg) dry thrust.

In the autumn of 1961 the Warsaw Pact held a fly-off to select a standard basic jet trainer for use by all members of the Warsaw Pact alliance. Given the history of Warsaw Pact aircraft procurement, selection of the Soviet type might have seemed a foregone conclusion, but in fact the Czechoslovakian Aero L-29 Delfin was adopted. Production began in 1963 and over the next 12 years more than 3,600 examples were built.

By modern standards the L-29 (NATO reporting name "Maya") seems dated, a situation reflected in poor sales results on the open market. All Pact allies except Poland operate the Delfin, but the only other sales scored were to Egypt, Guinea, Nigeria, Syria and Uganda. Total export sales were probably no more than 200 aircraft.

Performance of the L-29 is modest. Emphasis in the original Warsaw Pact specification lay in demands for simple maintenance and the ability to use grass strips. A top speed of only 350+kt (650+km/hr) was demanded, and the Delfin in practice manages 353kt (655km/hr)—well below the 400 to 450kt (740 to 830km/hr) achieved by Western types. This low performance is partly due to the low thrust of the L-29 engine—either a 1,960lb (890kg) Motorlet M 701 or S-50 turbojet of indigenous design. Like most of its contemporaries, the L-29 has an empty weight of around 2.5 tonnes, but has only about two-thirds the thrust.

Several variants were devised, including L-29A Akrobat single-seat aerobatic aircraft and the two-seat L-29R light-strike version with underwing stores and a nose-mounted camera. Neither saw large-scale production, but the presence of two underwing hardpoints of 200lb (90kg) capacity gave the standard aircraft a minimal but usable ground-attack capability. The aircraft is not fitted with internal guns, but can carry 7.62mm gun pods.

In general terms the L-29 meets the requirement to which it was designed, being able to operate from the roughest of Warsaw Pact airstrips, but the limited performance must make transition to advanced trainers difficult. Like such contemporary designs as the MB.326, Galeb and TS-11 Iskra, the view from the rear cockpit is poor. It is hardly surprising that most operators are now phasing the type out of service.

equipment could be used defensively to protect the aircraft or else in the training role to allow the MB.339 to act as a "friendly enemy" during the training of ECM and radar operators.

To improve the performance of the Veltro, Rolls-Royce has proposed the use of the new Viper 645, whose faster-rotating shaft and greater mass flow offer a useful 12 per cent extra thrust. Longer-term developments of the basic Veltro design are likely to include increased internal fuel and all-new engine—perhaps the two-shaft Garrett/Volvo TFE1042—or even a new super-critical wing.

Left: One of the prototype MB.339s demonstrating its capability in the weapon training role.

Below: Italian Air Force MB.339 trainer.

1. Single-seat cockpit of the MB.339K Veltro 2.
2. 30mm DEFA cannon and underwing hardpoints on the Veltro 2.

Below: Built in Czechoslovakia, the L-29 Delfin is used by other Warsaw Pact air forces, including (as here) that of Hungary.

Left: With flaps down an L-29 Delfin of the East German AF comes into land. The later L-39 is replacing this older aircraft.

Below: Egypt uses the L-29 for basic training and ground attack; 100 remain in service.

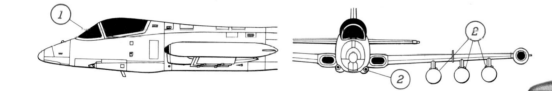

Aero L-39 Albatros

Type: basic trainer.
Specifications: length, 40ft 5in (12.32m); span, 31ft 0in (9.46m); height, 15ft 5in (4.72m); weight (take-off), 10,075lb (4,570kg).
Max speed: 420kt (780km/hr).
Service ceiling: 11,500ft (3,350m).
Range: 460nm (850km).
Armament: see text.
Powerplant: one Walter Titan turbojet rated at 3,790lb (1,720kg) dry thrust.

First flight of the L-39, successor to the L-29 Delfin, took place on 4 November 1968, but production deliveries did not begin until late 1972. Part of this delay seems to have been caused by the engine installation. In order to cope with the increased weight of the new design, Aero engineers selected the Ivchenko AI-25-TL two-shaft turbofan of 3,790lb (1,720kg) thrust, an uprated version of the engine which powers the Yak-40 feederliner. This engine is locally manufactured by Motorlet. In the course of development the L-39 intakes were increased in size and lengthened, indicative of powerplant/intake compatibility problems.

The increased thrust is partly offset by the heavier weight of the new design. Maximum speed at altitude is only 420kt (780km/hr),

while the sea-level rate of climb is only 4,330ft/min (1.320m/min)—some two-thirds that of the MB.339 and less than 40 per cent that of Alpha Jet (admittedly a more modern aircraft). Two ventral air brakes are automatically extended as the airspeed nears Mach 0.8.

Internal fuel capacity is 232 Imperial gallons (1,055l), contained in five bag tanks within the fuselage, supplemented by the contents of two wingtip tanks each holding 22 Imperial gallons (100l). These wingtip tanks are non-jettisonable, and also house the taxiing lights. Up to 20 seconds of inverted flight is possible.

In 1972 the L-39 was selected as an L-29 replacement by the Soviet Union, Czechoslovakia and East Germany. Service deliveries began in 1974. Like the earlier L-29, the L-39 has had limited export success beyond the "captive market" of the Warsaw Pact. Afghanistan, Iraq and Libya have bought a total of less than 100 examples, and Iraq is known to be shopping for a more advanced aircraft in the Hawk/Alpha

Jet class. Low performance plus the poor view from the rear cockpit have probably told against the type.

Three versions have been produced. Standard two-seat trainer is the L-39C, but the L-39ZO armed version bought by Iraq and Libya has reinforced wings with a total of four hardpoints. Definitive attack version is the L-39Z, with reinforced wing and undercarriage, plus a ventrally mounted GSh-23 gun pack with a total of 150 rounds. An ASP-3 NMu-39Z gyro gunsight is provided in the front cockpit.

The Z version has four underwing hardpoints. All can carry weapons, but the inboard pylons can handle 33 or 77 Imperial gallon (150 or 350l) drop tanks. The inboard hardpoints are stressed to handle loads of up to 1,100lb (500kg), while the outboard pylons can take up to 550lb (250kg) each. Weaponry

which can be carried includes bombs, 16-round UB-16-57 rocket-launchers, a daylight reconnaissance pod containing five cameras (port inboard pylon only) and AA-2 Atoll heat-seeking air-to-air missiles (outboard pylons). The L-39 forms part of a training system comprising the TL-39 flight simulator, the AKZ-KL-39 vehicle-mounted automatic test equipment and the NK-TL-29/39 ejection seat training rig.

Aérospatiale SA.316B/SA.319B Alouette III

Data for Alouette III
Type: multi-role utility helicopter.
Specifications: length, 32ft 11in (10.03m); height, 9ft 10in (3.0m); rotor diameter, 36ft 2in (11.02m); weight (maximum take-off), 4,850lb (2,200kg).
Max speed: 113kt (210km/hr).
Range: 290nm (540km).
Powerplant: one Turboméca Artouste IIIB turboshaft rated at 570shp (425kW).

More than 60 nations operate the Alouette I or II helicopter, making it by far the most successful European rotary-wing design. The original Alouette II was developed by the Sud Aviation company and flew on 12 March 1955. Powered by the 360shp (270kW)

Turboméca Artouste II turboshaft engine, the design was a simple yet effective five-seat aircraft. A thousand were built before production ended in 1975.

The SE 3160 Alouette III, which flew four years later, is a larger design whose cabin seats seven. Powerplant in this case is the Artouste IIIB derated to 570shp (425kW), giving the aircraft a higher performance. This aircraft remained in production until 1969. A strengthened transmission, greater all-up weight and heavier payload marked the SA.316B version, which first flew in June 1968, and two years later became the main production version, supplanting the SE 3160. Optional armament includes a 7.62mm machine-gun plus 1,000

rounds of ammunition, a 20mm MG 151/20 cannon, 68mm rocket pods, and four AS.11 or two AS.12 wire-guided air-to-surface missiles, plus the associated stabilised sight.

The search for additional power gave rise to two further variants. The SA 315B Lama combines a modified and strengthened Alouette II airframe with the engine, rotor and other dynamic components of the Alouette III.

This combination results in a machine ideally suited to "hot and high" conditions, and is licence-built in India as the Hindustan Aeronautics Cheetah. Assembly by HAL, using imported French components, began in 1972, but by 1976-7 aircraft were being built from scratch. HAL also manufactures the SA 316B under the designation Chetak, and has produced an armed version equipped with boom-mounted air-to-surface

Below left: French Aéronavale Alouette III used for SAR and carrier plane-guard duties.

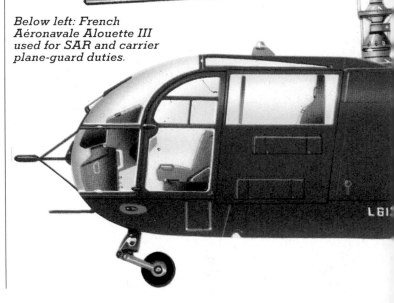

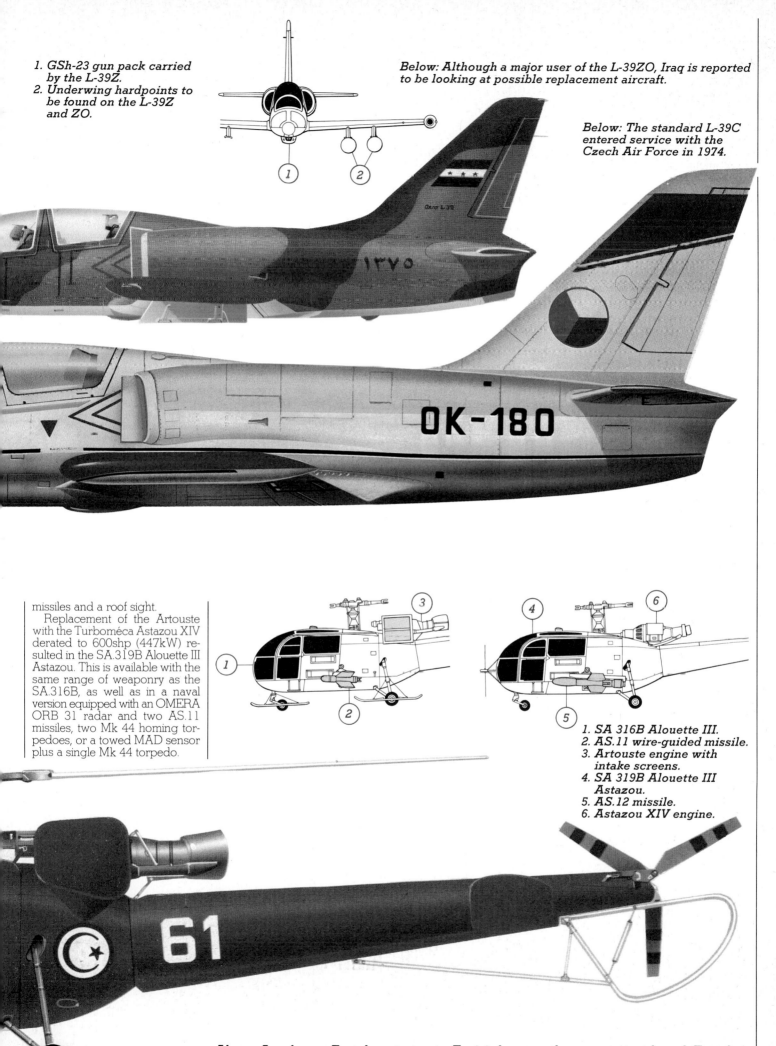

1. GSh-23 gun pack carried by the L-39Z.
2. Underwing hardpoints to be found on the L-39Z and ZO.

Below: Although a major user of the L-39ZO, Iraq is reported to be looking at possible replacement aircraft.

Below: The standard L-39C entered service with the Czech Air Force in 1974.

OK-180

missiles and a roof sight.

Replacement of the Artouste with the Turboméca Astazou XIV derated to 600shp (447kW) resulted in the SA.319B Alouette III Astazou. This is available with the same range of weaponry as the SA.316B, as well as in a naval version equipped with an OMERA ORB 31 radar and two AS.11 missiles, two Mk 44 homing torpedoes, or a towed MAD sensor plus a single Mk 44 torpedo.

1. SA 316B Alouette III.
2. AS.11 wire-guided missile.
3. Artouste engine with intake screens.
4. SA 319B Alouette III Astazou.
5. AS.12 missile.
6. Astazou XIV engine.

Above: As a former French protectorate, Tunisia has over the years recieved much French aid, including six Alouette IIIs (SA.316B liaison helicopter shown here) and the earlier Alouette IIs.

Aérospatiale CM.170 Magister

Data for CM.170
Type: basic trainer.
Specifications: length, 33ft 0in (10.06m); span, 39ft 10in (12.15m); height, 9ft 2in (2.8m); weight (normal take-off), 6,835lb (3,100kg).
Max speed: 386kt (715km/hr).
Service ceiling: 36,100ft (11,000m).
Range: 500nm (940km).
Armament: see text.
Powerplant: two Turboméca Marbore IIA turbojets each rated at 880lb (400kg) dry thrust.

Even by jet-trainer standards, the C.170 is a lightweight, tipping the scales at a mere 4,740lb (2,150kg) when empty and 7,055lb (3,200kg) at maximum take-off weight. The design had two unusual features—twin engines and a "butterfly" or "vee" tail having only two diagonally inclined surfaces.

Most basic trainers present the pupil pilot with only a single engine to look after, but the Magister started service life with two Turboméca Marbore IIA turbojets of 880lb (400kg) thrust each. The later Super Magister version used two 1,058lb (480kg) Marbore VIs engines.

In a "butterfly" tail both surfaces act in pitch and yaw, but each surface must carry higher tail loads than with a conventional tail assembly. For this reason the configuration is rarely used, but at the limited speed range of the Magister it works efficiently enough.

The Magister has acquired the reputation of being a "pilot's aeroplane", with good handling qualities. It was widely exported, a total of 916 being built on three production lines in West Germany, Finland and Israel.

Basic French Air Force variant was the CM.170, but the tail-hooked CM.175 Zephyr was developed for Aéronavale carrier training. Two 7.5mm or 7.62mm machine-guns could be mounted in the nose, complete with 200 rounds of ammunition per gun. Underwing hardpoints were provided for stores, although the aircraft's light weight resulted in a small payload. Two 55lb (25kg) bombs or two 18-round launch pods for 37mm rockets could be carried. Despite these limitations, the Israeli Air Force made large-scale use of the type in the light-attack role during the 1967 Middle East war. The aircraft proved effective, but casualties were heavy.

In the late 1970s an attempt was made to upgrade the basic design in the hope of winning a Magister-replacement contract from the French Air Force. A revised front fuselage provided the stepped tandem seating now widely favoured for trainers, while the engine bays were redesigned to house two Turboméca Astafan IIg turbofans of 1,740lb (790kg) thrust. Four wing hardpoints were provided—two with 330lb (150kg) capacity and two rated at 550lb (250kg). No domestic or export orders were forthcoming, despite the low price, so development was suspended after a single prototype had flown.

Bedek Aviation Amit
Israel has launched its own revised Magister—the Bedek Aviation Amit. This is a refurbished CM.175 with a new cockpit and ejector seats, replacement hydraulic and electrical systems, new avionics and Marbore VI turbojets. IDFAF Magisters are being re-worked as Amits.

Below: Two-seat Magisters of an Armée de l'Air training unit. This is one of the few V-tailed aircraft in service.

Aérospatiale SA.321 Super Frelon

Data for SA 321G
Type: heavy-duty helicopter.
Specifications: fuselage length, 63ft 8in (19.4m); height 22ft 2in (6.76m); rotor diameter, 62ft 0in (18.9m); weight (maximum take-off), 28,660lb (13,000kg)
Max cruising speed: 134kt (248km).
Range: 440nm (815km).
Maximum payload: 11,000lb (5,000kg).
Powerplant: three Turboméca Turmo IIIC turboshafts each rated at 1,570shp (1,170kW).

Although an Aérospatiale design, Super Frelon was developed in co-operation with Sikorsky, who assisted in the design of the rotor systems, and Fiat, who tackled the main gearbox and transmission. The end-product is the largest helicopter to be built in quantity in Western Europe. The prototype flew on 28 May 1963, and production began two years later. By the end of 1980, 99 aircraft had been sold, and most had been delivered. The future of the line depends on fresh customers coming forward for this 13-tonne aircraft, which has already been exported to China, Iran, Iraq, Israel, Libya and South Africa.

Five military versions have been developed, along with the civil SA 321F. Most numerous is the SA 321Ja utility version, able to carry up to 8,800lb (4,000kg) of cargo or 27 passengers in its cabin, or external loads of up to 11,000lb (5,000kg). The broadly similar 321L is operated by the South African Air Force.

Israel's 321K force was ordered to provide a heavy-lift transport capability, but has been used in the assault role. On 29 December 1968 Israeli Super Frelons took part on the raid on Beirut airport, and were also used on 26 December 1969 during a commando raid against Egypt to airlift a captured Soviet P-12 "Spoon Rest" radar. IDFAF Super Frelons carried assault forces and demolition squads on deep-penetration raids into Egypt against Mag Hammadi power station and the Quena dam on 31 October 1968, and on a 36-hour raid against the island of Shadwan in the Gulf of Suez on 22 January 1970. Israel is currently re-engining its Super Frelon fleet with 1,870shp (1,394kW) General Electric T58-16 engines.

The 321G ASW version was the first to enter production. It carries a 360 degree search radar, Doppler navigation radar, dunking sonar and up to four homing torpedoes. French Navy examples are being updated: the earlier ORB Heracles I radar is being replaced by the more powerful Heracles II. This version serves with Flottille 32F and includes among its duties the "de-lousing" of French navy ballistic-missile submarines as these vessels leave port to begin operational patrols.

During the recent war with Iran, Iraqi Super Frelons armed with AM.39 Exocet missiles are reported to have been used in combat against Iranian fast-attack craft, sinking at least one vessel. Libya operates the SA 321M.

Left: Attached to the side of this Aéronavale SA.321G Super Frelon operating as a trials aircraft is a sea-skimming AM39 Exocet anti-shipping missile. This version of the helicopter is operated by Flot.32F based at Lanveoc-Poulmic. A total of 24 machines were built.

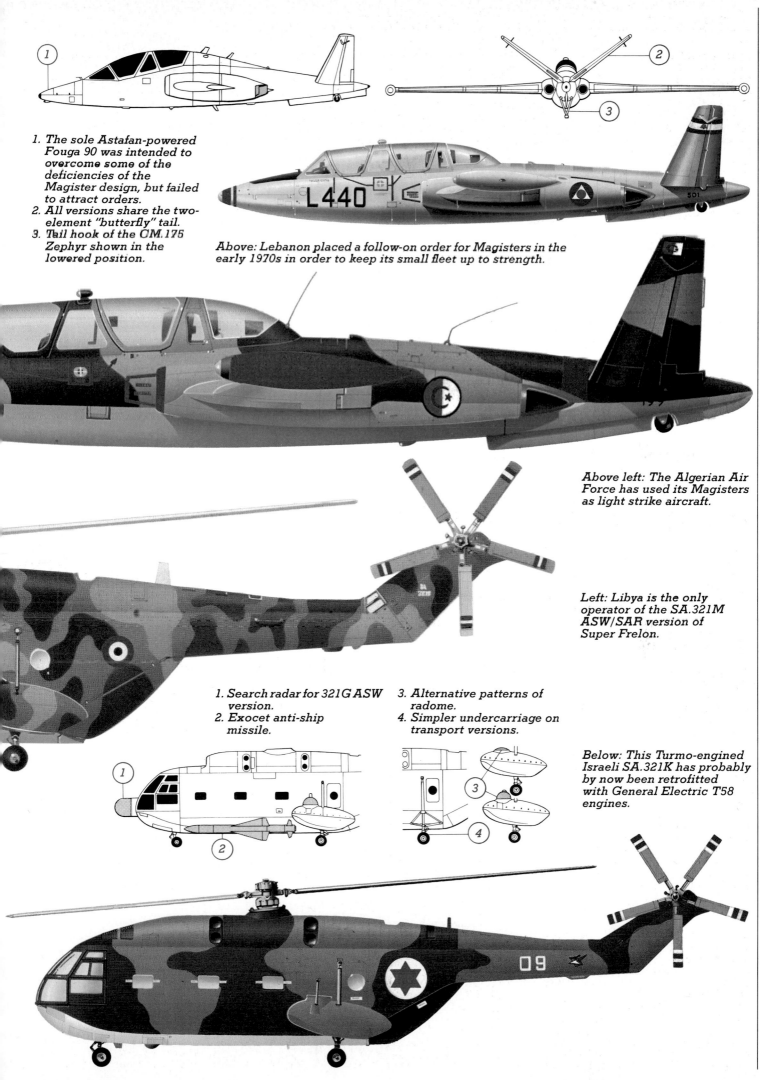

1. The sole Astafan-powered Fouga 90 was intended to overcome some of the deficiencies of the Magister design, but failed to attract orders.
2. All versions share the two-element "butterfly" tail.
3. Tail hook of the CM.175 Zephyr shown in the lowered position.

Above: Lebanon placed a follow-on order for Magisters in the early 1970s in order to keep its small fleet up to strength.

Above left: The Algerian Air Force has used its Magisters as light strike aircraft.

Left: Libya is the only operator of the SA.321M ASW/SAR version of Super Frelon.

1. Search radar for 321G ASW version.
2. Exocet anti-ship missile.
3. Alternative patterns of radome.
4. Simpler undercarriage on transport versions.

Below: This Turmo-engined Israeli SA.321K has probably by now been retrofitted with General Electric T58 engines.

19

Aérospatiale SA.330 Puma and AS.332 Super Puma

Data for SA.330L
Type: medium transport helicopter.
Specifications: fuselage length, 63ft 8in (19.4m); height, 16ft 10in (5.14m); rotor diameter, 49ft (15.0m); weight (maximum take-off), 16,315lb (7,400kg).
Max cruising speed: 146kt (271km/hr).
Range: 309nm (572km).
Powerplant: two Turboméca Turmo IVC turboshafts each rated at 1,575 shp (1,175kW).

SA 330 Puma was designed in the early 1960s by what was then Sud Aviation in order to meet a French Army requirement. As part of the 1967 Anglo-French helicopter deal, the UK agreed to join the project, ordering Puma for the Royal Air Force as a replacement for the inadequate Bristol Belvedere. About 30 per cent of the production work on the airframe and engines was tackled by Westland and Rolls-Royce, working in partnership with Aérospatiale and Turboméca. Initial production concentrated on three versions—the SA 330B (French Army), SA 330C (export) and SA 330E (Royal Air Force). The French army modernised its fleet in the late 1970s to improve the IFR performance, fitting new rotor blades and a Nadir navigation system.

Throughout its life Puma has been uprated and re-engined. Initial aircraft were powered by the Turmo IIIC-4 of 1,384shp (1,032kW) but this was replaced by the 1,417shp (1,057kW) Turmo IVA on the SA 330H and Turmo IVC 1,575shp (1,175kW) on the SA 330L. In most atmospheric conditions the IVC engine reaches full rpm limit before exceeding torque or exhaust temperature limits.

In 1978 the SA 330J civil version became the first helicopter outside the Soviet Union to be certified for all-weather use. The engine intakes on the 330M—military equivalent to the J—are extended and protect the engines against sea spray and sand. A hydraulic braking system can bring the nose and tail rotors to a halt 15 seconds after engine shut-down.

Puma is intended to go "in harm's way". The lower sections of the primary fuel tanks have self-sealing walls capable of coping with small-arms fire. The cabin can carry up to 16 soldiers in the normal configuration (20 in a high-density layout) or 12 casualties (six on stretchers). Large sliding doors are provided on both sides of the cabin, while a removable panel at the rear allows over-size loads to be carried.

Development of the larger AS 332 Super Puma was an Aérospatiale programme, necessitating lengthening of the nose, fitting a new undercarriage of greater wheelbase, and coupling 1,780shp (1,327kW) Turboméca Malinka engines to composite-blade nose and tail rotors of improved design. Plans to fit a Gazelle-type fenestron tail rotor were abandoned after flight trials with the experimental AS 331Z, but the Super Puma tail boom carries a ventral fin. The new undercarriage has single-wheel main gears in place of the twin-wheel units used on the standard Puma, plus a "kneeling" capability to reduce hangar height requirements, and optional folding tail-boom for ship-board use. The revised design offers better protection against hostile fire and a greater degree of protection for the occupants in a crash.

Super Puma is available in four versions—the short and long-nosed AS 332B and M models for army use and shore or ship-based naval configurations. Shore-based Super Pumas would detect and designate surface targets by means of a chin-mounted Omera ORB.32-14 radar, then attack with two Aérospatiale AM.39 Exocet missiles. Ship-board AS 332Ls carry the same radar, plus an Alcatel HS.12 dunking sonar and two homing torpedoes, but the ASW equipment could be removed in a few hours and replaced by Exocets.

Above: First prototype of the AS.332 Super Puma.

Aérospatiale SA.341/342 Gazelle

Data for SA.314G
Type: general-purpose helicopter.
Specifications: fuselage length, 31ft 3in (9.53m); height 10ft 3in (3.15m); rotor diameter; 34ft 5in (10.5m); weight (maximum take-off), 4,000lb (1,800kg).
Max cruising speed: 142kt (264km/hr).
Range: 361nm (670km).
Powerplant: one Turboméca Astazou IIIA turboshaft rated at 592shp (442kW).

Originally conceived as a replacement for the French Army Alouette, the SA 341 Gazelle uses the powerplant and transmission system of the earlier aircraft, coupled to an all-new five-seat fully-enclosed fuselage incorporating a 13-blade fenestron or shrouded tail rotor. The main rotor is a rigid Bolkow-type three-blade unit. Britain joined the project in the final design stages and the type is built on two production lines by Aérospatiale and Westland. A third production line was set up by Soko in Yugoslavia.

Initial versions included the SA 341A and B (British Army), C (Royal Navy), D and E (Royal Air Force), F (French Army), H (export). First of the more powerful versions was the SA 342K, in which the normal 592shp (442kW) Turboméca Astazou IIIA, IIIC or IIIN (depending on customer) was replaced by an Astazou XIVH. The latter engine has the same maximum power output as the earlier but is "flat-rated" and able to produce full power continuously without temperature or altitude restrictions. The SA 342J has an Astazou XIVM engine, improved fenestron, and higher maximum take-off weight. Developed for the French ALAT (Aviation Légère de l'Armée de Terre), the SA 342M carries the HOT anti-tank missile and associated SFIM gyro-stabilised roof sight.

Gazelle can fulfil a wide number of military roles. Armament currently includes forward-firing machine guns and AS.11 command-guided missiles, as well as the semi-automatic command to line-of-sight HOT, mentioned earlier. One or two stretchers can be carried in the post side of the cabin, and the aircraft can also be fitted with a rescue hoist. As a cargo carrier, it can lift an external slung load of 1,540lb (700kg).

As the aircraft matures, various armed forces are adapting it to carry a range of weapons. Egypt plans to assemble Gazelle under licence at the Arab Organisation of Industrialisation plant and to fit these aircraft with TOW anti-tank missiles. France's 2nd Parachute Regiment has retrofitted 20mm GIAT cannon to some of its aircraft, while the British Army is fitting its fleet with Ferranti AF532 gyro-stabilised roof sights for long-range target identification. Spaces have been left within the sight for a CRT module capable of injecting infra-red imagery from a future FLIR sensor mounted either within a modified version of the sight head or in a separate stabilised platform. Provision has also been made for an add-on laser designator to operate via the sight-stabilised head.

Gazelle has been widely sold in the Arab world, and Iraqi examples have probably seen combat in the recent war with Iran. Experience to date has shown that the aircraft's small size, high agility and rounded shape make it difficult to observe visually or by radar. With the advent of infra-red target-tracking systems, more attention will probably be paid in future to reducing the IR signature by means of suppressors and special paint finishes.

Right: SA.341M features:
1. *Roof-mounted missile sight.*
2. *HOT wired-guided missiles (two per side).*

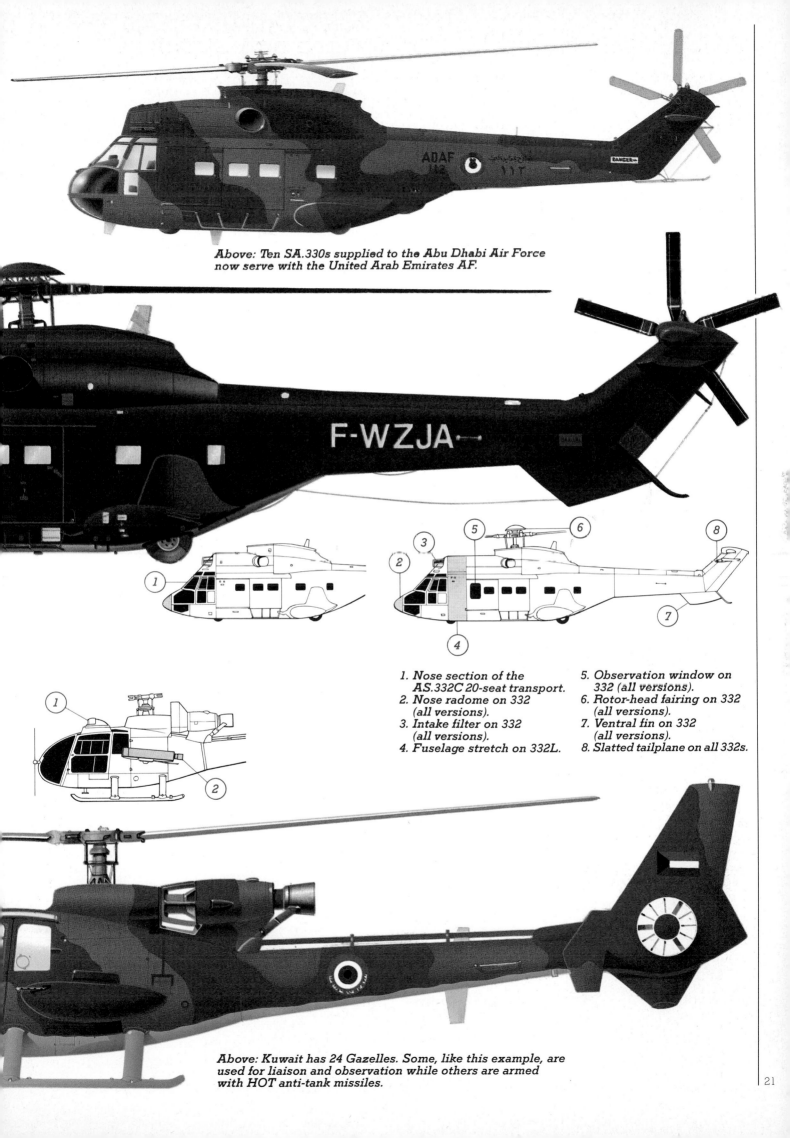

Above: Ten SA.330s supplied to the Abu Dhabi Air Force now serve with the United Arab Emirates AF.

1. Nose section of the AS.332C 20-seat transport.
2. Nose radome on 332 (all versions).
3. Intake filter on 332 (all versions).
4. Fuselage stretch on 332L.
5. Observation window on 332 (all versions).
6. Rotor-head fairing on 332 (all versions).
7. Ventral fin on 332 (all versions).
8. Slatted tailplane on all 332s.

Above: Kuwait has 24 Gazelles. Some, like this example, are used for liaison and observation while others are armed with HOT anti-tank missiles.

Aérospatiale AS. 365 Dauphin 2

Data for AS 365F.
Type: anti-ship helicopter.
Specifications: Fuselage length, 39ft 10in (12.15m); height 11ft 5in (3.47m); rotor diameter, 39ft 2in (11.93m); weight (maximum take-off), 8,580lb (3,900kg).
Max cruising speed: 150kt (306km/hr).
Range: (tactical radius with two AS.15TT) 165nm (305km).
Powerplant: two Turboméca Arriel IC turboshafts each rated at 710shp (530kW).

Launch order for the SA.365F Dauphin 2 and its Aérospatiale AS.15 TT missile armament was placed by Saudi Arabia, which plans to procure a batch of 24 for naval use. The first four to be delivered will carry an OMERA ORB 32 search radar and will be used for search and rescue purposes, but the remainder will be fitted out with the Thomson-CSF Agrion 15 radar and Aérospatiale AS.15TT anti-ship missiles.

Although similar in appearance to the earlier civilian SA.360 Dauphin, the Dauphin 2 is virtually a new design, some 90 per cent of its internal components being different. Approximately 20 per cent of the structure is made from composite materials. First version to fly was the AS.356N, a civil model which took to the air on 31 March 1979. Like Gazelle, Dauphin 2 uses a fenestron tail rotor. The main rotor is a four-blade unit with carbon-fibre spars and skin. Power is provided by two Turbo-méca Arriel IC 710shp (530kW)

turboshafts mounted on either side of the main rotor drive shaft— a feature which should minimise the chances of a single projectile strike disabling both engines.

Basically similar to the SA.365N, the SA.365F has outriggers on either side of the lower fuselage to carry the warload of four AS.15TT rounds. Agrion is based on the Iguane set used by the Atlantic NG maritime-patrol aircraft. The antenna is carried on a stabilised mounting beneath the aircraft nose to ensure a 360 degree field of view, and the set can track up to ten targets simultaneously while scanning for more.

Using the Agrion radar, the SA.365F will also be able to locate targets for Saudi warships equipped with Otomat anti-ship missiles and to provide mid-course guidance signals for Otomat. Aérospatiale has also developed a dedicated ASW version of Dauphin 2. This carries an Omera ORB.32D search radar plus Alcatel dunking sonar, or

else the Agrion 15 plus a Crouzet towed MAD sensor and two homing torpedoes.

Another military Dauphin 2 development is the SA.365M, which can carry up to 12 troops in the assault role. In this version the fuselage outriggers would carry four-round launchers for the Euromissile HOT or 22-round SNEB launchers for 68mm unguided rockets. On the mock-up of this variant a Venus stabilised night sight was shown mounted in the extreme nose. A thermal imager within the Venus sight

feeds direct into the optics of the roof-mounted day sight, so that the missile-aimer can choose between visual and IR images at the throw of a switch. The pilot's position has no built-in night sight; he will use night-vision goggles. During trials of the Venus system in 1981, using an SA.365H test-bed, HOT rounds hit a 7.5 × 7.5ft (2.3 × 2.3m) target at ranges of more than 2,500 yards (2,300m) in total darkness. Shots were fired in both good weather and a fine rain.

Agusta A 109A Hirundo

Type: general-purpose helicopter.
Dimensions: Fuselage length, 35ft 1in (10.7m); height 10ft 10in (3.3m); rotor diameter, 36ft 1in (11.0m); weight (maximum take-off), 5,730lb (2,600kg).
Max cruising speed: 155kt (287km/hr).
Range: 320nm (593km).
Powerplant: two Allison 250-C20B turboshafts each rated at 400shp (298kW).

Development of the A 109A began in the late 1960s, and the prototype flew on 4 August 1971. Early production aircraft delivered from 1976 onwards were civil, but the first military versions were supplied to the Italian army in 1977—five examples tested as utility aircraft capable of carrying up to seven troops and as anti-tank helicopters equipped with the Hughes TOW anti-tank missile. Missile firings went well, 12 hits being scored with the first 12 rounds. Argentina became the first military operator, ordering a batch of nine, while the Italian army took an option on 60 examples.

Agusta has proposed a series of military versions which can incorporate a range of features such as dual controls, armoured seats, a non-retractable under-carriage for shipboard use, a strengthened floor for cargo, external cargo hook, rescue hoist, auxiliary fuel tanks, crashproof fuel tanks, emergency flotation equipment, radar altimeter, infra-red suppression system, and radar.

Using these features, military versions can be customised for many applications. For light attack, A 109s could be armed with door-, pintle-, or externally-mounted machine-guns, or launchers for unguided rockets. Scout aircraft would be more lightly armed but fitted with stabilised sighting systems. The cabin is large enough to carry the avionics and crew members needed to create ECM and ESM variants, while naval aircraft could be fitted out for radar, AS.12 or AM.10 missiles for anti-shipping strikes, and G-2 mid-course guidance equipment for the surface-launched Oto Melara/Matra Otomat missile. By bulging the cabin walls, Agusta can offer a custom-built medical

evacuation variant able to carry two casualties on stretchers.

The Italian army has an operational requirement for an anti-tank helicopter, but is likely to adopt the heavier A 129. Customers looking for something less expensive may well select the A 109, which can carry four TOW rounds plus a nose-mounted sighting system.

The A 109 Mk2 version offers better "hot-and-high" perform-

ance, having an uprated transmission and improved tail-rotor driveshaft, new pattern of oil cooler and higher-pressure hydraulics. A follow-on design designated A 110 is being studied.

Right: Variants of the A 109:
1. Search radar on maritime version.
2. Flotation bags.
3. Sensors on EW version.
4. Chin sight on anti-tank version, which has . . .
5. Weapon pylons for rockets or gunpods, and . . .
6. TOW missiles (two per side).

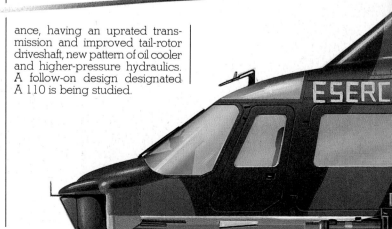

Left: Unmarked SA.360 Dauphin on trials in the anti-armour role, with guided missiles, all-weather sensors and roof-mounted sight. Like most modern anti-tank helicopters, it carries the HOT missiles in four-barrel containers. The Dauphin could become a very important battlefield helicopter by the end of this decade.

Below: The United States Coast Guard operates Dauphin 2 under the designation HH-65A Dolphin.

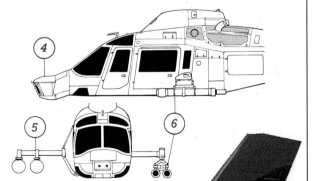

COAST GUARD

Above: The Italian Army has tested several TOW-armed A 109A helicopters, scoring an impressive 12 hits with the first 12 rounds fired.

Agusta A 129 Mangusta

Type: anti-tank helicopter.
Specifications: fuselage length, 40ft 3in (12.27m); height 10ft 10in (3.31m); rotor diameter, 39ft 0in (11.9m); weight (maximum take-off), 8,085lb (3,655kg).
Max cruising speed: 135kt (270km/hr).
Endurance: 2.5 hours.
Powerplant: two Rolls-Royce Gem 2-3 turboshafts each rated at 808shp (602kW).

A 129 Mangusta (Mongoose) is based on the experience gained with the A 109. The influence of the former may be seen in the rear fuselage, but the front section owes much to designs such as the US AH-1 Cobra.

Mangusta will rely on a combination of small size and agility for its survival. Only the cockpit and vital parts of the engines are armoured, but the aircraft is designed to survive a single 0.5in (12.7mm) calibre strike on virtually any part of the airframe, the largest vulnerable point being the approximately 1.0sq. ft (900sq. cm) of canopy area necessary to give the crew adequate view outside. The crew sit in armoured seats—gunner in the front cockpit with the pilot in the rear raised cockpit. Both have flat-surface low glint canopies.

Main and tail rotor blades are made from composites. Like the fuselage, the main rotor blades are designed to withstand 0.5in-calibre fire, while the rotor head does not contain lubricated bearings.

Two independent fuel systems are fitted, and can be cross-fed if necessary. Tanks and fuel lines are self-sealing, and the entire design is intended to offer high standard of crash resistance.

Heart of the avionics installation is a digital multiplex system built by Harris Corporation. This will control the engines, communications, navigation, fire-control and other systems. Offensive systems are likely to consist of up to eight TOW missiles, along with a nose-mounted sight incorporating a laser rangefinder and FLIR, but the use of up to eight Hellfire "fire-and-forget" missiles, along with a Martin-Marietta mast-mounted sight and night-vision system, has also been proposed.

Four prototypes are planned, plus a dynamic-test airframe. The aircraft will be powered by two Rolls-Royce Gem 2-3 turboshafts of 808shp (602kW), but Agusta has designed the airframe to accommodate a range of single- or twin-engined installations, including a single General Electric T700.

Original plans had called for the use of Lycoming LTS101-850 engines, but the switch to the British unit—which will be licence-built by Piaggio—helped offset a rise in aircraft weight and may avoid US embargoes affecting export prospects.

First flight date has been set for May 1983, and the aircraft should enter operational service with the Italian army in 1985. The Italian army has plans to acquire at least 60 for two anti-tank squadrons, and may well procure a further 30 aircraft in order to form a third.

Italy plans to operate the aircraft in the mountainous north-eastern

Antonov An-12 Cub

Type: heavy tactical transport.
Specifications: length, 108ft 7in (33.1m); span, 124ft 8in (38.0m); height (normal take-off), 34ft 6in (10.53m); weight, 121,475lb (55,100kg).
Max speed: 419kt (777km/hr).
Service ceiling: 33,500ft (10,200m).
Range: (maximum payload), 1,942nm (3,600km).
Powerplant: four Ivchenko AI-20K turboprops each rated at 4,000shp (2,983kW).

The basic An-12BP transport is known to NATO as "Cub-A" and can carry up to 20 tonnes of freight, vehicles such as the PT76 amphibious tank and ZSU-23-4 Shilka self-propelled anti-aircraft gun, or 100 paratroops. Access to the main cabin is via a ramp door at the rear. On most Western "beaver-tailed" types the forward (lower) section of such doors are hinged at the forward end, allowing them to be lowered to act as a loading ramp, but on the Cub the lower section is divided into two longitudinal halves which fold internally, an arrangement that seems needlessly cumbersome. Trucks may be able to back up to the open tail, but they could do so equally well given a Hercules-style tail ramp. If bulky loads must be taken aboard, a detachable ramp must be used.

Like most Soviet military transports, the An-12 has a tail-gun

Above: The An-12 undercarriage copes with any surface.

position fitted with two 23mm Nudelmann-Richter NR-23 weapons and a Gamma tail-warning system. The latter is probably a rearward-facing radar, and its antenna is mounted at the base of the tail fin and directly above the gunner's position. A chin-mounted radome covers the navigation radar, one model of which is the I-band set known to NATO as "Toad Stool". Late-production aircraft have a larger radome covering a new pattern of radar. This may have been retrofitted to the rest of the fleet. On a Western aircraft of this size the controls would be powered, but the Antonov team followed Soviet practice in fitting simple manual controls.

The An-12 was derived from the civil An-10 "Cat", but seems to have avoided the latter's structural and directional-control problems. According to Western intelligence sources, the cabin is not pressurised, limiting the cruising altitude during trooping flights, and forcing the An-12 to fly at altitudes below the optimum for the Ivchenko AI-20K turboprop powerplants.

India successfully used the An-12 as a night bomber during the 1973 Indo-Pakistan War, carrying bombs within the fuselage and releasing them out of the rear door. Such primitive operating techniques rely on the opposition being poorly equipped with ground radar and radar-guided interceptors. One Pakistani Mirage 5 pilot attempting a night interception is reported to have narrowly avoided colliding with an intruding "Cub".

At least two variants have been developed for EW duties. "Cub-B" carries a payload of Elint

equipment such as monitoring receivers, signal-processing equipment and recorders, and may be recognised by the large number of extra antennas. "Cub-C" is a dedicated stand-off jamming (ECM) aircraft, whose antennas are mounted on the fuselage, in a tail radome which replaces the gunner's position and in a ventral fairings located ahead of and behind the main undercarriage.

Unlike the Lockheed C-130 Hercules, which it resembles in both size and configuration, the An-12 is no longer in production in its country of origin, the line having closed in 1973 after delivering some 850 examples, 550 of which remain in Soviet service. "Cub" is expected to remain in Soviet service through the 1980s. China builds a version known as the Yun-8, which could well serve the air arm of the PLA until the end of the century.

part of the country, so Mangusta is designed to meet its specification at altitudes of up to 6,100ft (2,000m). This feature might help sell the type to Third World operators. Agusta still hopes to sell A 129 within NATO, particularly since the future of the only other West European anti-tank helicopter project—the Franco/German PAH-2—is in doubt. Target unit cost of A 129 is $2 million to $3 million.

Right: Model showing the general appearance of the A 129 Mangusta (Mongoose) helicopter.

Above: Mangusta is Western Europe's first custom-designed anti-tank helicopter. The Italian army has ordered 60 to begin with, and other NATO nations are likely to be among the customers.

Below: Cub-C ECM aircraft with:
1. *Equipment fairings with radomes.*
2. *Tail ramp as fitted on transport versions.*
3. *Radome replacing tail gunner's position.*

Above: No longer in production in the Soviet Union, Soviet Air Force An-12 Cubs are slowly being phased out in favour of the jet-powered Ilyushin Il-76.

Above: The large Indian Air Force transport force has a heavy-lift element including two squadrons of An-12s for Himalayan support duties.

Antonov An-22 Antheus

Type: heavy strategic transport
Specifications: length, 190ft (57.9m); span, 211ft 4in (64.4m); height, 41ft 1in (12.53m); weight (maximum take-off), 550,000lb (250,000kg).
Max speed: 399kt (740km/hr).
Service ceiling: 30,000ft (9,100m).
Range: (maximum payload) 2,700nm (5,000km).
Powerplant: four Kuznetsov NK-12MA turboshafts each rated at 15,000shp (11,186kW).

When favoured Soviet client states ask for urgent shipments of arms, the Soviet Air Force's An-22 fleet will almost certainly help deliver the goods. Airports in Egypt, Libya, Peru, Somalia and Vietnam have received this giant transport, which never fails to play a significant role in major Warsaw Pact exercises. Even main battle tanks such as the T-72 and T-80, or bulky missile systems such as the SA-4 Ganef, can travel by air if the An-22 is available.

Pilots transferred from the An-12 "Cub" to the larger An-22 Antheus—known to NATO as "Cock"—must at first be somewhat in awe of their new mount. The An-22 can take off at weights of up to 550,000lb (250,000kg) under the power of four 15,000shp Kuznetsov NK-12MA turboprops with contra-rotating propellers, and carry up to 176,000lb (43,000kg) of freight. Wing loading can be up to 150lb/sq. ft (730kg/sq.m)—well above the 90lb/sq.ft (440kg/sq.m) which would be typical of a fully loaded An-12 or C-130 Hercules.

Such a high wing loading on a transport intended to operate out of rough strips seems too much at first sight, but the Antonov team fitted large double-slotted trailing edge flaps to the An-22 wing and provided more than 0.09shp of engine power for each pound of take-off weight. Tyre pressure of the 14 undercarriage wheels is reported to be variable in flight in order to match the conditions at any air strip.

The main cabin of the An-22 is fully pressurised, and is fitted with a tail door whose lower section can be lowered to form a loading ramp. Four travelling gantries running on a roof-mounted rail system can move cargo loads of up to 5,500lb (2,500kg). Gantry rails are also fitted to the outside of the upper section of the tail door. This door section is hinged at its aft end and swings upwards when opened, so that its rails form an extension of the main system, allowing cargo to be lifted from the ground or from vehicles parked close in under the aircraft tail.

Two radars are fitted to the An-22. One set mounted in a chin position beneath the traditional Soviet glazed navigator's position is used for ground mapping, while a second in a nose radome is almost certainly a weather radar. Normal crew is five or six although there is accommodation for up to 29 personnel in a small cabin aft

of the flight deck. As is the case with all Soviet military transport air-crew, some crew members are trained to perform simple maintenance tasks on the aircraft.

The type remains the heavy-lifter of the Soviet air transport fleet, some 50 examples remaining in Soviet Air Force service. About 85 were built, and some serve with Aeroflot, where they remain available as reserve military transports. Several have been lost, some while on overseas duty, but there is no evidence of technical problems with the type. A wide-body An-40 jet-powered replacement is under development according to reports from the US.

Antonov An-24, -26, -30 and -32

Data for An-26
Type: light tactical transport.
Specifications: length, 78ft 1in (23.8m); span, 95ft 9in (29.2m); height, 28ft 1in (8.57m); weight (normal take-off), 50,700lb (23,000kg).
Max speed: 290kt (537km/hr).
Service ceiling: 24,600ft (7,500m).
Range: (maximum payload) 595nm (1,100km).
Powerplant: two Ivchenko AI-24VT turboprops each rated at 2,820shp (2,130kW).

Standard transport version is the An-24V, but for military purposes the An-24T was soon produced, with a ventral freight door at the tail. The An-24RT is similar to the T version but has an RU 19A-300 auxiliary turbojet in the starboard engine nacelle. Trials probably showed that the freight door was no substitute for a tail ramp, so neither the T nor the RT were built in large numbers.

First demonstrated in 1969, the definitive AN-26 "Curl" has a redesigned rear fuselage incorporating an upward-swept tail and rear door/loading ramp. In addition to the normal frontally hinged opening mode, the An-26 door can be disconnected, then lowered and moved forward and beneath the fuselage by an actuation mechanism. This can be done on the ground to facilitate loading from trucks or in flight to give a clear exit for paratroops. A large airdrop observation blister is fitted to the cockpit port wall.

Above: Eight-blade propellers tested on the An-24.

Improvements to the design resulted in the current An-26B version, which is equipped to carry up to three standard freight pallets.

Export sales of the An-24 and An-26 have gone well, particularly in the Third World, where the basic simplicity of the aircraft does not overstrain local maintenance skills and facilities. "Hot-and-high" performance remains limited, and at least one former operator never flew the aircraft with a full load, but split large payloads between two aircraft. Strakes were fitted beneath the rear fuselage as a result of development flying, but directional handling is alleged to remain poor. Other reports speak of gearbox failures on the Ivchenko AI-24 powerplants.

Ultimate version of the An-24 series at the time of writing was the An-32 "Cline". Based on the An-26, this solves the "hot-and-high" problem by the sheer brute force of 5,180shp (3,862kW) Ivchenko AI-20M turboprops. At a maximum take-off weight of 57,300lb (26,000kg) these give the An-32 a total of 0.18shp for every pound of weight. An An-32 can operate out of airfields up to 14,750ft (4,500m) in altitude.

In order to provide sufficient ground clearance for the massive 15ft 5in (4.7m) propellers needed to handle the increased power, the new engine nacelles are mounted above the wing, but an underwing fairing—effectively a dummy nacelle—is still needed to house the main undercarriage. An APU mounted at the rear of the starboard fairing may be used on the ground at basic airstrips.

The An-32 seems to have been a "private venture" by the Antonov bureau, since an Indian Air Force order, placed some three years after first flight, was apparently the first to be received. Hindustan Aeronautics is expected to build up to 95 under licence, and the type will replace Indian Air Force C-47 and C-119 transports. According to the Indian Air Force, cost of the An-32 is about half that of its obvious competitor, the DHC-5D Buffalo.

Like most Soviet transports, the cabin of the An-26 (as for -32) is fitted with a built-in electrically actuated conveyor system. The An-32 is fitted with an internal cargo hoist of 4,400lb (2,000kg) capacity.

An-30 "Clank" is a specialised aerial survey development of the An-24/26. The nose is extensively glazed to give the navigator a good forward and lateral view, while the cabin, which includes a photographic darkroom, can carry survey cameras or other sensors operating via glazed viewing ports.

An eight-blade propeller has been flight-tested on the An-24, and is reported to produce less noise and vibration than the normal four-blade model.

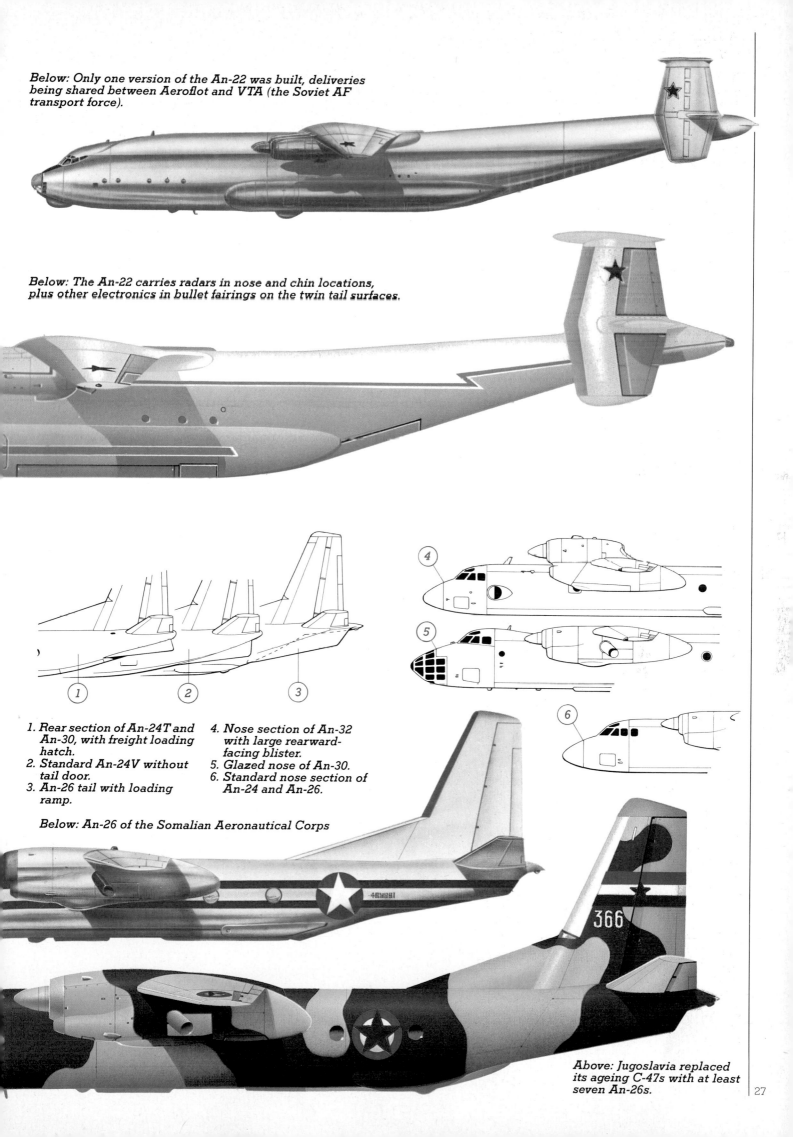

Below: Only one version of the An-22 was built, deliveries being shared between Aeroflot and VTA (the Soviet AF transport force).

Below: The An-22 carries radars in nose and chin locations, plus other electronics in bullet fairings on the twin tail surfaces.

1. Rear section of An-24T and An-30, with freight loading hatch.
2. Standard An-24V without tail door.
3. An-26 tail with loading ramp.
4. Nose section of An-32 with large rearward-facing blister.
5. Glazed nose of An-30.
6. Standard nose section of An-24 and An-26.

Below: An-26 of the Somalian Aeronautical Corps

Above: Jugoslavia replaced its ageing C-47s with at least seven An-26s.

Antonov An-72 Coaler

Type: light tactical transport.
Specifications: length, 87ft 2in (26.58m); span, 84ft 9in (25.83m); height, 27ft 0in (8.23m); weight (maximum take-off), 72,700lb (33,000kg).
Max speed: 410kt (760km/hr).
Range: (maximum payload) 540nm (1,000km).
Max payload: 22,000lb (10,000kg).
Powerplant: two Lotarev D-36 turbofans each rated at 14,330lb (6,510kg) dry thrust.

Developed as a Stol replacement for the An-26, the An-72 "Coaler" first flew in December 1977. Similar in concept to the earlier Boeing YC-14, the An-72 has engines mounted above the wing, whence their efflux can blow over the wing surface and down over the flaps, increasing the lift by means of the Coanda effect. The engines are Lotarev D-36 three-shaft turbofans of 14,330lb (6,510kg) thrust.

Most Soviet high-wing transports have a few degrees of dihedral on the outer wing section, but in the case of the An-72 this is very marked, amounting to around ten degrees. Full-span leading edge slats are fitted to the wing leading edge, while double-slotted trailing-edge flaps are fitted on the inboard section. The outboard flaps are triple-slotted. Spoilers located ahead of the flaps are used to destroy lift after touchdown. These are deployed automatically, being linked to load-sensing switches on the undercarriage. The original prototype had two large ventral fins near the tail, which were omitted on the second example, but production aircraft will probably have these restored, although they may be smaller in size.

The inboard flaps and wing surface profit from the upper-surface blowing produced by the engine exhaust, although Oleg Antonov is reported as saying that the overwing engine location was chosen to minimise the risk of foreign-object damage rather than to blow the wing upper surface and flaps. Deflectors fitted on either side of the engine exhausts serve to "spread" the efflux over the largest possible area of the wing upper surface and flaps.

Skin and flaps aft of the exhausts are manufactured from titanium.

A two-man crew is standard, although provision has been made for a flight engineer, should he be required. The nose radome can house a weather radar, and at least one of the An-72 prototypes was fitted with a Doppler navigation system. The undercarriage is fitted with low-pressure tyres suitable for rough-strip use. With a light cargo load, the An-72 has a take-off speed of only 81kt (150km/hr)

and needs a run of only 1,500ft (450m). Given 3,300ft (1,000m) of runway, an An-72 can get airborne at weights of up to 58,400lb (26,500kg), but this rises to 72,700lb (33,000kg) on a 4,900ft (1,500m) strip. Touchdown speed is 90kt (165km/hr).

Different types of tail door/ramp were tested on the prototypes, but *Jane's All the World's Aircraft 1981-2* reports Antonov suggesting that production aircraft might have an An-26-style door.

Bell 214

Data for 214ST
Type: utility helicopter.
Specifications: fuselage length, 50ft 0in (15.24m); height, 15ft 11in (4.84m); rotor diameter, 52ft 0in (15.85m); weight (maximum take-off), 17,200lb (7,800kg).
Max speed: 135kt (250km/hr).
Range: 421nm (780km).
Powerplant: two General Electric CT7-2A turboshafts, each rated at 1,625shp (1,210kW).

Development of the "Noda-Matic" vibration-damping suspension system in 1970s allowed Bell to increase the engine power of future variants of the UH-1 "Huey" family concept. The Model 214 has a strengthened airframe based on that of the UH-1H, plus the broad-bladed main rotor pioneered by the UH-1C & E, coupled to a more powerful engine. Much of the technology came from the experimental Model 309 King-Cobra, but Bell soon replaced the Lycoming 1,900shp (1,415kW) T53-L-702 used in the prototype 214 HueyPlus with the even more powerful T55-L-7C.

The resulting aircraft attracted a large order from Iran, so Bell re-engined the type once again, substituting the General Electric LTC4B-8D, flat-rated at 2,250shp (1,675kW) to maintain performance under "hot-and-high" conditions. Deliveries of the resulting 214A to what was then the Imperial Iranian Army began in 1975, and 287 were supplied. These remain in

service at Isfahan, and on paper form the largest numerical component of Iranian transport helicopter strength. In practice, the US Government arms embargo on Iran has badly affected serviceability, and some reports suggest that less than 50 were available for operational use as the war with Iraq settled into a long stalemate during 1981.

Iran planned to build the 214A under licence, and when Bell introduced the improved 214ST, powered by two 1,625shp (1,212kW) T700-GE-T1C engines, this model was selected for indigenous production. After the Iranian revolution, this deal was cancelled by the new Government, but Bell continued to develop the type as a private venture. In November 1979 the company committed itself to production of a batch of 100, with deliveries beginning in early 1982. The

214ST will also be built in Japan by Mitsui.

Reports that the Spanish Air Force has taken options on a number of 214STs for SAR duties had not been confirmed as this book was in preparation, but Bell was known to be studying the possibility of fitting a automated navigation and flight-control system for an SAR version at the request of an undisclosed potential customer.

Above: Prototype An-72 on flight test.

Left: The final configuration of the Soviet Air Force's An-72s has not yet been revealed, but the end product will be used to replace propeller-driven transports such as the An-26.

Right: Bell 214C in pre-revolution Imperial Iranian Air Force markings. This model was used for SAR duties.

Below: Originally supplied to what was then the Imperial Iranian Air Force, the Bell 214 fleet was still operational in sufficient numbers to participate in the 1980/82 war with Iraq.

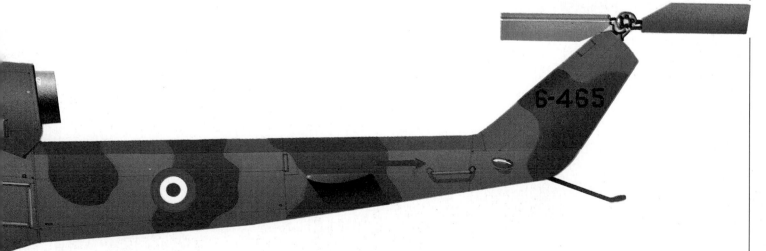

Bell 412

Type: utility helicopter.
Specifications: fuselage length: 42ft 5in (12.92m); height, 14ft 2in (4.32m); rotor diameter, 46ft 0in (14.02m); weight (maximum) take-off), 11,600lb (5,260kg).
Max speed: 124kt (230km/hr).
Range: 227nm (420km).
Powerplant: one Pratt & Whitney Canada PT6T-3B-1 turboshaft rated at 1,308shp (975kW).

Bell has traditionally been a manufacturer of twin-bladed helicopters, and until 1979 had flown multi-blade helicopters only for experimental purposes. In creating the 412 Bell took the Model 212/UH-1N and fitted two Pratt & Whitney Canada PT6T-3B engines and a four-blade rotor.

The PT6T-3B is an improved version of the "coupled-engine" powerplant used by the UH-1N. It offers better power output in an emergency if one of the power sections which drives the common gearbox and drive shaft fails or must be shut down. The blades of the new rotor are similar to those of the earlier UH-1N, having a glass fibre spar and skin, Nomex core and leading edge abrasion strip made from stainless steel and titanium. One improvement is the moulding into the blade of a lighting-protection mesh. The tail rotor is a two-bladed semi-rigid unit with interchangeable aluminium blades. These have a honeycomb core and stainless steel leading-edge strip.

The main rotor can fold when the aircraft is on the ground, so that the hanger requirements are similar to those of the UH-1N. Being four-bladed, it generates less vibration and noise than the two-bladed unit. As a utility aircraft, the 412 can carry 14 fully equipped troops over a range of 200nm (370km), with a 20-minute reserve, and evacuate six stretcher cases. Attention has been given to crew survivability. The fuel tanks are crash-resistant, while the landing gear and aircrew seats have been designed to absorb impact energy in the event of a crash. The airframe structure was designed to incorporate integral maintenance steps and handgrips in order to reduce the amount of support equipment required in the field. Venezuela was the first military customer for the 412 when the Air Force ordered two for utility duties.

Having built the earlier 212, Agusta decided to come in on the 412 programme, building civil and military versions. The Italian company offers a number of arma-

Bell OH-58 Kiowa

Data for OH-58C
Type: light observation helicopter.
Specifications: fuselage length, 32ft 7in (9.93m); height, 9ft 6in (2.91m); rotor diameter, 35ft 4in (10.77m); weight (maximum take-off), 3,000lb (1,360kg).
Max speed: 120kt (222km/hr).
Range (armed scout mission): 264nm (490km).
Armament: various combinations of guns or rockets.
Powerplant: one Allison T63-A-720 turboshaft rated at 420 shp (313kW).

One of the few aircraft to lose a competitive fly-off competition, only to win years later in a second round of evaluations, the OH-58 has also had a successful career in civil guise as the Model 206 JetRanger. The type first flew as the OH-4A in an attempt to meet what hindsight suggests was an unrealistic US Army Light Observation Helicopter requirement for a single type to fill the close-support, casevac, observation, reconnaissance and light transport roles. After selection of the Hughes OH-6 had been made, Bell redesigned the aircraft as the five-seat JetRanger and launched it on a successful civil career.

When the US Army reopened the LOH competition in 1968, the Bell design was selected and orders placed for 2,200 aircraft similar to the civil version but having a larger rotor. A year later the OH-58A Kiowa was in action in Vietnam. Modification of these aircraft to the improved OH-58C standard began in 1978. An up-rated Allison T63-A-720 of 420shp (313kW) gave 30 per cent more power than the original T63-A700 to improve "hot-and-high" performance, while the signature of the aircraft was reduced by fitting a flat-panel anti-glint canopy and an infra-red suppressor.

In the autumn of 1981 Bell was declared winner of the US Army Helicopter Improvement Programme (AHIP), and will rebuild 720 Kiowas to the new standard. This involves re-engining the aircraft with a 650shp (485kW) Allison 250-C30R turboshaft, fitting a new rotor with four composite blades, and adding new avionics, including a McDonnell Douglas mast-mounted sight incorporating a long-range TV sensor, FLIR and laser ranger-designator. The new rotor will provide the manoeuvrability needed for nap-of-the-earth flight plus low levels of vibration which will not disturb the sensors. The cockpit has also been completely redesigned with multi-function CRT displays in order to reduce crew workload. For air-to-air use, Stinger missiles will be carried in two-round launch pods.

Since the civil JetRanger had been developed to create the larger LongRanger, Bell was able to militarise the latter in 1980 in order to offer a new multi-role helicopter designated Texas-Ranger. Able to fill transport, casevac, SAR and anti-tank roles, the new aircraft can be fitted with an add-on TOW installation. Four rounds are carried ready for use, with four more reload rounds being carried in the cabin. The roof-mounted missile sight is a day-only unit based on that developed for the British Army's Lynx, and operates in conjunction with a pallet-mounted electronics pack located in the cabin.

Right: TexasRanger, a Model 206 with longer fuselage, fires TOW missile.

ment combinations on the AB 412. Scout, and reconnaissance aircraft can be armed with two door-mounted 7.62 machineguns and two 7.62mm gun pods, plus 10,000 rounds of ammunition. For fire-support missions, a single 20mm cannon may be mounted in the door and up to 5,200 rounds of ammunition carried. Other armed configurations proposed by Agusta are the carriage of 19-round launchers for 2.75in unguided rockets or AS.11 air-to-surface missiles. The aircraft can also be used for minelaying, carrying a dispenser for up to 200 anti-tank mines or 1,900 anti-personnel mines as an underslung load.

Above: *Agusta-built Bell 412 in the markings of the Italian Army air corps (Aviazione Leggera dell'Esercito). A total of 14 troops may be carried in the cabin.*

Below: *Bell CH-136 (OH-58 Kiowa) of the Canadian Armed Forces. The national markings are repeated in French on the other side of the fuselage.*

Below: *Agusta-Bell 206A (Hkp6) of the Swedish Army. Note the different antenna arrangement compared with that of the Canadian aircraft shown above, and the rear-view mirror beneath the nose.*

Above: *Model 406 AHIP with:*
1. *McDonnell Douglas mast-mounted sight with TV, FLIR and laser ranger.*
2. *Four-bladed main rotor of composite construction.*
3. *Infra-red suppressor on exhaust of uprated engine (Allison 250-C30R).*
4. *Launch tubes for General Dynamics Stinger heat-seeking missiles for air-to-air combat.*

Bell AH-1 HueyCobra

Data for AH-1S
Type: anti-tank helicopter.
Specifications: fuselage length, 44ft 7in (13.59m); height, 14ft 5in (4.41m); rotor diameter, 40ft 0in (13.41m); weight (normal take-off), 9,975lb (4,524kg).
Max speed: 123kt (228km/hr).
Range: 274nm (507km).
Armament: eight TOW missiles plus 20mm or 30mm turret-mounted cannon.
Powerplant: one Avco Lycoming T53-L-703 turboshaft rated at 1,800shp (1,340kW).

If the armoured formations of the Warsaw Pact were to roll west-wards in the mid-1980s, one of the most significant threats to their progress, apart from the nightmare of battlefield nuclear weapons, will be the anti-tank helicopter. The most numerically important of these is the Bell AH-1 HueyCobra.

Simple arithmetic shows the impact the AH-1 would have on Warsaw Pact tank strength. Each of the more than 900 US Army AH-1S helicopters will carry eight TOW missiles, weapons which have demonstrated a combat-proven kill rate of greater than 90 per cent. Even if only half the AH-1 force survives long enough to fire half its ammunition, the attackers will lose more than 2,000 tanks. NATO trials suggest that each helicopter will be able to kill anything from 12 to 19 hostile armoured fighting vehicles before being shot down. If this figure is correct, and the supplies of TOW missiles hold out, the US Army's AH-1 force has the potential to deal with more than 10,000 AFVs.

The AH-1 concept was born in the mid-1960s, when the need for an armed escort helicopter became apparent. The official solution to the problem — the Lockheed AH-65 Cheyenne — was abandoned in 1969, owing to technical problems and rising cost, but Bell had already devised its own private-venture offering by designing a gunship version of the UH-1 "Huey". Produced by mating the proven engine, transmission and rotor of the UH-1 with a new fuselage, incorporating a two-seat cockpit for the gunner (front) and pilot (rear), stub wings and a chin-mounted machine-gun turret, the resulting AH-1 flew for the first time on 7 November 1965. It was tested by the US Army that winter and ordered into production in April 1966. Within little more than 18 months, the AH-1 was in action in Vietnam. From this beginning Bell produced a new family of HueyCobra variants, which are still in production and a success story in their own right.

Initial model to be fielded was the AH-1G for the US Army. This combined the 1,100shp (820kW) Lycoming T53-L-13 engine with various forms of armament, such as M-28 turret armed with a 7.62mm machine-gun and 40mm grenade launcher, plus stub-wing mounted gun pods or 2.75in rockets. A total of 1,116 were built, and many were lost in more than one million flight hours of Vietnam service.

After flight tests of helicopter-mounted TOW missiles in a UH-1B, including combat firings against North Vietnamese tanks taking part in the 1972 invasion of South Vietnam, the US Army requested a TOW-armed AH-1. A total of 92 aircraft were modified to the AH-1Q standard, retaining the M-28 turret but with the addition of up to eight TOW rounds aimed by a gunner's helmet sight.

As tactics evolved, the AH-1G and Q were required to carry out stand-off hovering tactics and

nap-of-the-earth (NOE) flying, and the need for better vertical flight performance was soon apparent. All AH-1Q aircraft, plus a batch of 198 AH-1Gs, were therefore modified between 1976 and 1979 to the AH-1S standard, receiving an improved transmission and 1,800shp (1,342kW) T53-L-703 engine. Shortage of attack helicopters led the US Army to begin production of new-build AH-1S Step 1 aircraft in 1977. These differed from the rebuilt examples in having an improved instrument panel for NOE operations, a anti-glint canopy made up of flat transparencies, and revised avionics. The final 33 of the 100 built were fitted with composite rotor blades.

Step 2 aircraft had a 20 or 30mm gun turret, plus automatic compensation for off-axis firing and an improved stores-management system. After 98 had been delivered, production was switched to the Modernised AH-1S (Step 3) standard, with a new fire-control system incorporating improvements such as a laser rangefinder and tracker, ALR-39 RWR, ALQ-136 radar jammer, ALQ-144 IR jammer, and an IR suppressor on the engine. All US Army AH-1s will be brought up to this standard, although units based in Europe have reported minor structural problems with aircraft rebuilt from 20-year old AH-1G airframes, due to a combination of airframe age and the increased engine power.

Above: AH-1J SeaCobra of the US Marine Corps.

Below: AH-1 variants include:
1. AH-1G gunship with M-28 chin turret.
2. Addition of TOW missiles converted AH-1G to AH-1Q.
3. Short skid on AH-1GQ.
4. Addition of TOW converted the AH-1J

SeaCobra gunship to AH-1T standard.
5. Enlarged turret on AH-1J housing an M-197 three-barrelled 20mm cannon.
6. Twin-engine installation on AH-1J.
7. Original rotor blade tip.
8. Modified main rotor on AH-1S.

Optional equipment developed for the AH-1S includes the FACTS (FLIR-Augmented Cobra TOW Sight) which allows the gunner to cope with smoke or darkness, and LAAT (Laser-Augmented Airborne TOW) stabilised sight.

Bell has also test-flown the Model 249, which is based on the AH-1S but has a four-blade rotor similar to that used by the Bell 412. Studies have been carried into the possibility of fitting the AH-1S with the "fire-and-forget" Hellfire missile in place of TOW. HAH-IS units were deployed to Egypt during Operation Bright Star in 1980, performing well in the harsh desert environment. Some problems were experienced with sand contaminating the turret-mounted 20mm cannon, but this was found to be easily cured by spinning the barrel assembly at regular intervals.

Japan has evaluated the AH-1S and Fuji will build 54 under licence.

When the USMC evaluated the AH-1G, the need for greater engine power seemed obvious, so the AH-1J SeaCobra ordered by the Corps and later by Iran uses the 1,800shp (1,342kW) Pratt & Whitney Canada T400-CP-400 engine—a version of the dual-power section PT6T-3 used in the UH-1N "Huey". The nose turret of the AH-1J mounts a three-barrelled 20mm rotary cannon. Iranian AH-1Js were used against Iraqi armoured formations in the opening weeks of the Iran/Iraq war, a move which the Iraqis are reported to have countered by deploying ZSU-23-4 Shilka self-propelled anti-aircraft guns in forward positions and by massed fire from the turret-mounted heavy machine-guns carried by Soviet-designed tanks.

A further up-engining, with the 1,970shp (1,469kW) T400-WV-402 coupled to the dynamic system of the Bell 214, resulted in the AH-1T Improved SeaCobra, some of which have been modified by the addition of a TOW missile system. In 1980, an AH-1T was fitted with two General Electric T700-GE-700—an installation offering more than 3,200shp (2,380kW)—and test-flown. Bell has proposed a retrofit programme using these engines, plus an improved transmission and new composite rotor blades.

Below left: This Israeli Defence Force AH-1S is similar in build standard to the version supplied to Japan, complete with IR shroud over exhaust.

Left: AH-1S anti-tank helo with:
9. Universal 20mm gun turret.
10. Chin sight for TOW.
11. Flat-plate canopy.
12. Armoured glass protecting crew.
13. Infra-red suppressor on exhaust.
14. IR suppressor on export helos.

Left: Alternative gun turrets:
15. M-197 three-barrelled 20mm cannon.
16. 20mm Minigun.
17. Twin-turret M28 system housing the ...
18. M134 7.62mm Minigun and ...
19. M129 40mm grenade launcher.

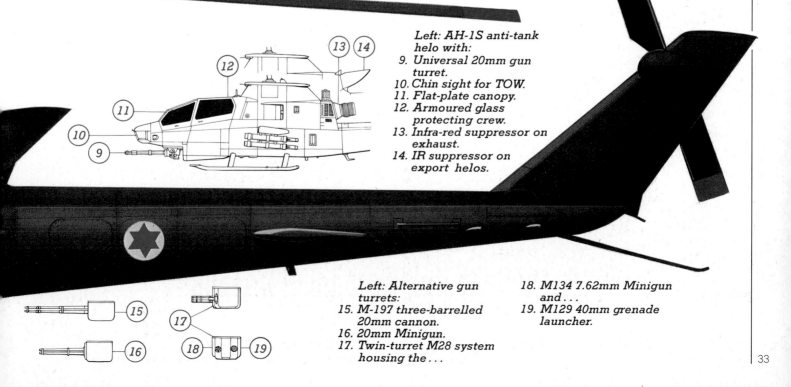

Bell UH-1 Iroquois

Data for UH-1H

Type: utility helicopter.

Specifications: Fuselage length, 41ft 1in (12.77m); height, 14ft 6in (4.41m); rotor diameter, 48ft 0in (14.63m); weight (normal take-off), 9,040lb (4,100kg).

Max speed: 110kt (204km/hr).

Range: 276nm (511km).

Max payload: 3,880lb (1,760kg).

Powerplant: one Avco Lycoming T53-L-13 turboshaft rated at 1,400shp (1,044kW).

When the XH-40 prototype took to the air for the first time on 22 October 1956, its designers could never in their wildest dreams have realised just how successful their latest creation would be. Quarter of a century later, the "Huey" is still in production and serving with the air arms of 66 nations.

The original H-40 was conceived as a six-seat utility helicopter. Powered by a single 700shp Lycoming T53-L-1, it had a weight of just over 5,000lb (2,200kg) loaded. Within seven years the H-40's descendants would already be powerful enough to lift a 5,000lb externally slung load. When finally committed to production in 1959, the basic aircraft was designated HU-1 (Helicopter Utility 1). This was soon changed to UH-1A, but by that time the nickname "Huey" had stuck.

Powerplant of the UH-1A was the Lycoming T53-L-5, and more than 700 aircraft were built. Some of these were among the first US Army rotary-wing aircraft to be sent to Vietnam. Several of the latter were armed with two 0.3in (7.62mm) machine guns and launchers for unguided rockets,

then pressed into service for close-support work.

From that time to the present the "Huey" development story has been one of ever-growing engine power and ever-increasing performance. The basic UH-1A with its 770shp engine was soon replaced by the UH-1B, which started life with the 960shp (715kW) T53-L-5 but later received the 1,100 shp (820kW) T53-L11.

The new version had an enlarged cabin able to accommodate seven passengers instead of six. Following the success of armed UH-1As, many UH-1Bs were to receive armament fits— two 0.30in (7.62mm) machine guns on each side of the cabin or 24-round rocket launchers in the same locations. The UH-1C which followed introduced a wide-chord pattern of main rotor blade and "door-hinge" rotor head. All these early "Hueys" were members of the Bell Model 204 family. This also included the T58-GE-3 powered UH-1F for the USAF (similar to the -1B but with 1,290shp of power), and the HH-1K search and rescue variant for the US Navy. The latter was powered by the 1,400shp (1,044kW) T53-L-13 turboshaft. Three UH-1M were used by the US Army to test night sensor systems.

Early "Hueys" had a maximum speed limitation of 110kt (204km/hr), but a new broad-blade pattern of main rotor allowed development in 1965 of the UH-1C for the US Army, followed by the UH-1E assault helicopter for the USMC and a series of USN types, including the UH-1L utility model, all capable of 140kt (220km/hr).

In 1961 Bell flew the UH-1D, a T53-L11-powered aircraft with a longer fuselage and cabin, extra fuel and a 4,000lb (1,800kg) payload. This soon became a major production model, and along with the 1,400shp (1,044kW) T53-L13-powered UH-1H played a major role in the Vietnam war.

These versions were part of the Bell Model 205 family, and led to civil variants such as the 205A-1.

In 1970 production of the UH-1N, first of the twin-engined "Hueys", began for the USAF. This was powered by a Pratt & Whitney Canada PT6T-3 Twin-Pac engine consisting of two independent PT-6 power units driving a single shaft via a common gearbox. Each section is rated at 900shp but the aircraft transmission cannot handle this amount of power. For normal use each

section is derated to only 645shp (481kW), but if one fails, the other can then deliver its full 900shp into the gearbox and transmission in order to sustain normal flight.

The US Army is still a major UH-1 user and plans to keep more than 2,500 UH-1Hs in service into the next century. This will necessitate the fleet being updated. Aircraft will receive modifications, including new rotor blades of composite construction, an improved transmission, new avionics such as the ALQ-39 RWR, ALQ-144 jammer, infrared suppressors to reduce vulnerability to heat-seeking missiles or infra-red target-tracking systems.

Some US Army UH-1H aircraft are being rebuilt as EH-1H EW aircraft, receiving the Quick Fix I or IA communications interception and jamming system. Japan's Ground Self-Defence Force plans to use the UH-1H for battlefield minelaying. Operational tests of a suitable mine are taking place and the system is due to enter service in 1983.

"Hueys" are still coming off the line, but no longer at the Bell plant. Agusta builds the AB 205, based on the UH-1D and H, while the UH-1N formed the basis of the AB 212. Dedicated naval versions of the latter are available in anti-ship and ASW configurations.

Other companies have completed local production of members of the UH-1 family. The UH-1D/H was built in Germany (Dornier), Japan (Fuji) and Taiwan (AIDC).

Beriev Be-12 (M-12) Tchaika

Type: maritime patrol amphibian.

Specifications: Length, 99ft 0in (30.17m); span, 97ft 5in (29.71m); height, 22ft 11in (7.0m); weight (maximum take-off), 29,450lb (64,925kg).

Max speed: 328kt (608km/hr).

Service ceiling: 37,000ft (11,280m).

Range (maximum): 2,150nm (4,000km).

Armament: see text.

Powerplant: two Ivchenko AI-20D turboprops each rated at 4,190ehp (3,124kW).

Although the Beriev design bureau has produced a series of amphibious aircraft for the Soviet Naval Air Force, the M-12 Tchaika will almost certainly be the last. A jet-powered Be-R-1 was produced in 1952, followed by a small evaluation batch of the swept-wing Be-10 "Mallow" in 1960-1, but the Be-12 (military designation M-12) was finally chosen to replace the veteran Be-6 "Madge".

Total production was probably

around 100 aircraft, and the type was deployed with the Black Sea and Northern Fleets. (Examples in Egyptian Air Force markings seen over the Mediterranean a decade ago were Soviet aircraft on detachment.) Approximately 80 remain in service, but with the land-based Il-38 taking over a major share of the ASW role, the M-12 has probably been relegated to second-line duties, such as SAR and fishery protection. Some may be retained, perhaps with updated systems, for use in tactical situations where an ability to alight on the water and conduct

a sonar search may be useful.

A weapons bay is located in the rear section of the fuselage, and two stores pylons are fitted to each wing. Hatches in the rear fuselage permit weapons to be loaded while the aircraft is afloat. At least 6,500lb (3,000kg) of stores may be carried; during record-breaking flights in 1974 an M-12

flew around a closed circuit of 1,080nm (2,000km) at a speed of 258kt (479km/hr) with a payload of 11,075lb (5,023kg). Homing torpedoes, depth charges and sonobuoys will be stored in the weapons bay, and air-to-surface missiles, unguided rockets or "iron" bombs may be carried on the pylons.

Left: From a distance, the light-coloured fitting on the roof of the "Huey" might be mistaken for an optical sight, but it is in fact a blade antenna.

Right: "Huey" and AH-1 gunship in close formation demonstrate the degree of commonality between the two designs.

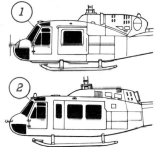

Left: Variants of the UH-1.
1. UH-1B with the original short fuselage.
2. UH-1H with longer cabin and modified housing for the T53-L-13 engine.

3. Agusta-built AB 212 ASW version with roof-mounted radome for search radar.
4. UH-1N Twin 212 with PT6T-3 engine.

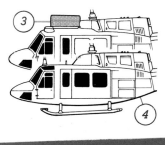

Left: This AB 212 ASW of the Italian Navy carries an earlier pattern of radar plus two homing torpedoes.

No details of the ASW avionics are available, but the aircraft sports a prominent MAD "sting" in the tail, and a forward-looking radar located in a nose-mounted "thimble" radome. Power for the avionics is generated by an APU located in the rear fuselage. According to one report, the aircraft carries a crew of five—two pilots, navigator, radar operator and MAD operator—but the range of simple avionics which such a small crew could handle would hardly warrant the use of an APU to generate additional electrical power.

Right: The sight of a flying boat on its flying run may evoke nostalgia, but in the Soviet Union as in the West, the days of such aircraft are virtually over.

Left: Beriev M-12 of the Soviet Naval Air Force (AVMF). The front-line career of these veterans is virtually over, but final retirement is probably a long way off.

Boeing B-52 Stratofortress

Data for B-52H

Type: heavy strategic bomber; also (B-52G) cruise missile carrier.
Specifications: length, 160ft 11in (49.05m); span, 185ft 0in (56.39m); height, 40ft 8in (12.4m); weight (maximum take-off), 488,000+lb (221,000+kg).
Max speed: 516kt (957km/hr).
Service ceiling: 55,000ft (16,700m).
Range (tactical radius on low-altitude mission): 950nm (1,760km), rising to 2,500nm (4,600km) at high altitude.
Armament: see text.
Powerplant: eight Pratt & Whitney TF33-P-3 turbofans each rated at 17,000lb (7,720kg) dry thrust.

Older than some of the aircrew who fly in them, the B-52s of the USAF are expected to serve until the end of the century, by which time most will be 40 years old. Most have already flown for more than 10,000 hours—a figure which increases by some 500 hours per year.

Current service versions are the B-52D, G and H, but the Ds will all have been retired by 1983, unless President Reagan reverses his 1981 decision to phase them out. The H model will continue in the traditional bombing role, armed with SRAM missiles and free-falling weapons, such as the B61 thermonuclear bomb, but the G force will be armed with 2,500km-range AGM-68B ALCM cruise missiles. Several hundred earlier B-52s are in storage and unlikely to fly again.

At best the continental USA will receive 30 minutes warning of a Soviet ICBM attack, but the use of SLBMs fired from submarines close to the US coast could cut this to 15 minutes or less. Since the B-52G and H force is tasked with the strategic strike mission, the bombers must be "flushed" into the air and well away from their home bases before the incoming warheads explode. All were retrofitted with cartridge starters in the mid-1970s so that the eight engines could be started simultaneously.

Structural and avionics modification of the B-52 has been a continuous process in order to maintain the big bomber's ability to penetrate to Soviet air space at low level and to keep its defensive systems abreast of current SAM and interceptor threats. In the past, bombers tended to become obsolete and be retired long before fatigue and other structural problems reared their head, but the projected B-52 flying life of 5,000 hours was exceeded in the early 1970s by even the youngest aircraft. The decision in the early 1960s to switch from the high-altitude role to low altitude placed further severe stress on the airframe.

An unfortunate choice of aluminium alloy for the lower section of the B-52G and H wing led to an inadequate fatigue life, so the wings were rebuilt, using a more stress-tolerant alloy. Other modifications strengthened the fuselage and vertical fin.

Initial B-52s delivered in the late 1950s had what is by current standards a modest ECM system—three different patterns of RWR, two chaff dispensers and an array of 14 ALT-6B jammers. Since then the defensive avionics have been regularly updated, and the G and H models currently carry Phase VI ECM systems, installed in the 1970s. A detailed listing of the systems carried is given in tabular form. Other ECM systems being fitted or planned for installation are the ITT ALQ-172 and new equipment intended to counter the Soviet SUAWACS early-warning aircraft.

Both the G and H models are being updated with new navigation and attack systems, while the former is also being converted to handle the AGM-68B ALCM cruise missile. The original B-52 navigation and bombing systems used vacuum tubes (valves to our UK readers), and was difficult to service, owing to the difficulty of obtaining spares. Beginning in 1980, these systems were replaced with modern solid-state electronics incorporating digital computers, all hardened against the effects of EMP from nuclear explosions. The entire suite is known as the Offensive Avionics System. Flight testing of the system began in September 1980 and the first 16 aircraft to be retrofitted were due to be operational by the end of 1982. Modification of the entire fleet will not be completed until 1990.

Basic components of OAS are a Honeywell ASN-131 inertial navigation system, Teledyne Ryan Doppler radar, IBM/Raytheon ASQ-38 bombing system, Honeywell radar altimeter and a modernised Norden radar. OAS incorporates terrain contour match-

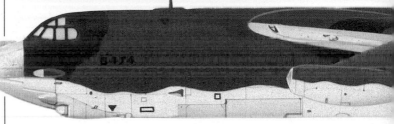

ing facilities similar to those of the ALCM cruise missile.

Communications are also being upgraded, with the bomber fleet receiving new VLF and LF systems.

The H model was selected for the deep-penetration role because it has the youngest airframes and is fitted with TF-33 turbofan engines instead of the more fuel-hungry J57 turbojet. Modifications to the B-52H will allow these aircraft to carry up to 84 Mk.82 500lb (230kg) bombs internally instead of the current 24, while a further 24 will be carried on underwing multiple-ejector pylons. Modified aircraft will be earmarked to support the US Rapid Deployment Force, making good the conventional bombing capability lost when the last B-52Ds are retired. Initial plans call for 35 aircraft to be modified.

In order to penetrate Soviet airspace, the B-52 force must fly at low level, a task not envisaged when the basic airframe was designed in the mid-1950s. There is no question of contour-following —the B-52 will skim from crest to crest at speeds of 352-65kt (652-76km/hr). In order to help the crew during low-level flight, the B-52G and H are fitted with ASQ-151 electro-optical viewing systems, which use FLIR and LLTV sensors mounted in chin turrets.

Deployment of the ALCM-armed B-52G is due to begin in December 1982. ALCM-equipped B-52Gs are due to become operational at a total of six bases, starting with Griffiss AFB in New York State. Each B-52G will initially carry 12 ALCMs, but the planned full complement is 20 rounds—eight in an internally mounted rotary launcher and 12 on underwing pylons.

In order to protect the ALCM against improved Soviet air defences, the missiles are to be fitted with an ECM system designed to counter the search radar of the SUAWACS. The ability of ALCM to penetrate Soviet defences is already being questioned. Tercom guidance relies on the missile locating itself on landfall, and some sources suggest that the number of locations along the Soviet coastline where the terrain is rugged enough to provide reliable guidance data is limited, and that air-defence systems are already being concentrated at such locations. In the long run ALCM may need a more capable type of guidance system.

Under the terms of the unratified SALT-2 treaty, bombers equipped to launch cruise missiles must be externally distinguishable from those which are not. In order to meet this requirement, the B-52G has been fitted with strakes—rounded fairings at the front end of the wing root. These fairings incorporate intakes for cooling air for part of the OAS avionics, and, as a useful bonus, improve aerodynamic efficiency by up to two per cent.

Above: The B-52D (with tall tail fin) is to be phased out, but the turbofan-engined B-52H (just above it) still operates as a penetrating bomber with free-falling weapons.

Left: B-52G with pylon-mounted AGM-68B ALCM cruise missiles and chin "blisters" for ASQ-151 FLIR and LLTV sensors.

B-52 Phase VI ECM equipment

Designation	Manufacturer	Equipment type	No. carried	Notes
ALE-20	various	16-round infra-red flare dispenser	12	Total of 192 flares carried
ALE-24	Lundy	Electro-mechanical chaff dispenser	8	Total of 1,125 chaff packages carried
ALQ-117	ITT	Noise & deception jammer	4	Operates in I & J bands (prob. 8-15 GHz)
ALQ-122	Motorola	False target generator	1	Counters Tu-126 "Moss" radar & SA-3 SAM
ALQ-153	Westinghouse	Tail-warning pulse-Doppler radar	1	
ALQ-155	Northrop	"Smart" power-management system	1	Controls up to eight jamming transmissions
ALR-20	Hallicrafters	Wide-band search receiver	1	Used to search for hostile transmissions
ALR-46	Itek	Radar-warning receiver	1	Covers E to J band (2-18 GHz)
ALT-16	Hallicrafters	Barrage jammer	2	Radiates noise over a wide frequency band
ALT-28	Hallicrafters	Noise-jamming transmitter	10	Developed from earlier ALT-13
ALT-32H	Hallicrafters	Noise-jamming transmitter	2	
ALT-32L	Hallicrafters	Noise-jamming transmitter	1	

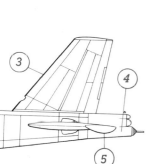

1. Tall tail fin and . . .
2. Tail gunner's position on B-52D.
3. B-52G/H short tail fin . . .
4. Remote-controlled guns, and . . .
5. Tail-warning radar pod.
6. Nose section of B-52D.
7. B-52G/H (original pattern).
8. B-52G/H (latest standard).

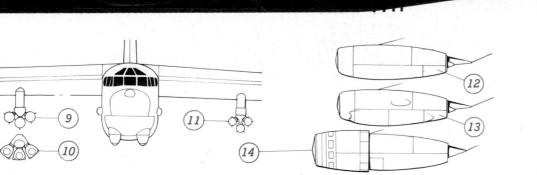

B-52 underwing stores . . .
9. Boeing AGM-86B SRAM missiles.
10. Boeing AGM-86B ALCM cruise missiles (on B-52G only).
11. 500lb (230kg) "iron" bombs. Current pattern of engine pod . . .
12. B-52D (for J57-P-19W or -29W turbojet).
13. B-52G (for J57-P-43WB turbojet).
14. B-52H (for TF-33-P-3 turbofan).

Boeing E-3A Sentry

Type: airborne warning and control systems (AWACS).
Specifications: length, 152ft 11ins (46.61m); span, 145ft 9in (44.42m); height, 41ft 4in (12.6m); weight (maximum take-off), 325,000lb (147,000kg).
Max speed: 460kt (855km/hr).
Service ceiling: 40,000ft (12,000m).
Powerplant: four Pratt & Whitney TF33 turbofans each rated at 21,000lb (9,540kg) dry thrust.

The E-3A can be used to monitor and identify aircraft at ranges of more than 200nm (370km), and to act as a mobile command and control centre for Tactical Air Command operations. The basic E-3A aircraft is based on the civil Boeing 707-720B transport, but has military Pratt & Whitney TF33 turbofans in place of the commercial powerplants. Following trials in the early 1970s with competing Hughes and Westinghouse radars in prototype aircraft designated EC-137D, the USAF selected the Westinghouse APY-1. Deliveries began in March 1977, and E-3As assumed an operational role in the North American Air Defences (NORAD) on 1 January 1979.

Basic configuration ordered by the USAF was the "Core E-3A" standard, but this was replaced on the production line from aircraft no. 24 onwards by an improved version described below. Earlier examples will be upgraded to the latter standard.

Since the provision of national airborne early-warning fleets was clearly too expensive for most of the NATO allies, plans were drawn up in the late 1970s for a multinational force of 18 aircraft. These needed a degree of maritime-surveillance capability, so Westinghouse began work on this in 1976 under a USAF contract. NATO also specified requirements for additional HF radio communications equipment and a radio teletype for maritime use, IDS tactical communications system, new data-processing equipment based on the IBM System 4 Pi Model CC-2 computer, and underwing hardpoints for defensive systems.

The new computer has a memory capacity of more than 665,000 words—more than five times that of the earlier CC-1 model specified by the USAF—and can carry out 1.25 million operations per second instead of 470,000. This gives the NATO-standard E-3A enormous data-processing speed and capacity, as well as the ability to initiate target tracks automatically. Official designation of the updated radar is APY-2.

Five basic operating modes are possible, and, like the APY-1, the -2 can change its operating mode for scan to scan, or even from one part of the scan to another. For maximum long-range performance, a low-PRF Beyond-the-Horizon mode may be used, but if good range resolution is required, the shorter-range pulse-Doppler non-elevation scan is used. In order to obtain elevation data, the radar can be operated in pulse-Doppler elevation scan mode, but this causes a further reduction in range performance. Targets radiating radar energy may be tracked by means of a passive mode, in which the radar acts purely as a receiver and thus does not betray its presence to the target. In maritime mode the threshold of the moving-target indication circuitry is reduced from 80kt (148km/hr) to zero, so that slow-moving or even stationary surface targets are displayed. A very short pulse is used in this mode, reducing the amount of sea clutter in the return signal.

Other modes are used for fault-finding, and to keep the radar on standby status and ready for immediate operation. The antenna rotates at 6rpm while the radar is operating, and at 0.25rpm while the set is on standby or shut down. Continuous rotation is necessary while in flight in order to keep the antenna bearing lubricated.

The technology used in the radar and data-processing hardware is of mid 1960s vintage and would not be too difficult to copy should an E-3A fall into unfriendly

Boeing E-4A/B Advanced Airborne Command Post

Type: airborne command post.
Specifications: length, 231ft 4in (70.51m); span, 195ft 8in (59.64m); height, 63ft 5in (19.33m); weight (maximum take-off), 775,000lb (351,500kg).
Max speed: Mach 0.99.
Powerplant: four General Electric F103 turbofans each rated at 52,500lb (23,850kg) dry thrust.

The USAF intends to deploy a total of six E-4 AABNCP (Advanced Airborne Command Post) aircraft by the mid-1980s. Boeing has delivered one E-4B and is currently rebuilding three E-4A aircraft to the B standard. Once this has been done, two more E-4Bs will be built to complete the fleet. The E-4s are currently based at Offutt Air Force Base in Nebraska, replacing the EC-135 Airborne Command Post.

Like the earlier aircraft, the E-4 is intended to carry staff tasked with strategic command and decision-making, acting as a backup to ground-based facilities whose destruction in the early stages of a nuclear conflict would be likely. To fulfil this role, the E-4 must carry an extensive array of data-processing and communications equipment. The E-4A was always seen as an interim aircraft, and was equipped with systems removed from earlier EC-135 aircraft. The use of a much larger airframe—basically a civil Boeing 747-200B with General Electric CF-650E (E-4A) or General Electric F103 turbofan engines—allowed a larger staff to be carried for a greater length of time. Available floor space in the new aircraft is 4,620 sq. ft (429sq. m)—almost three times that in the EC-135. Despite this, the amount of onboard data-processing remains limited.

Experience gained with the E-4A allowed the USAF to proceed with confidence on the definitive E-4B version, which has been extensively fitted out with new systems. With the aid of airborne-refuelling, an E-4B may remain airborne for up to 72 hours—a limit set by the endurance of the crew and by the amount of engine oil carried.

The equipment fit includes new SHF and LF/VLF communications equipment, capable of interfacing with military communications satellites such as FLTSAT-COM, and DFCS series. Antennas for these are located in a dorsal fairing not present on the earlier E-4A. An aircraft-mounted computer is used to aim the antenna within the fairing at the required satellite. The E-4B can communicate with the ground over a wide range of frequencies covering virtually the entire radio communication spectrum of 14kHz to 8.4GHz. Fourteen ground stations can handle traffic from the E-4, linking it into the main US ground-based communications networks.

Each aircraft is fitted with a retractable VLF wire antenna some 5 miles (8km) long and used by a total of 13 communications links. Much attention has been given to hardening the avionics against electro-magnetic pulse (EMP) effects produced by nuclear explosions, since trailing antennas could pick up EMP radiation.

At a later date the E-4B may receive equipment capable of receiving data directly from Defence Support Program early-warning and attack assessment satellites. An improved Airborne Launch Control System (ALCS) may also be fitted, allowing the AABCP to retarget Minuteman ICBMs. The existing ALCS allows Minuteman missiles to be launched on command from the E-4B. The launch codes are carried in memory units which are physically destroyed by an automatic system if power is removed for more than 3 minutes in order to guard against their being compromised in the event of an E-4 crashing.

The only other Boeing 747s in military service are the 11 747F aircraft in the inventory of the Iranian Air Force. Equipped for airborne refuelling, these were later joined by seven ex-TWA aircraft.

hands, but analysis and reverse-engineering of the system software would be a formidable undertaking. Should the system be compromised, the US could modify the software within weeks in order to modify the radar's operating characteristics.

On normal patrol duties the E-3A cruises at Mach 0.72 at an altitude of 29,000ft (8,800m). Under these conditions the radar has a range of just over 200nm (110km) against low-level targets. Sentry can remain on patrol for 9 to 11 hours, but this can be stretched to 22 hours by in-flight refuelling. The latter figure is limited by the capacity of the oil tank on the P&W TF33 engines.

No plans exist at the moment to fit USAF or NATO E-3As with ECM systems, but the hardpoints on the NATO-standard aircraft are suitable for chaff dispensers, while mountings and cabling have been fitted in the wing roots and leading edges to accommodate future ECM equipment and antennas.

The other customer to date has been Saudi Arabia, but in this case the aircraft has been slightly downgraded by the removal of highly classified systems such as JTIDS. The planned fleet of five E-3A will give better air-defence capability than would be possible with a network of 48 ground-based radars. The aircraft are due to enter service in 1986, and will be based initially at Dharan, later moving to a new airfield at Kharji.

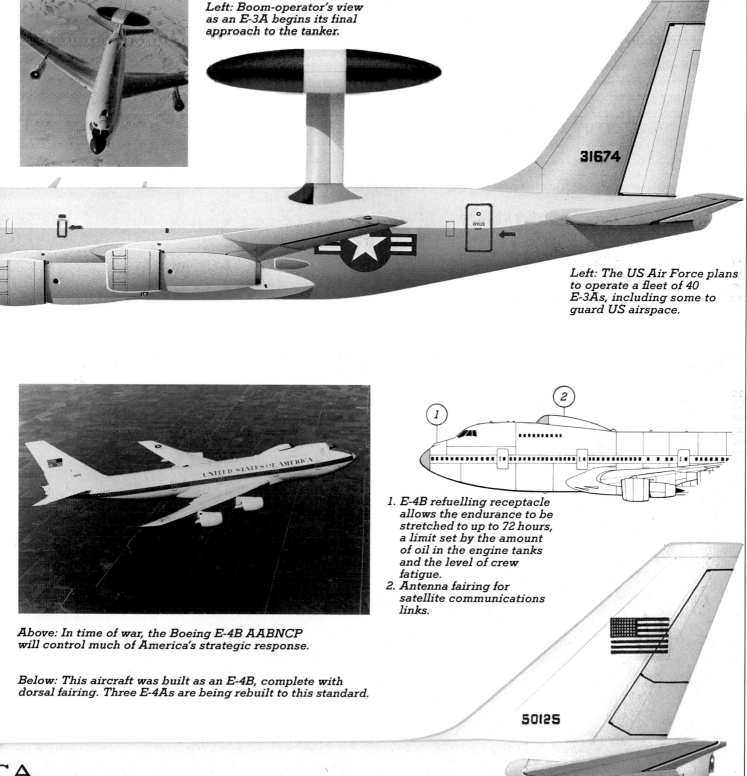

Left: Boom-operator's view as an E-3A begins its final approach to the tanker.

Left: The US Air Force plans to operate a fleet of 40 E-3As, including some to guard US airspace.

Above: In time of war, the Boeing E-4B AABNCP will control much of America's strategic response.

Below: This aircraft was built as an E-4B, complete with dorsal fairing. Three E-4As are being rebuilt to this standard.

1. E-4B refuelling receptacle allows the endurance to be stretched to up to 72 hours, a limit set by the amount of oil in the engine tanks and the level of crew fatigue.
2. Antenna fairing for satellite communications links.

Boeing KC-135 Stratotanker

Data for KC-135A
Type: tanker/transport; developed versions for special duties (see text).
Specifications: length, 134ft 6in (40.99m); span, 130ft 10in (39.88m); height, 41ft 8in (12.69m); weight (normal take-off), 301,600lb (136,800kg).
Max speed: 521kt (966km/hr).
Range (tactical radius with transfer of 74,000lb (33,500kg) of fuel): 2,000nm (3,700km).
Max payload: 31,200 US gallons (118,100l) of fuel.
Powerplant: four Pratt & Whitney J57-P-59W turbojets, each rated at 13,750lb (6,250kg) dry thrust.

Faced with the long series of Boeing "7-7" airliner designations from the original 707 to the latest 767, many people must have wondered what happened to the Boeing 717, since no such airliner has ever existed. Boeing in fact used the designation for the KC-135 Strato-tanker.

Despite the age of the basic aircraft, the KC-135 still serves as the main USAF flight-refuelling tanker, and will be supplemented rather than replaced by the newer KC-10A. A total of 732 tanker/transports were built between 1956 and 1966, plus others for such specialised roles as reconnaissance, elint and research.

In order to keep the fleet operational until the end of the century, Boeing's Wichita division has been engaged since the mid-1970s in replacing the lower wing skins as part of a life-extension programme. Until recently the standard powerplant remained the Pratt & Whitney JT-57-59W, a two-spool turbojet whose noise output did little to endear the type to local communities and whose "gas-guzzling" habits reflected a long-gone era of cheap fuel. To overcome both problems, the USAF plans to re-engine at least a portion of the fleet with turbofans.

The most obvious replacement powerplant was the General Electric/Snecma CFM-56, and Boeing was given a contract in 1980 to begin the conversion programme. Aircraft receiving the new powerplant will also have their hydraulic and electrical systems modified, and the resulting aircraft will be designated KC-135RE. Other current modifications include the installation of a night-refuelling floodlight at the top of the vertical fin, new avionics (including a Delco Electronics Fuel Savings Advisory System, which could cut fuel consumption by 2-4 per cent), and a nose and reel fuel transfer system located in the belly, just forward of the main landing gear.

Fifty-six KC-135As were converted into KC-135Q tankers capable of refuelling the Lockheed SR-71 force. These aircraft have additional avionics, plus fuel systems capable of handling JP-7 fuel.

A substantial number of KC-135s are now being flown by 14 units of the US Air National Guard. The only other operator of the type is the French Air Force, which acquired 12 KC-135Fs in 1964 for use with the Mirage IV bomber fleet. These aircraft remain in service and are being retrofitted with CFM-56 turbofans.

At least seven other air arms operate the Boeing 707. Saudi Arabia is scheduled to receive six KC-707 tankers, while second-hand examples of the civil 707 are now being offered to export customers by Pan American. In order to suit the latter to the tanker role, the wings will be strengthened and a three-point "probe-and-drogue" refuelling system added.

From the basic KC-135A configuration Boeing has created a family of special-purpose versions, the main currently operational variants being as in the table.

Designation	Role
EC-135A & L	Radio relay link
EC-135B	Range instrumentation a/c
EC-135C, H, J & K	Airborne command post
EC-135G	Airborne launch-control*
EC-135N	Spacecraft tracking
KC-135R	Reconnaissance
NKC-135	Trials aircraft
RC-135M & S	Elint?
RC-135T	Support & training
RC-135U, V & W	SLAR reconnaissance?
WC-135B	Weather reconnaissance

*for use with Minuteman ICBM force

Above right: C-135V with SLAR antennas on fuselage sides, fairings, blade antennas and wingtip HF probes.

Right: KC-135Q tankers carry the specialised JP-7 fuel required by the SR-71.

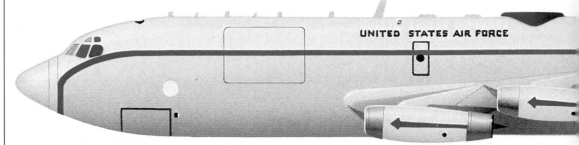

Above: Originally purchased for use with the Mirage IV nuclear bomber, this KC-135F plays host to France's latest Mach 2 design — the Mirage 2000 fighter.

Right: Turbofan-powered EC-135C airborne command post, one of 14 aircraft kept in service to supplement the larger and more modern E-4A and E-4B.

Below: The supply of 12 C-135F tanker/transports to France implied US approval of that nation's nuclear strike force.

38473

Below: The simple engine pods of this USAF KC-135 house J57-P-29W turbojets, noisy and fuel-hungry units due to be replaced by CFM-56 turbofans.

10274

Above: Formerly EC-135N, now C 135N, there are four of these USAF special electronic and test versions used for space range instrumentation.

1. Engine pods of KC-135A.
2. Experimental drag-reduction winglets.
3. Location of fuel-jettison pipe on non-tanker aircraft.
4. Engine pods for TF-33-powered EC-135C airborne command post.
5. CFM-56 turbofans on KC-135RE.
6. Sensor fairings on KC-135S.
7. Ventral camera pack on RC-135B.

Below: RC-135U reconnaissance aircraft of the 55th Strategic Reconnaissance Wing. Sensor equipment includes chin-mounted and under-fuselage radomes, rectangular fairing on fuselage side (probably for a sideways-looking sensor or radar), and an RC-135B-style camera installation beneath the tail section.

14849

U.S. AIR FO
4849

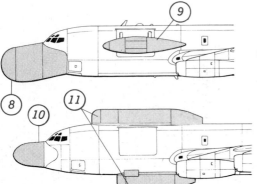
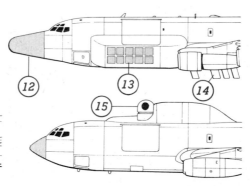

Left: KC-135 "specials":
EC-135N with
8. Nose radome.
9. Equipment fairing for optical tracker.
NKC-135A "Big Crow" with
10. Nose radome.
11. Fairings for trials equipment.
RC-135V with
12. Nose radome.
13. Multi-element antenna array for sideways-looking radar.
14. Blade antennas.
NKC-135A Airborne laser lab with
15. Steerable laser turret.

Boeing Vertol CH-46 Sea Knight

Data: for CH-46E
Type: multi-role naval helicopter.
Specifications: length, 44ft 10in (13.66m); height, 16ft 8in (5.09m); rotor diameter, 50ft 0in (15.24m); weight (maximum loaded), 21,400lb (9,700kg).
Range: (with 6,600lb payload) 94nm (175km).
Powerplants: two General Electric T58-GE-16 turboshafts each rated at 1,870shp (1,395kw).

Production of the Sea Knight by Boeing ended in the early 1970s, but the aircraft is still being built in Japan; 624 were supplied to the US Navy and Marines.

The original aircraft was designed by the Piaseckl Helicopter Corp. and offered to the US Army. This service soon switched its interest to the heavier CH-47 Chinook, but the USMC became the first military operator of the type—now designated the Boeing-Vertol Sea Knight. Basic version was the CH-46A, but this was succeeded by more powerful variants ending with the CH-46D. The USN was quick to adopt the type, procuring the UH-46A and D—basically similar to the CH-46A and D models—for ship replenishment, as well as the HH-46 for search & rescue.

Both services are upgrading their fleets. In creating the new CH-46E version, the USMC has installed 1,870shp (1,395kW) T58-16 turboshafts in place of the earlier lower-powered engines such as the 1,400shp (1,045kW) T58-GE-10 used in the CH-46D, glass-fibre rotor blades, crash resistant aircrew seats and fuel systems, plus improved rescue equipment.

During the mid-1980s, USN and USMC aircraft will be upgraded in a separate programme using retrofit kits to be provided by Boeing-Vertol. Goal of this project is to increase aircraft safety, reliability and maintainability. Canada operates two versions of the H-46 series under the designations CH-113 Labrador and CH-113A Voyageur. Both are being upgraded to an improved common standard with the addition of increased fuel capacity and equipment such as weather radar, an APU, and an external hoist for rescue operations.

Below: Canadian Armed Forces CH-113A Voyageur.

Boeing Vertol CH-47 Chinook

Data for CH-47C
Type: heavy transport helicopter.
Specifications: length, 51ft (15.54m); height, 18ft 7in (5.67m); rotor diameter, 60ft (18.29m); weight (max. take-off), 46,000lb (20,865kg).
Max speed: 164kt (304 km/hr.)
Range: (mission radius with 6,400lb internal payload) 100nm (185km).
Maximum payload: (external load) 23,200lb 10,550kg).
Powerplants: Two General Electric T55-L-11A turboshafts each rated at 3,750shp (2,795kW).

The basic Chinook design may be two decades old, but this twin-rotor helicopter remains one of the main heavy-lift helicopters in current production. It now serves with or has been ordered for the armed forces of at least 18 nations.

Current production model is the CH-47D and its derivatives, and earlier aircraft are being rebuilt to this standard. Initial production version was the CH-47A powered by two 2,200shp (1,640kW) Avco Lycoming T55-L-5 or 1,976shp (2,650kW) T55-L-7 turboshafts. This aircraft served with the armed forces of the USA and South Vietnam.

Experience with these early aircraft led to the installation of the higher-powered 2,850shp (2,125kW) T55-L-7C turboshaft driving a rotor with redesigned blades. These changes, plus aerodynamic improvements such as strakes on the aft fuselage and tail ramp/door, and a blunter design of rear rotor pylon, resulted in the CH-47B, which first entered service in the summer of 1967.

CH-47C was further developed, the choice of 3,750shp (3,750kW) T55-L-11A engines requiring the transmission to be upgraded in order to cope with the extra output. Fuel capacity was increased to meet the demands of these engines. Production deliveries of new-build CH-47Cs began in 1968, but existing US Army Chinooks of earlier type were rebuilt with the strengthened transmissions under an Army contract of May 1978.

It was inevitable that this heavyweight would see action in Southeast Asia. Some 900 Chinooks had been built by the early 1980s, and more than 550 of these saw action in the Vietnam war. In addition to being used as a troop and supply carrier, the Chinook acquired a reputation as a rescuer of downed aircraft. More than 11,000 damaged fixed-wing aircraft and helicopters were airlifted for eventual repair or salvage. Maximum payload of the CH-47C was 23,200lb (10,550kg), so fixed-wing aircraft sometimes had to be partially stripped down in order to lighten the load.

First flight of the CH-47D was in 1979, the three prototypes being a converted CH-47A, -47B and -47C respectively. All US Army Chinooks are to be updated to this standard, receiving T55-L-712 engines with an emergency rating of 4,500shp (3,350kW), and a new transmission able to cope with up to 5,600shp (7,500kW) of power. Glass fibre rotor blades are fitted along with an integral design of transmission lubrication and cooling system.

Since the CH-47D is obviously due to remain the standard US Army heavy-lift helicopter for some time to come, the design incorporates features such as modularised hydraulics, electrical systems with built-in redundancy, improved avionics and a redesigned cockpit intended to reduce pilot workload.

Canada's CH-147 version was based on the CH-47C, while the British Chinook HC.Mk 1 is largely based on the -47D model. British examples have T55-L-11C engines and provision for composite rotor blades. Current export version is the CH-47D-derived Model 414. The CH-47C was built under licence in Italy by Elicotteri Meridionali from 1970 onwards, and the first Italian-built equivalent to the CH-47D is due in 1983.

Above: RAF Chinook HC.1, until the advent of the new CH-47D the most advanced version of this medium-lift helicopter.

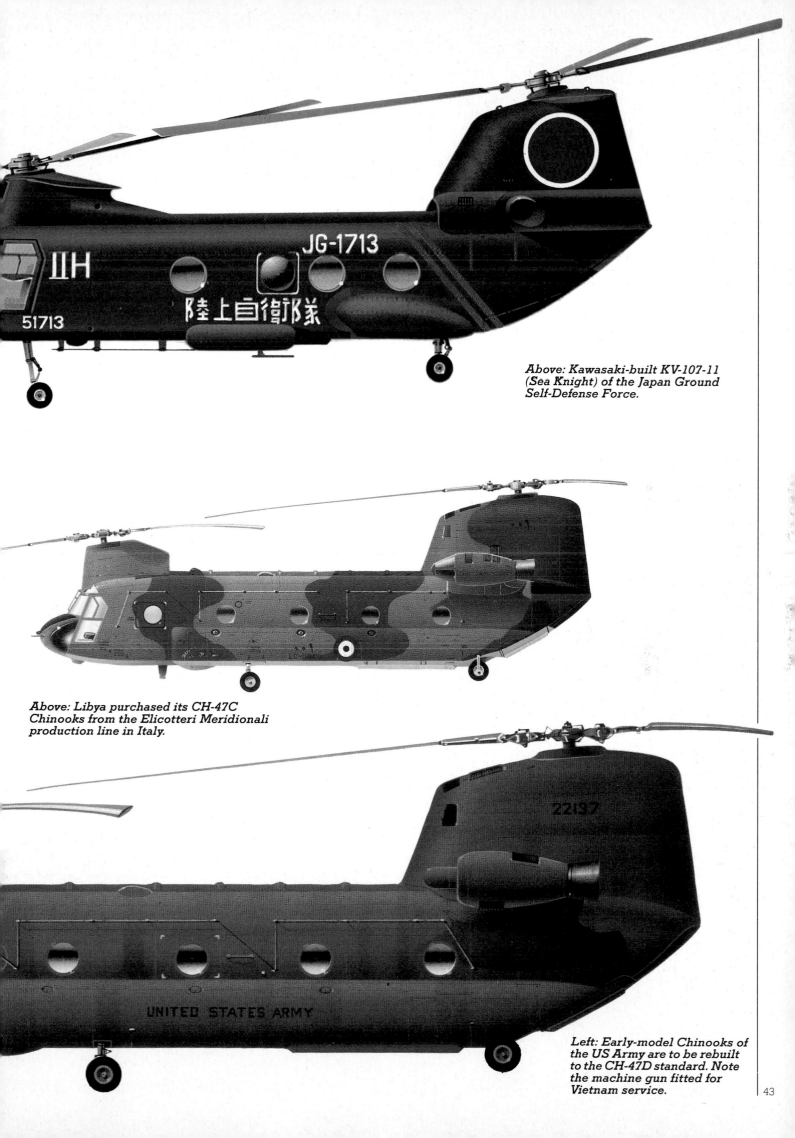

Above: Kawasaki-built KV-107-11 (Sea Knight) of the Japan Ground Self-Defense Force.

Above: Libya purchased its CH-47C Chinooks from the Elicotteri Meridionali production line in Italy.

Left: Early-model Chinooks of the US Army are to be rebuilt to the CH-47D standard. Note the machine gun fitted for Vietnam service.

Breguet Br.1050 Alize

Type: carrier-borne ASW aircraft.

Specifications: length, 45ft 6in (13.86m); span, 51ft 2in (15.6m); height, 15ft 7in (4.75m); weight (normal loaded), 18,100lb (8,250kg).

Max speed: 256kt (475km/hr).

Service ceiling: 20,500ft (6,250m).

Patrol endurance: with radome extended 5hr 12min.

Armament: see text.

Powerplant: one Rolls-Royce Dart RDa,.21 turboprop rated at 1,975shp.

Based on a late-1940s design for a carrier-based strike aircraft, the Breguet Alize still serves with the French Aéronavale on the carriers *Foch* and *Clemenceau*, and with the Indian Navy aboard the carrier *Vikrant*. Two Aéronavale units fly the Alize—Flottilles 4F and 6F. Being an ex-Royal Navy *Majestic*-class light carrier, *Vikrant* has limited hangar capacity, so the Indian Navy's 310 Sqn only deploys a single four-aircraft flight aboard the carrier.

Unlike its contemporary the Fairey Gannet (which used a twin-section Bristol Siddeley Mamba driving two contra-rotating airscrews), Alize is a single-engined

type powered by a Rolls-Royce Dart single-shaft turboprop. A total of 89 were built between 1957 and 1962, including two pre-production examples. France still has 39 examples in service, while India has 20, so the single-engine configuration does not seem to have resulted in an unduly high loss rate.

Considerable ingenuity was needed to create an effective ASW platform in so small an aircraft. The main weapons bay can carry an acoustic torpedo or three 350lb (160kg) depth charges, but the sonobuoys are located in the forward section of the wing nacelles (used to house the main undercarriage). Rockets, bombs, depth charges or wire-guided air-to-surface missiles may be mounted

on underwing pylons. The radar operator sits in front of the cockpit on the right-hand side, but the second sensor operator is located behind, a situation which may be less satisfactory than on larger aircraft, in which communications between operators is made easy by the use of side-by-side seating.

Having completed some 250,000 flying hours on the type,

the Aéronavale is now modernising 28 of its Alize fleet, replacing the earlier radar with the Thomson-CSF Iguane set used by the Atlantic NG, and adding an Omega navigation system and new ESM equipment. Revised aircraft are now in service, and the programme is due to be completed in 1983.

During the Indian occupation

British Aerospace BAe 748, Andover and Coastguarder

Type: light tactical transport; Coastguarder is maritime patrol version.

Specifications: length, 67ft 0in (20.42m); span, 102ft 6in (31.24m); height, 24ft 10in (7.57m); weight (maximum take-off), 46,500lb (21,100kg).

Max speed: 245kt (450km/hr).

Range (with 7,800lb (3,545kg) payload: 1,345nm (2,490km).

Max payload: 12,800lb (5,800kg).

Powerplant: two Rolls-Royce Dart 536-2, turboprops each rated at 2,280ehp (1,700kW).

Production of the BAe 748 is now concentrated on the Series 2B version, with extended wingspan, revised tail surfaces and Rolls-Royce Dart 536-2 engines. These changes give the aircraft a higher cruising speed and ceiling, improve take-off performance and increase the useful payload by 2,000lb (910kg).

Although the basic design of the aircraft was conceived as a DC-3 replacement for the airlines, more than 155 examples are now in military service with 18 nations. More than 50 of the aircraft built by BAe are custom-built military transports, with a large rear freight door and strengthened floor. The Andover CC-1 military freighter, with a kneeling undercarriage and tail door/ramp, was originally developed for Britain's Royal Air Force, but less than 20 remain in RAF service. Ten ex-

RAF Andovers are operated by the Royal New Zealand Air Force.

India has its own production line at the Kanpur division of Hindustan Aeronautics to supply aircraft for military and civil use, and the Indian Air Force operates more than 40 examples. Kanpur built its first 748 in 1961 and switched to the Series 2 in 1964. By the early 1980s Hindustan Aeronautics was building military freighters at a rate of four per year, and local production was expected to end in 1983.

In an attempt to meet the potential demand for maritime-patrol aircraft capable of policing 200-mile Exclusive Economic Zones, BAe devised the Coastguarder version, equipped with an MEL MAREC search radar in a dorsal radome, Doppler and Omega navigation systems and bubble transparencies for observers, plus optional equipment such as an IR linescan sensor. A prototype was prepared by converting an ex-airline 748 Series 2A, and this began a programme of flight tests in February 1977.

These trials confirmed that the aircraft could perform a useful maritime mission, but the market failed to respond with orders. BAe then decided to re-use the aircraft to create the prototype Series 2B 748, and to build a second prototype with a revised cabin layout. Moving the radar operator's position to the front of

the cabin left the rear section free for multi-role operations, allowing Coastguarder-configured aircraft to carry out secondary transport or SAR tasks. This revised aircraft was the outright winner of the Sea Search '81 competition held in the UK in 1981, but this success was not translated into immediate orders for the type.

BAe also offers an ASV/ASW version of Coastguarder, whose systems may be built up in modular form as dictated by the military budget or likely threat. At its most complex, this version could carry a tactical crew of seven—four operators to man consoles dedicated to communications/teletype, search radar, sonics, and ESM, two observers stationed at the team transparencies, and a single tactical co-ordinator seated at a fifth console.

Below: 21 Sqn of the Belgian Air Force operates three Military 748 transports. Note the prominent rear door.

of Goa in December 1961, Alizes flew reconnaissance missions, but the type saw combat during the 1971 war between India and Pakistan. Stationed in the Bay of Bengal, *Vikrant* used its Alizes to carry out continuous anti-submarine patrols at ranges of up to 70nm (130km) from the ship. One Alize was shot down by a Pakistan Air Force F-104 Starfighter, whose Sidewinder heat-seeking missile seems to have had no problem in homing on to the turboprop-powered aircraft which, incidentally, seems to have been land-based and not one of the *Vikrant's* complement.

Left: The Alize carrier-borne ASW aircraft serves with both the French and Indian navies.

INDIAN NAVY

Above: If Alize is to remain in Indian Navy service through the 1980s, an avionics update will surely be needed.

Left: The large freight door on this Brazilian AF HS.748 indicates it is a 2C version.

1. Large cargo door fitted to the 748 military freighter version.
2. Small rear door of Andover C.1.
3. Wingtips of the Series 1 and Series 2 aircraft and the original Coastguarder prototype.
4. Extended wingtips fitted to Series 2B aircraft and to the second Coastguarder prototype.

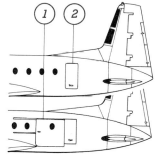

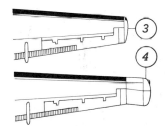

British Aerospace Harrier and Sea Harrier

Data for Sea Harrier
Type: carrier-borne V/Stol fighter; Harrier and AV8A are land-and carrier-based close support aircraft.
Specifications: length, 47ft 7in (14.5m); span, 25ft 3in (7.7m); height, 12ft 2in (3.71m); weight (maximum take-off), 25,000+lb (11,300+kg).
Max speed: 640kt (1,190km/hr).
Service ceiling: 50,000+ft (15,000+m).
Range (tactical radius on intercept mission): 400nm (750km).
Armament: 5,000+lb (2,700+kg) of ordnance plus two 30mm Aden cannon.
Powerplant: one Rolls-Royce Pegasus 104 vectored-thrust turbofan rated at 21,500lb (9,770kg) dry thrust.

Left: Two RAF Harrier GR.3s hug a Scottish hillside during a low-level training sortie. Under their wings are rocket packs outboard and drop tanks inboard.

Below right: The extended nose on RAF Harrier GR.3 fighters houses a Ferranti Type 106 laser ranger and marked-target seeker.

Thirteen years after first entering squadron service, and more than two decades since the pioneering Hawker P.1127 first flew, Harrier remains a controversial aircraft. Few air arms have chosen to adopt V/Stol, despite the growing range of anti-runway weapons which may be carried by the modern strike aircraft. The Royal Air Force remains a firm exponent of V/Stol operation, but the type's export success has hinged on its suitability for shipboard or amphibious use.

Harrier is capable of vertical take-off, but is rarely used in this manner, since short take-off runs substantially increase the range/payload performance. Vertical landing remains a useful facility, particularly if pilots fatigued by multiple sorties ever have to attempt a landing at an air base whose runways have been partially or totally destroyed.

The current RAF GR.3 is powered by a Rolls-Royce Pegasus 103 vectored-thrust turbofan offering 21,500lb (9,770kg) of thrust, and has a nose-mounted Ferranti Type 106 laser ranger and marked-target seeker, and Ferranti FE 541 nav-attack system.

The broadly similar AV-8A is a more austere aircraft, lacking the nav-attack systems of the Harrier but equipped with AIM-9 Sidewinder missiles for air-to-air combat. The USMC pioneered the use of "viffing" (vectoring in forward flight)—the technique of moving the nozzles during air-combat in order to permit the aircraft to perform manoeuvres which a conventional aircraft cannot duplicate. An unwary pilot attempting to get into firing position behind a wildly viffing Harrier or AV-8A is likely to find himself heading for a high-speed impact with the ground, for example, having been led into a situation which only a vectored-thrust aircraft can escape from.

Harrier and AV-8A have been criticised for having a poor view front and rear. Equipment at the bottom of the windscreen and the HUD itself tends to limit the forward view, while the large intakes tend to limit the view "over the shoulder".

Although both the RAF and USMC have lost a significant portion of their fleets through attrition, this reflects the stress of modern low-level high speed tactics rather than any shortcomings of the Harrier. The RAF considers the type's safety record to be good when compared to last generation designs such as the Hunter, and no one would suggest that the latter is in any way tricky to handle.

The USMC has compared AV-8A with the 1940s Vought Corsair which offered high performance but was unforgiving in the hands of poor pilots. Overoptimism in the light of early USMC experience with handpicked pilots led the USMC to consider AV-8A suitable for newly trained aircrew, but the attrition rate led the Corps to assign more experienced pilots to the type.

A developed Mk.5 version with a larger wing and extended intakes and front fuselage was proposed to the RAF, but was rejected in favour of the McDonnell Douglas AV-8B Harrier II.

Sea Harrier is a developed version of the basic Harrier rather than AV-8B. The avionics installation is completely revised, with the addition of a Ferranti Blue Fox radar in a nose radome, a Ferranti FIN 1040 self-aligning INS and digital computer for navigation. Royal Navy aircraft will carry AIM-9 Sidewinder missiles for air-to-air combat, but the Indian Navy examples will use the Matra R.550 Magic. The power-plant is a Rolls-Royce Pegasus 104 of 21,500lb (9,770kg) thrust. The cockpit has been raised, giving a better rear view, the revised nose section can be hinged to port for storage aboard ship, while magnesium alloy has been eliminated from the airframe as an anti-corrosion precaution for the naval environment. The reaction-control jets are more powerful than those on Harrier to give an extra margin of safety in the presence of inevitable air turbulence caused by ship superstructures, while the tailplane has been strengthened and given a larger degree of movement.

The aircraft entered Royal Navy service with 899 Squadron of the Fleet Air Arm, and will serve aboard Invincible-class light carriers, carrying out intercept, combat air patrol, anti-ship and strike missions. The Blue Fox radar has frequency agility, and was designed to detect large targets such as Backfire or the IL-38 May over the sea. Pulse-doppler techniques are not used, since this technique, although widely used in current-generation radars, is mainly intended to improve rejection of ground clutter.

The Indian Navy ordered eight Sea Harriers to replace the obsolescent Sea Hawk fighters formerly carried by the light carrier Vikrant. Should India proceed with plans to deploy a second carrier, a further Sea Harrier buy would be likely.

Sea Harrier often uses a 'ski-lift' ramp in order to improve take-off performance. Aircraft begin their take-off roll with the nozzles pointing aft, then apply a downward angle on reaching leading edge of the upward-curving ramp. This procedure sounds complex, but is easy to carry out in practice. Upward momentum so gained allows extra fuel or weaponry to be carried.

Sea Harrier had its combat debut around the Falkland Islands in May 1982. All but four of the RN Sea Harriers were deployed aboard the carriers Invincible and Hermes—a total of 28 aircraft. These were used both to provide fighter cover for the task force and for air-to-ground strikes. Harriers are credited with a total of 28 hostile aircraft downed in air-to-air combat without a single Argentinian "kill" being scored in return. The seven Sea Harriers lost fell victim to accidents or AAA fire. Immediately after the war, seven replacements were ordered, plus a further seven to increase the final strength of the force to around 40. Plans to sell the carrier Invincible to Australia have been officially shelved.

Above: Starboard break for two 800 Sqn Sea Harriers in pre-Falkland markings.

Left: Spain currently has nine AV-8As, but designates these AV-8S Matadors.

1. The Sea Harrier radome folds for carrier storage.
2. Two-seat cockpit of Harrier T.2.
3. Range of movement on vectoring nozzles.
4. Nose of original Harrier GR.1 without avionics housing.
5. Larger fin on T.2 trainer.
6. Larger ventral strake on T.2.
7. Extended tail boom on T.2 required to move control "puffer jet" further from centre of gravity.
8. Bolt-on wingtip extensions used on RAF long-range ferry flights.

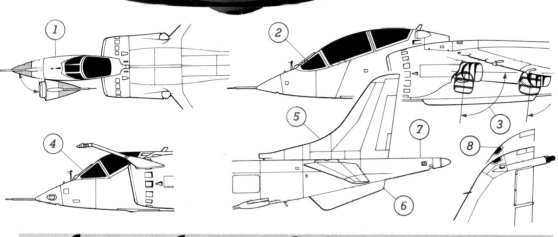

Left: Harrier GR.3 close-support aircraft of 1 Sqn, normally based at RAF Wittering, operating in Norway as part of NATO's Mobile Force. They have been given a coat of washable white paint over their standard grey/green camouflage which makes them difficult to detect when operating at low-level or dispersed on the ground.

Below: The raised cockpit canopy on Sea Harrier gives the rear vision required during air-to-air combat, while the nose radome houses a Blue Fox radar.

British Aerospace Hawk

Type: advanced trainer/light attack aircraft.
Specifications: length, 36ft 8in (11.17m); span, 30ft 10in (9.39m); height, 13ft 1in (3.99m); weight (maximum take-off), 17,085lb (7,750kg).
Max speed: Mach 0.88.
Service ceiling: 50,000ft (15,240m).
Range (tactical radius with a 5,600lb (2,545kg) weapon load): 300nm (556km).
Armament: one 30mm ADEN cannon in ventral pod, plus up to 5,660lb (2,560kg) of ordnance.
Powerplant: one Rolls-Royce/Turbomeca Adour Mk 851 turbofan rated at 5,340lb (2,430kg) dry thrust.

Developed as an advanced trainer for the Royal Air Force, Hawk must be considered a technological success and one which will probably feature in the export statistics of BAe for years to come. BAe may have failed to match the high-powered salesmanship of the French, which has taken the rival Alpha Jet to the top of the advanced trainer sales league, but has produced a true trainer with talons—an aircraft which is virtually a mini-Hunter.

Hawk is a good trainer, having handling characteristics which the RAF sum up as "it's an easy aircraft to fly ... but a difficult one to fly well". Full rudder is required to initiate and maintain a spin, and the aircraft takes about four seconds per turn. Maximum level speed is Mach 0.86-0.87 but this can be exceeded in a shallow dive. After some airframe buffet between Mach 0.88 and 0.95, the aircraft will exceed Mach 1.0, reaching a self-limiting speed of Mach 1.2 in a vertical dive.

The aircraft has a strong structure, having been designed to have a safe life of 6,000 flying hours, and has been cleared for operations to +8g and −4g. Hawk has exhibited an excellent safety record with the RAF in the advanced training role—one where attrition can sometimes be disturbingly high.

Initial predictions of potential export sales were perhaps optimistic, but BAe was not the only company to overestimate the short-term market for advanced trainers. Despite its undeniable qualities, it has had to fight hard for its share of the market. Hawk seems to have scored most of its successes with air arms which were looking for good strike potential, a pattern which may be repeated in future sales.

The RAF procured Hawk as a trainer, but part of the fleet is being modified to allow the carriage of AIM-9L Sidewinder missiles, so that these aircraft could be used to form supplementary air-defence squadrons in an emergency. In the attack role Hawk can carry up to 5,660lb (2,560kg) of ordnance. Nine 550lb (250kg) bombs have been carried at speeds of up to Mach 0.85.

Hawk was originally designed by Hawker Siddeley to meet an RAF requirement for a replacement for the Gnat. The resulting HS.1182 design was repeatedly refined in a multi-round design competition against the British Aircraft Corporation P.59 project before an order was finally placed in 1972. The designers always favoured the unreheated Rolls-Royce/Turbomeca Adour turbofan as a powerplant, although consideration was given to using the older but less expensive Rolls-Royce Viper turbojet.

There was no prototype—the initial aircraft were built to the planned production standard. All drawings were metric, Hawk being the first all-British aircraft to be built in this way. The first aircraft flew in August 1974, and deliveries to the RAF began at the end of 1976.

Gnat had a high-mounted wing and a narrow-track undercarriage retracting into the fuselage, but the Hawk designers opted to use a low-mounted wing which would permit the installation of a wide-track undercarriage more suitable for the rough handling of pupil pilots. This wing is built in one piece and attached to the fuselage by six bolts. The ailerons and moving tailplane are fully powered, while the vertical fin and rudder are mounted forward of the tailplane to ensure that the rudder is never completely blanked during a spin.

Until 1981 Hawk sales figures lagged behind those of Alpha Jet, a result of the zeal of Dassault sales teams in promoting Alpha Jet, particularly in areas of the world traditionally linked to French influence. When Hawk was announced the winner of the US Navy's evaluation of aircraft to meet its VTX-TS training requirement, it seemed at first sight that the type was on the verge of receiving its biggest-ever export order, but the US Congress ordered the USN to reopen the competition. Despite this move, Hawk remains a candidate.

During the various phases of the USN competition, BAe—working in conjunction with

McDonnell Douglas—devised the modifications necessary to fit Hawk to operational life aboard aircraft

British Aircraft Corporation Lightning

Data for F.6
Type: all-weather interceptor.
Specifications: length, 55ft 3in (16.84m); span, 34ft 10in (10.61m); height, 19ft 7in (5.97m); weight (maximum take-off), 41,700lb (18,954kg).
Max speed: Mach 2.3.
Service ceiling: 77,000ft (23,500m).
Range: 700nm (1,300km).
Armament: two Firestreak or Red Top plus 230mm Aden cannon.
Powerplant: two Rolls-Royce Avon 302 turbojets each rated at 15,680lb (7,110kg) thrust with afterburner.

Until the service debut of the F-14, F-15 and F-16, the Lightning was probably the most agile interceptor in Western service. Designed as a pure point-defence interceptor, the aircraft offers excellent manoeuvrability, being able to outfly most contemporary air-superiority types

Export prospects were badly affected by the short-sighted original specification to which the aircraft was designed. This called for a fast-climbing but short-ranged interceptor, a specification exclusively and narrowly tailored to the requirements of what was then Fighter Command of the Royal Air Force.

The original Mk.1 version carried a mere 7,500lb (3,400kg) of internal fuel in wing tanks, but this was later increased to 10,000+lb (4,545+kg) in the definitive Mk.6 version. Top speed of the F.6 is Mach 2.3 at altitude and Mach 1.2 at sea level. Touchdown speed is 140kt (260km/hr). Service ceiling is an impressive 77,000ft (23,400m).

For an aircraft weighing some 22 tonnes loaded, the Lightning interceptor carries a modest armament of two Red Top heat-seeking missiles and two 30mm Aden cannon with 120 rounds per gun. In the air-to-ground role, a maximum of 6,000lb (2,700kg) of ordnance could be carried, including 1,000lb (450kg) bombs, reconnaissance pods or up to 144 unguided rockets.

Royal Air Force Lightning strength has gradually diminished as the Jaguar strength has built up, allowing F-4 Phantoms to be switched from the strike role to interception duties. From the nine squadrons operational in the early 1970s the force has declined to two squadrons, plans to reform a third for home defence having been axed by the Conservative Government in 1981. In an emergency an extra squadron would be formed from Lightnings refurbished for service with the now-

carriers. The undercarriage was strengthened to cope with the higher loads associated with carrier landings, a tail hook was added beneath the rear fuselage, and provision was made for USN-style catapult launch. Two air-

Below: Indonesia was an early export customer for Hawk, ordering eight Mk 53 aircraft to replace its T-33s.

brakes would be mounted on either side of the rear fuselage in place of the current ventral pattern, and USN-compatible avionics and display systems would be fitted.

Latest version of Hawk to be offered on the world market is the Enhanced Ground Attack configuration, which would carry a nav-attack system incorporating a Ferranti laser rangefinder, Singer-Kearfott INS and Marconi Avionics HUD. For future versions, BAe has looked at the uprated -56 Adour engine or even an un-reheated version of the Turbo-Union RB.199. Like the proposed single-seat attack version, these remain paper studies at the time of writing.

Above: Hawk version proposed for US Navy VTX-TS requirement:
1. Carrier-type nose gear with larger wheel.
2. Reprofiled lower fuselage to stow nose gear.
3. Strengthened main gear.
4. Lateral air brakes.
5. Ventral fin and arrester hook.

Above: For weapons training, this Hawk of No1 Tactical Weapons Unit carries a belly-mounted cannon pack plus unguided rockets.

cancelled squadron, plus examples currently deployed in training.

In 1980 British Aerospace carried out a series of fatigue tests on a Lightning F.6 to clear the aircraft for the remainder of its operational career. Lightning was designed at a time when the likely threat was perceived to be the high-altitude bomber, but the type now has to carry out low-altitude interceptions.

Export Lightnings were sold to only two customers. Kuwait put its Lightning fleet into storage back in the mid-1970s, while Saudi Arabia is replacing its fleet with F-15C/D fighters.

Below: Despite its limited armament of two missiles and two cannon, the Lightning is well-liked by its pilots.

British Aerospace Nimrod

Data for Nimrod MR.2
Type: maritime patrol and ASW aircraft.
Specifications: length 126ft 9in (38.63m); span, 114ft 10in (35.00m); height, 28ft 8in (9.08m); weight (maximum take-off), 177,500lb (80,500kg).
Max speed: 500kt (926km/hr).
Service ceiling: 42,000ft (13,000m).
Endurance: 12 hours.
Armament: see text.
Powerplant: Four Rolls-Royce Spey 250 turbofans each rated at 12,140lb (5,520kg) dry thrust.

In the search for a replacement for the piston-engined Shackleton, the Royal Air Force considered designs ranging from derivatives of the CL-44 and Trident airliners to a four-engined Mach 2 variable-geometry aircraft.

The final RAF requirement was virtually written around the Breguet Atlantic, but Hawker Siddeley hastily prepared the HS.801 design to combine the wings and fuselage of the Comet airliner with the Rolls-Royce Spey 250 power-plant. An unpressurised ventral section was added to the fuselage in order to create the internal volume for a large unpressurised weapons bay.

A total of 46 production aircraft were ordered, and deliveries of the Nimrod MR.1 to the Royal Air Force began in 1969. Only five of the final batch of eight Nimrods were delivered as MR.1s; one became the prototype of the Nimrod Mk2, while the remaining two became prototypes for the airborne early-warning AEW.3.

Six RAF squadrons were equipped with Nimrod MR.1s, but one was disbanded in the late 1970s and its aircraft returned to BAe for rebuilding to the AEW.3 standard. Three examples of the Nimrod R.1 dedicated elint aircraft were issued to No 51 squadron—the RAF's specialist electronic-surveillance unit. This version of the aircraft can be recognised by the absence of the tail-mounted "sting", which houses the maritime aircraft's Emerson ASQ-10 MAD sensor.

Jet engines may burn more fuel than turboprop powerplants, but Nimrod is able to shut down one of its four engines after a high-speed flight to the patrol area. A second can then be throttled back, allowing the aircraft to proceed on the thrust of the remaining engines. Should either of the latter fail, the idling powerplant can be brought up to full thrust as a substitute. As the patrol continues and fuel is burned off, the point is reached where the Nimrod is light enough to be able to climb under the full power of a single

engine, and even the idling "spare" can be shut down.

Despite the low wing-loading, Nimrod gives a smooth ride at low level, while the low level of noise and vibration makes working conditions superior to those in a propeller-driven aircraft.

In order to maintain the effectiveness of the Nimrod force, the aircraft are being updated to the MR.2 standard. Deliveries of re-worked aircraft began in 1979.

Primary long-range sensor is the nose-mounted radar, and the EMI Searchwater radar with a Ferranti FM 1600D computer for data processing replaces the same company's ASV 21D set carried by the MR.1.

Also new to the MR.2 is the Marconi Avionics Central Tactical System, embodying the 920 ATC digital computer and Ferranti INS. Data from sonobuoys is handled by two of the new AQS-901 acoustic data-processing and display systems which are also made by Marconi Avionics. These latter units are fully independent and each can handle the output of up to four sonobuoys.

New ESM equipment made by Loral is carried in wingtip pods on the MR.2. This equipment supplements other ESM systems carried in the fin-top fairing—probably the same Thomson-CSF equipment as was fitted to the MR.1.

Ordnance carried in the Nimrod weapons bay includes the Stingray homing torpedo, iron bombs and US-supplied nuclear weapons for anti-submarine use. Standard or half-sized sonobuoys are released from launchers in the rear of the fuselage, the larger Sonics 1C type from the weapons bay.

By the spring of 1977 the UK had become disenchanted with protracted delays affecting NATO's plans for a West European E-3A force, so the decision was taken to develop an early-warning version of the Nimrod. The wisdom of this decision may be questionable in the light of slippages in timescale which have delayed the likely operational date to around the same time that NATO will begin E-3A operations, but the

British Aerospace Jet Provost and Strikemaster

Data for Strikemaster
Type: basic trainer/attack aircraft.
Specifications: length, 33ft 8in (10.27m); span, 36ft 10in (11.23m); height, 10ft 11in (3.34m); weight (maximum take-off), 11,500lb (5,200kg).
Max speed: 410kt (760km/hr).
Range: (hi-lo-hi with full weapon load) 215nm (398km).
Armament: two 7.62mm machine-guns plus a total of 3,000lb (1,350kg) of ordnance.
Powerplant: one Rolls-Royce Viper 534 turbojet rated at 3,140lb (1,430kg) dry thrust.

Production of the Jet Provost/Strikemaster ended in the late 1970s after a total of more than 200 aircraft had been supplied to 12 nations, and the type still remains the standard Royal Air Force basic trainer. Originally developed by Hunting and based on the earlier piston-engined Provost trainer, the Jet Provost flew for the first time in 1954. Following extended service trials, using a small batch of T.1 trainers,

the definitive T.3 was selected for RAF service. The equivalent export version was the T.51.

This was followed in 1961 by the more powerful T.4 version, which formed the basis of the T.52 export variant. Next step forward was the variant originally known as the BAC (British Aircraft Corporation) 145 or T.5, with a strengthened wing, pressurised cockpit and a lengthened nose housing additional avionics, followed by the armed BAC 167 version originally developed for Saudi Arabia and later more widely exported as the Strikemaster.

Almost inevitably, considering its purchase by Middle East air arms, the type soon saw combat, particularly during the Dhofar rebellion in Oman during the late 1960s and early to mid-1970s. At least three SOAF Strikemasters were lost to hits from Soviet-built SA-7 Grail man-portable surface-to-air missiles or AAA fire.

Strikemaster acquired a reputation of being reliable, and able to operate out of fairly primitive airstrips while carrying a useful

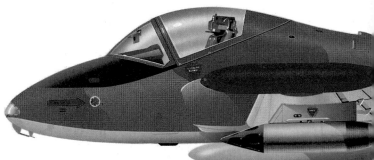

weapon load. Built-in armament consists of two forward-firing 7.62mm machine-guns, each with 550 rounds, plus a total of 3,000lb (1,350kg) of underwing stores on four underwing hardpoints. If heavier guns are required, Strikemaster can be fitted with an under-fuselage pack containing two 0.5inch machine-guns. The aircraft is normally flown with 48 Imperial gallons (827l) wingtip tanks.

The use of side-by-side seating went against the fashionable trends of the 1960s and 1970s, but it is interesting to note that the USAF has apparently decided that the eventual replacement for its side-by-side T-37 trainer should have the same cockpit configuration. In the attack role Strikemaster can be flown as a single-seater or an experienced pilot may be teamed with a newcomer in order to help the latter through his first few combat sorties.

Throughout its life the type has been frequently re-ordered by its many users. RAF T.3 and T.5 trainers were rebuilt in the mid-1970s to the T.3A and 5A standard, incorporating VOR, DME and ILS systems.

go-ahead was good news for the British avionics industry, since the resulting Nimrod AEW.3 carries the most complex electronics equipment ever fitted to an RAF front-line aircraft.

Original plans called for aircraft to be operational by 1982, but this date eventually slipped to 1983. Some consideration has been given to changing the aircraft's name in recognition of its new mission, but for the moment it remains the Nimrod AEW.3.

A total of 11 AEW.3 aircraft are being built, using Nimrod airframes originally manufactured for maritime-patrol use. Twin antenna assemblies for the Marconi Avionics search radar and Cossor Jubilee Guardsman IFF are moun-ted in nose and tail radomes, each covering 180-degree sector in azimuth. The revised rear fuselage is fitted with the standard Nimrod vertical fin, whose higher location gives better directional stability. Despite the size of the nose radome, it does not interfere with the forward view during take-off or landing.

High PRF radar transmissions are used to track high-speed aircraft targets, low PRFs being used against surface vessels. These modes can be interleaved as required from scan to scan. The radar is optimised for use over water, so forms a good operating partner for the APY-1 radar of the Boeing E-3A, since the latter was designed for over-land use. As a result, the combined fleet of Nimrod AEW.3 and E-3A aircraft available to NATO will give the alliance better early-warning facilities than would be possible with a single type. The two aircraft will be able to intercommunicate, initially using the NATO Link 11 system and later the JTIDS spread-spectrum equipment. The heat generated by the radar and other equipment is ten times that generated in the maritime Nimrod, so water/glycol or fluorcarbon liquid coolant is used to remove heat from the avionics and transfer it to the fuel contained in the wing tanks. Since the latter are normally the last tanks to be used during a Nimrod sortie, the wing acts as a giant radiator.

Left: In its MR.2 version, Nimrod is probably the world's most advanced maritime-patrol aircraft.

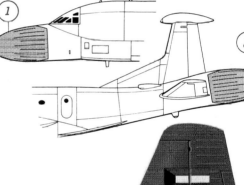

1. The nose radome on the AEW.3 does not interfere with forward vision during take-off and landing.
2. 180° radome for the rearward facing antenna on the AEW.3.

3. Flight-refuelling probe fitted for Falklands operations.
4. Radome on wing pod of R.1.
5. ESM wingtip pod on MR.2.
6. MAD tail "sting" on MR.1 and 2.
7. Tail radome on R.1.

1. Spin-recovery strake on RAF T.5 trainer.
2. Strikemaster carries a 7.62mm machine gun in the lower section of each intake.

Above: Nine Strikemaster Mk 83 remain in service with the Kuwait Air Force.

Below: Singapore received 16 Strikemaster Mk 84s in 1969. Five more were obtained from Oman.

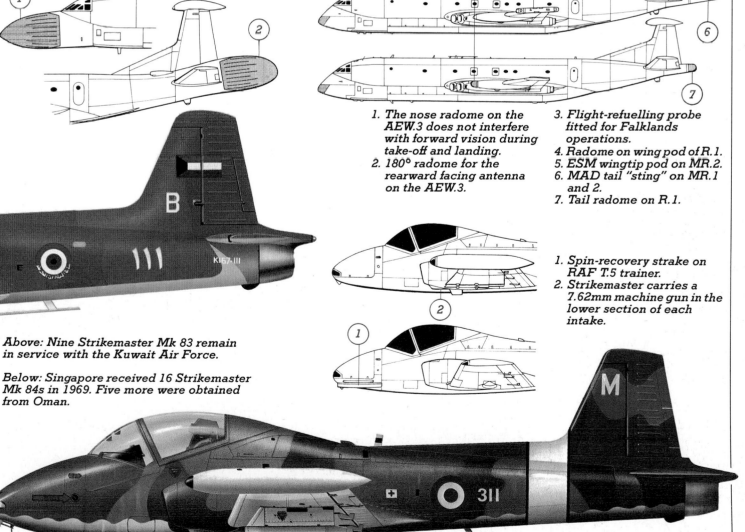

Canadair CL-41 Tutor and Tebuan

Data for CL-41A
Type: basic trainer & attack aircraft.
Specifications: length, 32ft 0in (9.75m); span, 36ft 6in (11.13m); height, 9ft 10in (2.84m); weight (maximum take-off), 7,397lb (3,355kg).
Max speed: 432kt (801km/hr).
Service ceiling: 43,000ft (13,100m).
Range (maximum): 820nm (1,520km).
Powerplant: one General Electric J85-CAN-40 turbojet rated at 2,633lb (1,195kg) dry thrust.

Never a large-scale export success — perhaps because of the competition posed by the BAe Jet Provost/Strikemaster and Cessna T-37 — the CL-41 Tutor remains in service with the Canadian armed forces and with the Malaysian Air Force. Begun as a private venture by Canadair, the type first flew in

1960. Three years later the first order was received from what was then the Royal Canadian Air Force for a total of 190 CL-41A aircraft powered by General Electric J85-CAN-40 turbojets of 2,850lb (1,290kg) thrust instead of the 2,400lb (1,090kg) Pratt & Whitney JT12A-5 used in the two prototypes. Production began in 1963 and the last Canadian example was delivered in 1966. Service designation was the CT-114 Tutor.

In the search for further orders Canadair created two further versions. The single CL-41R radar trainer had a new pattern of conical "needle" nose containing the NASARR radar system fitted to RCAF CF-104 Starfighters. This radar is based on that fitted to the F-104G but optimised for air-to-ground use.

Development of a light-attack version was an obvious move, but only 20 examples of the

resulting CL-41G were ordered by Malaysia, the sole customer to come forward. GE J85-J4 turbojets of 2,950lb (1,340kg) thrust replaced the earlier -CAN-40 version, the undercarriage was given larger-diameter wheels for rough-strip

operations, and six hardpoints capable of handling a total of 4,000lb (1,800kg) of ordnance were fitted to the wings. No built-in guns were provided, but provision has been made for external

gun pods to be carried.

In Malaysian service the CL-41G is designated Tebuan (Wasp). Deliveries began in 1967 and the type still serves in the attack and advanced training role with 6

Canadair CL-215

Type: utility amphibian.
Specifications: length, 65ft 0in (19.82m); span, 93ft 10in (28.60m); height (on land), 29ft 3in (8.92m); weight maximum take-off), 43,000lb (19,731kg).
Max speed: 185kt (345km/hr) at sea level.
Endurance: 12 hours.
Powerplant: two Pratt & Whitney R-2800-CA3 radials, each rated at 2,100shp (1,56kW).

Although not developed as a military aircraft, the CL-215 amphibian has an obvious potential in the search and rescue and coastal patrol roles. The only military operator to have placed an order is the Royal Thai Navy, but the CL-215 is also operated by the

governments of Greece, Jugoslavia and Spain. The prototype first flew on 23 October 1967, and carried out its first take-off from water seven months later. More than 65 aircraft have been built in four production batches, and the current production rate is one aircraft per month.

The design is a simple one, and the aircraft can operate from short airstrips or open stretches of smooth water such as bays or lakes. Take-off run on land is 2,600ft (800m) at a weight of 37,700lb (17,100kg), at which point the aircraft will have attained an altitude of 50ft (15). Operating from water at a weight of 37,000lb (16,820kg), the take-off run will be 2,740ft (835m). The aircraft is powered by two Pratt & Whitney

R-2800 CA3 18-cylinder radial engines of 2,100shp (1,566kW).

The CL-215's maximum endurance is 12 hours, which permits the aircraft to carry out a 6-hour patrol in a search area 400nm (750km) from base.

A conventional single-step-flying-boat hull is used, with a high-mounted one-piece wing and tall vertical tail fin. The main undercarriage is fully rectractable and of tricycle configuration, the nose unit retracting rearwards into the hull and the main units retracting into wells on the hull sides. Wingtip floats are provided, but these have been arranged to break away in a crash.

Normal crew complement of the basic aircraft is two pilots, seated side by side at dual controls,

but examples used for patrol or SAR work also carry a flight engineer, navigator and two observers. The latter are equipped with sliding seats which may be

CASA C-101 Aviojet

Type: basic/advanced trainer and strike aircraft.
Specifications: length, 40ft 2in (12.25m); span, 34ft 9in (10.60m); height, 13ft 11in (4.25m); weight (maximum take-off), 12,345lb (5,600kg).
Max speed: 428kt (793km/hr).
Service ceiling: 40,000ft (12,200m).
Range: 1,950nm (3,613km).
Armament: see text.
Powerplant: one Garrett TFE731-2-2J turbofan rated at 3,500lb (1,590kg) dry thrust.

In 1975 CASA was awarded a contract to develop a replacement for the Hispano Aviacion HA-200 jet trainer. Emphasis was placed in the contract on the need for the resulting design to be economical,

rather than on high performance, and the aircraft was to be capable of fulfilling weapons-training and light-strike roles. The prototype aircraft was to be in the hands of the user for service trials by the end of 1978.

During development the company turned to foreign companies for assistance. MBB was subcontracted to design the rear fuselage and tail section, while Northrop helped design the unswept wing and inlets. Garrett provided the TFE-731 non-after-burning turbofan engine, Hamilton Standard the air-conditioning and pressurisation system, and Martin-Baker the E10C zero-zero ejection seats. Dowty builds the nose wheel unit in the UK.

Avionics on Spanish Air Force

C-101s are largely from US suppliers such as Bendix, Collins, Magnavox and Sperry, but export customers may choose from a wider range of suppliers. Both cockpits are fitted with Saab-Scania RGS-2 gyro gunsights, while six under-wing hardpoints can be used to carry ordnance such as bombs, rockets or gun pods. A replaceable pack mounted beneath the rear cockpit can carry a range of equipment such as two 12.7mm heavy machine-guns, a single 30mm DEFA cannon, a reconnaissance camera or ECM systems.

Six prototypes were built. Two were used for fatigue testing, while four were flight-tested. First flight was on 27 June 1977 and all four were airborne within 10 months. Service trials began late in 1978.

Right: Performance of the C-101 is significantly lower than that of Hawk or Alpha Jet, but customers may be attracted by low acquisition and running costs.

An initial order for 60 aircraft placed by the Spanish Air Force has since been amended to cover a total of 88, while an unspecified export customer ordered eight. According to unofficial reports, the latter aircraft are for the Fuerza Aerea de Chile and will be locally assembled.

First deliveries to the Spanish Air Force were made in 1980, and production soon built up to three per month. Anticipating export orders, CASA installed sufficient

FM1125

Sqn and 9 Sqn respectively. Both are based at Kuantan, but attrition has reduced the complement of both units to eight aircraft each.

Canada still uses the Tutor as its basic trainer, students being assigned to the type after a short period of *ab initio* training on the CT-143 Musketeer II version of the piston-engined Beech Sundowner. Canadair reworked 156 surviving CL-41s in the late 1970s as part of an improvement/life-extension programme, fitting external fuel tanks, upgraded avionics and improvements to the canopy electrical system and engine-ice detection system.

1058

I NAVY

positioned at blister transparencies in the fuselage sides. SAR aircraft carry additional avionics such as an RCA AVQ-21 radar mounted in a nose radome, and a radar altimeter. In order to cope with the additional electrical load created by this equipment, two 800 VA inverters are fitted to SAR aircraft.

Above: The Royal Thai Navy took delivery of two CL-215 amphibians in 1978. These are based at Bangkok and are used for SAR missions.

XE25-04

EC-ZDI

production tooling to allow four a month to be built. Spanish Air Force examples are powered by the TFE731-2-2J of 3,500lb (1,585kg) thrust, but export aircraft will be fitted with the 3,700lb (1,680kg)-3-1J version of the engine.

In many respects the C-101 is lower in performance than many of its contemporaries, but offers excellent endurance and the prospect of long individual sorties or fewer refuellings. The TFE731 two-spool powerplant was originally devised for use on business jets, but the versions used in the C-101 have been modified to suit them to the demands of military flying such as inverted flight. This engine is of modular construction, has a geared front fan intended to optimise performance at all altitudes, and a bypass ratio of 2.66:1. Specific fuel consumption is 0.815lb/hr under high-altitude cruise conditions.

Four internal fuel tanks — one bag tank in the fuselage plus integral tanks in the outer sections of each wing and a third in the wing centre section — hold a total of 514 Imperial gallons (2,335l), an impressive fuel load for an aircraft of this size.

As a result, the C-101 has a ferry range of 1,950nm (3,610km) on internal fuel, and a tactical radius of 150nm (287km) in the fuel-demanding lo-lo-lo strike role.

Inevitably, this range performance has to be paid for in other respects, and the thrust-to-weight ratio of the CASA aircraft is markedly inferior to that of its rivals. At take-off weight in the 'clean' training configuration the C-101 has a thrust-to-weight ratio of only 0.33.

Although the current engine gives the aircraft a lower performance than many operators might require for the attack role, the bypass ratio should provide a low infra-red signature, making the type less vulnerable to IR-homing missiles.

53

CASA C-212 Aviocar

Type: light tactical transport.
Specifications: length, 49ft 9in (15.16m); span, 62ft 4in (19.00m); height, 20ft 8in (6.30m); weight (maximum take-off), 16,420lb (7,450kg).
Max speed: 202kt (374km/hr).
Range (with maximum payload): 220nm (408km).
Max speed: 202kt (374km/hr).
Range (with maximum payload): 220nm (408km).
Max payload: 6,100lb (2,770kg).
Powerplant: two Garrett TPE331-10-501C turboprops, each rated at 900shp (671kW).

Developed to replace elderly Spanish Air Force transports such as the C-47 and Ju-52, the C-212 has found a modest but steady market among Third World air arms. The first example flew on 26 March 1971, and damage to the aircraft sustained during a demonstration at that year's Paris Air Show did not significantly affect the programme. Deliveries to the Spanish Air Force began in May 1974, and production is currently running at four per month.

Initial military versions of the Series 100 aircraft were the C-212A transport (designated T.12 in Spanish service), C-212B (T-12A) photographic survey aircraft, C-212AV VIP transport and C-212E navigation trainer. CASA negotiated a licence agreement with Nurtanio Aircraft Industries in Indonesia, where the type entered production in 1976.

Since 1979 the basic aircraft standard has been the Series 200 — an improved version with more powerful TPE331-10 engines in

place of the earlier Garrett TPE331-5 units. Tailplane span is increased, while the structure and undercarriage have been strengthened to cope with the 15 per cent increase in maximum take-off weight. Production of the original Series 100 version has now ended both in Spain and at Nurtanio.

Transport versions can carry up to 24 fully equipped soldiers or 23 paratroops. Freight loads of up to 6,100lb (2,770kg) can be carried in the main cabin, while up to 12 stretcher cases and four medical attendants may be carried in the medevac role. Access to the main cabin is via two doors on the port side, plus a tail-mounted ramp/door which may be opened in flight for air-dropping of paratroops or cargo.

In addition to the normal transport version, the Series 200 is available in maritime patrol/ASW and Elint/ECM versions, both of which have attracted export orders. The maritime version can be easily

recognised by means of the new nose radome used to house the search radar, the fin-top antenna for the Omega radio-navigation system and by the number of extra antennas added to the fuselage. The avionics fit depends on the role selected. In the ASW aircraft three operators man cabin-mounted equipment consoles, while on the patrol version one crew member mans a radar console and two others are located at observation locations. The ASW version can be armed with sonobuoys, torpedoes, rockets and other weaponry.

Above: Spain operates a large fleet of CASA C-212 Series 100 and 200 STOL transports. These replaced the C-47 and Ju-52.

Above: Three Aviocars serve with 3 Sqn, of the Royal Jordanian Air Force, and are based at King Abdullah Air Base, Amman.

Cessna T-37 and A-37 Dragonfly

Data for A-37B
Type: basic trainer and attack aircraft.
Specifications: length, 29ft 3in (8.92m); span, 35ft 10in (10.93m); height, 8ft 10in (2.7m); weight (maximum take-off), 14,000lb (6,350kg).
Max speed: 440kt (814km/hr).
Service ceiling: 41,700ft (12,700m).
Range (with maximum weapons load): 400nm (740km).
Armament: one 7.62mm GAU-2 cannon plus up to 5,680lb (2,580kg) of ordnance.
Powerplant: two General Electric J58-17A turbojets, each rated at 2,850lb (1,295kg) dry thrust.

Cessna flew the first prototype of the T-37 basic trainer on 12 October 1954, and the first production T-37A followed on 27 September 1955. By the late 1950s the USAF saw the need for greater thrust, so decided to replace the 920lb (418kg) thrust Continental J69-T9 turbojets with the more powerful J69-T25 of 1,025lb (466kg) thrust. Additional avionics

such as UHF communications equipment were added at the same time, and the resulting T-37B flew in 1959. Existing T-37As were rebuilt to the new configuration, which became the standard USAF basic trainer, known to its crews as the "Tweety Bird" or simply "Tweet".

The type was widely exported, but the T-37C version devised in 1961 for delivery to foreign customers differed from the USAF version in having provision for underwing armament such as 0.5inch machine-gun pods, air-to-ground rockets or light bombs. By the time that production ended in 1975, more than 1,300 T-37s had been built. As a trainer, the type has been both popular and successful, although the lack of pressurisation has caused the USAF to limit its operational ceiling to 25,000ft (7,600m) instead of the achievable 42,000ft (12,700m).

In 1962 Cessna and the USAF began to study dedicated attack versions of the basic aircraft. Trials using the T-37C led to Cessna being given a contract to develop the YAT-37D trainer in a six-

month crash programme. The wings were strengthened to take six hardpoints — a total later increased to eight — and a 7.62mm GAU-2 minigun plus 1,500 rounds of ammunition were installed in the nose. Cockpit armour and self-sealing fuel tanks were added, along with additional avionics, while the undercarriage wheels and tyres were increased in size to cope with rough-field operations at the increased weight. General Electric J58-J2/5 turbojets derated to 2,400lb (1,090kg) thrust replaced the J69s, while wingtip tanks, each of 90 US gallons (340l) capacity, helped cope with the increased fuel demand.

Following trials in the USA, a batch of 39 A-37A Dragonfly aircraft were built by converting T-37B airframes, then sent to Vietnam for combat trials. Experience so gained was used to help produce the definitive A-37B version, 550 of which were built before production ended in 1975. These aircraft have a further-modified airframe and full-thrust J85-17A engines, allowing operations at still greater weights. Flak

curtains were fitted to the cockpit, and reticulated foam was added to the fuel tanks to protect against fire or explosion following strikes by incendiary anti-aircraft rounds.

A refuelling probe was added and the engine thrust line was moved slightly outwards and downwards to improve single-engine handling. By shutting down one engine in flight, A-37B crews can save fuel on the way out to and back from the combat area, thus increasing the tactical radius. Retractable intake screens may be swung into place in order to protect against foreign-object ingestion. These are normally used at take-off or landing, then retracted for the rest of the flight, but may also be used during low-level strafing runs to keep debris out of the engine.

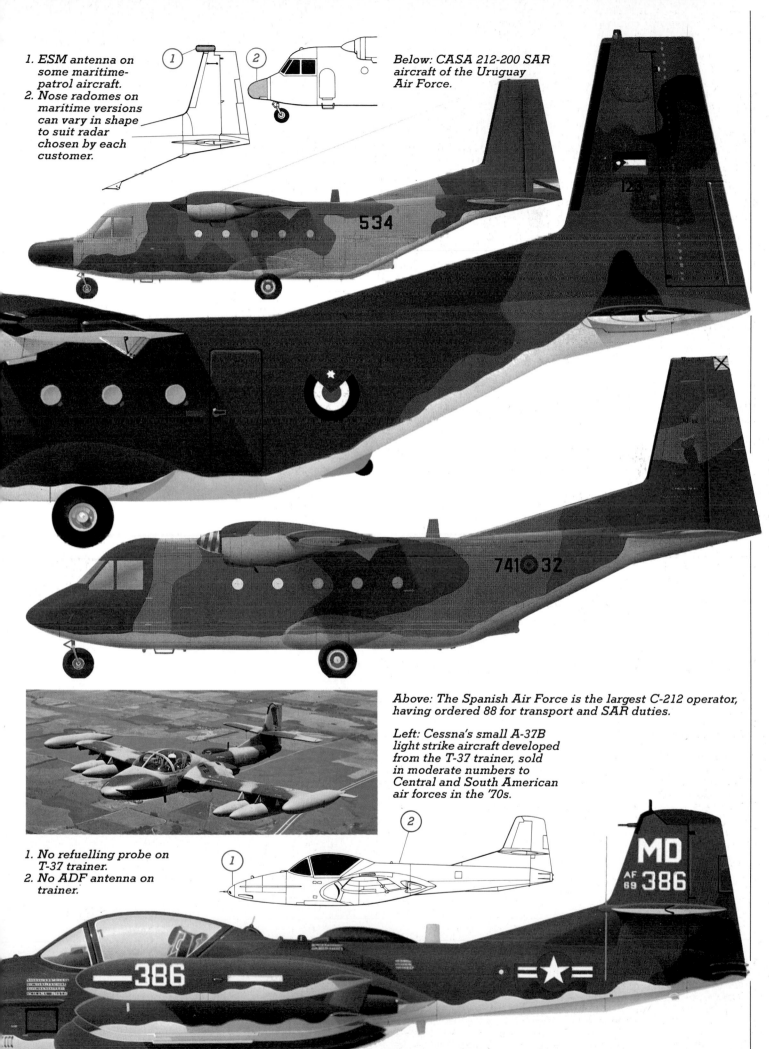

1. ESM antenna on some maritime-patrol aircraft.
2. Nose radomes on maritime versions can vary in shape to suit radar chosen by each customer.

Below: CASA 212-200 SAR aircraft of the Uruguay Air Force.

Above: The Spanish Air Force is the largest C-212 operator, having ordered 88 for transport and SAR duties.

Left: Cessna's small A-37B light strike aircraft developed from the T-37 trainer, sold in moderate numbers to Central and South American air forces in the '70s.

1. No refuelling probe on T-37 trainer.
2. No ADF antenna on trainer.

Above: A-37B Dragonfly of the Maryland-based 104th Tactical Fighter Squadron of the US Air National Guard.

Convair (General Dynamics) F-106 Delta Dart

Type: all-weather interceptor
Specifications: length, 70ft 9in (21.55m); span, 38ft 3in (11.67m); height, 20ft 3in (6.15m); weight (maximum take-off), 38,250lb (17,350kg).
Maximum speed: 1,325kt (2,455km/hr).
Service ceiling: 57,000ft (17,400m).
Range: (tactical radius) approx. 500nm (930km).
Armament: see text.
Powerplant: one Pratt & Whitney J75-17 turbojet of 17,200lb (7,820kg) dry thrust, 24,500lb (11,140kg) with afterburner, 26,500lb (12,050kg) with water injection.

Above: Delta Dart has completed two decades of US service.

For more than two decades the main interceptor guarding US airspace, the F-106 has now been relegated to service with the US Air National Guard. Originally conceived for service in the mid-1950s, the Delta Dart was delayed by a USAF decision to concentrate resources on the interim F-102 design. Problems with the engine and the complex MA-1 fire-control system delayed the first flight until 26 December 1956 and the type did not become fully operational until 1959.

Throughout its lifetime, the aircraft has been improved to match the current threat. The radar system has been improved and given additional ECCM facilities, while a solid-state Hughes computer replaced an earlier unit using tubes (valves to UK readers). A radar warning and homing system was added, and

an infra-red passive seeker was fitted on a retractable mounting positioned immediately ahead of the canopy. Both provide alternative methods of target detection and tracking.

Other modifications include a better ejection seat, solid-state TACAN and UHF radio, a one-piece canopy rear section substituted for the original hood in order to improve upward visibility, and a 20mm Vulcan cannon and "snap-shoot" gunsight added for short-range combat. Main missile armament is an array of Genie and Falcon missiles carried in a ventral weapons bay.

To ease the workload imposed on the single crew member, the cockpit contains a dual-ended control column whose left-hand grip contains controls for the

radar system while the right-hand unit carries controls for functions such as nosewheel steering, elevon trim, communications and armament. The radar display had one of the first CRTs capable of being observed under ambient lighting conditions.

Early in its career the F-106 set several altitude records and at one time held the official speed record. Time from brake release

Dassault-Breguet Atlantic

Type: maritime-patrol aircraft.
Specifications: length, 107ft 0in (32.62m); span, 122ft 4in (37.30m); height, 37ft 3in (11.35m); weight (maximum take-off), 100,090lb (45,400kg).
Max speed: 355kt (657km/hr).
Service ceiling: 30,000ft (9,150m).
Max endurance: 18 hours.
Armament: up to 6,600lb (3,000kg) of ordnance (see text).
Powerplants: four Rolls-Royce Tyne turboprops, each rated at 6,220ehp (4,638ekW).

Between 1964 and 1974 Breguet produced a total of 87 Atlantic maritime-patrol aircraft for the air forces of France, Germany, Italy

Force in the early 1960s.

By the mid-1970s France could see the need for a follow-on design to replace the Atlantic and also small numbers of ageing P-2 Neptunes still in NATO service, and decided that this could best be met by a new version of the Breguet aircraft. Design studies were carried out in 1977-8 and the Atlantic Nouvelle Generation (NG) programme was launched in September of the latter year.

The temptation to update the airframe was resisted, changes being limited to improvements in sealing, bonding and anti-corrosion treatment and similar minor modifications, which should improve the fatigue life of the

squadron of Atlantics in 1981.

Most of the changes will be in the avionics, the chin turret of the SAT/TRT FLIR sensor making the new aircraft immediately recognisable. Atlantic NG will carry a Thomson-CSF Iguane I-band radar with a retractable ventral radome containing an integrated radar/IFF antenna and offering track-while-scan performance on up to 100 targets. Antennas in the wingtips and in a fin-mounted pod feed the ARAR 13 ESM equipment, a passive receiver thought to cover the radar spectrum from 2.5 to 18.0GHz.

The prominent tail "sting" contains a Crouzet MAD sensor in-

lation will be linked via a digital data bus, while a Thomson-CSF Cimesa digital computer will process and collate the tactical data from the sensors ready for display to the crew.

Armament carried in the main weapons bay will include homing torpedoes, depth charges, or AM.39 Exocet anti-ship missiles. A smaller bay mounted further aft will carry up to 78 sonobuoys. These are likely to be a mixture of the TSM 8010 pattern carried by the Atlantic, plus the lighter, smaller and more capable TSM 8020 buoys.

and the Netherlands. Three Aéronavale aircraft were resold to Pakistan in the mid-1970s. The type thus came close to becoming the standard West European maritime patrol aircraft, and almost succeeded in attracting an order from Britain for the Royal Air

aircraft and make maintenance easier. These modifications include improvements to the elevator-control system, failures of which are reported to have caused several Atlantic crashes and led to the Royal Netherlands Navy temporarily grounding its single

corporating two detector elements whose outputs may be compared in order to measure the residual magnetic field of the aircraft, providing automatic compensation for changes due to different stores loadings.

All systems in the avionics instal-

to 40,000ft (12,200m) is less than four minutes for service aircraft.

The Delta Dart is definitely not for beginners. Initial approach is flown at more than 300 kt (556km/hr), touchdown speed being around 180 kt (334km/hr). If faced with the problem of landing at shorter than normal runways, pilots deploy the drag chute while still airborne in order to reduce the landing roll.

Below: The USAF Aerospace Defense Command was disbanded in 1980, and the last F-106s now serve with Tactical Air Command and the Air National Guard, usually with state of service displayed on their tailfins.

80780

AIR FORCE

Below: This Florida Air National Guard F-106A helps guard US airspace against the threat posed by the Cuban Air Force's recently-acquired MiG-23 Flogger strike aircraft.

Florida

72465

08

U.S. AIR FORCE

By converting existing airframes in order to create two prototypes, Dassault-Breguet was able to fly the first of these on 8 May, 1981. A total of 42 aircraft are required by the French Aéronavale, and deliveries are due to begin in 1986. Construction will be carried out by the international consortium which built the original Atlantics. This is made up of Aérospatiale and Dassault-Breguet (France), Dornier and MBB (West Germany), Aeritalia (Italy), Fokker (Netherlands), and SABCA and Sonaca (Netherlands).

None of the other Atlantic operators intends to procure the Atlantic NG, although West Germany plans some updating of its existing aircraft, having given Loval a $44 million contract for unspecified upgrading work.

Below: Atlantic New Generation development aircraft armed with Martel ASMs. Note ESM pods on the wing tips.

44

ATLANTIC
Louis Breguet

Left: 35 Atlantics serve with Flotille 21F, 22F, 23F and 24F of the French Aéronavale. From 1986 onwards they will replaced by the Atlantic NG.

44

44

MARINE

Left: External features of the Atlantic NG include a chin-mounted FLIR turret, dorsal antennas and new fin-top ESM.

Dassault-Breguet Etendard and Super Etendard

Type: ship-board fighter.
Specifications: length, 46ft 11in (14.31m); span, 31ft 6in (9.60m); height, 12ft 8in (3.86m); weight (max take-off), 26,500 (12,000kg).
Max speed: approx. Mach 1.
Service ceiling: 45,000ft (13,700m).
Armament: two 30mm DEFA cannon each with 125 rounds plus up to 4,600lb (2,100kg) of external ordnance.
Powerplant: one Snecma Atar 8K-50 turbojet rated at 11,025lb (5,010kg) of dry thrust.

Super Etendard, current ship-board strike aircraft of the French Aéronavale, is based on the earlier Etendard IV fighter and has about 90 per cent commonality with the earlier design. The two prototypes were built by converting Etendard IV airframes, and the first flew on 28 October, 1974, but the new type did not enter operational service with the Aeronavale until 1979.

Main differences between the Super Etendard and the Etendard IV are the fitment of an uprated engine, an improved wing and new avionics including nose radar. The Atar 8K-50 engine is a non-afterburning version of the powerplant used by the Mirage F.1C, and offers lower specific fuel consumption and increased thrust. The revised wing has an extended chord on the outer panels and is fitted with hydraulically-dropped leading edges. The new pattern of trailing edge flaps is of double-slotted form with greater travel. These modifications give the Super Etendard more lift and greater thrust than the Etendard IV.

Heart of the new avionics suite is the Thomson-CSF Agave I-band nose radar and Sagem-Kearfott ETNA inertial navigation-attack system. The new radar operates in conjunction with a Thomson-C3F VE-120 HUD, and the nose radome which shelters the inverse-Cassegrain main antenna gives the aircraft a fatter nose profile than the Etendard IV. In air-to-air mode, Agave can detect a fighter at between 10-15nm (18-28km), while detection range of a patrol boat is between 22-30nm (40-55km) in air-to-surface mode.

The Etendard IV was never exported and at the time this text was prepared less than ten remained in service with Flotille 16F. Sole export customer for the new version is the Argentinian Navy, which ordered 14 in 1979 for service on the carrier *25 de Mayo*. At least six examples had been delivered by April 1982, but deliveries were suspended by France following the Argentinian invasion of the Falkland Islands.

Super Etendard played no part in the invasion operation, having not yet embarked aboard the *25 de Mayo*, but had a dramatic combat debut shortly afterwards, when two aircraft attacked the British South Atlantic Battle Group using AM.39 Exocet missiles, sinking the modern Type 42 missile-destroyer HMS *Sheffield* and damaging the container ship *Atlantic Conveyor* (sunk later).

Financial constraints forced the French Navy to cut back its order from the planned 100 aircraft down to only 71. A reconnaissance version has been studied, but no go-ahead has been announced. Currently the French Navy operates Super Etendard from the carriers *Foch* and *Clemenceau*, but these vessels are likely to be replaced in the 1990s by two nuclear-powered carriers. In addition to the Exocet missiles mentioned above, Super Etendard can carry a full range of conventional weaponry including Magic missiles and bombs of up to 880lb (400kg) weight. Aeronavale aircraft can carry nuclear weapons such as the AN52 bomb and will be fitted with the A3MP stand-off missile.

Dassault-Breguet Mirage 5 and 50

Data for Mirage 50
Type: multi-role fighter.
Specifications: length, 51ft 0in (15.56m); span, 27ft 0in (8.22m); height, 14ft 9in (4.50m); weight (maximum take-off), 30,200lb (13,700kg).
Max speed: Mach 2.2.
Service ceiling: 59,000ft (18,000m).
Range: (lo-lo-lo tactical radius with two 400kg bombs), 340nm (630km).
Armament: two 30mm DEFA cannon with 125 rounds/gun plus up to 8,800lb (4,000kg) of ordnance.
Powerplant: one Snecma Atar turbojet 9K-50 rated at 11,055lb 9K-50 rated at 11,055lb (5,025kg) dry thrust, 15,870lb (7,210kg) with afterburner.

Development of the swept-wing Mirage F1 did not end the evolution of the delta-winged Mirage III. Development of the Mirage 5 was originally undertaken on the basis of Israeli experience with the IIIC. Given the clear weather conditions common in the Middle East, this operator was prepared to trade off avionics against internal fuel capacity and load-carrying ability. A new extended and slimmed nose replaced the existing assembly, and normally carried an Electronique Marcel Dassault Aida II radar. This simple set has a fixed forward-looking "lens" antenna and is used only for ranging. Seven hardpoints—two under each wing and three beneath the fuselage—are capable of carrying a total of more than 8,800lb (4,000kg) of ordnance, while the two 30mm DEFA cannon of the Mirage IIIE have been retained. Internal fuel capacity has been increased to 843 Imperial gallons (3,830l)—15 per cent more than in the IIIE.

Like the basic aircraft, the Mirage 5 generated a family of variants, including the 5-D two-seat trainer and the 5-R reconnaissance aircraft. The first aircraft flew in 1967 but the type was never to enter service with Israel. Delivery of the completed aircraft was embargoed in 1968, following the Israeli commando raid on Beirut airport.

In theory, such treatment of a customer should have crippled the type's export prospects, but in fact Dassault received orders for more than 500 from nations all around the world, a figure which includes 106 assembled in Belgium from a mixture of French and Belgian-manufactured components. The Mirage 5 was thus a large-scale export success in its own right, but not so the more powerful Mirage 50.

This latter programme seems to owe its origins to another politically embarrassing Dassault customer—the South African Air Force. This air arm began by operating the Mirage IIICZ, a variant of the original IIIC used by Israel and L'Armée de l'Air, but went on to operate the swept-wing F.1AZ. The latter uses the more powerful Atar 9K-50 turbojet, and this engine was installed in at least two South African versions of the delta-winged aircraft. The engine had already been test-flown in 1965 in the Mirage IIIC2 used to test the F1.C powerplant.

By combining this engine with the Mirage 5 airframe, Dassault was able to offer the Mirage 50 series. First example flew on 15 April 1979. Advantages over the Atar 9C-powered aircraft include a 15-20 per cent shorter take-off run, better acceleration, rate of climb and manoeuvrability, and the ability to carry more armament or fuel. First customer for the new type was Chile, whose Grupo 4 operates 16 from Rocas de Santo Domingo air base.

Clean take-off weight of the Mirage 50 is only 21,800lb (9,900kg), compared with the 24,000lb (10,900kg) typical for the Mirage F1.C, so the take-off thrust:weight ratio will be 0.72:1 instead of the 0.66:1 of the latter aircraft. Maximum sea-level climb rate is 36,400ft/min (11,100m/min). Internal fuel capacity is 764 Imperial gallons (3,475 l). The Atar 9K-50 has a lower fuel consumption than the 9C, improving the endurance of the Mirage 50, while the extra thrust improves survivability in the low-level attack role by offering extra speed.

Given this level of performance, it is difficult to believe that the type will not attract further orders. Large numbers of Mirage III operators will need to replace their existing fleets, and not all will be willing to invest in facilities for an all-new type such as the F1, or be able to afford the Mirage 2000. Dassault-Breguet is promoting the aircraft as suitable interim equipment for operators perceiving a requirement for the Mirage 2000 at some time in the future.

When first marketed, the Mirage 50 was offered with the Mirage 5 nose, complete with Aida radar, but Dassault now offers the aircraft with the Thomson-CSF Cyrano IVM multi-mode radar (a version of the set carried by the Mirage F1.C) or the same company's Agave radar

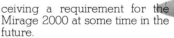

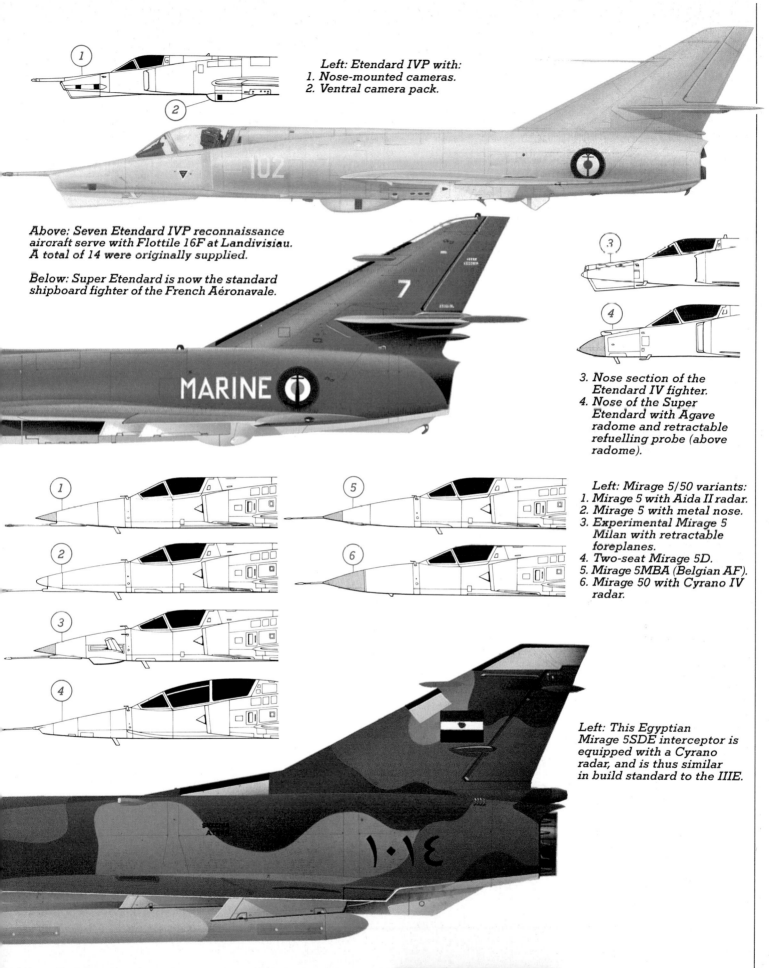

Left: Etendard IVP with:
1. *Nose-mounted cameras.*
2. *Ventral camera pack.*

Above: Seven Etendard IVP reconnaissance aircraft serve with Flottile 16F at Landivisiau. A total of 14 were originally supplied.

Below: Super Etendard is now the standard shipboard fighter of the French Aéronavale.

MARINE

3. *Nose section of the Etendard IV fighter.*
4. *Nose of the Super Etendard with Agave radome and retractable refuelling probe (above radome).*

Left: Mirage 5/50 variants:
1. *Mirage 5 with Aida II radar.*
2. *Mirage 5 with metal nose.*
3. *Experimental Mirage 5 Milan with retractable foreplanes.*
4. *Two-seat Mirage 5D.*
5. *Mirage 5MBA (Belgian AF).*
6. *Mirage 50 with Cyrano IV radar.*

Left: This Egyptian Mirage 5SDE interceptor is equipped with a Cyrano radar, and is thus similar in build standard to the IIIE.

from the Super Etendard.

It was almost inevitable that the Mirage 5 should fire its guns in anger, since the type is in service with a dozen nations. Libya operates one of the largest Mirage 5 fleets and has used the type in action against Egypt dur-ing a brief border conflict in 1977, and lost several during Egyptian attacks on El Adem air base. Zaire lost six in combat with invaders striking against Shaba province, but several of these were lost in crashes, not as a direct result of hostile action.

Left: Mirage 5 fighters for Israel were embargoed in 1968, and eventually delivered to the French Air Force as Mirage 5Fs. This 5F is lifting a heavy load of iron bombs plus a launcher for unguided rockets.

Dassault-Breguet Mirage III

Data for Mirage IIIE:
Type: single or two-seat tactical attack aircraft.
Specifications: length, 49ft 3in (15m); span, 27ft 0in (8.2m); height, 14ft 9in (4.5m); weight, (max. T.O.): 30,200lb (13,700kg).
Maximum speed: Mach 2.2 at altitude.
Service ceiling: 56,000ft (17,000m).
Range: (combat radius) 650nm (1,200km).
Armament: two 30mm DEFA cannon plus up to 8,800lb (4,000kg) of ordnance.
Powerplant: one SNECMA Atar 9C turbojet rated at 9,440lb (4,280kg) dry thrust, 13,670lb (6,200kg) with afterburner.

Dassault's ubiquitous delta managed to corner a major share of the market for first-generation Mach 2 fighters, obtaining the kind of export success which eluded the British Lightning and rivalling those of the US F-104 Starfighter. When the Israeli Air Force, original export customer for the type, used it to good effect in the now-legendary early-morning air strikes which opened the 1967 Middle East War, Dassault could not have asked for a more effective advertisement. Mirage became synonymous with "advanced fighter" and nation after nation placed orders in the years which followed.

Both the original non-afterburning five-tonne Mirage MD.550 aircraft and the subsequent Mirage II (an eight-tonne design powered by two afterburning Turboméca Gazebo engines) which flew in the mid-1950s were austere twin-engined designs of the type mooted as a result of Korean MiG-versus-Sabre air battles. In official circles it was still assumed that the F-86 avionics formula of a radar gunsight, IFF system and radio would be adaquate for supersonic combat.

Like other design teams, Dassault abandoned this simple concept to produce a heavier and better equipped aircraft capable of operating without the need for continuous ground control and with the potential of fulfilling other operational roles. The Mirage III-001 prototype was a private-venture design powered by a single afterburning Atar, demonstrating a top speed of Mach 1.6 within ten weeks of its first flight. Experience with this aircraft led to a French Air Force order for the even-heavier Mirage IIIA pre-production fighter which evolved into the Mirage IIIC.

First production examples were delivered in October 1960, but by then the design team was already hard at work on the Mirage IIIE variant intended for ground attack. This featured a stretched fuselage with extra internal fuel capacity and an uprated Atar engine with 13,670lb (6,200kg) thrust instead of the 13,225lb (6,000kg) unit fitted to the IIIC. It could be recognised by the fact that the rear of the canopy was roughly level with the intakes instead of being located behind the intakes.

In many respects the design of the delta Mirage family is highly conservative. The delta planform was probably the easiest pattern of wing to manufacture that would allow Mach 2 flight, since its 4.5% chord at the root allowed the wing to be around 15 inches (35cm) deep at that point. Until then, the best that Dassault designers could manage was the 6% chord 8-inch thick root of the swept-wing Super Mystere. In order to build a swept-wing Mach 2 Mirage, the design team would have had to create a wing less than six inches (15cm) thick at the root.

The tailless delta planform is not without disadvantages, explaining why only Dassault and IAI continue to make use of it. At low speeds, high angles of incidence are necessary in order to maintain lift. The trailing-edge flaps operate in the opposite sense to conventional elevators—in order to lift the nose the control surface must be deflected upwards. Since they effectively push the rear of the aircraft down, such surfaces are in effect reducing the total lift at the very time when maximum lift is required, so a pure-delta tends to require more runway than conventional fighters. Take-off run for the Mirage IIIE is therefore around 5,200 ft (1.6km), some 2.5 times that of the swept-wing Mirage F1.C and twice that of the MiG-21 tailed delta.

Dassault did attempt to overcome this problem in 1970 when a modified Mirage IIIE was flown with retractable canard foreplanes in an attempt to secure an order from Switzerland for a Venom replacement. Although low-speed manoeuvrability and climb rate were improved, and the take-off run cut by 2,000ft (600m), no customers came forward and the project was abandoned.

Although probably the most successful first-generation Mach 2 aircraft, the Mirage III is now somewhat dated. Basically it remains a good air-superiority design capable of meeting the needs of many customers, but is more limited in other roles. It may not offer the fine handling qualities of the early MiG-21—its most serious rival in the export market—but beats the Soviet fighter in most other respects.

The original Matra R.530 missile carried beneath the fuselage was designed back in the days when non-manoeuvring bombers flying at high altitude were seen as the primary threat. The Israeli Air Force tended to leave its rounds in storage, relying on the twin DEFA cannon during air-to-air combat.

With the arrival in service of the Matra R.550 Magic "dogfight" missile, most Mirage III operators have probably followed suit. The R.530 was once described to the author as being "good for re-fighting the Battle of Britain" but the newer weapon can be fired from aircraft pulling up to 6g. Magic is effective against targets anywhere in a forward sector ahead of the launch aircraft of at least 140 degrees and may "cross the bows" of the launch aircraft a mere 160ft (50m) ahead of the nose.

Standard nose radar of the Mirage III is the Thomson-CSF Cyrano II, an I/J-band set with a power output of 200kW. This can be used in search, tracking and air-to-ground modes, including terrain mapping. The navigation computer can accept up to 12 selected waypoints by means of punched cards but the complete installation lacks the all-weather ground-attack capability offered by more modern aircraft.

The Mirage III has had an active combat career. Israeli examples flew against Arab air arms during the 1970 War of Attrition and 1973 Yom Kippur War, South African aircraft have participated in anti-guerilla strikes into neighbouring territory, while Argentina lost many in 1982.

Above: Argentina has operated the Mirage IIIEA since 1972, but these aircraft suffered heavy attrition during attacks against the British task force during the Falklands campaign.

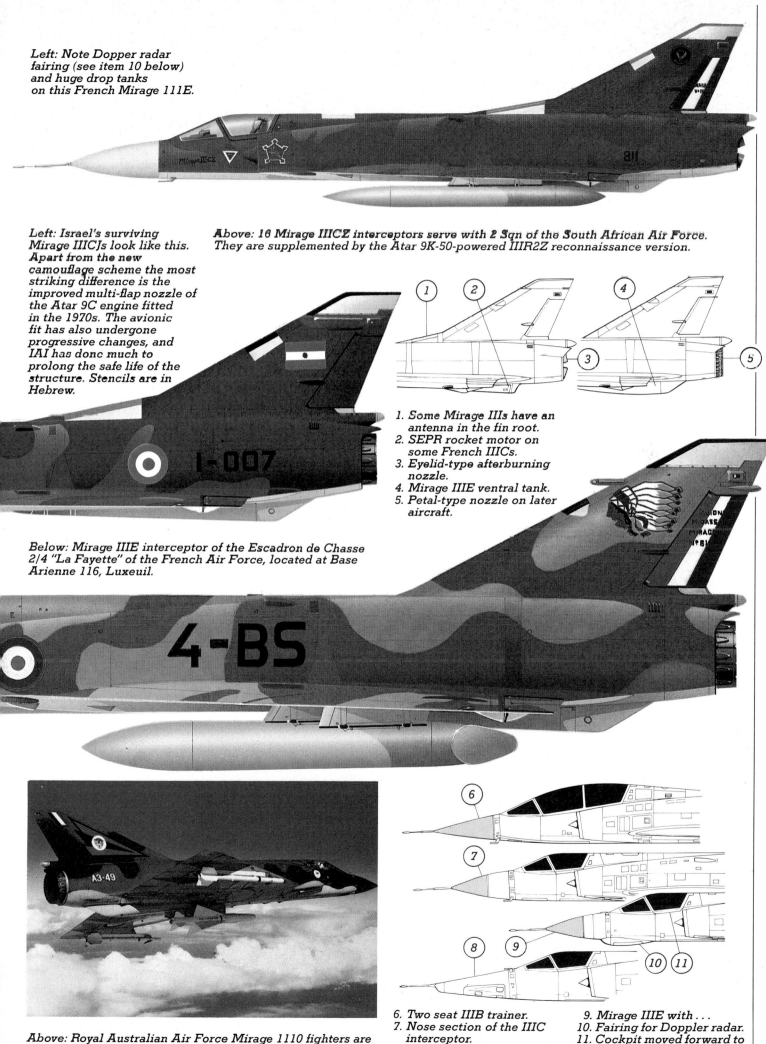

Left: Note Dopper radar fairing (see item 10 below) and huge drop tanks on this French Mirage 111E.

Left: Israel's surviving Mirage IIICJs look like this. Apart from the new camouflage scheme the most striking difference is the improved multi-flap nozzle of the Atar 9C engine fitted in the 1970s. The avionic fit has also undergone progressive changes, and IAI has done much to prolong the safe life of the structure. Stencils are in Hebrew.

Above: 16 Mirage IIICZ interceptors serve with 2 Sqn of the South African Air Force. They are supplemented by the Atar 9K-50-powered IIIR2Z reconnaissance version.

1. Some Mirage IIIs have an antenna in the fin root.
2. SEPR rocket motor on some French IIICs.
3. Eyelid-type afterburning nozzle.
4. Mirage IIIE ventral tank.
5. Petal-type nozzle on later aircraft.

Below: Mirage IIIE interceptor of the Escadron de Chasse 2/4 "La Fayette" of the French Air Force, located at Base Arienne 116, Luxeuil.

Above: Royal Australian Air Force Mirage 1110 fighters are soon to be replaced by the F/A-18A Hornet. Note the AIM-9 armament.

6. Two seat IIIB trainer.
7. Nose section of the IIIC interceptor.
8. IIIR reconnaissance aircraft.
9. Mirage IIIE with . . .
10. Fairing for Doppler radar.
11. Cockpit moved forward to make room for additional internal fuel.

Dassault-Breguet Mirage F.1

Data for Mirage F1.C

Specifications: length, 49ft 3in (15m); span, 27ft 7in (8.4m); height, 14ft. 9in (4.5m); weight, (max T.O.), 33,510lb (15,200kg).

Max speed: Mach 2.2.

Service ceiling: 67,000ft (20,000m).

Range: (typical interception tactical radius), 170nm (315km).

Armament: up to 12,700lb (5,800kg) of external ordnance plus two 30mm DEFA cannon.

Powerplant: rated at one Snecma Atar 9K turbojet rated at 11,060lb (5,027kg) dry thrust, 15,870lb (7,210kg) with afterburner.

By the early 1960s, the Dassault design team felt ready to tackle the engineering problems in producing a swept-back wing suitable for use at Mach 2. Although no formal requirement existed, the French Air Force could see the need for a multi-purpose fighter to replace the Mirage III.

Variable geometry prototypes were built and flown in 1967 (single engine) and 1971 (twin-engine) but it was a two-seat swept-wing design known as the Mirage F2 which first attracted French Air Force interest. In parallel with this project, Dassault created two single-seat variants powered by the Atar or TF-306 engine. When an order was finally placed in 1967, the French Air Force decided to adopt the Atar-powered single-seat Mirage F.1 design.

The design may have seemed pedestrian compared to the variable-geometry types, but in many ways it was the right aircraft at the right time. Dassault no doubt hoped that the new fighter would emulate the export success of the Mirage III, and there can be little doubt that the fixed-wing design was more attractive to most potential users than a more exotic offering would have been.

The cockpit layout may seem familiar to a Mirage III pilot, but the newer aircraft has little else in common with the delta design, although of similar size and weight. For a start, it has around 40 per cent more internal fuel thanks to the use of integral tankage in place of the earlier bag tanks. Use of the Snecma Atar 9K engine originally devised for the Mirage IV bomber gives 16 per cent more thrust, top speed of the F.1 being Mach 2.2 instead of Mach 2. Patrol endurance is trebled at high altitude, as is high-supersonic dash duration. At low level, the tactical range is doubled.

Use of the swept-back wing has allowed a 20 per cent decrease in approach speed and a 23 per cent reduction in the runway length required for take-off runs at maximum weight. According to Dassault, the Mirage F.1 has a "more than 80 per cent increase in typical manoeuvreability", while the smaller wing area gives a lower gust response and

smoother ride at low level.

The Thomson-CSF Cyrano IV radar offers many features not found in the Cyrano II fitted to the Mirage III. These include dogfight and home-on-jam modes. Target-detection range is doubled and the set can look down to 4 degrees below the horizon at 4,000ft before clutter from the terrain swamps the target signal.

Basic version adopted by the French Air Force is the Mirage F.1C, plus the F.1B two-seat trainer. Some aircraft are fitted with non-retractable in-flight re-fuelling probes to allow rapid overseas deployment. The F.1A is an attack version with simplified avionics and additional internal fuel, and was originally developed for South Africa.

An M53-powered version designated F.1E was test flown in the mid-1970s and unsuccessfully marketed as a NATO fighter, losing out to the General Dynamics F-16. This revised design offered attractive improvements in performance including Mach 2.5 dash, increased range and a 400ft reduction in take-off run in the clean condition.

Dassault now uses the F.1E designation for a multi-purpose version with upgraded avionics originally planned for the M.53-powered aircraft. The revised fit includes a Sagem-Kearfott inertial navigation system, EMD/Sagem Type 182 digital computer to handle navigational and attack computations, an improved version of the Cyrano IV radar offer-

ing terrain-clearance, air-to-ground ranging and fixed-target supression modes, and a cathode ray tube head-up display in place of the normal electro-mechanical design.

For reconnaissance purposes, the custom-designed F.1CR variant carries a payload of cameras within the fuselage but still retains the nose-mounted radar.

On a typical combat-air patrol mission with an armament of two Super 530 missiles, the F.1C would take off with afterburner engaged, then climb in military power (dry thrust) to a patrol height of 30,000ft. From a cruise speed of Mach 0.7, the aircraft could carry out a five-minute after-burning dash to engage a target.

On a peacetime aircraft identi-fication mission and carrying only its built-in 30mm cannon as arma-ment, the F1.C might make use of the following flight profile, using reheat at all times. After take-off and climb to medium altitude, the

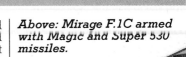

intercepter would build up speed further climb. Faced with a target at 40,000ft, the aircraft could be at that altitude and a speed of Mach 1.8 in just over six and a half minutes. Assuming an intruder some 170nm from the launch point, final interception would take place after a further 4.7 minutes of afterburning pursuit.

Up to 12,770lb of ordnance may be carried on seven hard points. In addition to the R.550 Magic dogfight missiles carried by the Mirage III series, the F.1C can carry two Matra Super 530

missiles. Able to carry out "snap-up" and "snap-down" attacks over a height range of almost plus or minus 30,000ft from medium altitude, this 550lb missile can engage targets out to a maxi-mum range of 19nm. Unlike Magic, it is not "fire-and-forget", since it uses semi-active radar homing rather than passive infra-red guid-

ance. During the flight time of the missile, the pilot must therefore keep the target illuminated using his Cyrano IV radar.

France has made some limited combat use of the F.1C in North Africa in air-to-ground strikes against Polisario guerilla forma-tions, while the Royal Moroccan Air Force has lost several to guerilla ground fire. Iraq examples have taken part in the war with Iran.

Above: Mirage F.1C armed with Magic and Super 530 missiles.

Above: F.1C interceptor of Escadron 2/5 "Ile de France" The basic aircraft operates up to 65,600ft (20,000m), but when fitted with the Super 530 missile can engage targets at higher altitudes. F.1C has more thurst, improved radar and better armament than Mirage IIIC which it has replaced in some units.

1. Mirage F.1R reconnaissance version with refuelling probe and ventral camera.
2. F.1C-200 with refuelling probe.
3. F.1AZ ground-attack version.
4. F.1B two-seat trainer.

Above: Ecuador's F.1JA fighters may have seen action during the brief clash with Peru in January 1981. They are based at Taura.

Above: Peacetime attrition has reduced the strength of Spain's F.1CE fleet from 66 to 44. All are based at Los Llanos.

Above: Ripple firing of unguided rockets from a Mirage F.1. Such weapons are still effective against ground targets.

Above: 3 Sqn of the South African Air Force is that nation's sole F.1CZ interceptor unit. 1 Sqn flies the F.1AZ ground-attack version.

5. Matra Super 530 missile. (The underwing mounting for the missiles reduces fuselage masking experienced on the Mirage IIIC's belly missile position.)
6. Matra R.550 Magic missile.
7. Antenna installation on Libyan aircraft only.
8. 1,700 litre drop tank.

63

Dassault-Breguet Mirage IV

Type: medium range supersonic bomber.
Specifications: length, 77ft 1in (23.5m); span, 38ft 10in (11.85m); height, 17ft 8in (5.4m); weight (maximum take-off), 73,800lb (33,500kg).
Max speed: Mach 2.2.
Service ceiling: 65,500ft (20,000m).
Range: (tactical radius with supersonic dash to target and subsonic return) 670nm (1,240km).
Armament: 70kT nuclear bomb or ASMP missile (see text) or up to 16,000lb (7,250kg) of ordnance.
Powerplants: two Snecma Atar 9K turbojets each rated at 15,430lb (7,010kg) with afterburning.

Of the 62 Mirage IV supersonic bombers built between 1964 and 1968 for service with General de Gaulle's Force de Frappe, 48 are still available for service. As the number of land-based intermediate range missiles and submarine-launched SLBMs has built up, the Mirage IV force has played a less important role in French strategic planning. Some bases were deactivated, but are still available for use in an emergency.

A total of 36 aircraft are currently assigned to the nuclear force, serving with EB 91 and 94, and are stationed in small groups at seven airfields—Avord, Cazaux, Istres, Luxeuil, Mont de Marsan, Orange, and St Dizier. Twelve aircraft located at Bordeaux-Merignac have been assigned to reconnaissance duties. Although lacking the performance of the USAF's SR-71 Blackbirds, these aircraft have carried out sorties in support of French operations to aid former colonies.

Basic weapon of the aircraft is a 70kT free-falling nuclear store, carried in a semi-flush mounting. By modern standards this weapon is obsolescent, but work has begun on converting some of the fleet to carry the Aérospatiale Air-Sol Moyenne Portée (ASMP) stand-off missile, allowing their active service lives to be extended. Only 15 aircraft were originally due for upgrading but the final number to be reworked has not yet been decided. Studies have shown that it will be less expensive to maintain a force of more than 15 aircraft entirely equipped with ASMP missiles than a larger fleet made up of converted and unmodified aircraft. ASMP is due to enter service in 1985.

As part of the ASMP modification programme, the aircraft will be fitted with a new Thomson-CSF air-to-surface radar designated Arcana. The role this will pay is not clear, other reports suggesting that the Electronique Marcel Dassault Antilope V radar will be used for target detection.

After launch from the parent aircraft, ASMP will fall to a safe distance, then ignite solid-propellent rocket boosters. The latter will bring it up to the speed at which its liquid-propellent ramjet can be in operation. Flight to the target will be under inertial guidance.

Tactical radius of the Mirage IV with in-flight refuelling is 2,100nm (4,000km) on a hi-lo sortie. ASMP will have a range of around 160nm (300km) if launched at high altitude, and just over 50nm (93m) at low altitude. Warhead yield will be 150kT. In theory the Mirage IV's large wing should give a rough ride at low level, but experience has shown that the aircraft performs well.

Dassault-Breguet Mirage 2000

Type: multi-role fighter.
Specifications: length, 47ft 1in (14.35m); span, 29ft. 6in (9.0m); weight (maximum take-off), 36,375lb (16,500kg).
Max speed: Mach 2.2+.
Service ceiling: 65,600ft (20,000m).
Range: (tactical radius with external tanks) 800nm (1,600km).
Armament: two 30mm DEFA 554 cannon with 125 rounds/gun plus up to 13,200lb (6,000kg) of missiles or other ordnance.
Powerplant: one Snecma M53 turbofan (see text).

Cancellation of the twin-engined Avion de Combat Futur programme in 1975 left the French Air Force without a next-generation fighter to replace its Mirage III and F.1C fleets. The Dassault team was quick to come up with a solution in the form of the Mirage 2000. A return to the delta planform by the Dassault designers came as a suprise in a world where delta wings were traditionally seen as the way to make a supersonic wing only if the local aircraft industry was incapable of turning out a swept design. Dassault designers were not being backward, however, studies having shown that if used in conjunction with artificial stability and the latest developments in aerodynamics, the delta was still an effective way of creating a Mach 2 design.

The new wing may offer extra lift, but in order to pack the required performance into a Mirage III-sized airframe, the thrust-weight ratio had to be improved. Political considerations almost certainly ruled out the use of a foreign engine, and the best that French industry could offer was the Snecma M53 turbofan under development for the now-abandoned ACF programme. This offered an afterburning thrust of around 10 tonnes. Composite materials based on carbon fibre or boron offered weight reduction in the airframe, giving the new fighter the desired combat thrust: weight ratio of greater than unity.

Use of a digital quadruply fly-by-wire flight control system gives the Mirage 2000 good handling characteristics at both low and high speeds, despite the reduced level of aerodynamic stability inherent in the basic design of the aircraft. Prototypes have flown at speeds from a mere 50kt (93km/hr) to more than Mach 2.

When "tamed" by the flight-control system, the aircraft's relaxed stability gives good manoeuvrability at subsonic and supersonic speeds. No mechanical back-up control system is fitted, although an emergency fifth channel powered from an independent battery could get the aircraft back to base in the event of the main system being knocked out by combat damage or EMP effects from nuclear explosions.

The first prototype flew on 10 March, 1978, only two years and three months after the project began. A second followed six months later, a third in April 1979 and the fourth not until May 1980. The latter was representative of a production aircraft, and its completion may have been delayed by modifications resulting from experience with the earlier aircraft.

Like the earlier Mirages, the 2000 is designed as a multi-purpose airframe capable of being customised into interceptor, attack, reconnaissance and trainer versions. Basic version is the Mirage 2000 interceptor, which will normally carry a payload of two R.550 Magic dogfight missiles plus two of the longer-ranged Super 530D SAR-guided weapons. The latter are capable of carrying out "snap-up" attacks on targets flying up to 16,000ft (5,000m) above the launch aircraft, allowing the latter to engage targets flying at 75,000ft (23,000m). It can also "snap-down" from a medium patrol altitude, allowing the Mirage 2000 to engage low-flying intruders.

The first 2000B two-seat version flew for the first time in 1980. This is intended for the training role, but a two-seat cockpit will also be fitted to the next variant—the 2000N low-altitude strike aircraft. This is due to fly in 1983 and to enter service with the Armée de l'Air in 1986. The airframe will be strengthened for flight at speeds of up to 600kt (1,110km/hr) at a height of only 200ft (60m) above the terrain. Such a demanding role also requires new avionics, so the aircraft will carry an Electro-nique Marcel Dassault Antilope V terrain-following radar in place of the current Thomson-CSF set, two SAGEM inertial platforms, a Thomson-CSF colour CRT display and additional but classified ECM systems.

Armament of this version will include the Aérospatiale ASMP ramjet-powered missile currently under development. In the same performance class as the USAF's Boeing SRAM, this will carry a nuclear payload over ranges of up to 200km (124 miles), ensuring that the aircraft never has to tackle the terminal defences around the target. There is no question of this missile being exported, but it remains to be seen whether a conventionally armed version of the 2000N is developed for export.

Development difficulties with the M53 engine and with the Thomson-CSF/Electronique Marcel Dassault RDI radar have delayed the programme by about two years, and the first examples are not due to enter French Air Force service until 1984. Early production planes will be fitted

Below: Only 36 Mirage IV remain operational in the nuclear strike role. Some will exchange their belly-mounted nuclear bombs (shown here) for the new Air-Sol Moyenne Portée ramjet-powered standoff missile; others will be phased out. Twelve further aircraft have been converted for reconnaissance.

Left: Despite its large wing area, the Mirage IV can carry out low-level dash to the target area.

Below: The first Mirage 2000 prototype flew only 27 months after the programme was launched, and was followed by three more single-seat prototypes and one two-seater.

with the Thomson-CSF RDM radar—a multi-role set originally devised for export versions of the Mirage 2000. This is a medium-PRF radar with modes for terrain-following, ground-mapping and sea search as well as air combat. The definitive RDI radar is a pulse-Doppler set having a high PRF and optimised for the interception role.

Another compromise in early aircraft is the use of the M53-5 engine of around 20,000lb (9,090kg) of afterburning thrust, instead of the definitive M53-P2 rated at almost 22,000lb (10,000kg). The more powerful engine will later be retrofitted to the entire French fleet, a modification which will require minor changes to the inlets.

First export customers were Egypt and India, both of which wish to assemble or even co-produce the aircraft. Both placed an initial order for 40 aircraft. India will take delivery of its first examples late in 1984 and may procure up to 150 aircraft. Egypt would like a larger fleet, but has problems in financing such an ambitious deal.

Above: Mirage 2000B trainer in the markings of Escadre de Chasse 10 based at Creil. Intended for training, this version has a two-seat cockpit and twin canopies.

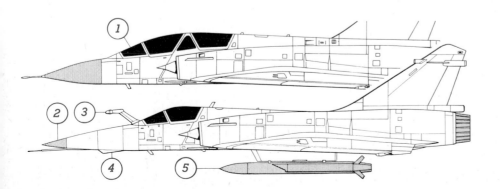

1. Mirage 2000B two-seat trainer.
2. Proposed single seat ground attack version with smaller radar plus . . .
3. Flight refuelling probe . . .
4. and laser marked-target seeker.
5. ASMP missile (on 2000N version only).

Dassault-Breguet Super Mirage 4000

Type: multi-role fighter.
Specifications: length, 61ft 4in (18.70m); span, 39ft 4in (12.0m); weight, (loaded), approx. 44,000lb (20,000kg).
Max speed: approx. Mach 2.2.
Powerplants: (prototype): two Snecma M53 turbofans each developing approx. 22,000lb (10,000kg) of afterburning thrust.

It seems barely credible that the Dassault-Breguet company has produced this heavy fighter as a company-funded private venture in the absence of funding or at least serious interest from a potential operator. Press reports continue to suggest that the aircraft is being developed with financial help from Saudi Arabia and will probably serve with that nation's air force. Saudi denials might carry more weight had the RSAF not shown significant interest in other long-range strike aircraft such as the Panavia Tornado.

Development of the Super Mirage was announced in December 1975, and the sole prototype flew for the first time on March 9, 1979. With typical French elan, the aircraft was taken to Mach 1.2 on that first flight and to Mach 2.2 on its sixth. Since then testing has continued at a modest pace, but has received little publicity. According to the company, much of the desired engineering data can be obtained from the Mirage 2000 programme.

In practical terms, the Super Mirage 4000 is a scaled up version of the basic Mirage 2000, but about twice the weight, with three times the internal fuel capacity, and powered by a pair of the Snecma M53 single-shaft turbofans used in the smaller aircraft. The Mirage 2000 has small strakes on the upper section of the inlet trucking, but the larger aircraft is fitted with variable-incidence foreplanes of highly-swept planform. These may be linked to the fly-by-wire active flight-control system required to cope with the negative stability created by an aft-positioned centre of gravity.

The design has been optimised for the low-altitude penetration-strike role, but would also form a good basis for a heavy interceptor in the class of the F-15 Eagle. The large nose section offers more space for a radar than that available in the Mirage 2000, and could house an antenna more than 30in (approximately 80cm) in diameter.

A radar of this size would give an interceptor version the ability to detect targets at ranges of up to 75-80 miles (120-130km) but there is no sign of such a radar emerging from the French electronics industry. The prototype has been fitted with the multi-mode Thomson-CSF RDM set used in the smaller aircraft.

Dassault-Breguet will not be able to carry out a significant amount of work on the Super Mirage 4000 navigation and attack systems unless a customer orders the type. Design and integration of the systems to be fitted will be difficult until a customer defines the task which he expects the aircraft to fulfil.

For the moment, the prototype is basically an aerodynamic test vehicle largely devoid of military systems, but sufficient to give a potential customer "hands-on" experience of the type. Unless a launch order is placed within the next year or so, it is difficult to avoid the conclusion that the aircraft seems destined to join the long series of Dassault "one-off" prototypes which never saw military service.

Dassault-Breguet/Dornier Alpha Jet

Data for Alpha Jet E
Type: Advanced trainer.
Specifications: length, 40ft 4in (12.29m); span, 29ft 11in (9.11m); height, 13ft 9in (4.19m); weight (maximum take-off), 16,500lb (7,500kg).
Max speed: Mach 0.85.
Service ceiling: 48,000ft (14,600m).
Range: (high-altitude tactical radius); 664nm (1,230km).
Armament: up to 4,960lb (2,250kg) of ordnance plus an under-fuselage gun pack.
Powerplants: two Snecma/Turbomeca Larzac 04-C5 turbojets each rated at 2,976lb (1,345kg) of dry thrust.

After a protracted development programme, this trainer and light strike aircraft has now settled down in service with the French and West German Air Forces and with a growing number of export customers. Vigorous sales promotion has resulted in a steady stream of orders.

The design was drawn up to meet a 1969 Franco/German requirement for an advanced trainer and light-strike/reconnaissance aircraft, and the first prototype flew on 26 October, 1973. West Germany delayed the production go-ahead, but this was finally given in March 1975, and production deliveries of the trainer version started in 1978.

The aircraft seems to have had more than its fair share of teething troubles, problems with the canopy and engines being reported. Early production engines could not be kept at maximum thrust for pro-longed periods, and the failure of Luftwaffe pilots to observe this restriction led to the German fleet being grounded after cracks were found in the combustion chamber of one engine. Modifications were quickly introduced to overcome this problem.

The most widely-adopted version of the aircraft is the Alpha Jet E (Ecole) trainer. France is the largest user, but the same model has also been sold to most export customers.

Two attack versions have already been devised and may be joined by a third. The first of these is the Alpha Jet A (Appui) attack aircraft operated by the West German Luftwaffe. This has a more complex avionics suite than the simple fit of the E model, including a Kaiser/VDO KM 808 HUD, Litef LDN Doppler navigation system and LR-1416 computer, Lear Siegler LSI 600E attitude and heading system, and Elettronica ECM equipment. Luftwaffe aircraft may also be used as 'Hind-killers', tests having shown that Alpha Jet's good low-altitude manoeuvrability makes it effective against assault helicopters.

Whether such a simply-equipped aircraft could survive in a NATO Central Front conflict is debatable. The East German LSK air arm seems to have no illusions that armed trainers can be used in the region — its operational fleet consists largely of MiG-21s. Dassault-Breguet has pressed ahead with its own MS2 strike version. This is equipped with a comprehensive system of French avionics including a Thomson-CSF VE 110C HUD and TMV 630 laser ranger, plus a Sagem Uliss 81 inertial platform, and has been ordered by Egypt and at least one other customer. Egypt plans to assemble 19 of its 30 aircraft at Helwan. The MS2 could also be adopted as a future weapons-training aircraft for the French Air Force.

Both partners may co-operate on yet another strike version — a single-seat aircraft for export markets — but no go-ahead decision had been taken by the end of 1981.

All Alpha Jets have a total of five hardpoints — two under each wing and one beneath the fuselage. These can carry a total of up to 5,000lb (2,250kg) of ordnance. No internal cannon is fitted but a belly-mounted gun pack containing a 30mm ADEN cannon plus 150 rounds of ammunition is available. (Luftwaffe gun packs carry a 27mm Mauser.)

Several Alpha Jets are being used as trials aircraft for different research programmes. Dornier has developed and flown a transonic wing of super-critical section on an Alpha Jet A. This is fitted with leading and trailing-edge manoeuvring flaps which are pre-set on the ground before take-off, but later flights may see the fitting of an actuation system capable of altering the flap settings in flight. Another A model has been fitted with vertical control surfaces on the underwing pylons so that it can be used as a testbed for direct sideforce flight tests. Dornier is also building a carbon-fibre wing which is due for flight testing in late 1982 or early 1983.

Left: Seen here alongside a single-engined Mirage 2000, the twin engined Super Mirage 4000 (rear) uses much of the technology of the smaller aircraft. Although a Dassault private-venture, the 4000 first flew using M53 turbofans "borrowed" from the French Air Force Mirage 2000 programme.

Below: Based on the aerodynamics and technology of the smaller Mirage 2000, the twin-engined Super Mirage 4000 has been flying in prototype form since March 1979.

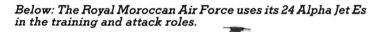

Below: The Royal Moroccan Air Force uses its 24 Alpha Jet Es in the training and attack roles.

Below: West German Luftwaffe Alpha Jet A of Jagdbombergeschwader 49 complete with ventral 27mm Mauser gun pack.

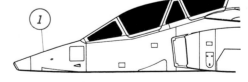

1. Nose section of Alpha Jet MS2 improved close-support aircraft ordered by Egypt. A laser rangefinder is mounted behind the optical port in the extreme front end.

Above: Alpha Jet E of the French Air Force Groupement-Ecole 314.

DH Canada DHC-4 Caribou

Type: STOL tactical transport.
Specifications: length, 72ft 7in (22.13m); span, 85ft. 7in (29.15m); height, 31ft 9in (9.70m); weight (max take-off); 28,500lb (12,900kg).
Max speed: 187kt (347km/hr).
Service ceiling: 24,800ft (7,500m).
Range (with max payload), 210nm (390km).
Maximum payload, 8,740lb (3,965kg).
Powerplants: two Pratt & Whitney R-2000-D5-7M2 radials each rated at 1,450hp.

De Havilland Canada has made STOL transports a company speciality, scoring a series of export successes with aircraft whose ability to operate in and out of short rough airstrips has become legendary. Having developed its expertise with the light Beaver and Otter designs, the company began work on the DHC-4 in 1956 with the aim of creating what is virtually a STOL equivalent of the C-47/DC-3.

The prototype flew for the first time in July 1958, backed by a US Army order for five aircraft and an initial Canadian armed forces order for two. The use of piston engines in a mid-1950s design might have seemed technically backward, but the choice was a wise one, particularly since piston engines can be maintained with simpler servicing facilities than those demanded by turboprops.

The design of the DHC-4 is basically simple. A large cabin capable of housing up to 32 soldiers or a payload of almost four tonnes was mounted beneath a large wing of cranked design. To ease loading and unloading, the rear fuselage was swept upwards to the tail giving the aircraft an instantly recognisable profile. The rear cargo door acts as a loading ramp, and can cope with loads of up to 6,720lb (3,050kg) in weight.

Although in theory forbidden to operate aircraft of more than 5,000lb empty weight, the US Army was keen to adopt the DHC-4. After receiving permission from the US Secretary of Defense, it placed orders for 159 examples. Several US Army aircraft were given to the Indian Air Force during the border clashes with China in the early 1960s. The Indian fleet was eventually to number 20, and these aircraft were subjected to some of the worst "hot and high" conditions in the world.

The US made extensive use of the DHC-4 in Vietnam, but in 1967 the aircraft were transferred from the Army to the USAF and re-designated C-7A or C-7B. Canada replaced its DHC-4 fleet with the newer DHC-5, selling the now-surplus aircraft to new operators in the Third World. Production ended in 1973 after more than 300 had been built, and more than 100 aircraft still serve with ten air arms.

Above: C-7A Caribou of the 94th TAW, Air Force Reserve, based at Dobbins AFB, Ga. It has a weather radar nose.

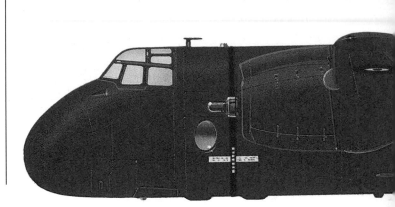

DH Canada DHC-5 Buffalo

Data for DHC-5D
Type: STOL tactical transport.
Specifications: length, 79ft 0in (24.08m); span, 96ft 0in (29.26m); height, 28ft 8in (8.73m); weight (max take-off), 49,200lb (22,300kg).
Max speed: 250kt (465km/hr).
Service ceiling: 25,000ft (7,600m).
Range (with max payload): 600nm (1,110km).
Maximum payload: 18,000lb (8,000kg).
Powerplants: two General Electric CT64-820-4 turboprops each rated at 3,130shp (2,330kW).

Although the US Army was never to procure the DHC-5, it provided the impetus for launching the programme when it issued a request for proposals in 1962 for a 41-seat STOL tactical transport. The Canadian company won a US Army contract to develop the DHC-5, costs being split three ways between the customer, the company, and the Canadian Government.

In appearance, the DHC-5 reflects its DHC-4 ancestry, having the same basic configuration. The wing is no longer cranked, but the section outboard of the General Electric T64 turboprops has a slight anhedral.

Four aircraft were supplied to the US Army for evaluation, but no production order followed. The Canadian armed forces ordered 15 examples, six of which now operate as maritime-patrol aircraft, but the production line closed in the early 1970s after delivering 24 aircraft to Brazil and 16 to Peru.

After drawing up plans for uprated DHC-5B and -5C models capable of meeting an Indian Air Force requirement, DHC decided to re-open the line in 1974 to build an improved DHC-5D model. This has 3,130shp (2.340kW) GE T64-415 turboprops in place of the earlier 2,650shp (1,976kW) units, and has attracted a steady stream of small orders for quantities varying from one to seven examples. These currently keep production running at around one aircraft per month.

The new powerplant is flat rated up to a temperature of 92°F (33°C) instead of 59°F (15°C), so it is not surprising that most of the orders for the DHC-5D have come from countries having desert or tropical terrain.

Several Buffaloes have been used as testbeds for experimental work in the USA. One was fitted with an air-cushion landing system in the mid-1970s, while NASA's Ames research centre rebuilt another with a new wing whose upper surface was blown by four turbofan engines. This is used as a testbed for research into quiet STOL techniques applicable to future transports.

Right: de Havilland Canada have twice put the DHC-5 Buffalo into production. The pilot of this Canadian-operated example is just flaring out on landing with the stick back and the large full-span slotted flaps down.

Right: Many of Canada's DHC-5A Buffaloes (designated C-115) are now used as maritime-patrol aircraft.

Above: Tactical twin sums up the Caribou. In RAAF service they operate with 35 and 38 Sqn at Richmond AFB, NSW.

Above: India has worked its small force of DHC-4 transports hard. This example has no nose radar.

Above: Two DHC-5D Buffaloes supplied in the mid-1960s are the main tactical transports of the Force Aerienne Togolaise. These aircraft were originally built for Zaire.

EH Industries (Westland/Agusta) EH 101

Type: ASW helicopter.
Specification: rotor diameter, 60ft (18.3m); weight (max take-off), 28,600lb (13,000kg).
Max speed: 164kt (304km/hr).
range: approx 1,000nm (1,800km).
Armament and Powerplant: see text.

This projected naval helicopter has its origins in design studies carried out during the mid-1970s to determine the optimum replacement for the Royal Navy's Westland Sea King ASW helicopters. By the summer of 1978, the Ministry of Defence had selected the Westland WG.34 design for development, but it was soon decided to attempt a collaborative venture with Italy, whose Navy had a broadly similar requirement.

The resulting EH 101 design is slightly smaller than Sea King but carries a heavier payload and better sensors. In Royal Navy Service it will operate largely from ships and must be able to withstand operating conditions in the North Atlantic. Italian aircraft will mostly be shore-based, operating over the Mediterranean. Both versions are due to enter service around 1990.

A joint company known as EH Industries has been set up to undertake the development, construction and marketing of the aircraft. The Italian Government has already earmarked funding for the first three years of work on the project, while Westland is providing a total of £2.75 million.

Project definition work began in the summer of 1981 and prototypes are under construction. First flight is expected in mid-1985. These first aircraft will be powered by three General Electric T700 turboshaft engines driving a main rotor with composite blades of advanced geometry. The transmission will be rated at 4,550hp, and an alternative engine may be selected for production aircraft.

Normal crew will consist of a pilot, observer and acoustics operator, and it is likely that each nation will install its own choice of avionics and weaponry. Ferranti is developing the Blue Kestrel track-while-scan radar for the aircraft. This set will have a short pulse length and high duty ratio, reducing the effect of aircraft height on effective detection range.

Like the Sea King, EH 101 is likely to be offered as a tactical transport. In this role, maximum take-off weight would be around 30,000lb (13,600kg), and up to 31 fully equipped troops could be carried.

1. A tactical transport version of the EH 101 is likely to be developed. This would be able to carry up to 31 troops and would have an undercarriage retracting into fairings on the fuselage sides.
2. The ASW version will be able to launch anti-ship missiles such as Kormoran or Exocet, using . . .

English Electric Canberra

Data for B (I). 12
Type: light bomber and interdictor.
Specifications: length 65ft 6in (19.95m); span 63ft 11in (19.5m); height, 15ft 7in (4.72m); weight (maximum take-off), 56,250lb (25,500kg).
Max speed: Mach 0.83.
Service ceiling: 48,000ft (14,600m).
Range: (tactical radius at low level) 700nm (1,300km).
Armament: four 20mm Hispano cannon, plus up to 3,000lb (1,350kg) of ordnance in the weapons bay and 2,000lb (900kg) carried on external hardpoints.
Powerplants: two Rolls-Royce Avon 109 turbojets, each rated at 7,500lb (3,400kg) of dry thrust.

This light bomber still serves in a front-line role with eight air arms, but only in small numbers. Since the type first entered operational service with the Royal Air Force in the early 1950s, it has seen much action. RAF Canberras took part in bombing operations against Egyptian targets in 1956, Indian aircraft saw action against Pakistan in 1965 and 1971, aircraft of the South African Air Force and what was formerly the Rhodesian Air Force were used against guerrilla targets in surrounding countries, Ethiopian aircraft took part in the battles against Somali forces in the disputed Ogaden region, while Argentinian examples saw action against the British fleet during the Falklands crisis of 1982.

The latter operation showed that this aircraft now lacks effectiveness in the face of modern air defences. Most Argentinian aircraft approaching the British South Atlantic battle group were generally unable to break through the defensive screen of Sea Harrier fighters from the formation's aircraft carriers.

To judge the aircraft by its performance in 1982 is unfair, since the Argentinian aircrews were having to cope with defences such as V/Stol fighters and surface-to-air missiles which did not exist when the original design was drawn up more than three decades ago. When the Canberra was developed, Bomber Command of the Royal Air Force still operated a large bomber fleet, and the new jet was intended to be suitable for mass production at minimum cost.

Refinements such as a swept wing, as used on the contemporary Boeing B-47, were eschewed in favour of a simple straight-wing design powered by two Rolls-Royce Avons. The basic concept owed much to the earlier de Havilland Mosquito, relying on speed, high altitude and manoeuvrability to penetrate hostile defences.

By the mid-1950s high-altitude operations were no longer possible in the face of modern defences, so a family of specialised intruder versions were equipped with ventral gun pack containing four 20mm cannon, plus unguided rockets, AS.30 air-to-surface missiles on underwing hardpoints and iron bombs in the weapons bay and under the wings.

Many aircraft still serve in second-line duties with the air forces of Britain, France and West Germany. Tasks which the aircraft still handles include reconnaissance, target-towing, and ECM training.

Below: Canberra bombers of the Argentine Air Force saw little action during the Falklands crisis. This veteran aircraft lacked the performance needed to cope with Sea Harrier and SAM defences.

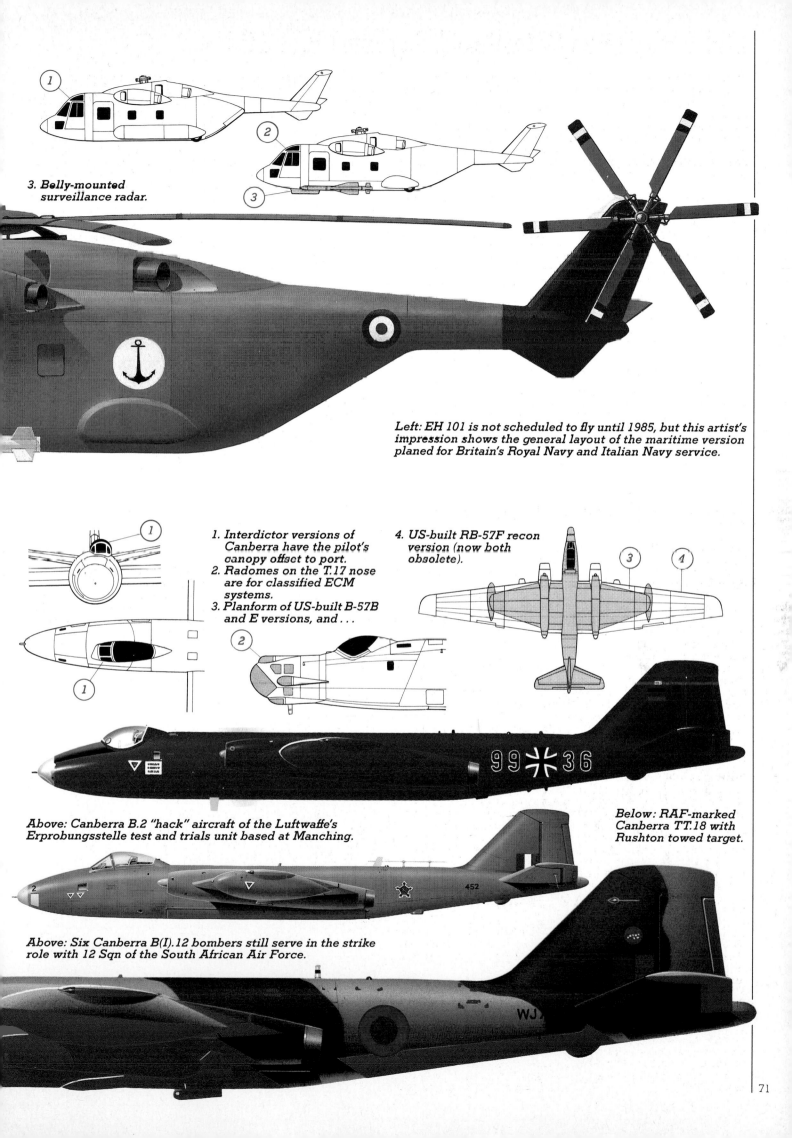

3. Belly-mounted
surveillance radar.

Left: EH 101 is not scheduled to fly until 1985, but this artist's impression shows the general layout of the maritime version planed for Britain's Royal Navy and Italian Navy service.

1. Interdictor versions of Canberra have the pilot's canopy offset to port.
2. Radomes on the T.17 nose are for classified ECM systems.
3. Planform of US-built B-57B and E versions, and . . .
4. US-built RB-57F recon version (now both obsolete).

Above: Canberra B.2 "hack" aircraft of the Luftwaffe's Erprobungsstelle test and trials unit based at Manching.

Below: RAF-marked Canberra TT.18 with Rushton towed target.

Above: Six Canberra B(I).12 bombers still serve in the strike role with 12 Sqn of the South African Air Force.

Fairchild Republic A-10 Thunderbolt II

Type: close-support aircraft.
Specifications: length, 53ft 4in (16.3m); span, 57ft 6in (17.5m); height, 14ft 8in (4.37m); weight (max. T.O.) 50,000lb (22,680kg).
Max speed: 385kt (713km/hr).
Service ceiling: 41,000ft (12,500m).
Range: (tactical radius with 1.8 hour loiter), 250nm (460km).
Armament: one 30mm GAU-8/A cannon plus up to 16,000lb of ordnance on 11 hardpoints.
Powerplant: two General Electric TF34 turbofans each rated at 9,065lb (4,120kg) dry thrust.

One of the greatest lessons which the USAF learned from Vietnam was that close support was an art in its own right, not an undemanding role which could be filled by whatever aircraft could be spared. As F-4 Phantoms and F-100 Super Sabres released their ordnance loads, "Charlie" often seemed to be not quite at the impact point. Hard-worked aircrew did their best to cope, but a supersonic jet fighter on a fast pass is hardly the optimum platform for accurate weapons delivery against front-line targets. According to the USAF, the A-10A, an aircraft whose concept was born during the South-East Asian conflict, is very much the right platform for the job.

Function was allowed to dictate shape, so the A-10 has turned out unlike any previous US attack aircraft. Its pilots love it, but cynics suggest that it may not be able to find its target in Europe's less than optimum weather, and that while it is making the attempt, Warsaw Pact fighter pilots will have a "turkey shoot" against these 400kt aircraft. A more realistic view lies somewhere between these extremes.

Everything that can be done to ensure survivability has been done. The pilot sits in an armoured "bathtub" of titanium, control systems are fully duplicated, and the engines have been widely spaced apart to ensure that both cannot be knocked out with a single minor hit.

The fuel tanks are filled with reticulated foam to minimise the risk of fire if the aircraft is hit, while fuel lines not protected by armour are fitted with self-sealing covers.

Another of the lessons from Vietnam was that twin-engined types may be safer during peacetime operations when they stand a good chance of coming home should an engine fail, but in combat the hit which knocks out one engine may directly or indirectly kill the other also. In a cramped engine bay, projectile fragments or damaged engine blades do not have to travel far to cause critical damage to the second engine. On the A-10, the twin turbofans are widely separated.

Even the position of the twin tail fins serves a purpose. At many aspect angles they screen the hot jetpipes of the engines from infra-red missile attack. Contrary to the popular belief, heat-seeking missiles do not home on to the hot exhaust but on to the hot metal of jetpipes. Engine efflux does act as a source of infra-red energy, but as a wavelength less easily detected by current homing head sensors.

Only the most prejudiced eye could describe the A-10 as an attractive aircraft, but some of its simplicity of line is due to the fact that components are interchangeable between port and starboard to ease the logistics problem during wartime. Fewer individual types of spares will need to be stocked, cutting down on the number of components to be stockpiled and making the cannibalisation of damaged aircraft easy.

Main armament of the A-10 is the fuselage-mounted 30mm GAU-8/A Avenger cannon, a weapon designed to destroy main battle tanks by penetrating the relatively thin armour on the sides, top and rear of the hull. Cannon of 30mm calibre have been used since the 1930s, current patterns including the widely used British ADEN and French DEFA.

As anyone who has watched the GAU-8/A being test-fired will readily testify, the new gun is in a different class of firepower. Being of the multi-barrelled Gatling type it can fire at up to 4,200 rounds per minute instead of the 1,400 to 1,800 rounds per minute of conventional cannon. The complete round is much larger than that of the ADEN/DEFA in order to house the propellant charge since the US gun fires its projectiles at 3,500ft/sec. (1.066m/sec) rather than the more typical 2,500-2,800ft/sec (750-850m/sec).

The A-10 can also carry AGM-65A and B Maverick electro-optical guided missiles as well as the newer imaging infra-red AGM-65D version. Conventional bombs and unguided rockets may also be carried but the GAU-8/A and Maverick remain the prime tank-killers.

Back in the mid-1970s, publicity films for the A-10 showed it executing steep dive attacks against targets from medium altitude, the sort of tactics which the medium and short-range surface-to-air missile has made impossible. This may have been a legacy from Vietnam, but is now a thing of the past. USAF A-10 pilots will take their mounts as low as possible, as at least one journalist discovered in the late 1970s when the slipstream from a low-flying A-10 snatched the notepad out of his hands!

The aircraft is undeniably big—almost the same size as a 1940-vintage B-25 bomber—but the pilots plan to use its high manoeuvrability in combat, using terrain masking to avoid the attentions of fighters and SAMs. Even the Soviet ZSU-23-4 Shilka self-propelled anti-aircraft gun can be countered by means of flight paths which pose higher crossing rates than its turret can manage.

Avionics fit of the current aircraft is austere to say the least. Pilots used to radar and inertial navigation systems must feel lonely in the A-10. The view from the cockpit is superb, but many of the systems one associates with a

front-line combat aircraft are not present.

At the moment, the main aid to help aircrew find the target is the Martin Marietta Pave Penny laser marked-target seeker, which is mounted on a short pylon on the lower starboard side of the fuselage. This is due to be supplemented by the same company's LANTIRN night-attack system and a Litton inertial navigation system.

LANTIRN will be mounted in two under-fuselage pods. One will contain a combined forward-looking infra-red (FLIR) sensor and laser designator/ranger plus the associated stabilisation optics, dual-mode automatic target tracker plus automatic target-recognition and Maverick target-handling facilities. The other will house a Ku-band terrain-following radar which will be used to present terrain-following data via the head-up display. The latter is a develop-

ment by Marconi Avionics and uses diffractive optics to present the pilot with wide field-of-view FLIR imagery so that the terrain ahead may be viewed even by night. LANTIRN equipment is due to enter production in 1985.

No aircraft can be made invulnerable, and any A-10 receiving a full burst from a ZSU-23-4 or a hit from a SAM will almost certainly be downed. In practice, however, many aircraft are lost as a result of minor hits by a few cannon shells, projectile fragments or even small-arms fire. One F-111 was lost over Hanoi during the Vietnam War when it received a hit so minor that the first the crew knew of it was the illumination of cockpit warning indicators followed by obvious control difficulties. Given this level of damage, an A-10 would have probably made it back to base to fight again another day.

Below: The grey camouflage scheme carried by this Davis-Monthan based A-10A was not adopted for operational aircraft.

Below: This "JAWS" camouflage scheme was rejected in favour of two-tone greengrey.

1. Over the angles shown shaded, the tail fins prevent the seeker head of an approaching infra-red guided missile from "seeing" the hot area of the TF34 turbofans.
2. Taller pattern of tail fin fitted to the experimental night adverse-weather version.
3. See notes 1. above.
4. Two-seat cockpit of two-seat trainer and night adverse-weather versions.
5. Definitive radome for projected night/adverse weather version.

Above: Maverick-armed A-10A of 34th TFW.

Above: The sole night adverse-weather test aircraft carried pod-mounted radar and FLIR systems beneath the wing.

FMA IA-58/66 Pucará

Data for IA-58B
Type: counter-insurgency aircraft.
Specifications: length, 46ft 9in (14.25m); span, 47ft 7in (14.5m); height, 17ft 7in (5.36m); weight (maximum take-off), 15,000lb (6,800kg).
Max speed: 252kt (467km/hr).
Service ceiling: 24,275ft (7,400m).
Range: 730nm (1,350km).
Armament: see text.
Powerplant: two Turbomeca Astazou XVI G each rated at 1,022ehp (760kW).

Left: Strangely, the Fuerza Aerea Argentina made little attempt at camouflaging their force of Pucarás during the Falklands war. Most retained an overall grey finish.

Production of the Pucará at FMA's Cordoba works is concentrated on the improved IA-58B Pucará Bravo. Similar to the earlier -58A, this has a deepened forward fuselage capable of housing the nose armament of two 30mm DEFA 553 cannon plus four 7.62mm machine-guns, and is fitted with upgraded avionics.

Originally known as the Delphin, the IA-58 started life in the mid-1960s, but progress was slow. An unpowered prototype flew in late 1967 and was used to check the aerodynamic configuration. The powered AX-02 prototype, which followed in September 1970, used two Garrett TPE331 turboprops, but the second prototype saw a switch to the definitive Turbomeca Astazou XVI G engine.

Production deliveries began in the mid-1970s, a total of 60 IA-58A aircraft being ordered by the Fuerza Aerea Argentina. By the early 1980s production settled down to a rate of two aircraft per month, and the type was in service with the III Brigada Aerea at Reconquista air base.

Combat debut was in 1976, when this unit flew Pucará sorties against communist guerrilla groups operating in Tucuman in the north-western part of the country. The IA-58A carries two 20mm Hispano cannon supplemented by four 7.62mm FN Browning machine-guns in the nose, and up to 3,600lb (1,600kg) of ordnance on one ventral hardpoint and two underwing pylons. Counter-insurgency aircraft fly low and slow enough to be engaged with small-arms fire, so armour is fitted to the cockpit floor and vital components of the twin XVIG Astazou engines.

Development of the more powerful IA-58B started a year later, and the prototype flew on 15 May 1979. Forty were ordered by the Air Force, and FMA tooled up to begin production in 1981.

Only export customer to order Pucará is Uruguay, which ordered six IA-58A for delivery in 1981. Argentina based a small force of Pucarás on the Falkland Islands during the brief 1982 occupation, and used them to attack the counter-invading British forces. Several were shot down, while others were knocked out by air attacks or naval gunfire. More were destroyed during a night attack on the airstrip at Pebble Island by the Special Air Service.

FMA IA-63

Type: basic and advanced trainer.
Specifications: length, 35ft 10in (10.93m); span, 31ft 9in (9.69m); height, 14ft 0in (4.28m); weight (clean), 7,695lb (3,490kg).
Max speed: Mach 0.75 (estimated).
Service ceiling: (estimated) 45,900ft (14,000m).
Powerplant: see text

First flight of this single-engined basic and advanced jet trainer is scheduled for October 1983, and the type is expected to enter service with the Fuerza Aerea Argentina in 1985. For a company the size of FMA, this modest trainer is a major project, a fact which is reflected in the pace of the programme.

Design work began back in 1979, and work on the first of four prototypes in March 1981. Two further airframes are being built for static testing. Assistance with the design is being provided by Dornier, a fact which may explain a more than passing resemblance to the Alpha Jet.

No decision has been taken on the definitive powerplant. FMA intends to fit the first three prototypes with the Garrett TFE731-2 turbofan of 3,700lb (1,680kg) thrust, but plans to install a 3,400lb (1,545kg) thrust Pratt & Whitney Canada JT15D5 in the third.

No attempt has been made to cut design corners—although the first Argentinian jet aircraft since the 1950s, the IA-63 will have a super-critical wing section, pressurised two-seat tandem cockpit with Martin-Baker Mk8 lightweight ejection seats. Dual controls will be provided, and, in keeping with current design practice, the rear seat is raised to give the instructor an acceptable forward view. The cockpit will be air-conditioned and pressurised.

FMA intends to give the IA-63 the ability to fly inverted for up to 20 seconds and optional provision for underwing armament. In clean configuration the design is stressed to take +6 to −3g. Maximum level speed should be a respectable Mach 0.7, and the design has a limiting Mach number of 0.8.

Airbrakes will be located on either side of the fuselage, while the inboard section of the shoulder-mounted wing will be fitted with two-segment flaps. The underwing hardpoints will be plumbed for drop tanks, and with the latter fitted the IA-63 will have a range of 1,350nm (2,500km).

Argentina plans to procure at

Below: The deepened front fuselage of the IA-58B houses two 30mm DEFA cannon. This version could be joined in service by the Garrett TPE331-powered IA-66 variant now being test-flown.

Below: Argentinian IA-58A Pucarás were based on the Falkland Islands during the brief 1982 military occupation. Many were destroyed on the ground.

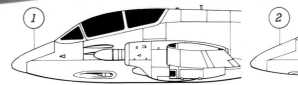

Above: IA-58 Pucará armed with rocket packs and guns. A number of these aircraft saw action in the Falklands.

1. Astazou-powered IA-58B Pucará.
2. Prototype IA-66 is an IA-58A re-engined with Garrett TPE331-11-601W turboprops.

least 80 examples for service with the Air Force, where the type will replace the MS.760 Paris trainers which currently serve at Cordoba air base. Export prospects may be less promising, in view of the range of similar aircraft already being offered by larger companies.

Below: Resembling the Alpha Jet, the sleek-lined prototype IA-63 trainer is scheduled to fly in 1983.

Fokker F27 Troopship and F27 Maritime

Data for F27 Maritime
Type: maritime-patrol aircraft.
Specifications: length, 77ft 3in (23.56m); span, 95ft 2in (29.0m); height, 28ft 6in (8.70m); weight (maximum take-off), 45,000lb (20,400kg).
Max speed: 259kt (480 km/hr).
Service ceiling: 29,500ft (9,000m).
Endurance: 10-12 hours.
Powerplant: two Rolls-Royce Dart turboprops each rated at 2,320shp (1,730kW).

Developed from the Mk 400 version of the well-proven airliner, the 400M—formerly known as the Troopship—can carry up to 46 paratroops, or airlift 24 stretcher cases in the medevac role. The doors on either side of the fuselage have been increased in size for use by paratroops, and canvas seats are arranged down either side of the interior. If the aircraft is required only for cargo-carrying, skid strips and tie-down fittings can be provided.

The Mk 500M is no longer in production. Based on the Mk 500 airliner, this has a stretched fuselage capable of housing 50 paratroops or 30 stretcher cases. No specific military version of the Mk 600 airliner was offered, but this version is operated by Algeria, Argentina, Benin, Ghana, Iran and the Ivory Coast. Dimensionally similar to the 400M, this has a large cargo door. Small numbers of earlier F27 versions such as the Mk 100 and Mk 200 are in military service with some operators.

Two features make the F27 attractive to military operators. With more than 480 on order or in service around the world, spares and support are easily available. Production is expected to continue through the 1990s, so further orders may be placed at any time to replace attrition losses or to increase fleet size. The high wing and low-set fuselage result in the lower sill of the dispatch doors of the 400M version being only 4ft (1.22m) above the ground, the corresponding figure for the airliner configuration being approximately 3ft 3in (1.0m). This makes cargo loading easy, particularly at austerely-equipped airfields.

Two specialised versions of the F27 are also on offer. The 400M is available equipped as an aerial survey aircraft, complete with cartographic cameras operating through optically-flat windows. These may be interfaced with an inertial navigation system so that the negatives produced indicate the position of the aircraft when each frame was exposed.

F27 Maritime is the Fokker offering in the slowly developing maritime-patrol market. A Litton APS-504 (V2) radar is used as the primary search sensor, its antenna being located in a ventral radome. Blister transparencies are located on either side of the aft fuselage for the use of visual observers.

Standard navigation system is the Litton LTN-72 INS, but customers can specify alternatives if required. A fuel tank in the centre of the wing (optional on civil F27s) and two external tanks on

underwing pylons give a total fuel capacity of 2,050 Imp gall (9,325 litres), giving the aircraft an endurance of ten to twelve hours. The prototype flew in 1976 and eleven have now been sold.

Folland Gnat/HAL Ajeet

Type: light fighter.
Specifications: length, 29ft 8in (8.94m); span, 22ft 1in (6.73m); height, 8ft 1in (2.46m); weight (maximum take-off), 9,200lb (4,170kg).
Max speed: 622kt (1,152km/hr).
Service ceiling: 45,000ft (13,720m).
Range: (tactical radius) 120-130nm. (195-204km).
Armament: two 30mm ADEN Mk4 cannon plus up to 1,500lb (680kg) of ordnance on four underwing hardpoints.
Powerplant: one Rolls-Royce Orpheus 701 turbojet of 4,500lb (2,050kg) dry thrust.

Based on the Folland Gnat light fighter, Ajeet was designed to overcome some of the problems displayed by the earlier aircraft.

In combat against Pakistan Air Force F-104 Starfighters and F-86 Sabres, the Gnat proved to be an agile and hard-to-hit adversary before large numbers of MiG-21s became available in the 1970s.

In 1972 the Indian Air Force published its requirement for an improved Gnat. This was originally conceived as an interceptor, but emphasis was later placed on ground-attack capability. Improvements were made to the unsatisfactory controls and hydraulics, a new "wet" wing with integral fuel tanks was devised, the avionics were updated and Martin-Baker Mk GF4 ejection seats installed instead of the Folland-designed Type 2G. Since the new wing tanks eliminated the need to carry external tanks on the underwing hardpoints, this means that the latter could be used to carry various weapons.

The first prototypes were built from the last two Gnat airframes to come down the Hindustan production line. They flew in 1975, joining two modified Gnats which were being used to test systems for the Mk 2. Production of the aircraft—now named Ajeet—began in 1976 to meet an Indian Air Force requirement for 80 examples. Production is running at around 20 per year and should soon be completed. It is scheduled to serve with four IAF squadrons.

Development of a two-seat training version was begun in 1976 and the type was scheduled to fly in 1981. The fuselage is stretched forward and aft of the wings to help provide room for the second cockpit, which is slightly raised.

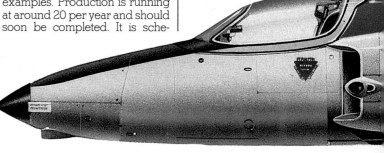

Fuji T1

Data for T-1B
Type: basic and intermediate trainer.
Specifications: length, 39ft 9in (12.12m); wingspan, 34ft 5in (10.5m); height, 11ft 0in (3.35m); weight (loaded), 9,680lb (4,390kg).
Max speed: 450kt (834km/hr).
Service ceiling: 39,400ft (12,000m).
Armament: up to 1,500lb (680kg) of ordnance, plus provision for Sidewinder missiles and one nose-mounted 0.5 inch Browning machine gun.
Powerplant: one Ishikawajima-Harima J3-3 turbojet rated at 3,087lb (1,400kg) dry thrust.

This basic/intermediate jet trainer still plays a major role with the Air Training Command of the Japan Air Self-Defense Force. Some 50 aircraft still serve with 13 Wing at Ashiya.

First flight was on 19 January 1958, and service deliveries of the T-1A version began in May 1960. The airframe was based on the F-86 Sabre, but the new forward fuselage—which retains the F-86-style nose intake—housed the pupil and instructor in tandem seats under a single canopy.

Original plans had called for the T-1 to be powered by a locally-developed Ishikawajima-Harima J3 single-shaft turbojet, but delays with this unit caused the T-1A to be delivered with the Rolls-Royce (Bristol) Orpheus 805 engine. Derated to 4,000lb (1,810kg) thrust, this engine resulted in the T-1A being somewhat overpowered. The top speed of 499kt (925km/hr) was determined by the thick section of the wing and the use of servo-tab controls, rather than by lack of engine thrust.

By 1960, the Japanese engine was ready for operational use, and the J3-powered T-1B flew for the first time in May of that year. Service deliveries of this version followed in 1961. Production ended in 1963 after a total of 66 had been built—two prototypes, four pre-series, 40 T-1A and 20 T-1B.

Several schemes for improved T-1 versions were mooted but only the T-1C was to fly. This was powered by the Ishikawajima-Harima J3-7 engine of 3,078lb (1,400kg) thrust. Despite flight trials with two prototypes in the early 1960s, this version was not adopted for service.

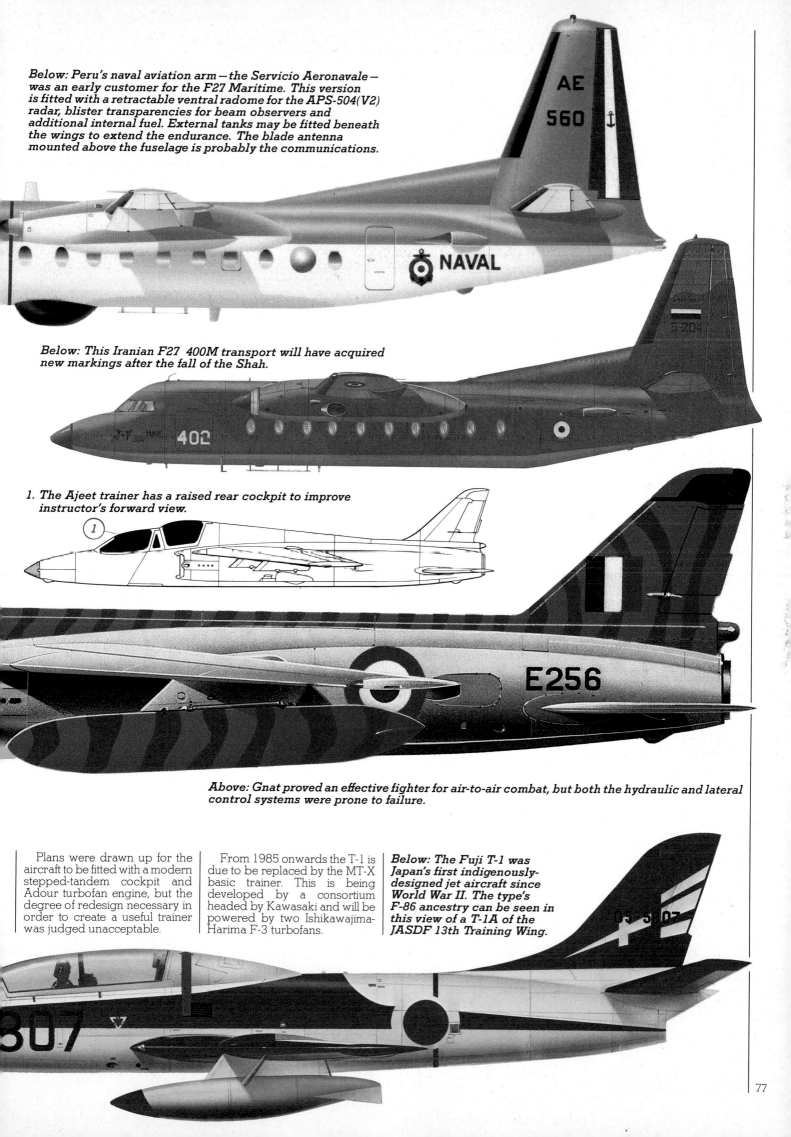

Below: Peru's naval aviation arm—the Servicio Aeronavale—was an early customer for the F27 Maritime. This version is fitted with a retractable ventral radome for the APS-504(V2) radar, blister transparencies for beam observers and additional internal fuel. External tanks may be fitted beneath the wings to extend the endurance. The blade antenna mounted above the fuselage is probably the communications.

NAVAL

Below: This Iranian F27 400M transport will have acquired new markings after the fall of the Shah.

1. The Ajeet trainer has a raised rear cockpit to improve instructor's forward view.

Above: Gnat proved an effective fighter for air-to-air combat, but both the hydraulic and lateral control systems were prone to failure.

Plans were drawn up for the aircraft to be fitted with a modern stepped-tandem cockpit and Adour turbofan engine, but the degree of redesign necessary in order to create a useful trainer was judged unacceptable.

From 1985 onwards the T-1 is due to be replaced by the MT-X basic trainer. This is being developed by a consortium headed by Kawasaki and will be powered by two Ishikawajima-Harima F-3 turbofans.

Below: The Fuji T-1 was Japan's first indigenously-designed jet aircraft since World War II. The type's F-86 ancestry can be seen in this view of a T-1A of the JASDF 13th Training Wing.

General Dynamics F-16 Fighting Falcon

Data for F-16A
Type: multi-role air-combat fighter and attack aircraft.
Specifications: length, 49ft 6in (15.09m); span, (excluding AAMs), 31ft 0in (9.45m); height, 16ft 8½in (5.09m); weight (maximum take-off), 35,400lb (16,057kg).
Max speed: Mach 2.
Service ceiling: in fighter mission, about 60,000ft (18.3km).
Range: Tac radius, over 575 miles (925km), ferry range, over 2,415 miles (3,890km).
Armament: one 20mm M61A-1 gun with 515 rounds; centreline plus six underwing pylons for virtually every kind of tactical store up to limit of 20,450lb (9276kg), with limit for 9g combat of 11,950lb (5,420kg).
Powerplant: one Pratt & Whitney F100-PW-200 augmented turbofan each rated at approximately 15,000lb (6,800kg) dry thrust, and at 23,810lb (10,800kg) with afterburner.

Perhaps the best, and certainly most cost/effective, tactical combat aircraft of the 1980s, the F-16 began life as a mere technology demonstrator. In 1972 the USAF, concerned at the price of the F-15, decided to initiate an LWF (lightweight fighter) programme to see to what extent it would be possible to build a smaller and cheaper aircraft that could still fulfil USAF fighter missions. The resulting General Dynamics 401, flown in February 1974, won over the rival Northrop and was further developed into the slightly larger YF-16. Today this is above all other aircraft the fighter that excites pilots and demonstrates what air combat—and the delivery of air/ground ordnance—is all about.

What transformed the prototype demonstrator into the most

multiple redundancy throughout in order that the high-authority stabilization system should function at all times. The concept also reduces trim drag, especially in tight manoeuvres or at supersonic speeds, and the stubby unswept wings have variable camber created by powered leading- and trailing-edge flaps which are set to commanded angles (up, zero or various down-angles) according to the flight regime. From the moment the pilot climbs up beside the snake-like nose and settles into the cockpit he becomes "part of the airplane", nestled in a reclining seat that enables him to pull well over 8g without a trace of grey-out or tunnel vision, which usually makes itself felt at much less severe load factors. He rests his right arm on the side coaming

Above: F-16A with AN/ASQ probe on one wing and AIM-9L on the other.

of ordnance. As for accurate delivery, those who were misled by the original LWF concept have been startled at the F-16's in-

Above: F-16A of 306 Sqn, Royal Netherlands Air Force, based at Volkel.

service record of bad-weather navigation and weapons delivery, which surpasses that of all other types in the USAF.

Deliveries to the USAF began in August 1978, and by 1983 about 700 will have been accepted by the USAF, Belgium, Denmark, Netherlands, Norway, Israel, Egypt and other customers such as Venezuela and Pakistan. The total planned USAF buy is 1,388 including 204 two-seat F-16Bs with 17 per cent less internal fuel. From 1977 the Sparrow and Sky Flash radar-guided AAMs were successfully fired, though these are not yet normally carried to supplement the close-range AIM-9J or -9L Sidewinders that form part of almost every mission load. The centreline usually carries an ALQ-119 or similar ECM pod, and in 1982 aircraft in service were being updated under a Multi-Stage Improvement Program which by 1984 will fit Fighting Falcons for precision strike, night attack, beyond-visual-range interception and possibly multi-sensor recon missions. New equipment includes improved displays, the Lantirn nav/attack system, the ASPJ (air-

borne self-protection jammer) and the ability to launch the Amraam (Sparrow-successor) medium-range AAM at multiple targets in rapid succession. The fully modified aircraft will be designated F-16C and (two-seat) F-16D.

GD has also flown an F-16 with large canard surfaces for direct-force control, enabling it to change line of flight (for example on weapon delivery) without changing its attitude. Other aircraft have flown with the F101DFE engine, giving enhanced performance, and with the older J79-119 turbojet to provide a cheaper fighter for export. Most exciting of all, the F-16E is the prototype of a new family with no separate horizontal tail, but with a large new wing and longer fuselage. This is expected to lead to a new F-16 having twice the payload/range of the existing aircraft.

numerous fighter of the NATO nations was the emergence of a market in 1974 by nations wishing to replace the F-104. On 7 June 1975 Belgium, Denmark, the Netherlands and Norway jointly announced selection of the F-16, and as a result a major multi-national manufacturing scheme was set up to build both the aircraft and its advanced afterburning engine in the five countries (the fifth being the USA, which of course also retains production of every part of the F-16s for its own air force and many foreign customers).

From the outset the F-16 was configured to take into account the concept of relaxed static stability (which makes a fighter more manoeuvrable), with powerful flight controls signalled by electric fly-by-wire systems which require

and flies the aircraft with a small sidestick which hardly moves, but commands manoeuvres according to the force the pilot exerts. His left hand stays on the throttle, and his eyes mostly look through the bright display of the British (Marconi Avionics) HUD, either in air combat or in surface attack.

Thanks to the tremendous specific excess power, which determines the surplus power available to give a fighter agility, the F-16 can outmanoeuvre almost any other aircraft in the sky. The routine limit is 9g, set by an inbuilt limiter which conserves airframe life. It is possible to hold 7g for over a minute, except at the highest transonic speed at sea level where the limit comes down to a sustained 6g. Even at these tremendous manoeuvre levels the F-16 can carry very heavy loads

Above: F-16B two-seater evaluated at Hill AFB in 1980. The A-10 style "Lizard" paint scheme could be adopted for aircraft based in Europe.

Right: Norwegian F-16s carry a braking parachute in the extended tail housing. RNeth.AF aircraft have a Rapport III ECM system in the same location.

1. Two-seat F-16B trainer.
2. Canard-controlled AFTI/F-16
3. Instrumentation pack on AFTI/F-16 only.
4. Extended rear fuselage of F-16/79.
5. Modified equipment fairing on Norwegian aircraft.

GENERAL DYNAMICS
F-16/79
50752

Above: One aircraft has been flown with a single-shaft J79 turbojet in place of the normal F100 turbofan.

6. Planform of F 16A.
7. Extended fuselage and cranked arrow wing of the F-16E. This first flew on July 3, 1982, from Carswell AFB, Fort Worth, Texas. During this flight a speed of Mach 0.9 was achieved.

HL
AF 78 096

8. Standard tailplane.
9. Graphite/epoxy tailplane of increased size fitted to late-production aircraft.

275

General Dynamics F-111

Data for F-111F

Type: F-111, all-weather attack aircraft; EF-111A, ECM tac-jammer.

Specifications: length, 73ft 6in (22.4m); span, (swept), 31ft 11½in (9.74m); (fully spread), 63ft 0in (19.2m); height, 17ft 1½in (5.22m); weight (maximum take-off), 100,000lb (45,359kg).

Max speed: clean, Mach 2.2 hi, Mach 1.2 lo.

Service ceiling: 60,000ft (18.3km).

Range: with external fuel, 2,925 miles (4,707km).

Armament: internal bay for two B-43 nuclear bombs or one B-43 and one 20mm M61A-1 gun; six underwing pylons for normal maximum of 29,000lb (13,154kg) of conventional bombs or other stores.

Powerplant: two Pratt & Whitney TF30-P-100 turbofans each rated at 25,100lb (11,385kg) with afterburner

Intended to become the world-wide standard tactical fighter, the F-111 incorporated all the new technical advances of the late 1950s such as variable-geometry "swing wings", augmented turbofan engines, inflight refuelling for rapid global deployment and advanced radar and missile armament. Unfortunately the USAF Tactical Air Command planners demanded tremendous ranges, both in the attack mission and for inter-theatre ferry, while the 1961 Defence Secretary insisted on a common design being developed to meet a parallel need for a new interceptor for the Navy. There followed years of political acrimony over the contract award, combined with terrible development problems which killed off the Navy model and left the USAF F-111 an overweight monster which never served in the fighter role.

This obscured the fact that even the first production model, the F-111A, which reached user squadrons in 1967, was the world's best tactical bomber, able to carry heavy loads and deliver them over long ranges in any weather with great precision, making blind first-pass attacks on a point target after approaching in the terrain-following mode automatically following the ground contours to stay under hostile radars. Even today no other aircraft can do this, apart from the Su-24 and Tornado IDS; and one has only to look at the Su-24 and MiG-23 family to see the influence this classic design exerted.

Having accepted that the F-111 was really a bomber, the same Defence Secretary wisely bought the FB-111A model for Strategic Air Command to replace the B-58 and old B-52s, despite its limited range even with flight refuelling. The FB established a good record of bombing accuracy and also carries the precision-guided SRAM both in

bomb bay and on wing pylons. The TAC machine, however, took years to mature. The F-111A had many shortcomings, only a few of which were rectified in the F-111E which equips the 20th TFW based at RAF Upper Heyford, England. The F-111C for the RAAF has the long-span wing and stronger main gears of the FB but flies in a tactical role and is also having to double as a recon platform, four of them having removable pallets. The F-111D was equipped at fantastic cost with a different avionic system, but the ultimate model is the F-111F with much more powerful engines and avionics giving most of the D capability at much less cost; this equips the 48th TFW at RAF Lakenheath.

Instead of thousands, GD built only 562 of all models. Since 1970 the F-111 has been vital to the USAF in having the ability to deliver a considerable bombload over a radius of more than 1,000 miles (1,600km) at any time of day or night, navigating with great accuracy and making a final attack at up to Mach 1.2 with a reasonable standard of defensive electronics including an ALQ-119 pod hung under the rear fuselage. Crews generally like the side-by-seating of pilot (left) and navigator (right), despite the asymmetric

Above: The F-111D — seen here releasing twelve Mk 82 bombs — featured improved avionics, but only 96 examples were built.

vision of each man. Having been planned as a fighter the F-111 is above average in low-level manoeuvrability, and can carry an internal gun. But the emphasis is entirely on the attack mission, and since 1978 new weapons have included the big GBU-15 glide bomb with precision guidance, while squadrons also been issued with the Pave Tack pod for installation under the weapon bay to provide target acquisition, designation and tracking, from very low altitudes if necessary, for precision missiles guided by laser, infra-red or EO (electro-optical) means. So far this large pod has been installed only on the F-111F, the older F-111A and E being updated with other new equipment including a modern digital computer, inertial

navigation system and cockpit control/display set.

Through sheer negligence the NATO countries have allowed the Soviet Union to gain a commanding lead in EW (electronic warfare) in almost every type of warfare. The superior avionics and ECM built into Soviet attack aircraft have no Western counterpart, despite efforts by Westinghouse, Loral, Magnavox, Cutler-Hammer and other companies, apart from the US Navy's EA-6B used at sea. For land warfare a new high-power ECM jamming platform was desperately needed, and in 1972 the decision was taken to rebuild F-111As to serve in this role. The job was assigned to Grumman, which not only created the EA-6B but was a major associate on the F-111. The

first of two EF-111A prototypes flew on 10 March 1977, proving the external configuration with a long canoe radome along the belly, housing the aerials of the ALQ-99E jammer system, and the fin-cap pod inside which are the receivers. The ALQ-99E is virtually the same as the installation carried in the EA-6B but no additional crew are needed, the whole three-ton installation being managed by the EWO (electronic-warfare officer) in the right-hand seat. Grumman is converting 42 aircraft to EF standard; the first production machine flew in June 1981. Popularly called Electric Foxes, from their initials, they would be vital in any future conflict in Europe or any other theatre involving modern air defence systems.

1. Wing stores on swivelling pylons.
2. Wing fully forward.
3. Wing fully swept.
4. Longer span wings used on F-111C and FB-111A only.

5. Vertical fin of the EF-111A tac-jammer "Electric Fox" version with built-in antennas and fin-top radome.

6. Standard-pattern vertical fin on all other versions.

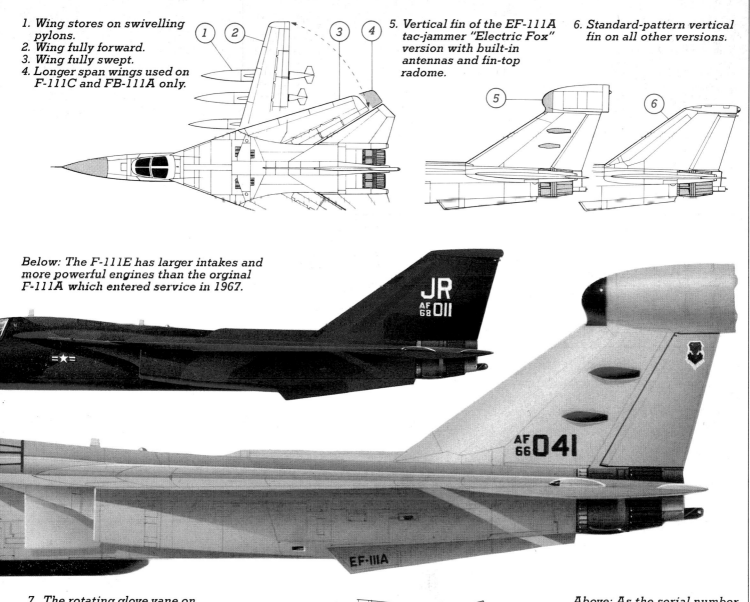

Below: The F-111E has larger intakes and more powerful engines than the orginal F-111A which entered service in 1967.

7. The rotating glove vane on all models is coupled to the wing leading-edge slats.
8. M61 ventral gun on the F-111D.
9. Revised "Triple-Plow" intake used on the F-111C, D, E and F versions.
10. Ventral radome on the EF-111A.
11. Early-pattern intake with vertical splitter plate used on the F-111A.

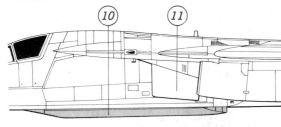

Above: As the serial number 66-041 on this EF-111A indicates, these special ECM aircraft are rebuilt F-111As.

Below: FB-111A bomber assigned to the Second Air Force, Strategic Air Command.

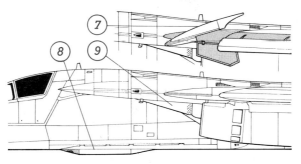

Grumman A-6 Intruder and EA-6B Prowler

Data for A-6E.

Type: A-6, all-weather carrier-based attack aircraft; EA-6B, carrier-based ECM jammer platform.

Specifications: length, 54ft 9in (16.69m); span, 53ft 0in (16.15m); height, 16ft 2in (4.93m); weight (maximum take-off), 60,400lb (27,397kg).

Max speed: 644mph (1,037km/h).

Service ceiling: 42,500ft (12,955m).

Range: with max external load, 1,013 miles (1,631km); max fuel, 3,250 miles (5,231km).

Armament: maximum of 18,000lb (8,164kg) on five external pylons each with a rating of 3,600lb (1,633kg); typical bombload, 30 bombs of 500lb (227kg) in clusters of six.

Powerplant: two Pratt & Whitney J52-PW-8B turbojets each rated at 9,300lb (4,220kg) dry thrust

Despite the lessons of Korea, the United States did little to procure all-weather attack aircraft, the only example (apart from the prototypes of the B-57G) being this subsonic twin-jet for the US Navy and Marine Corps. Developed much later than the basically similar British Buccaneer, it did not have the advanced airframe of the latter (which uses transonic blowing to reduce the size of the wing and tailplane) and thus has a long-span wing which is not suitable for full-throttle attack at low level. At the same time, if the crew can take the rough ride of such a wing near sea level, the airframe certainly can. Grumman always built aircraft like battleships, and the A-6 has to be so strong to make accelerated cat launches and arrested no-flare landings that a high-speed bombing run hardly affects the structural fatigue life.

Again unlike the British counterpart, the A-6 was designed to hang its bombs externally. Maximum bombload is impresive, and though similar weights can in theory be carried by even such small modern fighters as the F-16, the A-6 actually carried these loads in years of action in southeast Asia, and over substantial mission ranges. The fuselage has a tadpole shape, the vast nose being filled by the radars and navigation and weapon-delivery systems, with the crew of two almost side-by-side, the bombardier/navigator being at a slightly lower level and just to the rear on the right. They climb aboard up folding stairways forming part of the inlet duct outer skin on each side, the engines being hung on the fuselage immediately below the wing roots. Grumman abandoned tilting jetpipes, the engines being installed with a modest fixed downward slant. Originally there were airbrakes behind the nozzles on the rear fuselage, but in the current model, the streng-

thened and better-equipped A-6E, these are removed. The wing-tips, however, have always carried surfaces which look like ailerons but which are in fact airbrakes, splitting to open above and below. Roll control is by long spoilers, and the folding wings carry almost full-span flaps along the leading and trailing edge. These make the A-6 pleasant to fly at low speeds even at very high weights. Though devoid of self-defence armament, the A-6E has fair defensive electronics, and combined with good manoeuvrability has always given Intruder crews confidence in their ability to penetrate hostile territory.

In the original A-6A, which entered service in February 1963, the vast radome concealed two radars, a large Norden APQ-92 search set and a small Naval Avionics APQ-88 for tracking. The outputs were combined on the Kaiser analog vertical display in the cockpit, giving the pilot a kind of 3-D picture of the scene ahead even at night or in bad weather. A subsystem called Diane (Digital integrated attack nav equipment) helped by processing the inputs from the sensors and the main nav systems (inertial plus doppler) and the radar altimeter for terrain-following, and outputted precise solutions for flying the aircraft and delivering weapons. It all worked after a fashion, but crew workload was very high,

and maintenance burden appalling. With the A-6E the system was torn apart and replaced by a single much better multi-mode radar, the Norden APQ-148, throwing out the track radar hardly anyone ever used. The computer was replaced by a newer IBM solid-state box and the cockpit display was improved, the whole kit being backed up by a signal-data convertor and armament control unit that old-time A-6 crews say cuts the workload by three-quarters. Grumman also made the A-6E even stronger.

The E-type entered service in 1972, a bit late for Vietnam, but has since demonstrated its delivery capability beyond doubt. It is quite old as a basic type, but about a dozen are still being made each year and are expected to continue to come off the line at

this rate for the next several years.

By 1981 various updates were increasing A-6 capability. A simple add-on is the Harpoon cruise missile, six of which can be carried. The first 50 aircraft were operating with this long-range anti-ship weapon by early 1982, with the rest of the force due to follow in batches over the next few years. This gives the A-6 the option of hitting major surface ships from a stand-off range of almost 70 miles (110km), which is outside the effective radius of all known ship-to-air weapon systems. The other major update is fitting Tram (target recognition and attack multi-sensor), which adds stabilized laser and infra-red devices in a turret under the nose.

Grumman is to demonstrate the possibility of greatly enhanced flight performance by flying an A-6 with General Electric F404 engines in place of the pedestrian J52s. It so happens that a more powerful version of J52, the PW-408A rated at 11,200lb (5,080kg), is fitted to the EA-6B Prowler which until the advent of the EF-111A was the only really comprehensive and effective ECM aircraft in the West. Standard aboard all US Navy carriers and also flown by Marine units, the Prowler is a much-modified A-6 with a stretched forward fuselage seating two added backseaters to manage the ALQ-99 EW system. This groups passive receivers and

their aerials in a fin-cap pod and the powerful jammers, each tuned to a different waveband, in up to five external pods hung on the pylons. Each pod is self-powered by a windmill generator and most contain two transmitters covering up to eight frequency bands.

Above: Each one of the underwing jamming pods carried by this EA-6B Prowler contains two jamming transmitters.

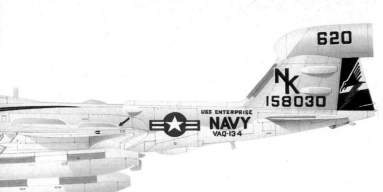

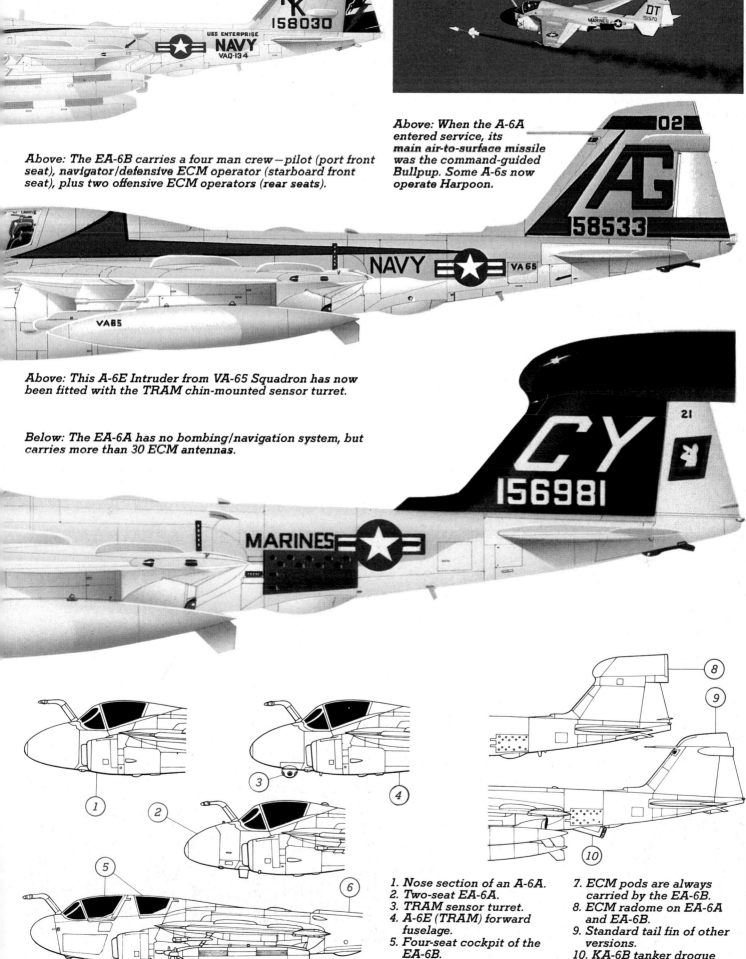

Above: The EA-6B carries a four man crew—pilot (port front seat), navigator/defensive ECM operator (starboard front seat), plus two offensive ECM operators (rear seats).

Above: When the A-6A entered service, its main air-to-surface missile was the command-guided Bullpup. Some A-6s now operate Harpoon.

Above: This A-6E Intruder from VA-65 Squadron has now been fitted with the TRAM chin-mounted sensor turret.

Below: The EA-6A has no bombing/navigation system, but carries more than 30 ECM antennas.

1. Nose section of an A-6A.
2. Two-seat EA-6A.
3. TRAM sensor turret.
4. A-6E (TRAM) forward fuselage.
5. Four-seat cockpit of the EA-6B.
6. Extended fin-root antenna on EA-6B.
7. ECM pods are always carried by the EA-6B.
8. ECM radome on EA-6A and EA-6B.
9. Standard tail fin of other versions.
10. KA-6B tanker drogue fairing.

Grumman E-2 Hawkeye

Data for E-2C.
Type: carrier-based early-warning and control aircraft; C-2, COD.
Specifications: length, 57ft 6¾in (17.54m); span, 80ft 7in (24.56m); height, 18ft 3¾in (5.58m); weight (maximum take-off), 51,817lb (23,503kg).
Max speed: 374mph (602km/h).
Service ceiling: 30,800ft (9,390m).
Range: 1,605 miles (2,583km).
Armament: None.
Powerplant: two Allison T56-A-425 turboprops each rated at 4,910ehp (3,660ekW)

Since 1975 there has been a great intensification in worldwide interest in AEW (airborne early warning) and Awacs-type platforms, following belated recognition of the fact that they can multiply the effectiveness of an air force and also do a great deal for armies and navies. Major land-based platforms in this class are outside the practical limits of most air forces, both on the grounds of budget and manning; but the compact E-2 Hawkeye had to fit into an aircraft carrier and thus automatically becomes more manageable. It has already sold to Israel and Japan, been evaluated by France and been offered to Egypt, in all cases for operation from land airfields.

Grumman was the original pioneer of the seagoing AEW aircraft, with the AF-2W Guardian and later the twin-engined E-1B Tracer in which the radar was put above the fuselage instead of below. By the late 1950s increasing demands and possibilities led to the design of the W2F, predecessor of today's Hawkeye, which was (with various species of Super Constellation) the first aircraft to have the new style of rotodome, in which the aerial is itself given a streamlined circular fairing instead of being accommodated inside a radome. At the same time, the size of aircraft needed to accommodate the General Electric APS-96 radar was such that considerable design ingenuity was needed. Four fins and rudders are used, all mounted at 90° to the dihedralled tailplane and all well below the wake of the saucer-like rotodome. The long-span wings fold about skewed hinges to swing down and to the rear to be stowed on each side of the rear fuselage, upper surfaces outward, like the World War 2 Avenger. The nose and tail do not fold, but after completing a mission the rotodome is retracted a short distance downwards to clear the hangar roof below decks. In flight the rotodome is set at a positive angle of incidence to lift at least its own weight.

As the Hawkeye has a modest performance it can have pneumatic boot deicers, alternately inflated by compressed air and allowed to deflate to break off any ice. These black "boots" extend along all leading edges and around the rotodome. The latter normally rotates once every 10 seconds when in operation, and the radar gives surveillance from an on-station height of 30,000ft (9.15km) within a radius of 300 miles (480km). Ten years into the programme the APS-96 was replaced by the much more advanced APS-125 with ARPS (advanced radar processing system) to give vastly better discrimination and detection capability over both land and water, the aircraft designation being changed to E-2C. This model entered service in 1973 and remains the standard "eyes" of the US Navy at sea.

As a flying machine the E-2C poses few problems. The Allison turboprops, basically similar to those of the C-130 and P-3, run at constant speed and thus accommodate demands for changes in power level immediately, the only delay being that due to changes in propeller pitch. All flight controls are fully powered, and even with full internal fuel (12,400lb, 5,624kg) the Hawkeye can be aerobatted almost like a fighter, though avoiding negative-g manoeuvres. Cat launches use the nose-tow system, pulling on the steerable twin-wheel nose gear, the single main wheels retracting forward and rotating 90° to lie flat in the bottom of the nacelles under the engines and behind the oil coolers. The approach speed with Fowler flaps down is a mere 102 knots (189km/h), and at the rear is the A-frame arrester hook and retractable tailskid.

The flight crew of two pilots occupy a broad airline-type flight

Top: Newly-built Hawkeye on flight test near the factory.

Above: C-2A of USN Tac Support Squadron 50.

deck. Behind them, amidst the mass of radar racking and the high-capacity vapour-cycle cooling system, the radiator for which is housed in a large duct above the fuselage, is the pressurized ATDS (airborne tac data system) compartment, mainly aft of the wing under the radar. This is the nerve centre of the aircraft, manned by the combat info centre officer, air control officer and radar operator. Here are grouped not only the pictures from the main radar but also over 30 other avionic interfaces, including particularly advanced communications systems and passive detection systems to give a picture of targets, tracks or trajectories and signal emissions, all duly processed and where appropriate with IFF interrogation replies. PDS (passive detection system) aerials point to front and rear from the nose and tail and to each side from the tips of the tailplane.

How good is the E-2C at its vital job? Clearly it meets the requirements of the US Navy, and production is trickling on steadily with the 95th E-2C due to be delivered in 1987. Its crews are enthusiastic, and Grumman has found them valuable sales aids in their not-unsuccessful efforts to sell the aircraft to foreign buyers who have no carriers. It would be possible, with the same radar and engines, to build a slightly more efficient platform if it did not have to operate from a carrier, but existing export customers have been happy to take the machine as it is. A mission can last six hours, and at a radius of 200 miles (322km) the time on station at 30,000ft can be almost 4 h. This is much shorter than the 10 h at this radius of the E-3A and Nimrod, but Grumman claim about a 2:1 difference in acquisition cost and operating cost. Data processing in the E-2C is adequate, with the ability simultaneously to

track more than 250 aerial targets and control more than 30 intercepts. Objects "as small as a cruise missile" can be tracked at 115 miles (185km).

The TE-2C is a training version. The C-2A Greyhound, which uses a similar airframe with a transport fuselage with rear ramp door, is the standard US Navy COD (carrier on-board delivery) transport. It carries 10,000lb (4,536kg) of cargo or up to 39 passengers, and the possibility of the US-3A Viking being adopted was eliminated by the 1982 decision to add 39 Greyhounds to the existing fleet of 17.

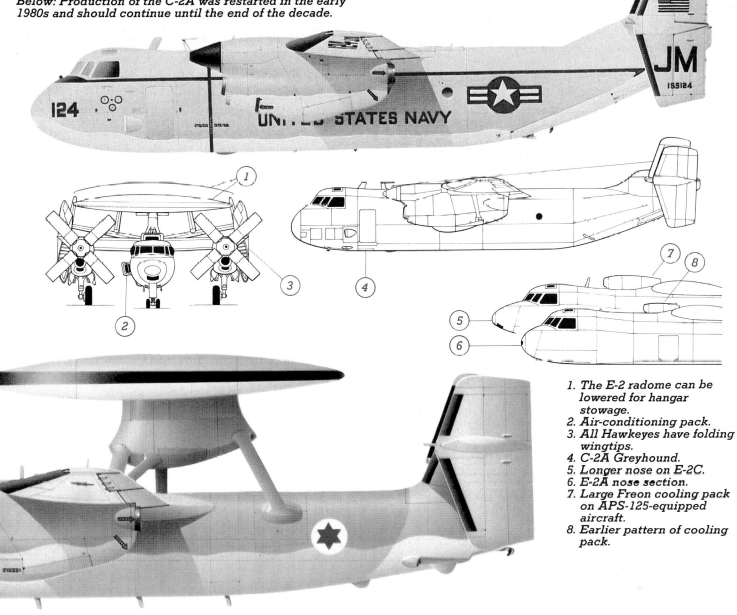

Below: Production of the C-2A was restarted in the early 1980s and should continue until the end of the decade.

1. The E-2 radome can be lowered for hangar stowage.
2. Air-conditioning pack.
3. All Hawkeyes have folding wingtips.
4. C-2A Greyhound.
5. Longer nose on E-2C.
6. E-2A nose section.
7. Large Freon cooling pack on APS-125-equipped aircraft.
8. Earlier pattern of cooling pack.

Above: Israeli Hawkeyes have been used to guide Kfir and F-15 fighters engaging Syrian Air Force MiG-21s and -23s.

Below: This early-production E-2C has been updated with the APS-125 ARPS (advanced radar processing system).

Grumman F-14 Tomcat

Data for F-14A
Type: multi-role fighter for carrier operation.
Specifications: length, 62ft 8in (19.1m); span (swept), 38ft 2½in (11.65m); (spread) 64ft 1½in (19.54m); height, 16ft 0in (4.88m); weight (maximum take-off), 74,348lb (33,724kg).
Max speed: Mach 2.4.
Service ceiling: over 50,000ft (15.24km).
Range: intercept mission, about 2,000 miles (3,200km).
Armament: one 20mm M61A-1 gun with 675 rounds, four Sparrow AAMs on lower edges of inlet ducts partially submerged, or four Phoenix AAMs on special belly pallets, plus two wing pylons each for one Phoenix or Sparrow and one Sidewinder or two Sidewinder; in surface-attack mode up to 14,500lb (6,577kg) of assorted ordnance can be carried externally, including the AAMs.
Powerplant: two Pratt & Whitney TF30-PW-414 turbofans each rated at 20,900lb (9,480kg) with maximum after-burner.

When in 1967 it seemed likely that the GD/Grumman F-111B might collapse as a programme, the chief associate contractor, Grumman, began detailed design of a possible replacement tailored exclusively to the Navy mission. The gamble paid off and in January Grumman won the VFX competition and flew the prototype Tomcat on 21 December 1970. Though a large and costly aircraft, without too much power from its engines, it was from the start extremely capable and versatile. Normally operated in the fleet defence mission, in the CAP (combat air patrol) and DLI (deck-launched intercept) modes, it has greater proven intercept capability than any other aircraft in service. This stems from the large and powerful Hughes radar and missiles, which were designed together as a new weapon system as far back as 1960 but still have no equal in 1983.

The AWG-9 radar and Phoenix AAM stemmed from the system flown in the YF-12 Blackbird interceptor and were originally flown on the F-111B. Compared with that unfortunate aircraft the F-14 has dramatically higher performance, despite the fact that, contrary to prediction and in the face of all Grumman could do, the weight has climbed as high as that of the cancelled machine while engine thrust has remained the same. The intended programme began with the F-14A, first delivered to Navy squadrons in October 1972, and was intended quickly to move on to the F-14B with much more powerful engines, and thence to the F-14C with new avionics as well. In fact, though the first of two F-14Bs flew successfully in 1973, this was cancelled.

Cost-escalation almost wrecked the programme, and has restricted the introduction of improvements other than a succession of engine modifications to overcome prolonged difficulties with blade retention and other features.

Despite this, the basic design was so good that for a decade the F-14A has admirably filled the role of US Navy shipboard fighter, and is one of very few aircraft to have an MSP (Mach sweep programmer) which automatically varies the sweep angle of the wings according to the mission demands, giving wide span for efficient cruise, various intermediate positions for combat (with rapid variation when necessary for high-rate manoeuvres) and maximum sweep of 68° for low-level attack on surface targets. One of the few obvious deficiencies of the original aircraft was that, except in a prolonged war situation, it was impossible to make use of the radar and AAM range of over 100 miles (161km). Potentially hostile targets had to be allowed to approach to within a small fraction of this distance for positive identification, nullifying the range advantage. Since 1981 the Navy has been slowly introducing the Northrop TCS (TV camera set), installed under the nose, which automatically seeks, locks-on to and displays the visual characteristics of other aircraft at distances many times normal visual limits. Both pilot and naval flight officer (the backseater) have a TCS display, and it enables them to take combat decisions at the earliest possible moment. Another add-on for 49 aircraft is the TARPS (tactical air recon pod system) which fills the hollow belly with advanced recon sensors. Further updates to the basic combat avionics are being introduced with the F-14C, to be delivered from 1983.

The Iranians bought 80 F-14As similar to the USN machine except for ECM installations, and complete with Phoenix missiles. Little has been heard of them in the war with Iraq, and though a few are still flying they can probably be largely discounted as a fighting force because of lack of spares and support.

Without trying to "knock" a fine combat aircraft, the objective in the VFX programme was to produce "a high-performance lightweight fighter with a gross weight of no more than 50,000lb". By first flight the weight with no external weapons except four Sparrows had climbed to 53,000lb, and then it went via 55,000 to today's figure of 59,372lb (26,930kg). This is despite the usable internal fuel having come down slightly to 16,200lb, which is good compared with the 13,455lb of the F-15C and 11,000lb of the F/A-18A, but less than half that of the F-111B which the F-14 replaced. In practice this has proved no

problem, and external fuel provisions are trivial and almost never used, though the flight-refuelling probe (full retractable, into the right side of the nose) is used frequently.

The published range limit for the AWG-9 radar is 195 miles (315km) against large aerial targets, with 75 miles more practical for a hostile fighter. The radar processor is competent enough to track 24 aerial targets simultaneously, and to guide six Phoenix (or other missiles) towards any six selected targets almost simultaneously. This TWS (track while scan) capability is sustained in the presence of strong enemy jamming and other countermeasures, and is very greatly enhanced in the improved AIM-54C Phoenix which began to replace the original AIM-54A in 1982. By this time the F-14A had almost replaced the F-4J and F-4S in the embarked carrier air wings, with 11 of 13 wings fully converted. About 430 Tomcats had been delivered out of 491 programmed, and the Reagan administration hopes considerably to increase this total.

Above: Like all Kittyhawk-class carriers, John F. Kennedy carries 24 Tomcats. One went overboard in 1976, but the US Navy fished it up before the Soviets could get to it to study the AWG-9 radar.

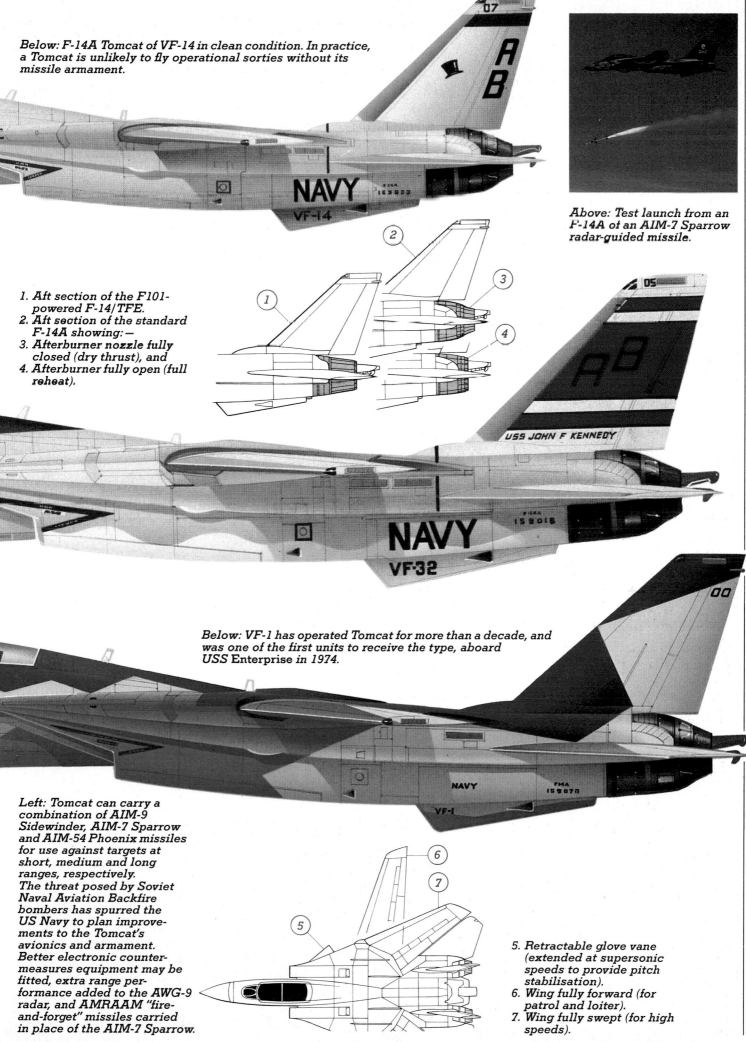

Below: F-14A Tomcat of VF-14 in clean condition. In practice, a Tomcat is unlikely to fly operational sorties without its missile armament.

Above: Test launch from an F-14A of an AIM-7 Sparrow radar-guided missile.

1. Aft section of the F101-powered F-14/TFE.
2. Aft section of the standard F-14A showing:—
3. Afterburner nozzle fully closed (dry thrust), and
4. Afterburner fully open (full reheat).

Below: VF-1 has operated Tomcat for more than a decade, and was one of the first units to receive the type, aboard USS Enterprise in 1974.

Left: Tomcat can carry a combination of AIM-9 Sidewinder, AIM-7 Sparrow and AIM-54 Phoenix missiles for use against targets at short, medium and long ranges, respectively. The threat posed by Soviet Naval Aviation Backfire bombers has spurred the US Navy to plan improvements to the Tomcat's avionics and armament. Better electronic counter-measures equipment may be fitted, extra range performance added to the AWG-9 radar, and AMRAAM "fire-and-forget" missiles carried in place of the AIM-7 Sparrow.

5. Retractable glove vane (extended at supersonic speeds to provide pitch stabilisation).
6. Wing fully forward (for patrol and loiter).
7. Wing fully swept (for high speeds).

87

Grumman OV-1 Mohawk

Data for OV-ID on SLAR mission.
Type: OV-1, tactical reconnaissance; RV-1, electronic intelligence.
Specifications: length, (with SLAR), 44ft 11in (13.69m); span, 48ft 0in (14.63m); height, 12ft 8in (3.86m); weight (maximum take-off), 18,109lb (8,214kg).
Max speed: 289mph (465km/h).
Service ceiling: 25,000ft (7.6km).
Range: 944 miles (1,520km).
Armament: usually none.
Powerplant: two Avco Lycoming T53-L-701 turbo-props each rated at 1,400shp (1,044kW).

Conceived in the late 1950s, the Mohawk is a unique high-performance observation platform for use by the USA (US Army) to study the enemy in land battles. This has been the role of aircraft since balloons were used at the battle of Fleurus in 1794. The output has been in the role of verbal reports, hastily scribbled written messages hurled from the cockpit, photographic film, and with the Mohawk it moved on with the addition of infra-red linescan and SLAR radar. The basic problem of what kind of platform to create was thorny, and perhaps never quite solved.

Grumman's G-134 aircraft is smaller and much lighter than a jet fighter, and though it seats two husky troops in side-by-side Martin-Baker seats, with extensive cockpit armour against small-arms fire, it has a take-off and landing run of a mere 600ft (180m) and is designed to use

any reasonably flat bit of ground near the front line. The basic problem remains, that even though the Mohawk is extremely agile and can be flung into tight turns round a tree at over 200 knots, it can be shot down by the kind of weapons possessed by all modern armies. For example, though the large front windshields are described as "bullet resistant", ordinary machine-gun fire can penetrate the bulged side windows, though flak curtains can if necessary be pulled across. Even the aircraft systems, such as fuel and engines, are vulnerable to ordinary bullets. This calls into question whether a much smaller and probably faster RPV might not be more cost/effective.

The original OV-1A was packed with tactical navigation and communications for flight in all weathers, and had cameras with flares for night use. Up to 3,700lb (1,678kg) of stores (supply packs or ordnance) could be hung under the wings on four pylons. The JOV-1A had six pylons for bombs or gun pods, while the OV-1B did away with airbrakes and dual controls but added a long SLAR pod. The OV-1C had the UAS-4 infra-red sensor instead of SLAR, but the OV-1D was a quick-change model with either sensor

to which most (over 100) B and C models were converted. This was the final new-build model, the last of 375 being delivered in 1970.

The Mohawk has proved popular, and remains in use with continual efforts to improve value by adding sensors and defensive electronics. The 12 RV-1D models

Left: The US Army still operates some 200 Mohawks, mostly OV-1Ds or earlier aircraft rebuilt to this standard.

are rebuilt OV-1Bs for permanent use in the Elint role, with various passive receivers, analysers and recorders of unknown or hostile signals. The EV-1E designation applies to 16 OV-1B rebuilds with ALQ-133 Quick Look II surveillance radar, ventral and wingtip EW pods and much extra Elint gear. Two of these were supplied to Israel. Conversions continue, and about 20 rebuilt OV-1s have been supplied to several east Asian countries.

Grumman S-2 Tracker

Data for S-2E
Type: ASW aircraft designed for carrier operation.
Specifications: length, 43ft 6in (13.26m); span, 72ft 7in (22.13m); height, 16ft 7in (5.06m); weight (maximum take-off), 29,150lb (13,222kg).
Max speed: 267mph (430km/h).
Service ceiling: 21,000ft (6.4km).
Range: 1,300 miles (2,095km).
Armament: internal bay for two Mk 44 or 46 (or similar acoustic-homing AS type) torpedoes or two depth bombs or four depth charges; six underwing pylons for 5in rockets, 250lb (227kg) bombs, AS.12 or other guided missiles or (for ferrying only) additional torpedoes.
Powerplant: two Wright R-1820-82WA Cyclone piston engines each rated at 1,525hp (1,140kW).

First flown over 30 years ago (4 December 1952) as the S2F-1, the Tracker was the first effective hunter/killer ASW platform for operation from carriers of the US Navy. Its 3,000hp enabled it to carry both sensors and weapons and thus combine the missions which had previously demanded a team of two aircraft, one a hunter and the other a killer.

Again, its piston engines and long-span wings enabled it to operate safely from small ASW carriers, freeing the giant attack carriers for other types, and this automatically enabled it to use even the poorest military airfields in customer countries.

There were many versions with progressively updated equipment, as well as the C-1A Trader COD transport and E-1B Tracer radar early-warning platform, but the only models in use today are the S-2E (best of the ASW variants) and a few earlier types, notably the original S-2A version pensioned-off by the original user and sold to many users, where over the years variable amounts of updating have been performed. All S-2 variants have a basic crew of four, the co-pilot on the right of the cockpit doing most of the navigation and the so-called radar operators in the rear seats also handling the other sensors such as a retractable MAD boom in the rear fuselage, 60 echo-sounding charges dropped in sequence from the fuselage as part of the Julie active echo-ranging system and AQA-3 Jezebel passive long-range acoustic search equipment. The rear of each engine nacelle houses 16 sonobuoys ejected on command, a searchlight is normally fitted outboard under the right

wing, and an ALD-3 DF set is carried to pinpoint radio signals emanating from submarines.

Of course, the S-2 also has some capability against surface ships, though large torpedoes cannot normally be carried. In the environments where Trackers find themselves today, however, they are efficient and effective. In the Falklands crisis of 1982, the six old S-2A's of the Argentine Navy did not see action, but in local limited-war type conflicts, concerned with such duties as anti-terrorist patrol, anti-smuggling, fisheries protection, frontier patrol of exclusive economic zones and action against polluting tankers the S-2 plays a useful role at modest cost. It combines fair performance with an endurance of some nine hours even when lumbered with several tons of

obsolescent but usually functioning avionics.

As for their use against modern nuclear submarines, this is another matter entirely. It is staggering that the S-2E did not even reach the US Navy until 1962, and that Grumman continued to build until 1968. By that time the S-2 as a basic vehicle was totally unable to meet the great challenge of modern submarines, which call for vastly greater sensor power (demanding greater airborne bulk, if not weight) able to cover greater volumes of ocean down to great depths, and computers able to handle far more info at higher bit rates. The S-2 could never begin to meet the requirements even if gutted and re-equipped with some of the gear carried by the S-3 (it could not accommodate more than half of it within the existing fuselage).

Below: The OV-1D's elongated avionics pod can carry a sideways-looking antenna capable of high resolution in the azimuth plane.

UNITED STATES ARMY

Left: The early JOV-1A armed version could carry a range of ordnance including unguided rockets.

Below: Several NATO nations operated Tracker. This example served with the Netherlands Naval Air Service.

169   S-2A-169   KON. MARINE

Left: For more than a decade the piston-engined Tracker played a significant role in US anti-submarine warfare plans.

23   4123   海上自衛隊   14

Above right: The Japanese Maritime Self-Defence Force (JMSDF) is replacing its S-2F with locally-built P-3 Orions.

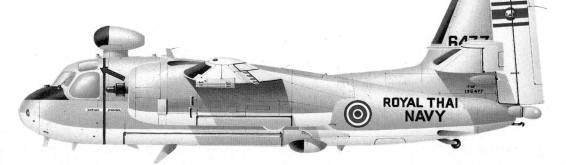

6477   135477   ROYAL THAI NAVY

Left: Thailand still operates ten S-2A Trackers. Used for ASW and general maritime patrol duties, these aircraft are based at Bangkok.

Handley Page Victor

Type: flight-refuelling tanker.
Specifications: length, 114ft 11in (35.05m); span, 117ft 0in (35.69m; height, 28ft 1in (8.58m).
Max speed: approx. 525kt (970km/hr).
Service ceiling: 50,000ft + (15,300m +).
Range: 4,000nm (7,400km/hr).
Payload: 91,000lb (41,000kg) of fuel.
Powerplant: four Rolls-Royce Conway Mk201 turbofans, each rated at 20,600lb (9,360kg) of dry thrust.

Left: A Victor K Mk2 of 57 Sqn refuels a Tornado during development trials of the latter aircraft. The earlier Victor K Mk1 did not have the fuselage-mounted hose-and-drogue unit.

Standard flight-refuelling tanker of the Royal Air Force since 1965, the Victor was originally developed in the 1950s as a strategic bomber. When the earlier RAF fleet of Valiant tankers was grounded at the end of 1964, owing to wing-spar fatigue cracks, several examples of the Victor B1 bomber were hastily converted into an interim tanker designated B (K) Mk1A, by the fitting of underwing hose-and-drogue refuelling pods.

The immediate problem solved, Handley Page devised a more elegant installation to be installed on the remainder of the B1s earmarked for conversion, and the resulting K Mk1 and Mk1A aircraft followed in 1966. These were equipped with a three-point re-fuelling system.

Definitive tanker version is the K Mk2, an adaptation of the Conway-powered B2 bomber, but the conversion work was carried out not by Handley Page but by the Manchester division of what was then Hawker Siddeley Aviation. Handley Page had gone into liquidation in 1969.

In order to maximise the service life of these aircraft, structural modifications were carried out, including the removal of the outer 3ft 6in (1.07m) of each wingtip. Avionic systems associated with the bomber role were stripped out and two extra fuel tanks of 16,000lb (7,300kg) capacity installed in the bomb bay. A total of 24 aircraft were converted, and the type entered RAF service in 1974. Like the K Mk1, these carried two underwing refuelling pods plus a third refuelling hose in the fuselage. Having more powerful engines, they did not suffer from the "hot and high" limitations experienced by the K Mk1.

During the second half of the 1970s these aircraft were the sole RAF tankers, the K Mk1 having been retired. By the early 1980s the airframes were starting to show their age. As this text was in preparation, a review of the likely airframe life was under way in the light of the 1982 defence cuts and plans to deploy tanker versions of the VC10 transport.

Hawker Siddeley Buccaneer

Data for S.2
Type: low-level strike aircraft.
Specifications: length, 63ft 5in (19.33m); span, 44ft 0in (13.41m); height, 16ft 3in (4.95m); weight (maximum take-off), 62,000lb (28,200kg).
Max speed: Mach 0.85 at sea level.
Service ceiling: at least 40,000ft (12,200m).
Range: (hi-lo-hi) 2,000nm (3,700km).
Armament: 4,000lb (1,800kg) of ordnance in the weapons bay plus up to 12,000lb (5,500kg) on underwing hardpoints.
Powerplants: two Rolls-Royce Spey 101 turbofans each rated at 11,250lb (5,100kg) of dry thrust.

Above: Buccaneer S.2B of the Royal Air Force in desert camouflage. The fitting on the outer wing pylon is the carrier for lightweight practice bombs.

Originally developed as a low-level strike bomber for use from Royal Navy carriers, the Buccaneer now operates from land bases with the Royal Air Force and the South African Air Force. The turbojet-powered S.1 model has long been retired, surviving examples being Spey-powered S.2B versions, some of which originally served with the Royal Navy.

Technically, the aircraft was a successful design, and one which should have been built in large numbers as a Canberra replacement. Inter-service rivalry and desire to obtain the Mach 2 TSR.2 or F-111K prevented any large-scale RAF purchase, while the very effectiveness of the aircraft caused successive UK Governments to be cool towards attempts to export the type. A Conservative Government allowed South Africa to purchase 16 aircraft, but a later Labour Government refused to supply a further batch or even to replace one aircraft which crashed in transit. Not surprisingly, no further customers came forward.

Greatest weakness of the type is its analogue avionics of late 1950s vintage. These systems, including the Ferranti Airpass III nose radar, were designed for the naval role and in no way even remotely approach the performance of the digital equipment carried by the contemporary Grumman A-6. Piecemeal replacement of individual items of equipment with digital equivalents would have been difficult, as was discovered when Buccaneer was used as a testbed for Tornado avionics. The aircraft really needed an extensive refitting with modern all-digital systems which would have allowed it to remain in front-line service until the mid-1990s. Some examples will serve this long to supplement the Tornado force, but only in the anti-shipping role and retaining the analogue systems.

The massively-strong structure of Buccaneer allowed pilots to fly at the lowest altitudes with impunity. The first time that its portly form graced the flight line at Nellis AFB in Nevada during a mid-1970s Red Flag air-combat exercise, USAF F-15 pilots were confident of their ability to deal with such a large slow-flying type. Practical experience over the next few days was a sorry tale for the Eagle pilots, who at first found the Buccaneers almost impossible to detect. The first "kill" was scored when a disorientated Buccaneer crew carried out a pop-up manoeuvre in order to locate themselves. The experience so gained helped other USAF crews locate and kill the British aircraft, but the Eagles never achieved the large-scale successes confidently predicted.

Such triumphs were to be marred in 1980 when a Buccaneer manoeuvring at low altitude during a Red Flag exercise in order to avoid interception lost a wing and crashed. Inspection of the fleet showed that almost half had serious fatigue problems due to the higher level of stresses associated with overland operations. Inspection and minor repairs restored most of the fleet to operational status. A repair scheme was devised for the more badly-fatigued examples, but one squadron was forced to disband.

Below: Victor was originally developed as a strategic bomber. Aircraft such as this Blue Steel-armed B.2 were rebuilt as tankers during the 1970s.

Above: Victor K Mk2 of 55 Sqn, Royal Air Force. With Victors showing their age somewhat, the RAF's aerial refuelling capability is to be augmented with modified VC10s.

Left: An RAF Phantom refuels from a Victor K Mk2.

XV352

Left: Buccaneer S.2B trials aircraft carrying a Paveway laser guided bomb under the port wing. Note the bulged bomb bay of this version and the pre-toned down scheme.

Below: Six Buccaneer S.50 bombers still serve with 24 Sqn of the South African Air Force, at the Command headquarters, Waterkloof. They are fitted with auxiliary rockets for hot-and-high take-offs.

423

Hawker Siddeley Hunter

Data for FGA.9
Type: single-seat fighter-bomber.
Specifications: length, 45ft 10in (13.98m); span, 33ft 8in (10.26m); height, 13ft 2in (4.26m); weight (max. take-off), 24,000lb (10,880kg).
Max speed: (in level flight) Mach 0.94.
Service ceiling: 50,000ft (15,300m).
Range: 370nm (690km).
Armament: four 30mm ADEN cannon plus up to 2,000lb (900kg) of ordnance.
Powerplant: one Rolls-Royce Avon 207 turbojet rated at 10,150lb (4,600kg) dry thrust.

More than a dozen nations still operate a total of more than 500 Hunters, and the type remains popular with its crews and operators. As aircraft were phased out during the 1960s and 1970s by their original owners, British Aircraft Corporation repurchased as many as possible for rework and resale to new and existing operators.

In the course of a long career Hunter has often fired its guns in anger. Indian Hunters saw combat in both Indo-Pakistan wars, showing themselves more than a match for the F-86F Sabre. Iraqi and Jordanian examples fought in the 1967 Yom Kippur war, although the Jordanian examples were virtually wiped out during Israeli strikes against their bases. South

African Hunters have taken part in anti-guerilla strikes into the territory of that nation's neighbours, while Hunters of what was then the Rhodesian Air Force played a major role in the long guerilla war in that country.

Despite the arms embargo on Rhodesia, that air arm's Hunter fleet remained operational as a result of illicitly-purchased spares obtained from various sources. Much improvisation was doubtless required, and some Rhodesian Air Force Hunters may have been re-engined with Avons which came on to the market in the mid-1960s when Caravelle and Comet airliners went to the breakers. Both sides in the conflict recognised the Hunter's virtues—

the first Government of the newly-independent Zimbabwe was quick to order a "top-up" batch of five ex-Kenyan aircraft in order to maintain the strength of 1 Sqn. Most surviving Hunters are export models of the F.6 interceptor, FGA.9 ground-attack aircraft, or T.7 two-seat trainer. One of the few criticisms of the type has been that the armament of four 30mm ADEN cannon is too heavy for modern air-to-air combat, having been originally devised for use against Soviet jet bombers whose large airframes can probably absorb large amounts of combat damage. In the ground-attack role, the quadruple ADENs are a fair substitute for the General Electric GAU-8/A cannon carried

by the Fairchild A-10. The ADEN cannot match the armour-penetration capability of the US weapon, but four firing in concert will deliver more than 80 rounds per second.

The aircraft should not be thought of as a "poor man's fighter" since the largest operator is the highly professional Swiss Air Force whose attempts to find a suitable replacement have lasted for more than a decade and included the procurement of top-up batches of aircraft in the early 1970s. In 1981 the Swiss tested the Hunter's ability to carry the Hughes AGM-65 maverick smart missile on the outboard underwing hardpoints, an armament which may prove attractive to other operators.

Below: The Royal Navy uses two T.Mk 8M two-seat Hunters to train Sea Harrier pilots in the use of the Blue Fox radar. All trainer versions have side-by-side seating, as here.

Hawker Siddeley (Avro) Shackleton

Type: maritime reconnaissance aircraft.
Specifications: length, 87ft 3in (26.59m); span, 120ft 0in (36.58m); height, 16ft 9in (5.1m); weight (maximum take-off), 108,000lb (49,000kg).
Max speed: 237kt (439km/hr).
Service ceiling: 20,000ft (6,100m).
Endurance: 4hrs.
Armament: up to 10,000lb (4,500kg) of ordnance, including depth charges and homing torpedoes.
Powerplant: four Rolls-Royce Griffon 57A, each rated at 2,455hp (1,830kW).

With the new Nimrod AEW.3 aircraft coming into service with the Royal Air Force, replacing the piston-engined Shackleton AEW.2, the sole operator of this ageing descendant of the World War II Lancaster becomes the South African Air Force. Given the problem which this air arm has in obtaining equipment, it is impossible to predict how long these last examples will remain in service.

Work on the MR.3 started in 1954 to meet the requirements of Specification R.5/46. The new

type was intended to be a significant improvement over the earlier Mk1 and Mk2. A tricycle undercarriage was fitted, the dorsal gun turret was deleted to make room for a crew rest room, new clear-vision cockpit transparencies improved the aircrew's view of the outside world and the application of soundproofing to the fuselage interior attempted to screen the occupants from the noise output of the four Griffon engines. The MR.3 entered service with the RAF in 1957 and was to remain in British service until the early 1970s.

By then, even older Mk2 versions had been brought out of retirement and fitted with APS-20 radars removed from ex-Fleet Air Arm Gannet early-warning aircraft. The result was to serve as the only UK airborne early-warning aircraft until the 1980s, when the Nimrod AEW.3 was due to enter service, despite the fact that the APS-20 was so old that it had first seen service aboard AEW versions of the Skyraider. This strange combination of ancient airframe and totally obsolete radar may not have frightened the enemy, but did embarrass its operator, who politely declined a

Below: South Africa's veteran MR.3s are the last surviving maritime-patrol Shackletons. They were bought in 1957 and have since been resparred and updated to cope with the increasing submarine threat in South African waters.

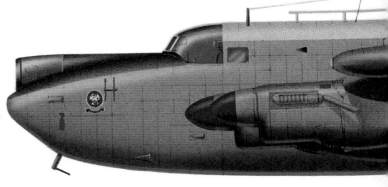

request in the late 1970s from the magazine *Flight International* for the opportunity to fly the type.

Shackleton MR.3 entered service with the South African Air Force in 1957, when eight were delivered to No.35 Sqn SAAF. These aircraft replaced earlier Sunderland MR Mk.5 flying boats, and were similar in build standard to RAF MR.3s in all but a few minor details—such as the astrodome being repositioned much

further aft, directly above the ventral "dustbin" retractable radome.

Like the British MR.3 fleet, the South African aircraft were progressively updated, but they never received the Viper auxiliary turbojets fitted to the outboard engine nacelles of RAF aircraft under the Phase 3 modification programme. The surviving aircraft were resparred in the 1970s and five still serve with 35 Sqn.

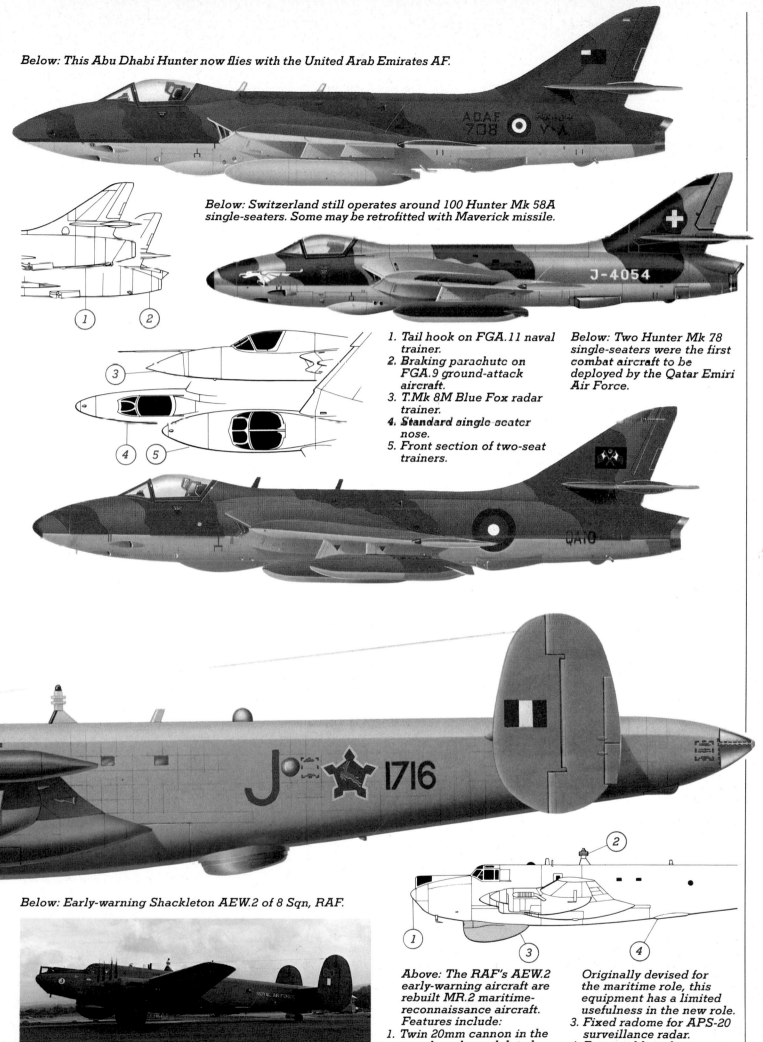

Below: This Abu Dhabi Hunter now flies with the United Arab Emirates AF.

Below: Switzerland still operates around 100 Hunter Mk 58A single-seaters. Some may be retrofitted with Maverick missile.

1. Tail hook on FGA.11 naval trainer.
2. Braking parachute on FGA.9 ground-attack aircraft.
3. T.Mk 8M Blue Fox radar trainer.
4. Standard single-seater nose.
5. Front section of two-seat trainers.

Below: Two Hunter Mk 78 single-seaters were the first combat aircraft to be deployed by the Qatar Emiri Air Force.

Below: Early-warning Shackleton AEW.2 of 8 Sqn, RAF.

Above: The RAF's AEW.2 early-warning aircraft are rebuilt MR.2 maritime-reconnaissance aircraft. Features include:
1. Twin 20mm cannon in the nose have been deleted.
2. Antenna for Orange Harvest ESM system.

Originally devised for the maritime role, this equipment has a limited usefulness in the new role.
3. Fixed radome for APS-20 surveillance radar.
4. Retractable radome installation for the original radar has been deleted.

Hawker Siddeley Vulcan

Data for B.2
Type: long-range medium bomber.
Specifications: length, 99ft 11in (30.45m); span, 111ft 0in (33.38m); height, 27ft 2in (8.28m); weight (max take-off), approx. 250,000lb (113,000kg).
Max speed: Mach 0.97 at height.
Service ceiling: approx. 65,000ft (20,000m).
Range: (loaded) approx. 4,000nm (7,400km).
Armament: up to 21,000lb of nuclear or conventional ordnance in the internal weapons bay.
Powerplant: four Rolls-Royce Olympus 301 turbojets each rated at 20,000lb (9,070kg) dry thrust.

Originally scheduled to be phased out of Royal Air Force service in 1982, these delta-winged bombers had a last minute reprieve as a result of the Argentinian invasion of the Falkland Islands in April of that year. Aircraft were hastily re-equipped for the delivery of conventional weaponry instead of the nuclear weapons which they had previously carried in support of NATO. A single aircraft delivered the opening shots in the British

campaign to re-capture the islands when it attacked the runway at Port Stanley.

Further raids were mounted prior to the British landings in an attempt to deny the Argentinian forces the use of the island's airstrips. The technique used was to attack at night from medium altitude, so that the bombers could not be engaged by light AAA fire or the "day-only" Tigercat SAM units. The bombs were aimed by radar, but the resulting accuracy seems to have been low. In the initial raid, only one bomb struck the runway.

Following a failure of its in-flight refuelling equipment one Vulcan was forced to land in Brazil. It was disarmed by the Brazilian authorities, refuelled, and allowed to return to Ascension Island.

The original B.1 version entered service with the RAF in 1957, but was later supplanted by the improved B.2. Both were originally devised as high-altitude bombers, but development was carried out so slowly that the threat posed by surface-to-air missiles required the aircraft to carry rocket-powered Blue Steel air-to-surface missiles as well as conventional free-falling

nuclear weapons. Soviet SAM strength eventually forced a switch to low-altitude tactics in the mid-1960s.

In theory, there seems no technical reason why the Vulcan could not have been given a B-52-style structural rebuild and new avionics fit in order to prolong its service life, but this would have been costly. For maximum effectiveness, the aircraft would have required new stand-off missiles— either the US-developed Boeing AGM-68B ALCM cruise missile or a British-designed equivalent, perhaps based on the British Aerospace Sea Eagle. Given the financial demands of the Tornado and Trident programmes, there was no way that funding for a Vulcan rebuild could be provided, so the RAF seems likely to abandon the long-range bombing mission.

Vulcan has had some avionics updating. To suit the aircraft to the low-level role, the General Dynamics APN-171 terrain-following radar was purchased from the USA. This lightweight radar operates in J-band and provides either a "fly-up" demand signal to the aircraft autopilot, or can provide instructions to the pilot via a simple cockpit-mounted indicator. Some updating of the ECM systems is also likely to have taken place, since part of the original installation was compromised by Soviet espionage.

The only other version still in service at the time of writing was the strategic-reconnaissance SR.2 operated by 27 Sqn since 1974.

Hindustan Aeronautics Kiran

Data for Mk 1A
Type: basic trainer.
Specifications: length, 34ft 9in (10.6m); span: 35ft 1in (10.7m); height, 11ft 11in (3.63m); weight (maximum take-off), 9,040lb (4,100kg).
Max speed: 375kt (695km/hr).
Service ceiling: 30,000ft (9,150m).
Range: 440nm (815km).
Armament: see text.
Powerplant: one Rolls-Royce Viper 11 turbojet rated at 2,500lb (1,140kg) dry thrust.

Much delayed by the higher priority given to the HF-24 Marut fighter project, Kiran remains in production, while the more ambitious Marut has passed through its own service career and been retired. The design is simple, with a configuration resembling that of the Jet Provost/Strikemaster. The project owes more to India's desire to maintain an effective indigenous aircraft design capability than to any desire on her part to advance the art of aeronautical engineering.

Design work began back in 1961, and the prototype flew four years later. Deliveries of a batch of 24 pre-production aircraft to the Indian Air Force began in 1968 and the production rate built up during the 1970s. Delays in the programme forced the IAF to procure an interim type, so a batch of 50 TS.11 Iskra was acquired in the mid-1970s.

Kiran is intended to serve both

as a basic trainer and as a weapons trainer/light-attack type. After delivering 119 examples of the basic Mk1, the HAL line switched to the Mk1A version, which has a hardpoint of 500lb (230kg) capacity under each wing. These can be used to carry a bomb, a HAL-built gun pod containing two 7.62mm FN machine-guns, or a seven-round rocket launcher. The hardpoints are plumbed, so 50 Imperial gallon (227l) drop tanks may be carried to supplement the normal 250 Imperial gallons (454l) of internal fuel.

The cockpit is air-conditioned and pressurised. Seating is side-by-side on Martin-Baker H4HA zero-altitude seats. An oxygen system is provided to allow high-altitude flight.

For armament training or light strike duties HAL has produced the Kiran Mk2, which first flew on 30 July 1976. An IAF order for 24 examples of this version was placed in 1981, and production deliveries should begin in 1983. A derated Orpheus 701 turbojet replaces the Viper II fitted to the basic aircraft, raising the installed thrust from 2,500lb (1,140kg) to 3,400lb (1,540kg), and the basic VHF radio and ADF avionics installation of the earlier marks is supplemented by a Ferranti navigation system and an Indian-built IFF system. An extra pair of hardpoints are fitted beneath the wings, and two 7.62mm machine-guns are mounted in the nose.

Above: The side-by-side trainer Kiran needs a take-off run of less than 1,500ft (450m).

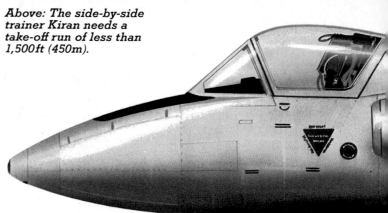

Left: A Vulcan B.2 bomber displays its double-delta planform during a low-altitude flight. Though they relinquished the role of nuclear deterrence to the Royal Navy's Polaris force in mid-1969, Vulcans can still carry free-fall nuclear bombs for low-level strike.

Below: Vulcan carried much of its defensive ECM equipment in the tail cone, but aircraft were retrofitted with radar-warning receivers whose antenna installation may be seen at the top of the vertical fin.

XL445

Below: Kiran Mk1A has two underwing hardpoints capable of carrying fuel tanks or ordnance. Kiran Mk2 is a development with extra hardpoints, specially intended for weapons training.

U753

Below: The Indian Air Force and Navy have a total of more than 170 Kirans for basic and weapons training. Advanced training is performed at the Air Force Academy, Hyderabad.

U762

Hughes OH-6A Cayuse and Model 500 Defender

Data: for 500MD
Type: multi-role light helicopter.
Specifications: length 23ft 0in (7.01m); weight, 8ft 11in (2.71in); rotor diameter, 26ft 5in (8.05m); weight (maximum take-off), approx. 3,000lb (1,360kg).
Max speed: 132kt 9244km/hr).
Range: 318nm (589km).
Armament: see text.
Powerplant: one Allison 250-C20B turboshaft rated at 420shp (313kW).

Deliveries of the OH-6A Cayuse began in September 1966 to meet a US Army requirement for 1,071 aircraft capable of carrying a two-man crew plus four equipped infantrymen, or up to 1,000lb (450kg) of cargo. The aircraft was selected for service in the controversial Light Observation Helicopter (LOH) competition of 1965, but was eventually to serve alongside the Bell OH-58A, a derivative of the OH-4A which it defeated in that contest. The US Army purchased 1,434 examples, while several hundred more were built for other customers by Hughes or foreign licencees. Normal OH-6A armament is an XM-27 7.62mm trainable gun system, an XM-75 grenade launcher or other payloads of up to 1,000lb (450kg).

four blades instead of the standard two-blade unit, the aircraft becomes the Quiet Advanced Scout Defender.

Basic TOW-armed anti-tank version is the 500MD TOW Defender used by Israel, Kenya and Korea. This model has a missile sight mounted on the port side of the nose, but the further-improved 500MD/MMS TOW variant introduces a mast-mounted missile sight. As its name suggests, 500MD/ASW Defender is for anti-submarine use. It carries the same ASQ-81 MAD sensor and Mk 46 torpedo armament as the original ASW model of the 500D.

Ultimate model to date is the 500MD Defender II introduced in 1980. This features a five-bladed main rotor and can be fitted with optional features such s the low-noise four-bladed tail

Below: Hughes is offering this configuration of Defender, complete with mast-mounted sight and TOW missiles, to a number of potential customers. None is known to have entered operational service.

rotor, infra-red exhaust suppressor, TOW (anti-tank) or Stinger (anti-helicopter) missiles, a 30mm Hughes Chain Gun, or a mast-mounted sight incorporating a laser rangefinder.

Japanese versions are built under licence by Kawasaki as the KV-107 series. The Japan Self-Defense Forces operate the KV-107II-4 26-seat tactical transport, KV-107/II-3 and /IIA-3 minesweepers and the KV-107/II-5 and /IIA-5 search and rescue versions. Kawasaki also offers civil versions and has exported SAR versions to the Swedish navy and the Government of Saudi Arabia. The Swedish examples are fitted with Rolls-Royce Gnome engines and are designated HKP-7.

By uprating the basic design during the mid-1960s, Hughes created the five-passenger civil Model 500, an aircraft powered by an 317shp (235kW) Allison 250-C18A turboshaft instead of the 252shp 188kW) T63-5A used in the OH-6A. This improved design was used in turn as the basis for a family of Model 500M military versions.

First to fly was the 500M, which entered service with the Colombian air force in 1968. In addition to the standard utility version this was also available in an ASW configuration ordered by the Spanish navy. The latter variant is equipped with a towed ASQ-81 MAD sensor and armed with two Mk 46 lightweight torpedoes.

The addition of features such as self-sealing fuel tanks, armour plating, hard-points for a range of armament such as TOW anti-tank missiles, plus an infra-red supressor for the engine exhaust led to the 500MD Defender multi-role version. Built by Hughes, BredaNardi (Italy) and Korean Air Lines (South Korea), this aircraft is available in several versions.

500MD Scout Defender, as its name suggests, is intended for observation and light-attack roles. It can carry a 7.62mm Minigun, a 30mm cannon, a 40mm grenade launcher or up to 14 2.75inch folding-fin unguided rockets. With the addition of a mast-mounted sight and silencing features such as a slower-turning tail rotor with

Left: Hughes 500MD Defender II armed with four TOW missiles and fitted with the associated nose sight. It has already been supplied to Kenya, South Korea and Israel and other orders are following. Its big advantage is its smallness and this will be enhanced with the new mast-mounted sight developed by Hughes which will mean the machine will have less need to expose itself to enemy fire.

Below: Israel operates 30 TOW-armed 500MD Defenders with nose-mounted sighting systems and two missiles on each side of the fuselage.

1. Battlefield support version of 500MD.
2. Mast-mounted sights.
3. Rocket launcher.
4. Stinger air-to-air missiles.
5. ASW version of 500MD.
6. Towed MAD sensor.
7. Radome for search radar.
8. Skid-mounted flotation bags.
9. Underslung homing torpedoes.
10. "T"-tail on 500MD.
11. Optional four-blade low-noise rotor for 500MD.
12. "V"-tail on OH-6 Cayuse.
13. Sight on TOW-armed 500MD.
14. Exhausts with infra-red suppression.
15. Two TOW rounds per side.
16. 30mm Chain Gun plus . . .
17. Sight available on 500MD.
18. Standard unsuppressed exhaust.

Above: Taiwan operates twelve shipboard 500MD anti-submarine helicopters with under-fuselage torpedo armament, nose-mounted search radar and a towed MAD "bird" sensor stowed on the starboard side of the fuselage.

Hughes AH-64 Apache

Type: Advanced attack helicopter.

Specifications: length of fuselage, 49ft 1½in (14.97m); diameter of main rotor, 48ft 0in (14.63m); height, over tail fin, 11ft 7½in (3.54m); weight (maximum take-off), 17,650lb (800kg).

Max speed: 192mph (309km/h).

Service ceiling: 20,500ft (6,250m).

Range: Internal fuel, 380 miles (611km); ferry range with external fuel, 1,121 miles (1,804km).

Armament: Hughes 30mm Chain Gun with 1,200 rounds, four pylons each carrying four Hellfire laser-guided anti-armour missiles or up to 76 folding-fin 2.75in rockets or a mix of Hell-fires and rockets.

Powerplant: Two 1,536shp (1,145kW) General Electric T700-GE-700 turboshaft engines with special IR-suppressing exhausts.

There are shades of Lockheed's AH-56A Cheyenne about this impressive helicopter, which is designed to be the definitive attack armed helicopter to live with front-line troops for extended periods and provide the precision fire-power needed at crucial points, especially against armour, by day or night and in any weather. The Cheyenne was intended to do just this, but ground to a halt from cost-escalation and the long time taken to solve the problems, and was replaced by the simpler and cheaper Cobra which Bell had developed privately. This time Bell was the loser in the original fly-off evaluation in 1975-6; curiously, while the losing Bell YAH-63 had the pilot sitting in front and the co-pilot/gunner in the rear cockpit, the Apache follows the Cobra configuration and sits the pilot behind the co-pilot/gunner. But the similarity with the Cheyenne lies in the area of almost ten years which must elapse between design of this helicopter and its receipt by the first user troops. This has had a terrible effect on the pro-gramme prices, and it will be surprising if the planned 536 can be afforded. The programme will probably be for 446, costing more than the estimate for the 536.

Moreover, though the Apache is designed to survive hostile fire from projectiles up to 23mm calibre, an extremely severe require-ment which is almost impossible to meet in full, it seems foolhardy to expose such a very costly vehicle to the firepower of a modern army which today almost certainly includes missiles (certainly in the case of WP armies), against which no effective defence is possible. It is all the stranger that the advanced sight systems are not on top of the rotor on a mast but in the tip of the nose, forcing the helicopter above the skyline in all combat situations, except in the fortunate case where there is a hill in the background.

These sight systems are the most interesting part of this intensely interesting vehicle. While the basic machine bristles with advanced powered and fly-by-wire flight controls, navaids, communications EW systems and crashworthy mechanical design, the nose con-tains a stabilized sight incorporating a FLIR, laser ranger and target designator and laser tracker, all managed by the co-pilot/gunner. It also contains the PNVS (pilot's night vision system) for blind sensing of the external scene, while both crew members have the IHADSS (integrated helmet and display sighting system) which moves with the wearer's head and speeds up target acquisition. With luck production Apaches could be seen by late 1983, with service entry in 1984.

IAR-93 Soko Orao

Type: close-support aircraft.

Specifications: length, 45ft 1in (13.99m); span, 31ft 7in (9.63m); height, 14ft 7in (4.45m); weight (max take-off), 23,150lb (10,500kg).

Max speed: 610kt (1,130km/hr).

Service ceiling: 42,600ft (13,000m).

Range: (hi-lo-hi tactical radius with 4,400lb ordnance load) 194nm (360km/hr).

Armament: two 23mm cannon plus up to 5,500lb (2,500kg) of ordnance on five hardpoints.

Powerplants: two Rolls-Royce Viper 633 turbojets each rated at 5,000lb (2,270kg) with afterburning.

Rarely does a member of the Warsaw Pact need to look beyond its allies in order to obtain military equipment, but one notable exception to this rule is the IAR-93 Orao twin-engined trainer/strike aircraft being jointly developed by Jugoslavia and Romania. The work is being handled by Soko and CNIAR respectively in the two countries. Most aircraft developed col-laboratively are given the same designation by all partners, but the two Balkan states have agreed to differ, the finished product being designated Orao by Yugo-slavia and IAR-93 by Romania.

The two Governments made the decision to collaborate back in 1971. Technical assistance was sought from the United Kingdom, the design being powered by two Rolls-Royce Viper turbojets and being fitted with Martin-Baker zero-zero ejection seats and other British sub-systems.

The first single-seat prototype flew in 1974 and was followed by at least two more. These were powered by two unreheated Vipers. A number of pre-production aircraft were built in both countries.

For production aircraft, an afterburning version of Viper designated Viper 633 was de-veloped. Based on the non-afterburning Viper 632 used to power the Aermacchi MB.326 and MB.339, this is now being made under licence in Jugoslavia and Romania.

Development has been slow, apparently due to technical problems including aircraft weight, and the initial production contract calls for a total of only 50 aircraft, 25 for each partner. Production deliveries were due to begin in the early 1980s, but no reports of service deployment have been received so far. Romania has a requirement for up to 125 ex-amples, but Jugoslavia is reported to be reluctant to take more than the initial 25.

The aircraft has a strong under-carriage suitable for rough-field operations, while the wings are fitted with leading edge slats and trailing-edge flaps to improve lift. Space has been provided in the nose for a simple ranging radar. Absence of detailed information of the avionics installation makes it difficult to assess the type's military effectiveness.

Left: Everything about the AH-64A is impressive — including the price tag. Rising costs resulted in delays in the first production order being placed. When the go-ahead was given, it was for a batch of only twelve.

Below left: Apache bristles with technological innovation, including the nose-mounted TADS/PNVS sight, belly-mounted 30mm Chain Gun, and the fire-and-forget Hellfire missiles.

Left: Although likely to accept fewer aircraft than Romania, Jugoslavia has been more inclined to release information on the project.

Above: This prototype Orao (Eagle) was built in Jugoslavia at the Soko plant. Production aircraft will be fitted with an afterburning version of the current Viper powerplants.

Ilyushin Il-18 Coot

Type: long-range transport
Specifications: length, 117ft 9in (35.9m); wingspan, 122ft 8in (37.4m); height, 33ft 4in (10.17m); weight (maximum take-off), 141,000lb (64,000kg).
Max cruising speed: 364kt (675km/hr).
Range: 3,500nm (6,500).
Max payload: 29,750lb (13,500lb).
Powerplants: four Ivchenko AI-20M turboprops each rated at 4,250shp (3,170kW).

Virtually a Soviet equivalent of the Bristol-Britannia, this four-engined airliner is in service with a large number of East European and Third World air arms as well as the Soviet air force. Having been designed as an airliner, it is not really suitable for flying military cargoes, but tends to serve in modest numbers as a personnel transport.

The type can be modified into a freighter by the addition of a wide cargo-loading door in the rear fuselage, and some strengthening of the floor, but such conversion work is currently carried out only in the Soviet Union. Aeroflot is having some of its fleet reworked, but there are no reports of military examples being modified.

Il-18 formed the basis of the Il-38 May maritime-patrol aircraft (see separate entry). A second military version is the ELINT aircraft designated "Coot-A" by NATO. This uses the airframe of the transport version, but modified to carry a wide range of sensors.

A cylindrical container approximately 33ft 7in (10.25m) long and 3ft 9in (1.15m) in diameter is carried beneath the forward fuselage. This probably contains the antenna system for a sideways-looking radar. Smaller canoe-shaped fairings on either side of the forward fuselage probably contain sideways-looking cameras or electro-optical sensors, since a door can be distinguished about a third of the way from the forward end.

Many antennas have been added, including two prominent blade antennas on the fuselage roof. Examination of the fuselage shows the presence of several light coloured rectangular panels. These are probably made from glass fibre, and act as radio transparencies for microwave antennas designed to sample Western radar transmissions and data links. As Aeroflot continues to phase out its aging Il-18 airliner fleet, other dedicated military versions can be expected.

Above: Like most Warsaw Pact air arms, the Polish Air Force operates a number of Il-18 Coot airliners as personnel transports. Heavy payloads travel by Antonov An-12.

Above right: Small numbers of Il-18 airliners are used as personnel and VIP transports by the Soviet Air Force.

Ilyushin Il-28/Harbin H-5 Beagle

Type: light bomber.
Specifications: length, 57ft 11in (17.65m); wingspan, 70ft 4in (21.45m) height, 22ft (6.7m); weight (maximum take-off), 46,700lb (21,200kg).
Max speed: 487kt (902km/hr).
Service ceiling: 40,350ft (12,300m).
Range: 1,300nm (2,400km).
Armament: up to 6,600lb (3,000kg) of ordnance, plus two fixed forward-firing NR-23 cannon and two in a tail turret.
Powerplants: two Klimov VK-1A turbojets each rated at 5,950lb (2,700kg) of dry thrust.

China is the only major operator which still uses this ageing design as a front-line bomber, with some 600 still in service. Third-World air arms such as Algeria, North Korea, Vietnam and South Yemen may field small numbers as token bomber forces, but against all but the most rudimentary air defences, the type must be regarded as obsolete. In Chinese service the aircraft is known as the H-5 Harbin.

The type first flew back in 1948, entering service two years later. Soviet production probably ended in 1960, but Chinese production is still under way at a low rate. A few Chinese examples have even been equipped for nuclear delivery, but this role must by now have largely been taken over by the larger and faster Harbin H-6 (Tu-16).

Like the British Canberra, the Il-28 was suitable for mass production and service in the hands of conscript aircrew and ground crew. Although widely exported to Eastern Europe and the Third World, it never acquired the popularity of the British aircraft. Second-hand Canberras will still find willing buyers, but there is little demand for the Il-28. Although the latter is a simple and robust design, it carries a lower payload than the Canberra, while the latter's lower wing loading pays dividends in better manoeuvrability and higher ceiling. The Il-28 may have sported a defensive tail position equipped with twin 23mm cannon, but this hardly compensated for the speed advantage enjoyed by the Canberra.

Undoubtedly, the type's main role is now that of a trainer. The Il-28U "Mascot" lacks the armament and ground-mapping radar of the basic bomber, but has a second cockpit fitted with dual controls mounted ahead of the standard cockpit in a hard nose section which replaces the normal glazed unit.

Other versions likely to soldier on through the 1980s are the Il-28T torpedo bomber and the Il-28R tactical reconnaissance aircraft, the latter with a payload of cameras and electronic sensors in the weapons bay. It is possible that China might prolong the service life of its bomber versions by modifying them for missile-launching should weapons become available.

Below: The Warsaw Pact air arms now use the Il-28 solely in "hack", trials and training roles. The type would not be effective in skies controlled by modern fighters.

Left: Coot-A's EW sensors and antennas include:
1. *Blade antennas — probably for long-range communications.*
2. *Equipment fairing, perhaps for long-range electro-optical viewing systems.*
3. *Under-fuselage pod, probably for SLAR*
4. *Ventral radomes.*

Below: The wire antenna running from the cockpit area of this Coot-A ELINT aircraft is probably for HF communications. For details of the equipment fit, see line drawing at the top of this page.

Above: More than 400 Harbin H-5 (Ilyushin-28) bombers are still China's main bombing force.

Below: In the Il-28U Mascot trainer, a second cockpit is provided in place of the navigator's glazed position.

Above: North Korea's 70 Il-28 Beagles make up a numerically strong bomber fleet but would be severely mauled by South Korea's F-5 fighters in any new Korean war.

Ilyushin Il-38 May

Type: maritime patrol aircraft.
Specifications: length, 129ft 10in (39.6m); span, 122ft 8in (37.4m); height, 33ft 4in (10.17m); weight (maximum take-off), 144,000lb (65,000kg).
Max speed: 347kt (645km/hr).
Patrol endurance: 12hr.
Armament: see text.
Powerplants: four Ivchenko AI-20M turboprops each rated at 4,250ehp (3,170ekW).

Assessment of this long-range maritime-patrol aircraft is made difficult by the almost total absence of information concerning its avionic systems. The basic aircraft is an adaptation of the Il-18 Coot airliner. Most obvious modification, apart from the tail-mounted MAD "sting" and dorsal radome, is the new forward location of the wing. This was required in order to offset the weight of additional equipment located in the rear fuselage, almost certainly that of the ordnance carried in the full-length fuselage bay.

Compared with the Lockheed Orion and BAe Nimrod, the Il-38 is a surprisingly "clean" design, free from many of the radomes and sensor systems which clutter the appearance of the Western

ASW aircraft but make them effective weapon platforms. Air inlets and outlets mounted on either side of the forward fuselage are probably inlets for a "sniffer" system designed to detect diesel exhaust, while the under-fuselage radome covers the antenna of a radar designated "Wet Eye" by NATO. This operates in J-band, its high frequency and resulting good angular resolution helping to reduce the effects of sea "clutter" in the radar returns. A small fin-top antenna may be for ESM purposes.

Sonobuoys carried in the weapons bay complete the sensor array, and offensive armament carried in the same location includes homing torpedoes, depth charges and probably nuclear depth bombs. The crew is thought to number 12, probably five on the flight deck and seven in a tactical station in the rear fuselage. The forward fuselage probably contains avionics racks.

Il-38 was first observed in 1971, and after a decade of service, a new version is long overdue. This could well be created by reworking existing aircraft, adding better radar and signal-processing equipment, LLTV or FLIR sensors, and antennas for satellite communications.

Ilyushin Il-76 Candid and SUAWACS

Type: long-range transport.
Specifications: length, 152ft 10in (46.6m); span, 165ft 8in (50.5m); height, 48ft 5in (14.75m); weight (maximum take-off), 375,000lb (170,000kg).
Max speed: 459kt (850km/hr).
Service ceiling: 51,000ft (15,500m).
Range: (with max payload) 2,700nm (5,000km).
Max payload: 88,000lb (40,000kg).
Powerplants: four Soloviev D-30KP turbofans, each rated at 26,455lb (12,030kg) dry thrust.

Superficially, the Ilyushin design resembles the Lockheed C-141 StarLifter, but the general specification more closely resembles that of the USAF's planned C-X transport. It can carry up to 70,000lb (31,820kg) of freight a distance of 3,100 miles (4,990km) in less than six hours, but is optimised for operations from short unpaved airstrips. Each of the main undercarriage units is equipped with eight wheels, while the nose unit has four. Tyre pressures may be varied from 36-73lb/sq.in (2.5 to 5 bars) in flight to match conditions at the destination airfield.

Like most Soviet transports, the Il-76 contains built-in cargo-handling equipment, including two overhead cranes, reducing

Above: Aeroflot Il-76 parked next to an Il-62M airliner. This example does not have the manned tail gun position of the military version.

dependence on ground facilities, while an APU in the port undercarriage fairing provides ground power both for this equipment and for engine starting. Normal crew complement of seven includes maintenance technicians capable of carrying out minor repairs in the field. The underside of the fuselage is reported to be strengthened to resist impact damage from stones or debris thrown up during take-off or landing at unpaved airstrips.

Il-76 marked the first Soviet use of US-style engine pods, but the engines are set well inboard to minimise the effects on handling of any engine failure. The wings are fitted with leading edge slats, triple-slotted trailing-edge flaps, and spoilers for low-speed roll control. The slats cover most of the leading edge, but are reported

to be troublesome in Siberian conditions, owing to icing.

First instance of the type being used outside the Soviet Union was in 1977, when large numbers formed part of the transport fleet which carried heavy military equipment to Ethiopia as part of the Soviet support that nation received in its war with Somalia. It has since been sold to Iraq, Syria and Libya.

Some Il-76 aircraft have been converted for use as tankers, but it is not clear whether the resulting configuration is in operational service. According to US sources, the tanker version may also have a secondary bomber role against targets protected only by low-grade air defences. The airframe also serves as the basis for the "SUAWACS" early-warning aircraft.

SUAWACS early-warning aircraft

As a result of experience gained with the Tu-126 Moss early-warning aircraft, Soviet radar designers felt ready by the late 1970s to embark on the development of a Soviet equivalent of the Boeing E-3A Sentry. Such a move had been widely anticipated by US Intelligence, which in the latter part of that decade monitored specific key areas of Soviet military research and development for the first signs that the necessary technology was emerging from Soviet laboratories.

As late as 1977 no clear evidence of what was inevitably to be dubbed "SUAWACS" had emerged. By the end of the decade a full-scale Soviet R&D programme was under way. Photographs taken by US reconnaissance satellites show that the basic airframe of the Il-76 Candid jet transport has been adapted for

Below: Operating from bases in the Soviet Union or in client states, the Il-38 regularly monitors Western naval operations.

Left: Il-38 with the forward section of the weapons bay open. The aircraft was probably in the act of dropping sonobuoys when intercepted by the Royal Air Force Nimrod MR.1 which took this photograph. Il-38 carries a range of weaponry, including homing torpedoes.

Below: Sole export customer for the Il-38 was the Indian Navy. Three serve with INAS 315 at Dabolim.

the new role by the addition of an AWACS-style radome mounted directly above the wing leading edge. A second smaller E-4-style dorsal fairing houses antennas used for satellite communications.

One potential weakness already identified by the USAF is that the tall T-tail of the Il-76 may create a slight "blind spot" in the azimuth coverage. The degree to which this is true is probably known only to the Soviet Air Force, since the practical effects of such obscuration are difficult to predict. US engineers will doubtless have investigated the phenomenon in laboratory studies, using millimetre wavelengths and carefully prepared scale models of the aircraft. Some sources report that the aircraft will utilise the airframe of the Il-86 Camber wide-bodied airliner, suggesting that the Il-76 installation may have been a test-bed made necessary by persistent delays experienced with the Il-86.

US intelligence has already obtained Elint data on the radar, allowing the planning of suitable ECM systems to begin. The set operates on frequencies of between 2.3-2.4 GHz, and analysis of the waveforms of the intercepted signals shows the sophistication of the technology used.

Construction and deployment are expected to be organised as a "crash" programme, with the first aircraft being fielded in 1983 or 1984 at the latest. The eventual fleet is expected to outnumber the USAF E-3A force, with at least 50 aircraft being operational by 1985-6.

Specific anti-SUAWACS countermeasures have already been studied. The approaches considered include the development of a new version of the Boeing SRAM air-launched missile, and the fitting of additional ECM equipment to the B-52H bomber and to US cruise missiles.

Above: Aeroflot's fleet of about 50 Il-76 transports forms a valuable reserve force for the Soviet Air Force.

Above: The Il-76 can probably operate out of airstrips no more than 2,800ft (850m) long. Maximum payload from longer runways is 88,000lb (40,000kg) of cargo or up to 140 troops.

Israel Aircraft Industries IAI 201 Arava

Type: light STOL utility transport.

Specifications: length, 42ft 9in (13.03m); span, 68ft 9in (20.96m); height, 17ft 1in (5.21m); weight (maximum take-off), 15,000lb (6,804kg).

Max speed: 203mph (326km/h).

Service ceiling: 25,000ft (7.6km).

Range: Max payload, 174 miles (280km); max fuel, 812 miles (1,306km).

Armament: provision for forward-firing machine guns, typically two 0.5in Browning in fuselage side packs, plus third gun (0.5 or rifle-calibre) at rear of nacelle on pintle mount; two pods each containing six 82mm rockets also on fuselage sides, additional to guns.

Powerplant: two 750shp Pratt & Whitney of Canada PT6A-34 turboprops each rated at 750shp (560kW).

At the start of the Yom Kippur war in October 1973 the Chel Ha'Avir (Israeli Air Force) had long been aware of the home-grown Arava, the prototype of which had flown as far back as November 1969. It was distinctly cool about the aircraft, emphasizing that it was no part of its job to foster the local aircraft industry (perhaps an odd stance in the circumstances). Nevertheless, as it urgently needed extra STOL transport capacity to try and get its forces into the right places during the national holiday, the Chel Ha' Avir commandeered a civil Arava 102 prototype, as well as two Arava 201 military examples that had been built for a foreign customer. It flogged the three machines to

death day and night throughout that bitter war and found them of tremendous value. It seemed they could go anywhere and carry anything, and never failed to remain serviceable. Rather to its surprise it found itself extolling the virtues of this robust utilitarian machine, and today has at least ten on active service.

The Arava was designed in the period 1964-67 as the first major aircraft to be designed in Israel. IAI (Israel Aircraft Industries) had only recently dared to take on the building of the Magister jet trainer, and to design and certificate a new type was a major challenge. The Arava was given a circular-section nacelle, 98in (2.5m) in diameter, unpressurized, with a swinging tail end but with para-dropping of troops or supplies through the rear left-side door. The tail is carried on booms, and the wing has double-slotted flaps, and short ailerons supplemented by spoilers. Handling is exemplary, and take-off and landing run can be in the order of 960ft (under 300m), at maximum weight carrying a payload of 5,184lb (2,351kg). Loads can include 24 troops, or 17 paratroops plus dispatcher or light vehicles, or 12 stretcher (litter) casualties and two attendants.

By 1983 the number sold was approaching 100. Some are of the maritime surveillance model, with various radars or other sensors. It is not known if any have been sold of the EW version (seen in model form), with a wide selection of pallet-mounted Elint, ECM and ESM installations including a ventral radar bin, aft-facing scanners on the rear hinged door(s) and numerous aerials sprouting from the airframe. A 60-kVA APU is carried to provide the required electrical power. All Aravas have comprehensive blind-flying instruments and avionics and most have ADF, VOR/ILS and weather radar.

Israel Aircraft Industries Lavi

Type: air-combat fighter and attack aircraft.

Specifications: length, in region of 50ft (15m); span, in region of 26ft (8m); weight (maximum take-off), in region of 32,000lb (14.5 tonnes).

Max speed: at least Mach 2 at high altitude.

Service ceiling: At least 56,000ft (17km).

Range: Combat radius in intercept mission, probably about 400 miles (650km); ferry range over 1,500 miles (2,400km).

Armament: will include an internal gun (possibly an M61A-1) and an external ordnance load of at least 10,000lb (4.5 tonnes) carried on seven pylons.

Powerplant: One Pratt & Whitney PW1120 augmented turbojet rated at 20,900lb (9,344kg) with afterburning.

Israel has yet to experience the pressures and problems of creating an air-combat aircraft from scratch, as she is trying to do in this programme. It is a very different undertaking from building on an established design to create the Kfir. It is a pity a collaborative programme could not have been achieved, the obvious partner being Sweden. A powerful foreign partner, probably American (McDonnell Douglas has been hinted), may yet be signed up; but the Lavi (Young Lion, ie a more mature beast than a mere Kfir) is a very long way from fruition. And the incredible statement made at the 1981 Paris Salon that the Israeli licensees of the engine then expected to begin production of the PW1230 "within 18 months" suggests that the planning is optimistic.

It would be logical to expect the Lavi to use some Mirage-derived technology, and it will probably have a wing based on that of the Kfir but with variable camber on both leading and trailing edges and a long root extension. The canard foreplane will be fully controllable by the quad fly-by-wire flight-control system and the whole aircraft will be designed to CCV (control-configured vehicle) technology, with relaxed static stability to increase agility and reduce trim drag. Compared with a swing-wing aircraft the large wing area must make it difficult to fly the vital ground-attack mission with acceptable pilot comfort, flying at about Mach 1 in the terrain-following mode, and it may be that such an attack is not being attempted. Nevertheless the first aircraft the Lavi is intended to replace (in 1986, but this looks optimistic) is the Skyhawk, in the attack mission. Only later, by about the end of the decade, will Lavis replace the F-4 Phantom. On present planning the Kfir will remain the air-combat fighter into the 1990s, but operational experience may turn this projected timetable on its head.

Below: Following its success during the 1973 Yom Kippur war, the Israel Aircraft Industries Arava has proved popular with the IDFAF. This IAI 201 version has been fitted out with 0.5in (12.7mm) Browning machine guns in packs on each side of the fuselage, plus launchers for 82mm unguided rockets.

4X-IAC

Right: Ground crew flight crew and infantry pose with a civil Arava commandeered for military duty during the 1973 Yom Kippur war.

The Skyhawk, continually updated with electronics and supported by high-power jamming aircraft, can do a good job in the attack role despite its age. The Kfir, however, despite its excellent qualities, cannot take on even today's F-16 with much hope of success, and there is a clear need for a new air-combat fighter for the Chel Ha'Avir to enter service long before the 1990s. Moreover

the cost and technical risk place grave uncertainties over the programme. It was halted in the winter 1981-82 and allowed to proceed only after a governmental review. There is a chance that a J79-powered Lavi might fly in 1984 (it has been said that the first of four prototypes will fly in 1983), but a PW1120-powered production machine is very much further away.

Below: Artist's impression of the new Lavi multi-purpose fighter.

779

Israel Aircraft Industries Kfir, Nesher and Dagger

Data for Kfir-C2
Type: fighter/bomber.
Specifications: length, including probe, 51ft 4¼in (15.65m); span, 26ft 11½in (8.22m); height, 14ft 11¾in (4.55m); weight (maximum take-off), 32,408lb (14.7 tonnes).
Max speed: short dash at high altitude, to Mach 2.3 (1,516mph, 2,440km/h).
Service ceiling: 58,000ft (17.68km).
Range: combat radius on CAP mission with three drop tanks, 434 miles (700km).
Armament: two 30mm DEFA 552 cannon each with 140 rounds; maximum of 9,468lb (4,295kg) of external ordnance on seven hardpoints, including two Shafrir 2 close-range AAMs under outer wings, two 1,000lb (454kg), four 500lb or similar bombs or one Rafael Luz ASM on centreline, two 1,000lb or six 500lb bombs under wings as alternative to cluster bombs, concrete dibbers, Maverick, Hobos or Shrike missiles, rocket pods, tanks or ECM pods.
Powerplant: one General Electric J79-J1E turbojet rated at 11,810lb (5,370kg) dry thrust, 17,900lb (8,120kg) with afterburner.

Back in the 1950s Israel Aircraft Industries had a dream of making fighters for the nation's defence, and by the mid-1960s it was clear the fighter would be the French Mirage III. Plans moved fairly slowly until the sudden termination of French support for Israel in October 1967. This not only prevented delivery of the paid-for Mirage 5s (developed largely to Israel's specification) but cut off support from the existing Mirage IIICJ force. By 1969 Project Black Curtain was examining the problems of redesigning the IIICJ to take a J79 engine, and a re-engined Mirage IIIB two-seater flew in September 1971. This led to a small re-engining programme of aircraft known by the name Salvo which was completed in 1972-3.

While this was in hand Israel managed to obtain complete sets of drawings for both the Mirage and the Atar 9C engine—slightly better than the 9B then in use in the IIICJ—and this immediately led to a temporary diversion of effort to a straight-forward manufacturing programme of an Atar-Mirage, the first of which flew as early as September 1969. Later named Nesher (Eagle), this model had an Elta radar derived from Cyrano II but adhered closely to the French original. At least 40 were delivered in 1971-3, many without radar apart from a small ranging sight of Aida type, as in the Mirage 5. After delivery of the much better Kfir the Neshers were withdrawn from service and most (reportedly 26) were sold to Argentina, where they were named Daggers.

By 1972 the J79 re-engining programme had moved on to use IAI-built airframes, producing additional aircraft and not just conversions. These new aircraft were named Barak (Lightning), and five saw action in the 1973 Yom Kippur war, with excellent results. But IAI could see that the marriage of Mirage III and J79 was a lash-up, and considerable fresh engineering effort went into producing a completely new and uncompromised aircraft, and this resulted in the first Kfir (Lion Cub) in about May 1974. This was based on the Mirage 5, with additional fuselage fuel and numerous engineering changes, on which IAI introduced more than 100 further improvements, the total number of engineering changes being 270.

Major features included an engine installation slightly further

refined over that of the Barak, with enlarged ducts, a new engine bay of reduced length, a dorsal fin with ram inlet, four auxiliary engine-bay cooling inlets, a completely revised cockpit and avionic installations, new extended nose of basically triangular cross-section, long-stroke landing gears and various changes to the systems, especially the fuel system. The Kfir-C1 was built in small numbers in 1973-4 in interceptor and attack versions differing in avionic features and with the former fitted with an Elta 2001B pulse-doppler radar.

Though an outstanding machine, the C1 was capable of further improvement, and by 1975 the C2 was in production. This introduced removable fixed-incidence swept canard fore-planes on the engine inlets, strakes along the lower sides of the nose, and extended dogtooth leading edges. These changes, which could with advantage have been on all delta Mirages, greatly improve combat manoeuvrability, especially at high weights, and also reduce take-off and landing distances, and improve vision at low speeds by greatly reducing the angle of attack. The approach is now made slower, with the nose almost on the horizon and without getting on the back of the drag curve. In the attack mission the gust response is dramatically reduced, and another improvement was to fit the later 2021 X-

band radar. These changes, and updated EW/ECM installations, have been largely retrofitted to earlier Kfirs. The Kfir-TC2 is a dual trainer with a longer downward-inclined nose.

Though not quite in the same class as the F-16 and (unconfirmed designation) MiG-29, both of which it may have to encounter in combat, the Kfir-C2 is a giant improvement over all other delta Mirage fighters and similar in capability the Mirage 2000, for roughly one-tenth the price (US

$5m compared with $50m). It is able to carry a great variety of weapons and deliver them reliably and accurately, and its flight performance and handling show no evident deficiencies. In the air-combat mode without external fuel it weighs just 20,700lb (9,390kg), giving a thrust/weight ratio at low level of 0.86, compared with 0.63 for a late delta Mirage III. The advantages of the aerodynamic changes have not been publicly quantified but are very considerable.

Left: The mission of this Kfir C-2 obviously calls for high manoeuvrability, since the detachable canard foreplanes have been fitted. Ground crew prepare to load bombs.

Above: Kfir C-2 in standard IDFAF dual-role camouflage, complete with orange/yellow identification markings on wings and fin. This aircraft was based at Hatzerim in the Negev during 1976.

Above: Kfir C-1 (note the absence of canard foreplanes) in markings attributed to 101 Sqn, the top IDFAF fighter unit.

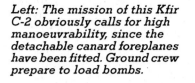

Left: Kfir C-2 (above) and C-1 (below).
1. *Horizontal strake on C-2 only.*
2. *Canard foreplanes of the C-2 may be detached for missions not requiring high manoeuvrability.*
3. *"Dog tooth" leading edge on wing of C-2 version. Like the simpler notched leading edge on the C-1, this acts as a low-drag equivalent of a wing fence.*
4. *Leading edge notch on C-1 only. During the late 1980s some aircraft were fitted with experimental wing fences.*

Left: Kfir C-2 development of the Mirage. Design was undertaken in secret after the 1967 war. Engine is American, avionics Israeli and the guns are French.

Below: Kfir C-2 in the two-tone grey air-superiority finish adopted in 1978. Note the absence of ID triangles.

Kaman SH-2 Seasprite

Data for SH-2F
Type: shipboard ASW/multi-role helicopter.
Specifications: length 40ft 6in (12.3m); height, 13ft 7in (4.14m); rotor diameter, 44ft 0in (13.41m); weight (normal take-off), 12,800lb (5,800kg).
Max speed: 143kt (265km/hr).
Range: 367nm (679km).
Armament: sonobuoys and homing torpedoes (see text).
Powerplants: two General Electric T58-GE-8F turboshafts each rated at 1,350shp (1,010kW).

Until the Sikorsky SH-60B Seahawk is available in significant numbers, Seasprite will remain the most important US Navy shipboard helicopter, serving in ASW, utility and search and rescue roles.

Original versions were the single-engined UH-2A and UH-2B utility aircraft. Both were rebuilt from 1967 onwards to the twin-engined UH-2C standard with two 1,250shp (932kW) General Electric T58-GE-8B turboshaft engines instead of one, nacelles being added on either side of the fuselage.

HH-2C was an armed search and rescue version of the UH-2C. Heavily armoured, it carried a chin-mounted 7.62mm Minigun, waist-mounted machine guns, an uprated transmission, four-bladed tail rotor and dual-wheel landing gear being added to handle the increased weight. The similar HH-2D was an SAR aircraft and did not carry armour or guns.

Main version in current service is the SH-2F LAMPS (Light Airborne Multi-Purpose System) variant used for ASW and for anti-ship surveillance and targeting. This model entered service in 1973, and a total of 88 were delivered by the end of the decade. Production was restarted in 1981 with a follow-on batch of 18 aircraft.

Sensors fitted to the SH-2F include a Canadian Marconi LN-66HP surveillance radar with a dorsally-mounted radome located directly beneath the cockpit, Texas Instruments ASQ-81 towed MAD, and ALR-66 ESM receiver. The aircraft entered service using SSQ-41

(passive) and -47 (active) sonobuoys but these are being replaced by newer Difar and Dicass patterns. Normal armament is a pair of homing torpedoes.

Earlier SH-2D and HH-2D aircraft have been updated to the SH-2F standard under a rebuild programme which ended in the spring of 1982. The SH-2F serves with eight USN squadrons, one or more aircraft being stationed on a wide range of cruisers, destroyers and frigates.

Despite its age, the design still has untapped potential. Back in 1973, Kaman tested a prototype SH-2F at a take-off weight 500lb (230kg) above the current limit, so payload or fuel capacity could yet be increased.

Kamov Ka-25 Hormone

Data for Hormone-A
Type: shipboard ASW helicopter.
Specifications: fuselage length, 32ft (9.75m); height, 17ft 7in (5.37m); rotor diameter, 51ft 8in (15.74m); weight (maximum take-off), 16,500lb (7,500kg).
Max cruising speed: 104kt (193km/hr).
Range: 217nm (400km).
Armament: see text.
Powerplant: two Glushenkov GTD-3 turboshafts each rated at 900shp (738kW).

For shipboard use, the Soviet Navy prefers to use helicopters fitted with co-axial rotors, since these can be made more compact than conventional designs. Aircraft of this type are a specialty of the Kamov bureau, whose Ka-25 is the current standard Soviet shipboard helicopter. The aircraft first flew in 1960, and approximately 450 were built during a production run which lasted from 1966 to 1975. Most remain in service.

Two versions have been identified. Hormone-A is the basic ASW aircraft equipped with a chin-mounted search radar, a towed MAD sensor and a dunking sonar. Most examples are of this variety, which seems a practical design hampered by inadequate sensors. Additional antennas and fairings have been added over the last decade, but the type still lacks night-vision equipment and the ability to operate its sonar in all weathers. Some aircraft have a

small fairing mounted immediately below the central tail fin. This immediately brings to mind the fairing beneath the tail boom of the Mi-14 Haze, but on the Kamov aircraft this cannot be dismissed as a float. A small cylindrical housing with a transparent upper section is mounted above the tail boom of many aircraft. This may house an electro-optical sensor. Hormone-A carries a crew made up of a pilot, co-pilot and two or three systems operators.

A small weapons bay in the cabin floor carries a payload which probably consists of sonobuoys, ASW torpedoes, nuclear depth bombs or other stores. Later models of ASW torpedo seem to be too large to fit within the bay, since some aircraft carry a rectangular under-fuselage weapons container. As part of an upgrading programme, the Ka-

25 is probably being fitted with "fire-and-forget" air-to-surface missiles.

Hormone-B is a more specialised aircraft recognisable by its larger chin radome and the presence of a retractable ventral radome. This aircraft is used to acquire targets for long-range anti-ship missiles.

Hormone has been used as the basis for a new ASW helicopter which first went to sea on the destroyer *Udaloy*. Assigned to reporting name "Helix" by NATO, stretched fuselage, improved sensors and probably a new powerplant and transmission.

Left: Hormone-A is the ASW version of the Kamov Ka-25, two of which are seen here on the carrier Moskva. *Flying is a Hormone-B with the more bulbous nose radome for Over-the-Horizon Targetting.*

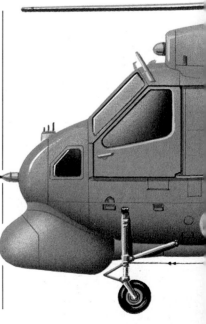

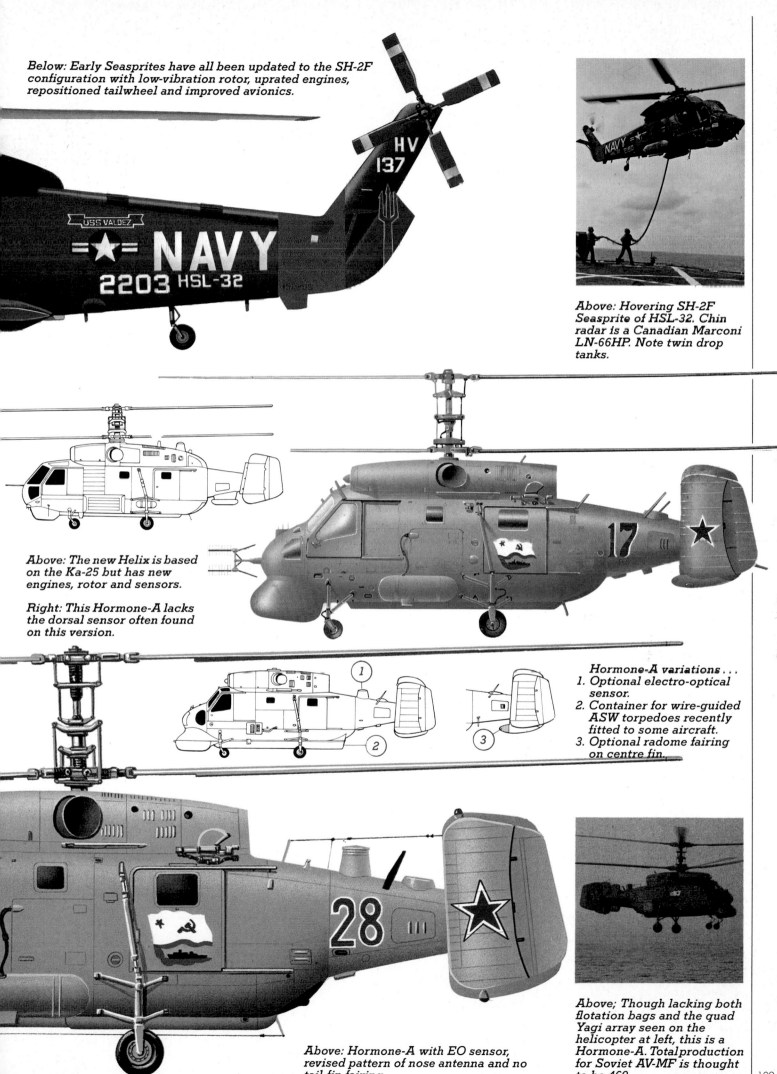

Below: Early Seasprites have all been updated to the SH-2F configuration with low-vibration rotor, uprated engines, repositioned tailwheel and improved avionics.

Above: Hovering SH-2F Seasprite of HSL-32. Chin radar is a Canadian Marconi LN-66HP. Note twin drop tanks.

Above: The new Helix is based on the Ka-25 but has new engines, rotor and sensors.

Right: This Hormone-A lacks the dorsal sensor often found on this version.

Hormone-A variations . . .
1. Optional electro-optical sensor.
2. Container for wire-guided ASW torpedoes recently fitted to some aircraft.
3. Optional radome fairing on centre fin.

Above: Hormone-A with EO sensor, revised pattern of nose antenna and no tail-fin fairing.

Above; Though lacking both flotation bags and the quad Yagi array seen on the helicopter at left, this is a Hormone-A. Total production for Soviet AV-MF is thought to be 460.

Kawasaki C-1A

Type: medium-range tactical transport.

Specifications: length, 95ft 2in (29.00m); span, 100ft 5in (30.60m); height, 32ft 9in (9.99m); weight (max take-off), 99,200lb (45,000kg).

Maximum speed: 435kt (806 km/hr).

Service ceiling: 38,000ft (11,600m).

Maximum payload: 26,200lb (11,900kg).

Range (with eight tonne payload), 700nm (1,300km).

Powerplants: two licence-built Pratt & Whitney JT8D-M-9 turbofans each rated at 14,500lb (6,600kg) of dry thrust.

Faced with the need to develop a tactical transport with all-up weight of around 30-40 tonnes, most designers would probably start with an unswept wing plus a pair of Rolls-Royce Tyne or Allison T56 turboprops, or even four GE T64 turboprops. In the quest for a C-46 replacement, Japan decided to be bold and opt for a swept wing and two Pratt & Whitney JT8D turbofans.

In the early 1960s none of the available transport designs met the JASDF's requirements. Despite the attractions of a C-130 purchase, the service drew up the requirements for an aircraft of indigenous design.

Two prototypes were built, the first flying on 12 November 1970. The original design had been prepared by the Nihon Airplane Manufacturing Company, but the actual manufacture of the aircraft was split up between Kawasaki, Fuji, Shin Meiwa Nippi and Sumitomo, with Kawasaki responsible for final assembly and flight test.

Flight testing was protracted, modifications being introduced in order to make the controls lighter and more effective and to reduce buffeting on the rear fuselage. The experience so gained was incorporated into two pre-production aircraft delivered in 1973/4.

The initial production contract had been awarded the previous March, but project costs were already rising, forcing a cutback in procurement from the planned 60 aircraft. Deliveries of production examples began late in 1974. By the time that production ended in 1981, 31 had been built.

As well as being expensive, the

Lockheed C-5 Galaxy

Type: heavy strategic transport

Specifications: length, 247ft 10in (75.54m); span, 222ft 8½in (67.88m); height, 65ft 1½in (19.85m); weight (maximum take-off) 769,000lb (348,810kg).

Max speed: 571mph (919km/h).

Service ceiling: at 615,000lb (278,964kg), 34,000ft (10.36km).

Range: with max payload, 3,749 miles (6,033km).

Armament: None.

Powerplant: four General Electric TF39-GE-1 turbofans each rated at 41,000lb (18,640kg) dry thrust.

Like the F-111 the C-5 was designed in the early 1960s as a giant example of Total Package Procurement in which one prime contractor was responsible for delivering a major working system which had to meet giant challenges. In this case the challenges were unprecedented range and payload, plus the ability to use rough unpaved airstrips.

In fact, the C-5A, the initial model, is the world's most capable strategic airlifter. It could hardly be otherwise when its colossal size and weight are considered, because its interior is larger than that of a Boeing 747 and has a level cargo floor at so-called truck-bed height, with straight-through loading and unloading of vast computer-controlled palletized loads, plus vehicles up to the size of battle tanks or large surveillance radars.

Up to 36 Type 463L pallets can be loaded, or three CH-47 Chinook

heavy transport helicopters, or two M-60 or Abrams M-1 tanks (the limitation in the latter case being weight). Normal maximum payload is 220,967lb (100,228kg). In the rare event of the C-5A being used as a trooper the number of seats usually provided is 75 at the rear of the upper deck and 270 on the lower deck. The entire nose swings up for front-in loading, and the rear of the hold is closed by a ramp door. The interior is pressurized and air-conditioned, and the landing gears have a total of 28 wheels to give the high

flotation necessary for off-runway operation. A flying boom inflight-refuelling receptacle is provided above the forward fuselage, and comprehensive avionics include inertial navigation and a large Norden multi-mode nose radar.

Part of the trouble in the original programme was the impossibility of meeting the severe demands for long range. This led to the structure being pared to the bone, and after the start of flight testing in June 1968 there were many snags including various structural failures (none catastrophic). By

Lockheed C-141 StarLifter

Data for C-141B

Type: strategic airlift transport.

Specifications: length, 168ft 4in (51.3m); span, 159ft 11in (48.74m); height, 39ft 3in (11.96m); weight (maximum take-off), 2.25g load factor, 343,000lb (155,580kg).

Max speed: Max cruise, 566mph (910km/h).

Service ceiling: 41,000ft (12.5km).

Range: with max payload, 2,935 miles (4,725km).

Armament: None.

Powerplant: four 21,000lb Pratt & Whitney TF33-P-7 turbofans each rated at 21,000lb (9,520kg) dry thrust.

Although this impressive and highly capable turbofan-engined airlifter has done a fantastic

job for Military Airlift Command since it entered service with the USAF in October 1964, it has frequently run out of available volume long before the payload limit was reached. During the Vietnam war the StarLifter (then existing only in a single form, the C-141A, of which 285 were constructed) was the backbone of the trans-Pacific airlift, carrying personnel and urgent supplies westbound and casualties eastbound.

Lockheed-Georgia carried out parametric studies and concluded that adding plugs ahead of and behind the wings, giving a total additional length of 23ft 4in (7.11m) would provide the most cost/effective solution to the problem of providing extra volume. A single aircraft was thus rebuilt, becoming

the first C-141B, and flown with the extended fuselage on 24 March 1977.

Subsequently a flight-test programme confirmed the validity of the modification, other changes including the addition of a universal inflight refuelling receptacle in the top of the forward fuselage, in a bulged fairing outside the pressurized structure. The first production C-141B was delivered on 4 December 1979, and the last of

271 rebuilds was delivered in May 1982. The complete rebuild programme cost $475 million, well under the estimated figure, and has increased MAC's airlift capacity by the equivalent of 90 extra StarLifters. Each C-141B can carry 13 pallets, instead of 10 previously, and a roughly proportionate increase in other loads. The C-141Bs were re-delivered as virtually new aircraft, with at least a 30,000-hour life ahead.

C-1 lacks range and payload performance. Long-range fuel tanks were fitted in the wing centre section of the last five aircraft in order to extend the range, but the JASDF now plans to supplement the C-1 with up to 14 Lockheed C-130. Most of the fleet serve with the Air Transport Wing at Miho.

Several C-1s serve in experimental roles. One will be used to test-fly the F-3 turbofan being developed for the Kawasaki KA-850 trainer, while another is being rebuilt by the National Aerospace Laboratory as an experimental four-engined Quiet Stol (QSTOL) transport similar in configuration to the Antonov An-72.

Left: High cost and limited range prevented the C-1 from being built in large numbers, but the design introduced Japanese industry to the technology of jet transports.

late 1970 a total of 30 Galaxies had flown, and 15 had been delivered to Military Airlift Command, but because of severe cost-escalation the number in the programme had to be cut from 115 to 81.

Subsequently the type established a great record with MAC, marred only by recurrent fatigue problems which severely limited safe airframe life and caused costly rectification which culminated in 1977 with the decision to re-wing the best 70 of 77 surviving aircraft. The first aircraft with a completely

new wing was returned to MAC in early 1981, and the cost of reconstructing the other 69 is put at about $1.5 billion. This programme is expected to continue until 1987.

Meanwhile in 1982 the Administration decided not to buy the C-17 (at present) but instead to fund 50 C-5B aircraft at a Lockheed price of $4.6 billion and a total programme cost of about $8 billion. The C-5Bs will have all the structural improvements and also improved TF39 engines, and are to be delivered in 1986-89.

Above: By 1987, the USAF will have rebuilt the wings of 70 C-5A Galaxies to overcome fatigue problems, and have returned the modified design to production as the C-5B.

Below: C-141A (No.4) were rebuilt to the C-141B (No.5) standard with:
1. In-flight refuelling receptacle.

2. Forward new fuselage section.
3. Aft new section.

Below: Rebuilt C-141B StarLifters are virtually new aircraft. In-flight refuelling receptacles allow long-range missions without en-route landing.

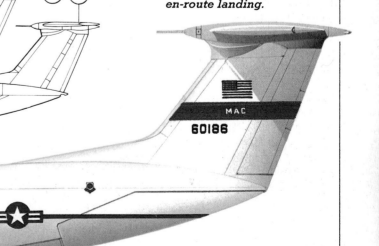

Lockheed C-130 Hercules

Type: airlift transport and multi-role platform.

Specifications: length, 97ft 9in (29.79m); span, 132ft 7in (40.41m); height, 38ft 3in (11.66m); weight (maximum take-off), 175,000lb (79,380kg).

Max speed: maximum cruise, 374mph (602km/h).

Service ceiling: at 130,000lb (58,970kg), 33,000ft (10km).

Range: With max payload, 2,487 miles (4,002km).

Armament: usually none.

Powerplant: Four 4,910ehp Allison T56-A-15 turboprops flat-rated at 4,50ehp (3,660ekW).

Universally known as the Herky Bird, the C-130 first flew in the summer of 1954, but today remains in full production long after several intended "C-130 replacements" have faded from the scene. When it appeared it was obviously the best airlifter in the world, designed to meet a 1952 requirement for USAF Tactical Air Command. What nobody then expected was that the basic design would have potential for so much growth, or to be so adaptable to fly totally different missions. The C-130 is probably the single most versatile transport aircraft flying today, and new versions for new missions keep appearing.

Today we take the C-130 configuration for granted, but when it was designed most military transports had sloping floors and small side doors, and lifting ability that was by comparison puny. With the C-130 the USAF gained an aircraft with electrifying performance from modern turboprops, a large cargo hold that was pressurized and air-conditioned yet had a full-section ramp door for straight-in loading, full-span integral tankage for long range, soft-field landing gear (fully retractable) and comprehensive avionics for all-weather flight and accurate navigation and precision airdrops of any kind of cargo.

It is fashionable today to sympathize with troops who have arrived by C-130, which in comparison with a jet takes longer to get there and subjects its occupants to noise and thrashing propeller vibration. It is hard to recall that when the C-130 was young it was the last word in speedy, quiet, smooth military airlift, a great and favourable contrast with its piston-engined contemporaries. Another feature which is still occasionally the subject of adverse comment is the landing gear, which has a track (distance between left and right main wheels) of 14ft 3in (4.34m). This is very small in comparison with the span and general size of the aircraft, but the C-130 has repeatedly demonstrated its ability to land on rough, narrow airstrips even in crosswind conditions without tipping over or digging in a wingtip.

Another possible problem is the cross section of the cargo hold which measures 10ft 3in (3.13m) wide and 9ft 2¾in (2.81m) high. These dimensions, which

are actually slightly greater than the maximum dimensions of the otherwise much larger C-141, are well attuned to the overall size of the C-130, to its payload capability and its original tactical missions. There would be no point in swelling the fuselage to accept a battle tank because the aircraft could not carry such a weight. At the same time, the average density assumed for military cargoes at the design stage was so high that, as soon as the C-130 was fitted with more powerful versions of the T56 engine (up from 3,750 to 4,050 and then over 4,500hp) to give it more payload, the users began to run out of available cargo volume. This was a problem initially with the commercial L-100 Hercules, which often carries low-density cargoes. By the 1980s it had spread to military models, and the Royal Air Force has had 30 of its original force of 66 Hercules rebuilt with a 100in (2.54m) plug section added ahead of the wing and a 80in (2.03m) plug aft of the wing, to convert them from Hercules C.1 standard to the C.3. This can carry seven standard cargo pallets instead of five, 128 troops instead of 93, or 93 stretcher (litter) patients (plus six attendants or sitting casualties) instead of only 70. Lockheed-Georgia Company is now producing new Herky Birds stretched to the same extended length for military customers, the first being for Indonesia

It is impossible here to list all the sub-types of C-130, which number more than 60 including special customer fits and post-delivery conversions. From the original C-130A stemmed the DC-130 drone/RPV director, RC-130 photo-survey model, JC-130 test-bed, NC-130 permanent test platforms, and AC-130A armed night gunship for ground attack. The more powerful, longer-ranged C-130B gave rise to the HC-130B search/rescue aircraft, VC-130 staff transport and weather-reconnaissance WC-130. The C-130E, built for MATS (today MAC) as a strategic airlifter,

versions. The LC-130F is a ski family for polar use, and the C-130G a Navy series of communications relay aircraft (Tacamo VLF submarine system) later styled EC-130G. The C-130H introduced the A-15 engine and gave rise to the AC-130H, HC-130H, KC-130H tanker, HC-130P for fuelling helicopters, EC-130Q Navy relay stations, KC-130R Marine tankers, LC-130R for the Antarctic, and RC-130S special (classified) recon platforms. The C-130K was the RAF Hercules C.1.

So far about 1,750 Hercules of all kinds have been sold, to over

brought a further incrase in fuel capacity and weight and became the baseline model and progenitor of the AC-130E gunship, DC-130E director, EC-130E Loran calibrator, HC-130E for search/rescue MC-130E missile carriers, and WC-130E weather con-

50 countries. The latest versions include a CAML (cargo aircraft minelayer system), a maritime patrol and rescue model and the EC-130ARE with a fin-mounted Awacs-type rotodome. The proposed twin-engined version has been shelved.

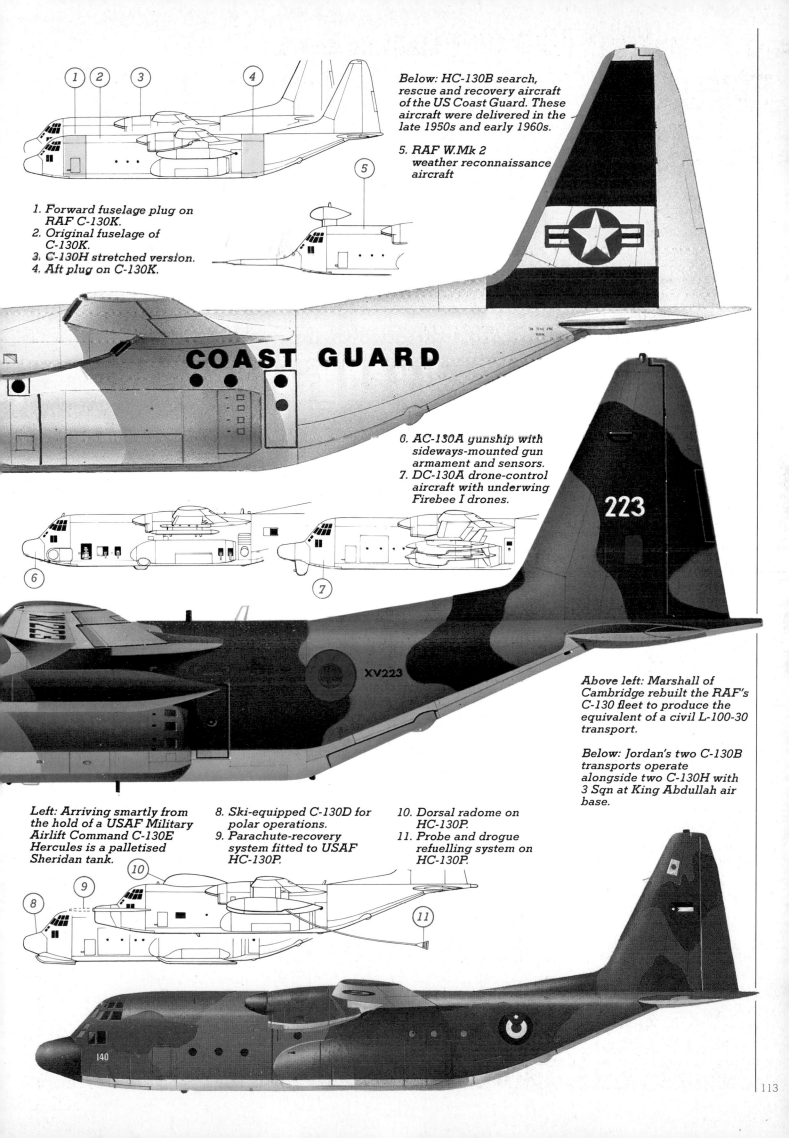

Below: HC-130B search, rescue and recovery aircraft of the US Coast Guard. These aircraft were delivered in the late 1950s and early 1960s.

1. Forward fuselage plug on RAF C-130K.
2. Original fuselage of C-130K.
3. C-130H stretched version.
4. Aft plug on C-130K.

5. RAF W.Mk 2 weather reconnaissance aircraft

6. AC-130A gunship with sideways-mounted gun armament and sensors.
7. DC-130A drone-control aircraft with underwing Firebee I drones.

COAST GUARD

Above left: Marshall of Cambridge rebuilt the RAF's C-130 fleet to produce the equivalent of a civil L-100-30 transport.

Below: Jordan's two C-130B transports operate alongside two C-130H with 3 Sqn at King Abdullah air base.

Left: Arriving smartly from the hold of a USAF Military Airlift Command C-130E Hercules is a palletised Sheridan tank.

8. Ski-equipped C-130D for polar operations.
9. Parachute-recovery system fitted to USAF HC-130P.

10. Dorsal radome on HC-130P.
11. Probe and drogue refuelling system on HC-130P.

Lockheed F-104 Starfighter

Data for F-104S

Type: 104G, attack and reconnaissance aircraft; 104S, interceptor.
Specifications: length, 54ft 9in (16.69m); span, without tip tanks, 21ft 11in (6.68m); height, 13ft 6in (4.11m); weight (maximum take-off), 31,000lb (14,060kg).
Max speed: 1,450 mph (2,330km/h, Mach 2.2).
Service ceiling: 58,000ft (17.7km).
Range: Combat radius, with max fuel, 775 miles (1,247km).
Armament: Nine hardpoints for external weapon load up to maximum of 7,500lb (3.4 tonnes), including two Sparrow or Aspide AAMs under wings and/or two Sidewinder AAMs under fuselage and either a Sidewinder or a tank on each tip; in place of Sparrow control electronics a 20mm M61A-1 gun can be installed in fuselage.
Powerplant: One General Electric J79-GE-19 turbojet rated at 11,810lb (5,370kg) dry thrust, 17,900lb (8,120kg) with afterburner.

Though it was carefully designed in the early 1950s as the best possible air-combat fighter, taking into account the lessons of the Korean war, the early F-104 Starfighter proved less successful in this role than its Soviet counterpart the MiG-21. Only small numbers of F-104A and C models were ever used by the US Air Force, and the number built would have been small had not Lockheed privately redesigned

the structure and avionics to fly low-level missions under inertial guidance carrying a nuclear bomb. This new aircraft, the F-104G, was the subject of large-scale orders by Germany's Luftwaffe, and thus sold also to many other air forces around the world, and was built under licence by international groups Germany, Holland, Belgium including Italy, Canada and Japan.

Several hundred F-104Gs remain in use with various forces, with variants including the RF-104G for reconnaissance, the TF-104 trainer family, the RTF-104 two-seaters for multi-sensor and electronic reconnaissance and the Canadian CF-104 configured for air/ground missions with extra fuel in place of an M61 gun.

Newest of all Starfighters are the F-104S interceptors developed jointly by Aeritalia and Lockheed and built under licence in Italy by the latter company. Its main features are an uprated engine, improved Autonetics R21G radar optimized for air/air combat, but also with air/ground mapping and terrain-following modes, a Martin-Baker IQ7A zero/zero seat, and a completely different spectrum of weapons including three types of guided AAM. In the Luftwaffe the F-

104G gained a bad reputation in popular hack by officers.
the 1960s because its totally unforgiving nature resulted in numerous fatalities among inexperienced pilots. In fact, the basic machine—despite its frightening, almost wingless appearance—is not inherently dangerous to a pilot who knows his job, and is frequently used as a

In the Aeronautica Militare Italiano the F-104S equips six Gruppi in the all-weather interceptor role and four in the fighter/

ground attack role, and has proved effective and popular. Though it certainly needs a good runway it has comprehensive all-weather avionics and an excellent range, its chief shortcoming being lack of precision air/ground delivery systems. Funding is now being scraped together to update the force for pinpoint navigation and air/ground delivery in all weathers, as well as adding a look-down mode in the air-combat role. Aeritalia built 165 of this model, plus 40 for Turkey.

Lockheed/Kawasaki P-2J

Type: maritime patrol aircraft
Specifications: length, 95ft 10⅜in (29.23m); span, over tanks, 101ft 3½in (30.87m); height, 29ft 3½in (8.93m); weight (maximum take-off), 75,000lb (34,019kg).
Maximum speed: with jets, 403mph (649km/h).
Service ceiling: 30,000ft (9.15km).
Range: 2,765 miles (4,450km).
Armament: internal bay for total stores load of 8,000lb (3,630kg); underwing attachments for 16 rockets.
Powerplant: Two 2,850ehp (2,130ekW) General Electric T64-IHI-10 turboprops made licence by Japanese group led by II II, plus two 3,085lb (1,400kg) II II J3-7C booster, turbojets used only for short bursts of high speed.

Though the Lockheed P-2 Neptune has faded from the front-line inventory of most major powers, the Japanese P-2J version is only now beginning to be replaced by the P-3C/Update II, which succeeded the P-2J on the Kawasaki

assembly line. The P-2J was based upon the P-2H which preceded it in JMSDF service. Design began in 1961, and it could be argued that by this time the P-2 as a basic platform was no longer adequate to carry modern sensors and systems. Bearing in mind that the first production P-2J did not fly until August 1969, and the last of 89 was not delivered until 1979, the whole programme begins to appear mistaken. It might have been an excellent aircraft had it been produced ten years earlier in timing.

Though the JMSDF were at pains to try to procure a much more modern aircraft than the P-2H, some of the considerable and expensive changes did little to enhance the operational effectiveness. Replacing the Turbo-Compound piston engines by turboprops saved weight which was nullified by the greater fuel consumption, and using the locally produced booster jets merely increased costs. The twin-wheel main gears are better than the large single wheels previously used, and the much

longer fuselage allowed a crew of 12 to operate in reasonable comfort with a better amidships tactical compartment housing the main navigation and sensor displays. By 1960 standards a

comprehensive suite of navigation and attack sensors was fitted, but this had to be updated in the course of the production programme to bring the equipment a little nearer to contemporary standard.
ASW sensors include the Julie/Jezebel acoustic system, ARR-52A (V) sonobuoy receiver and HSQ-101 MAD installation in the extended tailcone. The

search radar was originally the APS-80 (J) but this was improved to APS-80 (N) in later aircraft, though it is still an outdated set. By 1981 the P-2J force was beginning to be reduced by modifying

aircraft for other purposes, beginning with three conversions for electronic warfare, ECM jamming and target towing with the designation UP-2J. Further conversions were expected to follow, and by 1984 one aircraft is to be modified as a variable-stability platform for test-pilot training, replacing a P-2H. Replacement by the P-3C/Update II is to take place in 1982-88.

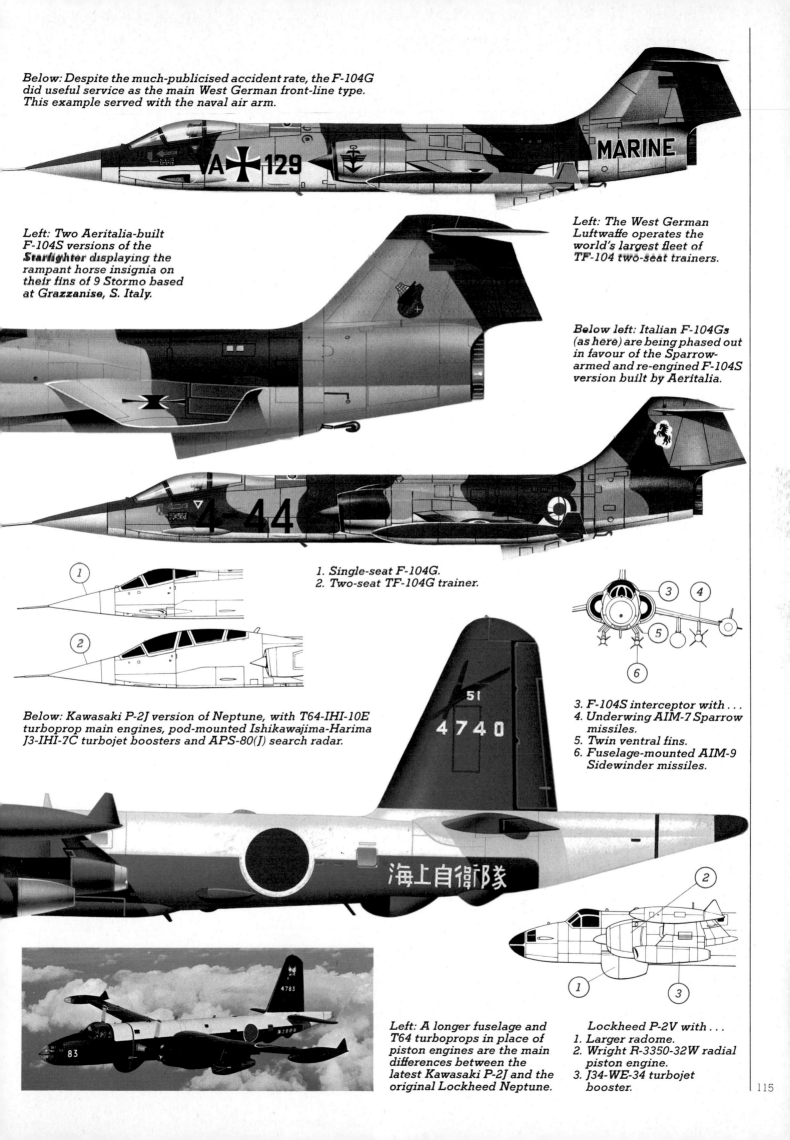

Below: Despite the much-publicised accident rate, the F-104G did useful service as the main West German front-line type. This example served with the naval air arm.

Left: Two Aeritalia-built F-104S versions of the Starfighter displaying the rampant horse insignia on their fins of 9 Stormo based at Grazzanise, S. Italy.

Left: The West German Luftwaffe operates the world's largest fleet of TF-104 two-seat trainers.

Below left: Italian F-104Gs (as here) are being phased out in favour of the Sparrow-armed and re-engined F-104S version built by Aeritalia.

1. Single-seat F-104G.
2. Two-seat TF-104G trainer.

3. F-104S interceptor with . . .
4. Underwing AIM-7 Sparrow missiles.
5. Twin ventral fins.
6. Fuselage-mounted AIM-9 Sidewinder missiles.

Below: Kawasaki P-2J version of Neptune, with T64-IHI-10E turboprop main engines, pod-mounted Ishikawajima-Harima J3-IHI-7C turbojet boosters and APS-80(J) search radar.

Left: A longer fuselage and T64 turboprops in place of piston engines are the main differences between the latest Kawasaki P-2J and the original Lockheed Neptune.

Lockheed P-2V with . . .
1. Larger radome.
2. Wright R-3350-32W radial piston engine.
3. J34-WE-34 turbojet booster.

Lockheed P-3 Orion

Data for P-3C
Type: maritime-patrol and ASW aircraft.
Specifications: length, 116ft 10in (35.61m); span, 99ft 8in (30.37m); height, 33ft 8in (10.29m); weight (maximum take-off), 135,000lb (61,200kg).
Max speed: 411kt (761km/hr).
Service ceiling: 28,300ft (8,600m).
Range: (with 3 hours on station) 1,350nm (2,500km).
Armament: sonobuoys plus various models of homing torpedo, mine and nuclear or conventional depth bomb.
Powerplant: four Allison T56 turboprops, each rated at 4,910ehp (3,660kW).

In external appearance only, the early Orions closely resemble today's P-3C, but, as is the case with all ASW types, the aircraft is simply a method of transporting weapons, sensors, data-processing equipment and operators. Equipment performance rather than aircraft performance is what determines combat effectiveness, and the Orion has been upgraded several times during its long career.

Earliest production P-3A aircraft used the ASA-16 electronic display from the earlier Neptune, the AQA-3A sonics-analysis system, ASQ-10A MAD sensor and APS-80 search radar. These aircraft could handle data from up to four sonobuoys at once, but an early modification substituted the AQA-5 equipment, which was capable of handling eight sonobuoys. By substituting 4,910ehp (3,660kW) Allison T56-A-14 turboprops for the earlier 4,500ehp T56-A-10W units and making minor changes to the avionics, Lockheed then produced the P-3B version, which was built in large numbers and exported to Australia, New Zealand and Norway.

Development of the avionics for the definitive P-3C version began in 1962, and prototype hardware was flying by 1967. It is not possible to convert P-3B aircraft to the C configuration. This basic suite has itself been the subject of several upgrading programmes.

Aircraft delivered since January 1975 have had improved avionics, such as an Omega navigation system, a more sensitive acoustic-processing system, a 393K-capacity magnetic drum data-storage system to increase the computer's memory size, additional tactical displays for the sensor operators, plus software improvements such as a new CM-2 computer language. The increased computer capacity allows a larger amount of acoustic information to be stored, along with a more comprehensive threat "library" of data and acoustic signatures. It also widens the range of tactical options available to the crew. This equipment standard is known as Update I.

Next stage was to add an infra-red detection system for target identification, the trainable turret containing sensors, wide-angle and "zoom" optics being located beneath the aircraft nose. An ARS-2 sonobuoy reference system, capable of measuring the relative position of each buoy by means of passive signal "time-of-arrival" techniques was also installed, along with facilities for the carriage and launch of Harpoon anti-ship missiles. Deliveries of this Update II version began in 1977.

Update III is currently under development and should enter production in 1984. This includes an extensive revision of the ASW avionics, such as replacing the current DIFAR sonobuoy receiver with a new unit, and installing a new acoustic processor. In order to cope with the electrical power load created by these systems, as well as the heat generated by their operation, the APU and cabin environmental control systems are to be improved. Update III is being developed under a programme which started back in 1978.

When Canada selected the P-3 in 1976, the version chosen was not the USN-standard P-3C but a customised version designated CP-140 Aurora. This combines the basic P-3 with avionics and sensors of the S-3 Viking carrier-based ASW aircraft. These systems include the APS-116 search radar, OL-5004 acoustics data processor, OL-5008/AA FLIR, OA-5154 MAD sensor and AYK-502 navigation/tactical computer. The cabin layout has also been modified to meet Canadian requirements, and provision has been made for the installation of sensor packs for tasks such as pollution-control or aerial survey in the weapons bay. Deliveries began in 1981.

Six P-3F Orions were supplied to what was then the Imperial Iranian Air Force during the mid-1970s. These were to have carried simplified avionics suitable for maritime patrol, but the final configuration included ASW equipment.

Specialised Orion variants include the WP-3A for weather reconnaissance, and the EP-3E Elint aircraft used to shadow Soviet naval units. The latter are rebuilt P-3A or B aircraft carrying

ALQ-110 and ALR-60 equipment for the interception and recording of radar and communications signals respectively.

Lockheed S-3A Viking

Type: carrier-based ASW aircraft.
Specifications: length, 53ft 4in (16.26m); span, 68ft 8in (20.93m); height, 22ft 9in (6.93m); weight (maximum take-off), 52,539lb (23,831kg).
Max speed: 518mph (834km/h).
Service ceiling: Over 35,000ft (10.7km).
Range: Over 2,303 miles (3,700km); ferry range, over 3,454 miles (5,560km).
Armament: Left/right split internal bay can house four Mk 36 destructors, four Mk 46 torpedoes, four Mk 82 bombs, two Mk 57 or four Mk 54 depth bombs, or four Mk 53 mines; two wing pylons can carry single or triple ejector racks for wide range of bombs, rocket pods, mines, cluster bombs, flare launchers, destructors or 250gal (1,136lit) auxiliary fuel tanks.
Powerplant: Two 9,275lb (4,207kg) General Electric TF34-GE-400A turbofans each rated at 9,275lb (4,207kg) dry thrust.

Thanks to the amazing longevity of the Grumman S-2 family the requirement for a replacement was not issued until 1968, and this enabled the winning design, the Lockheed S-3A, to be an extremely modern aircraft which packs a fantastic amount of systems, sensors and weapons into an airframe of small dimensions for easy carrier operation. Like the S-2 the S-3 is a high-wing twin-engined aircraft with a crew of four. There is no mid-fuselage tactical compartment; instead all four crew sit facing forward in Escapac zero/zero seats, the backseaters being called Senso (sensor operator) on the left and Tacco (tactical co-ordinator) on the right.

They control an array of ASW gear that is so modern in concept that it was adopted by the Canadian Armed Forces for its CP-140 (Orion) in preference to the latest P-3C/Update III systems. The main radar is the APS-116, by Texas Instruments, a totally new high-resolution set specially designed for overwater use. The ASQ-81, latest of the US Navy MAD detectors, is installed in a long boom which in the retracted position lies in the top of the rear fuselage as far forward as the wing. In the underside of the rear fuselage are launch tubes for 60 sonobuoys of the LOFAR, CASS, DICASS, R/O or BT types. ESM (electronic surveillance measures) includes passive receivers and instantaneous frequency measurers in pods on the wingtips. A retractable turret under the crew compartment houses the OR-89 FLIR (forward-looking infra-red). These and many other devices are all controlled by a central digital computer, a Univac 1832A.

Vikings, of which most of the airframe was constructed by associate contractor Vought, entered fleet service in 1974 and soon established a great reputation. Surprisingly there were no other production variants, nor export sales, and production was complete at 187 in 1978. Conversions were flown to US-3A COD transport and KS-3A tanker configuration, but the C-2A is returning to production in the COD role. The main force of 160 Vikings is, however, being updated to S-3B standard with improved acoustic and radar processing capacity, expanded ESM, a new sonobuoy receiver system and provision for the Harpoon anti-ship missile.

Above: The P-3C is the most advanced version of Orion in current US Navy service. Iran's P-3F (right) is similar in avionics. At least one of six delivered is still flying.

1. Rare experimental variant, NP-3B.
2. The P-3B has no chin turret.
3. Ventral sonobuoy launch tubes on P-3C.
4. Non-ASW version such as the EP-3E and WP-3A have no MAD tail "sting".

Left: 335 Sqn, Royal Norwegian Air Force operates seven P-3B.

●L🔵KK

Right: The early model P-3A remains in the US Navy service, but now serves only with Reserve units such as the squadrons of Atlantic and Pacific Reserve Wing.

PE
150606
NAVY

Left: The wings of the S-3 fold assymetrically for storage aboard USN aircraft carriers.

Below: US Navy S-3A Vikings are being updated to the S-3B standard, receiving improved avionics and armament. This aircraft has CoD containers under the wings.

1. KS-3A tanker with external tank on underwing pylon and refuelling drogue deployed.
2. Retractable refuelling probe on all versions.
3. Retractable turret for OR-89/AA FLIR on S-3A.
4. Proposed US-3A COD version.
5. Drogue unit on KS-3A.
6. Retractable MAD boom.

12
NH
7998
NAVY
VS-33

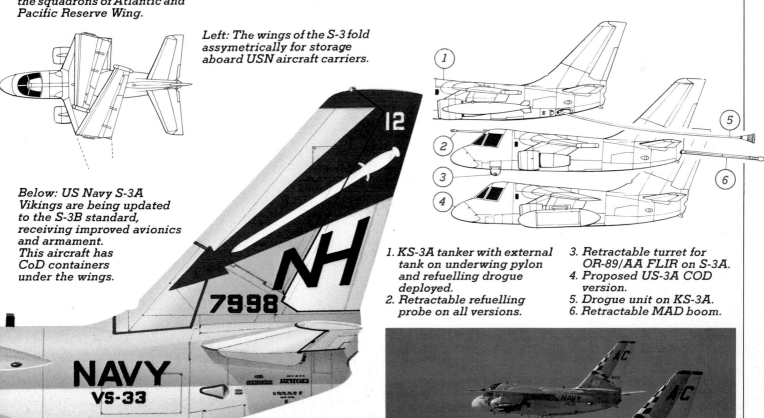

Right: S-3A Vikings from the carrier Saratoga cruise out to their patrol locations with MAD booms retracted.

Lockheed SR-71

Type: supersonic strategic reconnaissance aircraft.
Specifications: length, 107ft 5in (32.74m); span, 55ft 7in (16.94m); height, 18ft 6in (5.64m); weight (maximum take-off), 170,000lb (77,000kg).
Max speed: Mach 3+.
Service ceiling: approx. 86,000ft (26,000m).
Range: 2,600nm (4,800km).
Armament: none.
Powerplant: two Pratt & Whitney J58 turbojets, each rated at 32,500lb (14,700kg) thrust with afterburner.

Developed as a replacement for the US Central Intelligence Agency's fleet of U-2 reconnaissance aircraft, the Lockheed SR-71 was destined never to carry out "black" missions into Soviet airspace. Despite this, its fame as a reconnaissance type is guaranteed by its operations over many of the world's trouble spots, as well as the galaxy of absolute world speed records won during the 1970s. As this text was in preparation, the SR-71 had held the records for speed in a straight line, speed in a closed circuit and height in sustained flight since carrying out a "blitz" on the record book in July 1976.

Officially the SR-71 project grew out of USAF work on the YF-12 advanced interceptors, although it is possible that the fighter was in fact a spin-off from a reconnaissance/strike requirement. The YF-12A was the first version to be revealed in 1964. Soon afterwards President Johnson also revealed the existence of the "SR-71"—a designation thought to have resulted from a Presidential slip of the tongue. The new aircraft should have been designated RS-71 (Reconnaissance/Strike) instead of SR (Strategic Reconnaissance), but the latter became official, either due to confusion or the desire to play down the aircraft's planned strike role. If pod-mounted nuclear weapons are available for the SR-71, as was originally planned, no one is saying.

The YF-12A flew for the first time in April 1962, but had no real chance of ending up in quantity on USAF flight lines. Trials were carried out with the Hughes ASG-18 pulse-Doppler radar and AIM-47A missiles, then the type was transferred to research duties as a high-speed testbed.

First flight of the SR-71 took place on 22 January 1964, and production deliveries began in 1966. Estimates of the number built range from 21 to more than 30. Nominal strength of the only user—the 9th Strategic Reconnaissance Wing—is nine aircraft, but it is likely that others are in reserve.

Like the XB-70 bomber programme, the SR-71 project required a long series of technological developments to make Mach 3 flight possible. Materials, lubricants, powerplants, fuels and sub-systems all had to be created from scratch to create an aircraft whose performance eclipses that of the only known Soviet Mach 3 type—the MiG-25 Foxbat. When the aircraft cruises for prolonged periods at Mach 3, the external skin temperature rises to at least 450 degrees Centigrade, and to more than 1,000 degrees in areas where the thermal effects are severest.

The best structural material was found to be titanium, so this metal was used to fabricate more than 90 per cent of the aircraft structure and skin. Steel and high-temperature alloys developed for use in jet engines are also used. The dark paint finish used to help radiate heat away from the aircraft gave rise to the unofficial designation "Blackbird". To minimise structural weight, the margins of structural strength have been pared to a minimum. Had the YF-12 interceptor entered service, flight profiles would have been strictly "fast and straight" since violent manoeuvres would have been out of the question, even at low speed.

To power the aircraft, Pratt & Whitney created a massive single-spool turbojet capable of operating in a partial ramjet mode at Mach 3. Much of the air from the intakes bypasses the engine through a series of large-diameter ducts and is dumped into the afterburner. At Mach 3 the engine produces only some ten per cent of the total thrust, the remainder coming from the inlets and ejectors. The fuel used is designated JP-7 and has a low vapour pressure.

Owing to the large amount of structural expansion as the airframe heats and cools, it is impossible to achieve a perfect seal on the integral fuel tanks under all conditions. The tanks may be fuel-tight when hot, but while the aircraft is on the ground, the structure cools and contracts, creating leaks.

A complex automatic system controls the position of the engine nacelle inlet centrebodies. At high speeds this positioning is critical.

Lockheed T-33 and AT-33

Type: advanced trainer.
Specifications: length, 37ft 9in (11.48m); span, without tanks, 38ft 10½in (11.85m); height, 11ft 8in (3.55m); weight (maximum take-off), 14,442lb (6,441kg).
Max speed: 590mph (950km/h).
Service ceiling: 47,500ft (14.5km).
Range: 1,345 miles (2,165km).
Armament: if fitted, two 0.5in M-3 guns and two bombs or other stores of 1,000lb (454kg) each.
Powerplant: one Allison J33-A-35 turbojet rated at 5,200lb (2,360kg) dry thrust.

When Lockheed's "Mac" Short suggested the company should turn the F-80 Shooting Star (which in 1948 was becoming obsolescent) into a trainer, a colleague said "Hell, Mac, it's the best fighter we've got, why turn it into a dodo?" Short had his way, and the TF-80 (later T-33A) flew on 22 March 1948. Nobody could explain why it went faster than the fighter! Suffice to say the T-bird was an instant smash hit, and the 5,871 built was several times the F-80 total, not including 210 built under licence by Kawasaki in Japan and 656 with Nene engines built as Canadair Silver Stars in Canada. Large numbers were built for the Navy or transferred to that service as TV-2s (later T-33B), and the Navy later bought a much modified T2V SeaStar model, later restyled T-1A. Other variants include the AT-33 for close support, RT-33 for single-seat reconnaissance with electronic gear in the rear cockpit, and the DT-33 drone director.

An exact counterpart of the MiG-15UTI, the T-33 has a robust airframe, simple systems and relatively low operating costs, and for these reasons has endured to this day in minor air forces around the world. At all times handling has been enjoyable, the view through the very long clamshell canopy outstanding and endurance with 191gal (870-lit) Fletcher tanks on each wing tip adequate for useful training sorties or long ferry missions. Occasionally T-birds are still used for combat training, in a quasi-operational role, and in warfare in Ethiopia, Honduras and possibly other countries have been locally modified to carry different or additional weapons.

In 1980 there were, according to Lockheed spares records, something like 800 of all sub-types still in active use around the world. Since then the number has continued to fall, probably mainly through inability of the host government to procure spares rather than because of fatigue or other problems with the aircraft. In many air forces some T-33s are retained as popular hacks for liaison or for practice by senior officers, even after replacement as the standard jet trainer. More than 200 have been modified for target towing.

Right: RT-33 has . . .
1. *Modified nose with camera equipment.*
2. *Rear cockpit used to house electronics.*

Below: SR-71B two-seat trainer based at Beale AFB.

17956
1000th
SORTIE

U.S. AIR FORCE

956

Left: Mach 3 flight demands the complex aerodynamic shape seen here head-on.

1. Pod for J58-1 turbojet engine.
2. Strakes for additional lift.
3. Inward canted tail fins.

Should conditions not be correct, the inlet shock wave can suddenly move from its correct position, causing the engine to "unstart", yawing the aircraft violently.

First pilot to fly the SR-71 and be allowed to tell the tale in public was Robert Ropelewski, a staff member of the US trade magazine _Aviation Week & Space Technology_. In high-speed flight SR-71 crews rely on a stability augmentation system to reduce workload, he reported. Manoeuvring must be gradual, particularly if an inexperienced pilot is at the controls.

Fuel tanks must be used in a predefined sequence, moving the aircraft centre of gravity as speed builds up. Unwanted drag can eat into fuel reserves during high-speed cruise, so the aircraft is trimmed by transferring fuel forward or aft from one tank to another. Centre of gravity position is critical if elevon displacement and hence drag is to be minimised.

Since no effective replacement for the SR-71 is likely to enter service in the near future, the USAF is replacing some of the older avionic systems with a modern digital flight and inlet control system.

17955

Left: Side view of the SR-71A conceals the aircraft's complex shape.

955

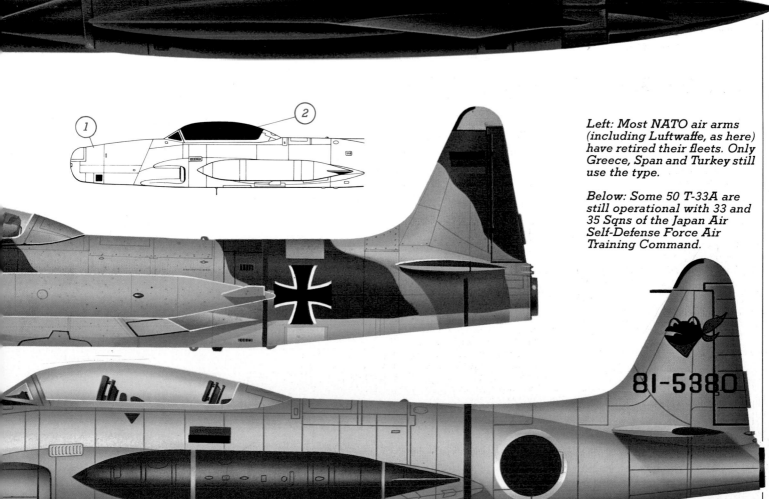

Left: Most NATO air arms (including Luftwaffe, as here) have retired their fleets. Only Greece, Span and Turkey still use the type.

Below: Some 50 T-33A are still operational with 33 and 35 Sqns of the Japan Air Self-Defense Force Air Training Command.

81-5380

Lockheed U-2 and TR-1

Data for TR-1
Type: U-2, clandestine recon and nine other roles depending on sub-type; TR-1, multi-sensor tac recon.
Specifications: length 63ft 0in (19.2m); span, 103ft 0in (31.39m); height, 16ft 0½in (4.89m); weight (maximum take-off), 40,000lb (18,143kg).
Maximum speed: over 430mph (692km/h) at very high altitude.
Service ceiling: 90,000ft (27.43km).
Range: more than 3,000 miles (4,830km).
Armament: none.
Powerplant: one Pratt & Whitney J75-P-13B turbojet, rated at 17,000lb (7,710kg) dry thrust.

No aircraft in history has a record remotely approaching that of the Lockheed U-2. Because it was created in total secrecy, and emerged upon the world as a mysterious high-flying aircraft cloaked in the guise of a civilian research machine for NASA, the only official statements were deliberately misleading ones. Only in the past few years has the scope and variety of the programme become apparent. Today it has given rise to the TR-1 series, a regular USAF surveillance platform ordered, funded and announced without subterfuge.

The original requirement of 1954 was for an aircraft able to fly so high that it could not be shot down, and thus could make overflights of foreign territory with impunity, carrying large optical cameras and, in later versions, other sensors. Lockheed's C.L. "Kelly" Johnson led a special team at the secure department known as The Skunk Works, and came up with a solution resembling a large metal sailplane with a J57 jet engine. To save weight the landing gear comprised two sets of main wheels in "bicycle" tandem arrangement on the centreline, plus small wing outriggers which after takeoff were jettisoned. The landing finished up on one of the downturned wingtips.

The designation U-2A was a cover, signifying a utility usage, and 48 were ordered in a hidden 1956 vote. Except for the first block an integral-tank wing was adopted to extend range, and early in the run, probably at the eighth aircraft, the 11,200lb-thrust J57 was replaced by the much

larger J75, the designation changing to U-2B. With integral-tank wings and extra fuel in tanks projecting ahead of the leading edge the U-2B could fly almost 4,000 miles in 9 hours at 90,000ft, using special low-volatility fuel and the pilot in a pressure-suit in a cockpit with features borrowed from the F-104, with a food warmer and spaceflight-type food tubes. Many operational missions took place over several Communist countries, but were abruptly halted on 1 May 1960 when a U-2B was shot down by a SAM near Sverdlovsk.

Lockheed built five U-2D two-seat derivatives of the U-2B used for missile monitoring, at least three Bs being converted. The WU-2A is a weather-recon rebuild of the A, and several Bs were rebuilt as U-2CT dual conversion trainers, painted white and with the instructor seated high to the rear, unlike the observer/systems operator in the D who is at the same level as the pilot. The CT was greatly needed, because the U-2 is one of the trickiest aircraft in the world to fly. It is built to such low factors the flight controls prohibit all but the gentlest manoeuvres, and in gusty conditions or crosswinds flying is prohibited. On the approach the speed is within three knots of the stall, yet the wings can flap significantly and keeping them level on the ground requires intense concentration. The JU-2D and WU-2D were test and upper-atmosphere rebuilds.

With 1968 serials, 25 Bs were reconstructed as U-2R multi-sensor and electronic recon platforms, with a much larger airframe increasing gross weight from 15,850/17,270lb to a new high of 29,000lb and dramatically raising fuel/equipment payload from around 5,100lb to 12,000lb (5,443kg). Many versions failed to materialise, but the R was so useful that tooling was retained, and in 1980 production restarted on a derivative of the R designated TR-1A (single-seat) and TR-1B (two-seat), along with a civil ER-2 (single-seat) and TR-1B (two-seat), (Earth-resources) surveillance platform produced for NASA.

The chief new sensor in the TR-1A is an ASARS (advanced synthetic-aperture radar system), in the form of a unique UPD-X side-looking radar which behaves—as do all synthetic-aperture systems—as if it had a

gigantic aerial scanner by emitting waves at spaced sequences along the aircraft's track. Thus the ASARS has the discrimination and picture resolution that would be obtained by a scanner hundreds of metres in diameter. In addition a very comprehensive ECM suite is carried, together with over 2,400lb (1,089kg) of other special electronics housed in two giant 23ft pods on the wings, far larger than the auxiliary tanks of the U-2B. Additional mission equipment, including some of the largest avionics and sensors, are in a modular nose section which is detachable, in a Q-Bay aft of the cockpit and in a smaller E-Bay between the Q-Bay and the forward main gear bay. Further mission equipment is housed in the lower rear fuselage and in the tailcone.

The stated purpose of the TR-1A is "to provide continuously available, day or night, high-altitude surveillance of the battle area in direct support of the US and Allied ground forces in time of peace, crises and war situations". It replaces the defunct Compass Cope large RPV which was intended for the same duty in the European theatre. The USAF plans to deploy 33 TR-1As, plus two TR-1Bs, in 1981-84. They will not be used only in Europe, but that is clearly the area where surveillance of potentially hostile territory is most crucial, to give warning of impending attack. Without crossing a hostile frontier the TR-1 could look 35 miles (55km) into the foreign territory, simultaneously transmitting the resulting radar imagery to the ground via a data link.

Above: Externally similar to the current TR-1, the U-2R was built in the late 1960s. This version introduced the stretched fuselage, "wet" wing and underwing payload pods. The vertical fin was mounted on a dorsal equipment fairing, while the front and rear undercarriage units were repositioned.

Below: U-2CT conversion trainer based at Davis-Monthan AFB and used by the 100th Strategic Reconnaissance Wing. Like all CT models, this is a rebuilt U-2B reconnaissance aircraft with a second cockpit mounted on top of the forward fuselage.

66692

Above: U-2R with modified nose and underwing pods for mission electronics.

1. General configuration of the U-2R and TR-1.
2. Underwing equipment pods for sensors, recorders and other systems.
3. U-2C single-seater with dorsal equipment fairing.
4. Nose section of the U-2CT

trainer. The location of the front cockpit is unchanged from the single-seat models.
5. U-2D with sensor systems located in an equipment bay directly behind the cockpit.

Below: U-2A based at Edwards AFB. Note the smaller air intakes for the J57 turbojet fitted to these early models.

66701

U.S. AIR FORCE

80-1066

Below: Although similar in appearance to the U-2R, the TR-1 carries more advanced sensors and ECM systems, plus more internal fuel.

MBB BO 105

Data for BO 105C
Type: multi-role all-weather helicopter.
Specifications: length, 14ft 1in (4.3m); height, 9ft 10in (3.00m); rotor diameter, 32ft 3in (9.84m); weight (max take-off), 5,300lb (2,400kg).
Max speed: 145kt (270km/hr).
Range: (with max payload); 355nm (656m).
Powerplants: two Allison 250-C20B turboshafts each rated at 420shp (313kW).

This light utility helicopter first flew in the mid-1960s as a civil design. All versions are highly manoeuvrable due to the use of an advanced rotor. This has a titanium hub and flexible glass fibre blades.

On most helicopters, the blades on the main rotor are fixed to the rotor head via complex hinge assemblies. On the BO 105, the

improved tail rotor was fitted along with a more impact-resistant undercarriage. Deliveries of the resulting BO 105M started in 1980 to meet an order for 227 aircraft to replace the German Army's Alouette II fleet.

This version was also used as the basis of the German Army's BO 105P anti-tank helicopter (also designated PAH-1). Pylons for HOT anti-tank missiles are added to the fuselage sides, a SFIM stabilised sight is fitted to the cabin roof, while a Singer ASN-124 Doppler radar is used for navigation.

Seven squadrons are planned. Three anti-tank regiments will each operate two PAH-1 squadrons, while the seventh unit will be attached to No 6 Panzer Grenadier Division for unspecified "special duties". Each aircraft can

carry six HOT missiles and has an endurance of up to 90 minutes. Since the planned Franco/German PAH-2 anti-tank helicopter seems unlikely to be built, PAH-1 should have a long career with the German forces. Further aircraft could be ordered to maintain or even increase fleet strength once deliveries of the 212 currently on order are completed in 1983.

Most bizarre BO 105 variant is probably the aircraft being used as a testbed for the SFIM Ophelia stabilised sight. This uses mast mounted sensors whose location high above the main rotor earned the aircraft the nickname "Giraffe" and an appropriately-mottled paint scheme.

This aircraft first flew on 21 May 1981, and its spherical equipment fairing mounted some

2ft 11in (0.89m) above the rotor ensured that it was unlikely to be mistaken for any other BO 105 version. The sphere can be controlled from the cabin by means of a control stick on the instrument console, and is traversable through +_120° in azimuth and from -30° to +20° in elevation. Mounted within the sphere is the OPHELIA (Optique Platforme HELIcoptère Allemand) multichannel sensor package.

Ophelia was originally developed for the PAH-2 project. The sensor housing above the mast contains FLIR and TV viewing systems plus a laser rangefinder, all mounted on a stabilised platform. A second stabilised platform mounted beneath the nose carries a wide-angle FLIR system used for low-level navigation. This array of sensors is being tested

blades are connected to a forged titanium hub which has feathering hinges only, so the rotor can withstand negative "g" forces. This results in impressive manoeuvrability, since the aircraft can conduct conventional "pull-up" manoeuvres over obstacles, followed by a rapid "push-down" involving negative "g".

First model to achieve widespread military success was the BO 105C all-weather version. When the German Army decided to adopt an improved model as a light observation and liaison aircraft, the design was further refined. To suit it for the military role, the transmission was uprated, the fuel system and main rotor were made more damage-resistant, and an

Below: A sight to chill a tank commander's heart; an MBB BO 105 armed with HOT anti-armour missiles rises over a tree line. Destined for the Federal German Army, this machine has yet to receive its camouflage.

with various types of head-up and head-down displays and a helmet sight.

The BO 105 is being assembled under licence by CASA in Spain, NAM in the Philippines, and Nurtanio in Indonesia. The Spanish Army uses the aircraft in the communication, observation and anti-tank roles. Several serve as liaison aircraft with the Philippines Navy, while the Army's Aviation Battalion is thought likely to order an anti-tank version. BO 105s are in service with all three Indonesian armed forces.

Right: The Federal German Army is receiving 212 BO 105P anti-tank helicopters to equip three Army Corps regiments. Each BO 105P is armed with six HOT missiles, aimed from a roof-mounted sight.

Above left: PAH-1 (BO 105P) anti-tank helicopter of the West German Army. The vertical fitting seen above the roof-mounted HOT missile sight is part of a blade antenna.

Left: BO 105 Giraffe:
1. *Ophelia stabilised TV/ FLIR/laser rangefinder installation in steerable spherical housing.*
2. *Roof-mounted sight.*

Above: The basic BO 105C utility helicopter lacks the missiles and sighting equipment carried by the 105P version. This aircraft is in the markings of 300 Sqn of the Royal Netherlands Air Force, which took delivery of 30 examples in 1976.

McDonnell Douglas A-4 Skyhawk

Data for A-4M
Type: light attack bomber.
Specifications: length, 40ft 4in (12.29m); span, 27ft 6in (8.38m); height, 15ft 0in (4.57m); weight (maximum take-off), 25,500lb (11,600kg).
Max speed: 583kt (1,080km/hr).
Service ceiling: 52,000ft (15,800m).
Range: 1,785nm (3,300km).
Armament: up to 9,100lb (4,100kg) of ordnance plus two 20mm cannon.
Powerplant: one Pratt & Whitney J52-P-408A turbojet rated at 11,200lb (5,100kg) dry thrust.

Time is starting to take its toll of what must surely be one of the classic aircraft of the 1960s and 1970s—Ed Heinemann's A-4 Skyhawk. More than 2,000 of the 2,960 examples built were delivered to the US forces, but within a few years of production ending, only a few hundred US examples were operational, most with Reserve units.

At the time of writing, two A-4-equipped attack squadrons remain in US Navy service, but the US Marine Corps still has 80 A-4Ms in the training role, and 68 A-4s pre-positioned in Europe for wartime use. Six squadrons of A-4E and A-4F still serve with the Marine Corps Air Reserve Force, while the US Naval Reserve still uses A-4L single-seaters and TA-4J trainers. Versions remaining in service with export customers are detailed below. Total number exported was just over 500.

The A-4E entered service in 1962, six years after the original A4D-1. It was the first model to replace the Wright J65 engine with the Pratt & Whitney J52 turbojet. The G is broadly similar, but was developed for the Royal Australian Navy, the first overseas customer to buy new-build aircraft.

Final version to be developed for the US Navy was the J52-P-8A-powered A-4F, the first Skyhawk to house a dorsal "hump" to house avionics. This version also introduced a zero-zero ejection seat and better protection against ground fire, while the installation of spoilers reduced the landing run.

Israel took delivery of its first A-4H aircraft in 1967. This too was based on the A-4E, but introduced a new pattern of square-tipped vertical fin with increased area. Twin 30mm DEFA cannon replaced the normal USN 20mm weapons. In the early 1970s these aircraft were modified by the fitting of the dorsal "hump" housing for avionics, first introduced on the A-4F.

The latter feature may also be seen on Royal New Zealand Air Force A-4K aircraft, a variant based on the A-4F but fitted with features such as a drag 'chute and radio installation revised to suit local requirements. Kuwait operates a small force of A-4KU

and TA-4KU (trainer) aircraft.

The A-4L is a modified A-4C fitted with an uprated engine. Originally developed for the US Navy Reserve, it also forms the main strike component of the Royal Malaysian Air Force.

Instead of following the US Navy lead in switching from the A-4 to the larger A-7 Corsair II, the US Marine Corps decided in 1969 to stay with the McDonnell Douglas aircraft. The A-4M Skyhawk II was specially developed to meet USMC requirements and was a major step forward in Skyhawk performance. The J52-P-408 powerplant gives 20 per cent more thrust than was available in the A-4F. This engine also minimised the smoke trail left by previous versions of the aircraft.

A new pattern of upward-hinging one-piece canopy gives better vision downwards and ahead of the aircraft, while up to 9,100lb (4,100kg) of ordnance may be carried on five hardpoints. The 20mm cannons have a total of 400 round of ammunition—twice the amount carried by earlier aircraft. A drag 'chute was in-

stalled beneath the rear fuselage. The A-4N was similar, but built for Israel.

The A-4P and Q were supplied to the Argentinian Air Force and Navy respectively; the latter service plans to withdraw the Q version from the aircraft carrier *25 de Mayo* and replace them with Super Etendards.

Singapore's A-4S is an updated version of the early B model, and the two-seat TA-4S features separate canopies for the pupil and instructor.

Although the aircraft is out of production, its qualities continue to attract customers for the dwindling number of second-hand aircraft available for resale. Few Skyhawks are now left in storage at Davis-Monthan AFB. The most likely source of aircraft for future customers is the current Israeli fleet of some 200 E, F, H and N models, most of which have been drastically rebuilt in that country.

Israel Aircraft Industries offers a complete Skyhawk-improvement package at a unit price of around $1.5 million, and aircraft can either be modified in Israel or reworked

locally by means of modification kits. Offensive capability is improved by fitting extra hardpoints and substituting 30mm cannon for the normal 20mm weapons, while the installation of IAI's WDNS-141 nav-attack system and HUD increases weapon-delivery accuracy.

An RWR gives warning of impending attack and the modified aircraft is fitted with chaff and flare dispensers plus an extended jetpipe intended to absorb the effects of an SA-7 missile strike. This latter feature was prompted by the number of Skyhawks which required emergency "surgery" after taking SA-7 hits during the 1973 war. To improve performance from short strips, a braking

parachute, dual disk brakes, a steerable nosewheel and lift dumpers are available.

For many operators Skyhawk remains irreplaceable, and the aircraft's manoevrability and ability to absorb battle damage are legendary. In his biography Heinemann recalls how early in the project's history "... we figured that the plane would have slightly better speed than the Soviet MiG-15 fighter". During the Vietnam war Lt T. R. Swartz of the US Navy outmanoeuvred and shot down a MiG-17, and several Israeli aircrew have also claimed MiG "kills".

In both conflicts many other pilots returned from sorties in badly damaged aircraft which stubbornly refused to surrender to the effects of anti-aircraft fire. Anyone seriously contemplating taking the type to war in the 1980s would be advised to fit IAI-style jetpipe extensions in order to cope with the SA-7 threat, but otherwise the aircraft remains as effective today as it was a quarter of a century ago.

Top: Israeli A-4E Skyhawk, the version built before the addition of the fuselage avionics bulge.

Above: Early A-4C Skyhawk of VA-83 being passed by a Phantom on USS Enterprise during the Vietnam war. Note low drag bombs under wing.

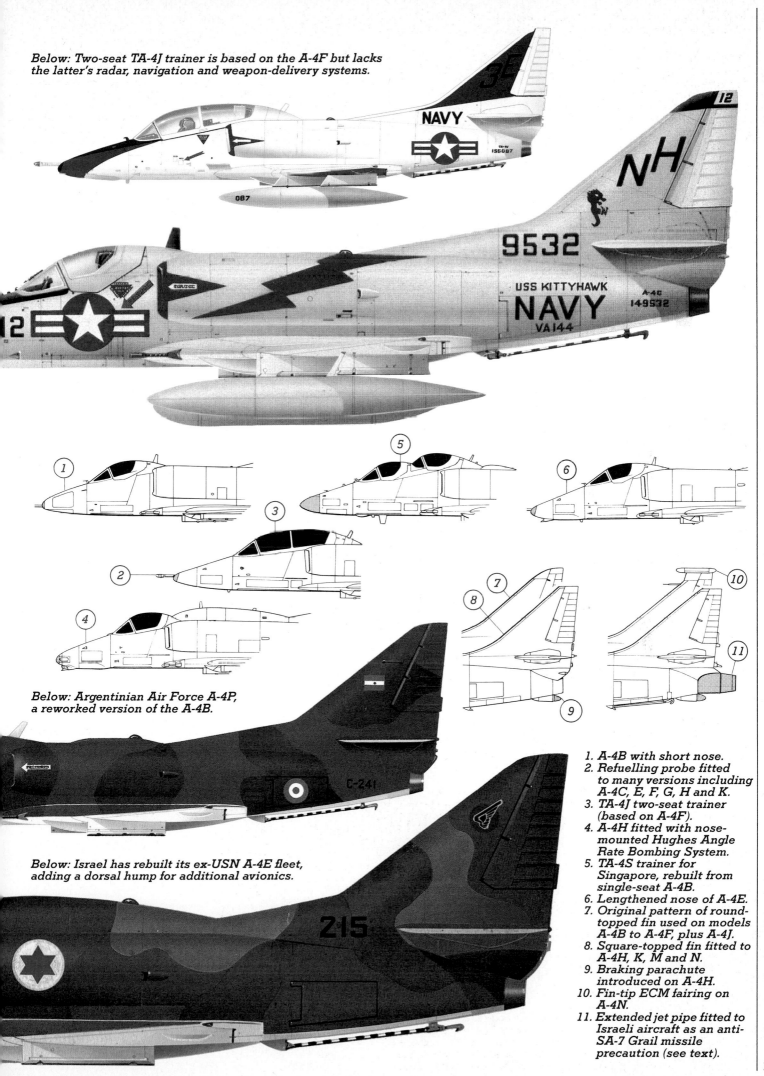

Below: Two-seat TA-4J trainer is based on the A-4F but lacks the latter's radar, navigation and weapon-delivery systems.

Below: Argentinian Air Force A-4P, a reworked version of the A-4B.

Below: Israel has rebuilt its ex-USN A-4E fleet, adding a dorsal hump for additional avionics.

1. A-4B with short nose.
2. Refuelling probe fitted to many versions including A-4C, E, F, G, H and K.
3. TA-4J two-seat trainer (based on A-4F).
4. A-4H fitted with nose-mounted Hughes Angle Rate Bombing System.
5. TA-4S trainer for Singapore, rebuilt from single-seat A-4B.
6. Lengthened nose of A-4E.
7. Original pattern of round-topped fin used on models A-4B to A-4F, plus A-4J.
8. Square-topped fin fitted to A-4H, K, M and N.
9. Braking parachute introduced on A-4H.
10. Fin-tip ECM fairing on A-4N.
11. Extended jet pipe fitted to Israeli aircraft as an anti-SA-7 Grail missile precaution (see text).

McDonnell Douglas F-4 Phantom II

Data for F-4E
Type: multi-role fighter.
Specifications: length, 63ft 0in (19.2m); span, 38ft ½in (11.77m); height, 16ft 5½in (5.02m); weight (maximum take-off), 61,795lb (28,030kg).
Max speed: High altitude, Sparrow AAMs only, 1,500mph (2,414km/h, Mach 2.27).
Service ceiling: 54,400ft (16.58km).
Range: ferry range, 1,978 miles (3,184km).
Armament: one 20mm M61A-1 gun under nose with 639 rounds, four Sparrow AAMs recessed under fuselage, and total external ordnance load up to 16,000lb (7,257kg) including virtually every tactical store, such as B-28,-43,-57 or -61 nuclear bombs, Falcon, Sidewinder, Amraam or Sky Flash AAMs, Bullpup, Walleye, Shrike, Standard ARM, Maverick, Paveway or Hobos ASMs, free-fall bombs and mines, cluster weapons, rocket pods, fire bombs, ECM pods, gun pods, spray tanks, fuel tanks, tow targets, camera (or other sensor) pods, Pave Knife pod or flares.
Powerplant: two 17,900lb (7,760kg) General Electric J79-GE-17A turbojets each rated at 11,810lb (5,370kg) dry thrust, 17,900lb (8,120kg) with afterburner.

For almost 20 years, from 1960 to 1980, the F-4 was the top fighter of the world, and the common standard against which other combat aircraft were judged. This is remarkable when it is considered that it was designed as a pure interceptor for use from aircraft carriers, was later used chiefly as an attack bomber and reconnaissance aircraft and was in any case exceptionally large for a fighter. Moreover, a run of stall/spin accidents in southeast Asia led at a late stage to the fitting of a slatted wing, while another combat deficiency—willingly accepted in 1960 when missiles were all the rage—was absence of an internal gun, which was not fitted in any version until the last to enter production, the F-4E.

The original production machine was the Navy F-4B, with Westinghouse APQ-72 radar in a large bulging nose radome, radar intercept officer seated behind and slightly above the pilot, blown flaps, and normal armament of four Sparrows, four Sidewinder close-range AAMs and a centre-line tank. In converting the F-4B for land use the USAF was at first restricted to changes considered essential, and these included complete dual controls (for a usual crew made up of two rated pilots), inertial navigation, more comprehensive air/ground bombing systems, and larger tyres and brakes. It was from this model

that the totally redesigned RF-4C dedicated recon platform was developed; by far the most advanced multi-sensor (but unarmed) aircraft of its day, it in turn was the basis of the RF-4B of the Marines. In 1964 the USAF was permitted to order a model tailored to its needs, and the resulting F-4D packaged largely new and improved navigation, weapon-aiming and defensive-electronic systems into the same airframe. For the first time the D model was more a bomber than a fighter, and a much more automated one than the manual F-4B.

Britain's Navy and RAF versions were a disappointment, despite their very powerful turbofan engines, but their high-lift features (such as a slotted tailplane and drooping ailerons) and also the versatile AWG-10 fire-control system were among many new features incorporated in the F-4J, the second-generation Navy/Marines model. The AWG-10 included the first pulse-doppler radar to go into service with an aircraft of the US Navy, coupled with a computer and many of the updated avionic items of the F-4D. Subsequently the J force were given the best EW/ECM systems of any Phantom, while 227 old F-4Bs were rebuilt as F-4Ns to almost the same standard. There were many sub-types and export models, but the most successful of all Phantoms had been the definitive Air Force model, the F-4E. This has a solid-state APQ-120 radar in a slim nose, M61 gun under the nose, slatted wing, extra rear-fuselage tank and more powerful engines, and overcomes all previous deficiencies.

Just how good the F-4E and its related variants—such as the Navy/Marines F-4S, an updated F-4J with a slightly different slatted wing—are depends upon the circumstance and the opposition. Compared with an F-16 or Mirage 2000 it looks cumber-

some and sluggish; even the F-18, which is its replacement in the Marine Corps and then the Navy, has demonstrated markedly smaller turning circle at all typical combat airspeeds, and the ability to pull much more g (such as just over 9) at much higher AOA, and to go on holding it at full power without losing speed or energy. The Phantom is a willing old warhorse but it comes from a much earlier generation, with less-efficient high lift systems, a high wing-loading and a power loading in the range 0.8 down to 0.55, while the modern dogfighter is considered lacking if the figure is not in excess of unity.

One of the Phantom's assets is its overall size and power, which enables it to carry heavy loads and fly long ranges. In the interdiction role its operational radius is 712 miles (1,145km)—not, of course, with a 16,000lb bomb-load—and this is exceeded only by very few aircraft such as the

Su-24 and F-111. It is large enough to carry a fully comprehensive kit of sensors for air/air and air/ground missions, EW suites to warn it of hostile radars, ECM pods to protect it, and excellent armour protection.

The F-4G Advanced Wild Weasel platform is at present the standard USAF defence suppression aircraft (116 in service) to assist tactical interdiction aircraft. Based on the F-4E, the G carries the McDonnell Douglas APR-38 radar homing and warning system, with the chief aerial (antenna) and other packages in a fin-cap pod and in a slim fairing that replaces the gun. Like previous Wild Weasel aircraft this version carries weapons, including Maverick, Standard ARM, Shrike and HARM (high-speed anti-radiation missile).

Above: F-4G Advanced Wild Weasel Phantom of the 35th TFW.

Above: Japan's Mitsubishi-built F-4EJs have a tail-warning radar and can carry the Japanese AAM-2 heat-seeking missile. They are being retrofitted with the APG-66 used in the F-16.

Below: RF-4E multi-sensor reconnaissance aircraft of the West German Luftwaffe. Other recon versions are the RF-4C and RF-4EJ.

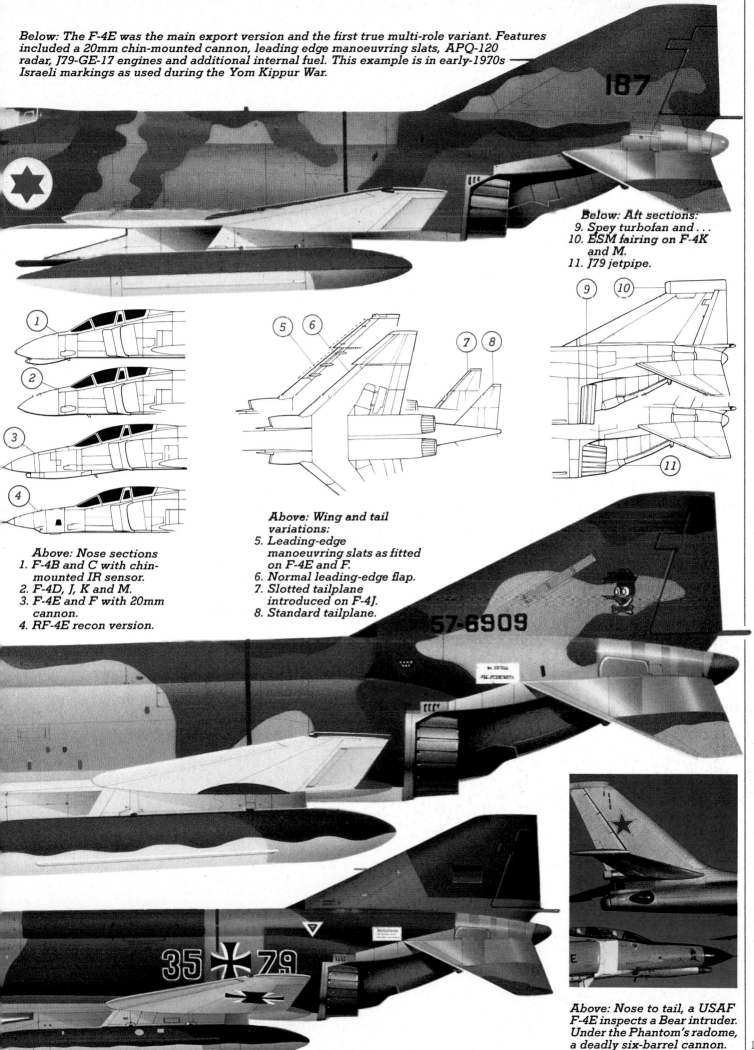

Below: The F-4E was the main export version and the first true multi-role variant. Features included a 20mm chin-mounted cannon, leading edge manoeuvring slats, APQ-120 radar, J79-GE-17 engines and additional internal fuel. This example is in early-1970s Israeli markings as used during the Yom Kippur War.

Below: Aft sections:
9. Spey turbofan and . . .
10. ESM fairing on F-4K and M.
11. J79 jetpipe.

Above: Nose sections
1. F-4B and C with chin-mounted IR sensor.
2. F-4D, J, K and M.
3. F-4E and F with 20mm cannon.
4. RF-4E recon version.

Above: Wing and tail variations:
5. Leading-edge manoeuvring slats as fitted on F-4E and F.
6. Normal leading-edge flap.
7. Slotted tailplane introduced on F-4J.
8. Standard tailplane.

Above: Nose to tail, a USAF F-4E inspects a Bear intruder. Under the Phantom's radome, a deadly six-barrel cannon.

McDonnell Douglas AV-8B/GR.Mk 5 Harrier II

Type: close-support and attack aircraft.

Specifications: length, 46ft 4in (14.12m); span, 30ft 4in (9.25m); height, 11ft 8in (3.56m); weight (maximum take-off), 29,750lb (13,494kg).

Max speed: 692mph (1,113km/h).

Service ceiling: 55,000ft (16.76km).

Range: ferry, with external tanks, 2,879 miles (4,633km).

Armament: two belly gun pods, either 25mm General Electric GAU-12/U or 30mm Aden; centreline pylon rated at 1,000lb (454kg) for tank, bombs or ECM pod, inboard wing pylons rated at 2,000lb (907kg), centre wing pylons at 1,000lb (454kg) and outer wing pylons at 630lb (286kg), four inner stations being plumbed for drop tanks and all being available for bombs, wide ranges of AAMs or ASMs, up to total disposable load limit (including fuel and injection water) of 7,000lb (3.4 tonnes) for vertical take-off or 17,000lb (7,711kg) for the standard rolling short take-off.

Powerplant: one Rolls-Royce Pegasus 11-21E, US designation F402-RR-404, vectored-thrust turbofan rated at 21,500lb (9,570kg) dry thrust.

When Britain foolishly pulled out of a joint Advanced Harrier development programme in 1975 the project was continued by McDonnell Aircraft as the AV-8B to meet the needs of the US Marine Corps. The resulting aircraft, which first flew in November 1978 in prototype form, is primarily what has critically been called "a bomb truck". In this role it is superb; it amply meets the needs of the US Marine Corps for a better STOVL (short take-off, vertical landing) close-support machine, and its payload/range capability is up by at least 100 per cent over the original Harrier, without any extra engine power. Part of the improvement stems from the large new graphite/epoxy wing, whose tankage boosts internal fuel by 50 per cent, part stems from the large plain flaps, part from the improved ventral strakes and retractable dam panel between the gun pods, and a very large part is due to the favourable induced airflow around the wing caused by the altered vectoring engine nozzles and their position relative to the wing.

This extremely useful machine enters Marine service in 1985, 336 being planned. By 1986 the first of 60 for the RAF, with designation Harrier GR.5, is also expected to be in use. The RAF had little choice, though on paper the British Harrier 5, with light-alloy wing of greater span, was a superior aircraft with higher speed and greater rate of turn in the close dogfight mode. The AV-8B does not meet all the RAF requirements, and even after local improvements to the wing/body junction is appreciably slower than the earlier Harriers. Even the addition of the BAe-developed Lerx (leading-edge root extension) does not bring air-combat agility up to the required level, but a little more may be done in this direction, and also to pull a little more thrust from the engine whilst reducing its running costs and improving component life. Certainly in the attack/recon role which has always been pre-eminent in the RAF Harrier squadrons the GR.5 will be roughly equivalent to two of the Brand X model.

The avionic standard of the GR.5 has yet to be settled, but will probably not include the Blue Fox radar of the Sea Harrier. All AV-8Bs do, however, have the latter's raised cockpit with all-round vision, as well as a laser inertial system, advanced HUD, completely redesigned cockpit displays and a refuelling probe.

Unquestionably the original design of Harrier was right for the ground-attack/recon mission, for which the smallest possible wing is desirable, but air combat calls for a large wing. So too does the STO technique, for at the start of Harrier design it was not fully appreciated that VTO would be very rare in practice, and that the normal operating mode would be a high-acceleration rolling take-off with the wing bearing about half the weight at the liftoff point, nozzles going to 50-55°.

Today the AV-8B and Harrier GR.5 form a solid basis for the next-generation V/STOL aircraft, and they have done so with virtually no attempt to increase the available engine power, which is central to the capability of such aircraft. Though there is a lingering feeling in the RAF that the aircraft is biased too much in favour of carrying heavy bomb loads, and insufficiently in favour

McDonnell Douglas F/A-18A Hornet

Data for F/A-18A

Type: carrier-based strike fighter.

Specifications: length, 56ft 0in (17.07m); span, excluding AAMs, 37ft 6in (11.43m); height, 15ft 3½in (4.66m); weight (maximum take-off), 47,000lb (21,319kg).

Max speed: clean, high altitude, about 1,188mph (1915km/h, Mach 1.8).

Service ceiling: 50,000ft (15.24km).

Range: attack radius 633 miles (1,019km); ferry range, 2,303 miles (3,706km).

Armament: one 20mm M61A-1 gun with 570 rounds; maximum external ordnance load of up to 17,000lb (7,710kg) on nine stations including wingtips for Sidewinder AAMs, outboard wing stations for wide range of stores including Sparrow or similar medium-range radar-guided AAMs, inboard wing stations for ASMs, tanks or other stores, and three fuselage stations for missiles, tanks, a FLIR pod, laser-spot tracker or other stores.

Powerplant: two General Electric F404-GE-400 augmented turbofans, described as "in 16,000lb (7,257kg) class".

detriment of the AV-8B and many other Navy programmes, the F/A-18A is a large programme totalling a planned 1,377 aircraft for the Navy and USMC to replace the F-4 and A-7.

After many problems and a major redesign of the wing and lateral control system the aircraft meets all numerical requirements, with only trivial exceptions, and in some respects is significantly superior. The original design was a navalized version of the Northrop YF-17, submitted in summer 1974 to meet a Navy VFAX requirement for a lightweight multi-mission fighter.

Finally the Navy contracted with McDonnell Douglas for the Hornet derived from the YF-17. Main differences were more powerful engines of greater bypass ratio, a wider fuselage with room for a very large main fuel tank along the centreline—which in fact lifts the Hornet rather out of the "lightweight" class—providing 4,400lb (2 tonnes) of extra fuel, a larger wing, a nose of increased volume to accommodate the Hughes APG-65

multi-mode radar (in some ways descended from the APG-63 of the F-15) with doppler beam sharpening to give enhanced resolution of the picture during the air/ground mapping mode.

After a great deal of professional test flying the Hornet eventually emerged as an outstanding aircraft to fly. The unswept wing has powerful variable camber, with a 30° drooping leading edge and a trailing edge made up of very large single-slotted flaps and powered ailerons all of which go to 45° on the landing approach. The flight control system is a quad-redundant fly-by-wire system, with two digital computers which among other things continuously programme the wing leading and trailing edges to the optimum setting (up or down) for each flight condition.

Roll control is by the differential tailplanes, supplemented under most conditions by the ailerons. The large wing-root extensions have axial slots which provide boundary layer control for stable flight at AOA up to 60°. Hotas (hands on throttle and stick) philosophy has been followed throughout, and most of the traditional cockpit instruments are replaced by three CRT displays and an information control panel.

The first Navy development squadron formed at NAS Lemoore in late 1980, Marine operational service started in late 1982, and the first Navy squadron in a carrier with the fleet is due in 1985. The original scheme of having an F-18A fighter version

| Funded at a high rate, to the

of high speed and high turn rate for dogfighting, the production machine will be pretty close to what the two customers wanted and a giant improvement in effectiveness over the AV-8A/GR.3. For the more distant future PCB (plenum-chamber burning) research has been picked up by Rolls-Royce where it was abandoned in 1964 and is expected to lead to augmented vectored Pegasus engines for supersonic derived designs, some of which may have a 'three-poster' jet configuration instead of four nozzles.

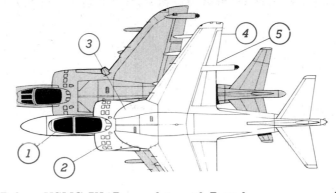

Left: AV-8A and AV-8B compared:
1. *Revised canopy giving better external view.*
2. *Redesigned air intake.*
3. *Leading-edge extensions.*
4. *New graphite/epoxy wing of greater span and area.*
5. *New location of undercarriage outrigger units.*

Below: USMC AV-8B complete with British-devised wing leading-edge root extensions.

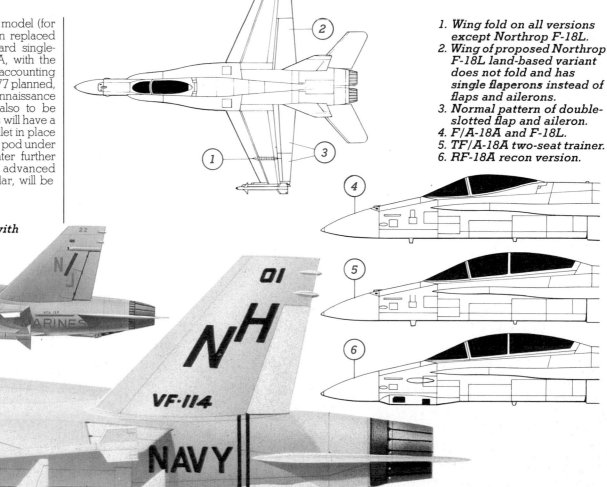

Above: YAV-8B prototype without LERXs.

and an A-18A attack model (for the Marines) has been replaced by a common standard single-seater called F/A-18A, with the TF/A-18A two-seater accounting for over 150 of the 1,377 planned, and the RF-18A reconnaissance version is expected also to be ordered by 1984. This will have a multi-sensor recon pallet in place of the gun, and a FLIR pod under the left inlet duct. Later further sensors, such as advanced synthetic-aperture radar, will be added.

Below: Two-seat TF/A-18A trainer with extended canopy.

1. *Wing fold on all versions except Northrop F-18L.*
2. *Wing of proposed Northrop F-18L land-based variant does not fold and has single flaperons instead of flaps and ailerons.*
3. *Normal pattern of double-slotted flap and aileron.*
4. *F/A-18A and F-18L.*
5. *TF/A-18A two-seat trainer.*
6. *RF-18A recon version.*

McDonnell Douglas F-15 Eagle

Data for F-15C
Type: single-seat all weather air superiority fighter.
Specifications: length, 63ft 9in (19.4m), span, 42ft 10in (13.1m), height, 18ft 6in (5.6m); weight (max T.O.), 68,000lb (30,840kg).
Max speed: Mach 2.5+.
Service ceiling: 63,000ft (19,200m).
Range (with in-flight refuelling): 2,500nm+ (4,600km+)
Armament: one 20mm M.61 cannon plus missiles on five hardpoints.
Powerplant: two Pratt & Whitney F100 turbofans each rated at 15,000lb (6,800kg) dry thrust, 25,000lb (11,350kg) with afterburner.

In many ways a lineal descendant of the P-51 Mustang, the F-15 Eagle is a true air-superiority fighter, the first to be developed in the United States since the F-86 Sabre. In the 1950s and 1960s, the concept of multi-role aircraft ruled supreme, but like the subsonic A-10, the F-15 saw a return to the concept of an aircraft optimised for a single role.

long-range target detection. In the early stages of an interception, radar data is usually presented on the Vertical Situation Display, a small head-down CRT mounted at the upper left-hand corner of the instrument panel, while the head-up display (HUD) is used at closer ranges. Radar controls are located on the throttles and control column so that the pilot can operate "head-up" while in combat, operating the radar without removing his hands from the controls. He may select to use the short or long-range missiles or the cannon using a switch on the throttles, and the radar will automatically adjust its scan pattern and present the appropriate information in the HUD.

Such is the speed of electronic

put this space to good use in a demonstration two-seat strike variant originally known as "Strike Eagle" but later referred to as the F-15E. Trials with this aircraft began in 1980 in the hope of attracting a USAF order. Strike Eagle can carry up to 16,000lb (7,300kg) of ordnance on five weapon stations.

Primary armament of the Eagle is the AIM-9L Sidewinder and larger AIM-7E Sparrow. Sidewinder has long been a combat-proven short-range weapon, but initial experience with earlier models of Sparrow during the Vietnam War were less succesful. When the missile worked, it proved effective, but many combat reports spoke of Sparrow rounds failing to guide. Further

become an "all-volunteer" air force, plus shortage of spares due to funding difficulties. By the end of 1979, the USAF reported that servicability was approaching 80 per cent, while a series of modifications to the engine and its control system had reduced the number of stall-stagnations.

Despite such engine problems, the F-15 remains the "Rolls-Royce" of air-superiority fighters. No other fighter in the East or West can match its combination of light wing loading, high thrust-to-weight ratio, long-range radar and radar-guided missiles. For the customer who needs the very best and whose defence budget can take the strain, the Eagle is likely to remain the ultimate fighter of the 1980s.

In only two respects did the design "come unstuck" by a move to advanced technology. The 25mm GAU-7/A Gatling-type gun firing caseless ammunition had to be abandoned for technical reasons and replaced by that old reliable standby the General Electric M61 20mm gun. The Pratt & Whitney F100 engine may also have pushed technology too far too soon. In terms of performance it is without a doubt the most advanced engine in the West and probably in the world, developing 25,000lb (11,350kg) of thrust in full afterburner for a total weight of only 3,085lb (1,400kg). Unfortunately, early engines proved liable to a phenomenon called "stall stagnation" whose effects have yet to be completely eliminated. The throttle cannot be operated with quite the freedom possible with earlier engines in certain parts of the flight envelope.

The pilot enjoys a good 360 degree view of the outside world through the large bubble canopy, while his Hughes APG-63 I/J-band radar handles the task of

development, that the APG-63 is already a candidate for upgrading. F-15C and D models have radars incorporating a programmable signal processor which will provide track-while-scan capability, high-resolution ground mapping, improved resistance to countermeasures and the ability to discriminate between individual aircraft in a tight formation when the latter is first detected at long range. Other improvements in the C and D models include the ability to carry an additional 2,000lb (900kg) of internal fuel plus Fastpack conformal fuel or sensor pallets on the fuselage sides.

There is sufficient space within the front fuselage and under the canopy to house a second crew member as the F-15B/D trainers demonstrate. McDonnell Douglas

development resulted in the improved and longer-ranged AIM-7F version used to arm the Eagle and other current-generation US fighters, while the monopulse-guided AIM-7M version will be even more resistant to ECM. Final proof of the combat effectiveness of the F-15/AIM-7F combination came in 1981 when the Israeli Air Force downed a Syrian MiG-25 Foxbat. Israeli aircraft have been used on several occasions against the Syrian Air Force, and flew "top cover" for the F-16s which damaged Iraq's Osirak nuclear reactor on June 7 1981.

Early operating experience with the USAF led to some adverse publicity due to low aircraft availability. Part of the problem was due to shortage of trained manpower in what had recently

Above: Single-seat F-15 Eagle in a climb. In point defence layout, it carries Sidewinders and Sparrows.

Above: The fuselage of the two-seat versions is the same length as that of the single-seat aircraft, but the canopy is modified to provide extra headroom for the second crewman.

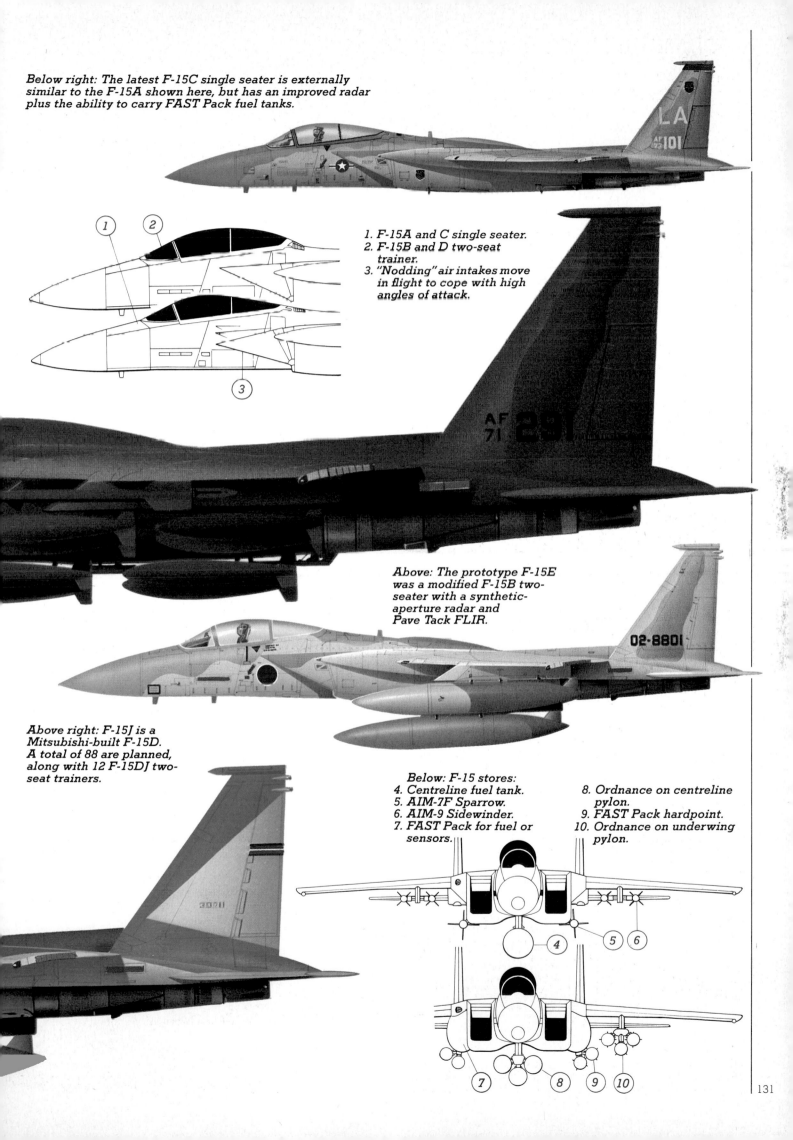

Below right: The latest F-15C single seater is externally similar to the F-15A shown here, but has an improved radar plus the ability to carry FAST Pack fuel tanks.

1. F-15A and C single seater.
2. F-15B and D two-seat trainer.
3. "Nodding" air intakes move in flight to cope with high angles of attack.

Above: The prototype F-15E was a modified F-15B two-seater with a synthetic-aperture radar and Pave Tack FLIR.

Above right: F-15J is a Mitsubishi-built F-15D. A total of 88 are planned, along with 12 F-15DJ two-seat trainers.

Below: F-15 stores:
4. Centreline fuel tank.
5. AIM-7F Sparrow.
6. AIM-9 Sidewinder.
7. FAST Pack for fuel or sensors.
8. Ordnance on centreline pylon.
9. FAST Pack hardpoint.
10. Ordnance on underwing pylon.

131

McDonnell Douglas KC-10A Extender

Type: strategic tanker and cargo aircraft.
Specifications: length, 181ft 7in (55.35m); span, 165ft 4½in (50.41m); height, 58ft 1in (17.7m); weight (maximum take-off), 590,000lb (267,620kg).
Max speed: 600mph (966km/h).
Service ceiling: 30,300ft (9,235m).
Range: 11,500 miles (18,500km).
Armament: None.
Powerplant: Three General Electric F103 (CF6-50C2) turbofans, each rated at 52,500lb (23,810kg) dry thrust.

Throughout the mid-1970s the US Air Force studied its requirement for an ATCA (advanced tanker/cargo aircraft) able to support the global deployment of TAC and other air units by carrying spares, crucial ground personnel and fuel for refuelling the unit aircraft en route. The DC-10-30CF was selected as the basis in late 1977, and the first KC-10A flew on 12 July 1980. At first procurement was on a trivial basis, typically two aircraft per fiscal year, but in early 1982, when six had been delivered and a further 10 were on order, the USAF was given permission to buy a further 44, to make up a force of 60. This is almost double the size of KC-10 force previously envisaged, and should have the not unimportant effect of enabling Douglas Aircraft to keep the type in production. Previously the absence of any DC-10 sale for 1983 delivery had made low-rate KC-10 manufacture too much of a financial burden, and the line was expected to close.

The KC-10A is an outstandingly capable aircraft. The forward end of the main cargo compartment can be equipped with seats for ground staff or other support personnel up to a maximum of almost 60. The main deck can carry 27 standard 463L cargo pallets, or 25 if access is needed from both sides of the compartment. Pallets and vehicles are loaded under computer control through a large side door (8ft 6in by 11ft 8in, 2.59 x 3.56m) on the left side well forward. Virtually all the fuel in the aircraft main fuel system, plus up to 117,829lb (53,446kg, 18,125 US gal) in seven flexible cells under the main floor can be transferred to receiver aircraft along the most advanced refuelling boom yet used. Developed by McDonnell Douglas, it has digital fly-by-wire control and can transfer fuel at up to 1,500 US gal (1,250 gal, 5,678 litres) per minute. A refuelling hosereel and drogue is also installed for probe-equipped aircraft, and the KC-10A Extender has a boom receptacle situated

Microturbo Microjet 200

Type: jet-powered basic trainer.
Specifications: length, 21ft 6in (6.55m); span, 24ft 10in (7.56m); height, 7ft 5in (2.3m); weight (max take-off), 2,530lb (1,150kg).
Max speed: 255kt (138km/hr).
Service ceiling: 30,000ft (9,100m).
Range: 540nm (1,000km).
Armament: none.
Powerplant: two Microturbo TRS 18 turbojets each rated at 290lb (132kg) dry thrust.

In a brave attempt to capture a share of the potential market for jet-powered ab initio trainers, Microturbo — a French manufacturer of small jet engines — decided to develop and test fly its own aircraft. The first prototype was built from wood and flew in 1980. Following flight trials, the company embarked on the definitive Microjet 200B design.

The design has many novel features. At first sight the aircraft appears to have no visible form of propulsion, since there are no obvious air inlets or jet pipe. To power the aircraft, Microturbo decided to use two of their TRS 18 single-shaft turbojets. The inlets for these are of flush NACA design, and take the form of rectangular cut-outs on the sides of the fuselage and just aft of the wing trailing edge. To the rear of these are the jetpipes, which protrude from either side of the fuselage.

Side-by-side seating was adopted, but in order to save space, the starboard seat is staggered some 22in (53cm) behind the port seat. According to Microturbo, this arrangement combines the best features of side-by-side and tandem layouts. There was no question of fitting cabin pressurisation in so small an aircraft, nor would this be needed for the type's likely duties, but an oxygen supply is provided and the cabin is both ventilated and heated. Ejection seats are not necessary in view of the aircraft's limited performance.

The wing is unswept and fitted with frise ailerons and single-slotted trailing edge flaps. The swept-back tailplane is of "V" configuration. Rarely used on military aircraft, this pattern of tail is satisfactory at low speeds.

The fuselage is of conventional light-alloy construction, but the wings and tailplane, together with their associated control surfaces are made from glass fibre/epoxy

Mikoyan MiG-15UTI Midget

Type: advanced trainer.
Specifications: length, 32ft 11in (10.04m); span, 33ft 1in (10.08m); height, 12ft 1in (3.70m); weight (maximum take-off), 11,900lb (5,400kg).
Max speed: 548kt (1,015km/hr).
Service ceiling: 47,980ft (14,600m).
Range: (with "slipper" tanks) 770nm (1,420km).
Armament: one 23mm cannon or 12.7mm machine-gun.
Powerplant: one Klimov VK-1 turbojet rated at 5,950lb (2,700kg) dry thrust.

"Extreme caution in aircraft handling" is hardly a phrase which a trainee pilot likes to see in the handling notes of his aircraft, but the warnings contained in the manual of Chinese-built versions of the MiG-15UTI advanced trainer make alarming reading, referring to "sudden and significant loss in stability... causing an uncontrollable condition of pitch-up" should the horizontal tail surfaces enter the region of downwash from the wing. When the student finally meets his new mount, it must come as a relief to find that the handling characteristics are less dangerous than the text-book suggests.

Originally devised as a conversion trainer for aircrew assigned to fly the MiG-15 fighter, the UTI later became the standard Warsaw Pact advanced trainer. For a large number of Third-World air arms, it still serves in this role. Despite the undoubted inexperience of some of the trainees assigned to it, the UTI seems effective for this purpose. Less than optimum flying characteristics are not an unacceptable quality for an advanced trainer to possess, particularly if the student has spent his previous career on more accommodating types.

The MiG-15 may have more than its fair share of vices, but it also has handling characteristics which remind a pilot of how the type was matched in its prime only by the F-86 Sabre. Radius of turn at medium speeds was small enough to give many a Sabre pilot an unpleasant experience, while stability at higher speeds remains good.

By Western standards the cockpit is an ergonomic slum, although some British aircraft of the 1940s and early 1950s were close rivals. Controls are scattered apparently at random around the cockpit, while the occupant of the rear seat has very limited headroom. Thanks to the barrel-shaped fuselage — a form dictated by the Klimov VK-1 centrifugal-flow turbojet (a derivative of the Rolls-Royce Nene) — the instructor has an acceptable forward view.

above the forward fuselage.

The basic refuelling mission can transfer 200,000lb (90.7 tonnes) of fuel to receiver aircraft at a distance of 2,200 miles (3,540km) from the KC-10's home base. Alternatively it can fly no less than 6,905 miles (11,112km) with a cargo load of 100,000lb (45.4 tonnes). In the Congressional hearings that preceded authorization of the programme it was pointed out that it would need 40 KC-135A tanker/cargo aircraft to refuel an F-4 fighter squadron deployed from the USA to Europe, plus almost as many carrying cargo, whereas the whole mission could be flown with the support of just 17 KC-10As, burning about 30 per cent as much fuel themselves. The KC-10A entered service in March 1981, and so far all have been placed under the authority of Strategic Air Command.

Below: The Advanced Aerial Refuelling Boom is located beneath the tail section of the KC-10A.

composites in order to save weight. Undercarriage and flap actuators are electrically powered.

Some attempt has been made to reproduce the control "feel" of a higher-performance aircraft, and the wing loading is deliberately high. As a result, says the company, combat pilots can carry out much of their training on the Microjet. Company studies suggest that the hourly flying costs will be literally a few per cent of the costs of a typical front-line aircraft.

Above: The prototype Microjet 200 was made of wood, but the 200B would be made from metal and composites.

Left: The MiG-15UTI is still the standard advanced trainer of the Polish Air Force.

Left: The paint finish on this Egyptian MiG—15UTI has long deteriorated from the pristine standard shown here.

Mikoyan MiG-17/Shenyang J-5 Fresco

Data for MiG-17F
Type: single-seat fighter.
Specifications: length 36ft 4in (11.09m); span, 31ft 7in (9.63m); height, 11ft (3.35m); weight (maximum take-off); 14,750lb (6,700kg).
Max speed: Mach 0.95.
Service ceiling: 54,500ft (16,600m).
Range: (with external fuel), 790nm (1,470km).
Armament: three Nudelmann-Richter NR-23 cannon plus up to 1,100lb (500kg) of ordnance on underwing hardpoints.
Powerplant: one Klimov VK-1 turbojet rated at 4,700lb (2,150kg) of dry thrust, 7,450lb (3,385kg) with afterburner.

At one time it was fashionable to decry the MiG-17 as a crude attempt to correct the worst deficiencies of the MiG-15, but pilots who have faced the type in combat speak of it with greater respect. It may be crudely engineered and not the easiest aircraft of its generation to fly, but its manoeuvrability and hard-hitting armament downed many a Mach 2 fighter in the skies over Vietnam and the Middle East.

One of the top-scoring Syrian pilots to emerge from the 1973 Yom Kippur War flew the Fresco. Starting with the mistaken assumption that his combat career against

Israeli Mirages and Phantoms was likely to be short, he boldly flew his MiG as closely as possible to his victims before opening fire with the aircraft's heavy cannons. Air aces from the Second or even First World War would doubtless have approved of such tactics, and the MiG-17 provided the performance required to carry them out in the 1970s.

The breaker's yard has probably claimed most if not all of the more specialised MiG-17s built, such as the missile-armed MiG-17PFU, but the basic day fighter and the uprated MiG-17F were widely exported. The latter was the most important variant, as it was fitted with an afterburning version of the Klimov VK-1 centrifugal turbojet.

Top speed in level flight is

Mach 0.95—a great improvement on the MiG-15's practical upper limit of Mach 0.86—and it can probably be dived supersonically. The aircraft has a reputation for ruggedness and is suitable for use from rough strips, qualities which led the Egyptian Air Force to use the type to good effect as a low-level fighter-bomber during the Yom Kippur War. Spinning characteristics are reported to be poor—an inheritance from the MiG-15. It is possible to recover from a spin, but, at lower altitudes, prompt ejection is said to be the

best tactic.

The Soviet Air Force never deployed a trainer version of the MiG-17, so pilots converting to the type were trained on the MiG-15UTI. Most export operators of the Fresco have followed this

Above: MiG-17F Fresco C of the Syrian air force.

Below: Hungarian Mig-17PF Fresco D.

scheme, but the standard advanced trainer of the Chinese Air Force is the J-5, a two-seat version of the J-5 (MiG-17). This is powered by a non-afterburning VK-1, and carries only a single 23mm cannon.

Mikoyan MiG-19/Shenyang J-6 Farmer

Data for Shenyang J-6
Specifications: Length, 41ft 4in (12.60m); span, 30ft 2in (9.20m); height, 12ft 9in (3.88m); weight, (maximum take-off), 19,200lb (8,700kg).
Max speed: Mach 1.3.
Service ceiling: 58,700ft (17,900).
Range: (combat radius with external tanks), 370nm (680km).
Armament: three 30mm NR-30 cannon plus two heat-seeking missiles or up to 2,200lb (1,000kg) of ordnance.
Powerplant: two Shenyang WP-6 turbojets each rated at 5,700lb (2,600kg) of dry thrust, 7,170lb (3,300kg) with afterburning.

Few examples of the Soviet-built Mikoyan MiG-19 remain in service, most having been replaced by the MiG-21 series, but the Chinese-built Shenyang J-6 copy seems assured of a long service career. The aircraft is still in production but at a rate well below the 30 per month capacity of the Shenyang plant. Most are probably export customers.

In Chinese service the aircraft is designated Type 6 Fighter, J-6 being a Western designation based on the Chinese original. Several versions have been developed. The basic J-6 interceptor is

based on the MiG-19S Farmer-C, the definitive day-fighter version created by the Mikoyan bureau. The Soviet original of this model flew in the mid-1950s, and many were supplied to China in knocked-down form for local assembly.

A licence agreement covering Chinese production was signed in 1958, but the first Chinese-built aircraft did not fly until December 1961. By the summer of the following year, J-6 interceptors were operational with the Chinese Air Force.

Chinese versions of the MiG-19SF and MiG-19PF followed during the 1960s. The former was basically an improved MiG-19S fitted with more powerful Tumanski R-9BF turbojets, but the PF has a longer fuselage and limited all-weather Scan Odd radar equipment. The main radar antenna was mounted in a small intake centrebody, while the antenna for ranging purposes was located in the upper inlet lip.

China did not directly copy the MiG-19PF, but seems to have developed its own variants. Not all have the lip-mounted ranging radar. Of those that do not, some have been fitted with a new pattern of inlet centrebody with a slim, sharply-pointed radome.

China operates a number of Farmers fitted with reconnaissance

cameras. One example flown to Taiwan by a defecting pilot was found on inspection to be a Soviet-built MiG-19—not the MiG-19R customised reconnaissance aircraft, but a Chinese conversion of a standard MiG-19 fighter. The Soviet Union did develop a two-seat MiG-19UTI trainer, but never adopted it for large-scale service. China has created its own equivalent—the FT-6 trainer.

Early in its career, the MiG-19 acquired a poor reputation in the West. Reports claimed that the engines were prone to flame-out at the slightest provocation and that the aircraft was difficult to fly with one engine out. Since then, widespread Pakistani and Egyptian use of the J-6 has shown the aircraft to be highly manoeuvrable and capable of outmanoeuvring many rivals, as well as outclimbing

Above: Alkali-armed MiG-19PM of the Polish Air Force.

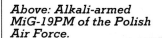

the MiG-21 or F-104. This performance is largely obtained by sheer brute force in the form of a thrust:weight ratio more typical of Mach 2 types, so endurance is correspondingly short.

The aircraft is well made, but requires frequent major overhaul—every 600 hours for the airframe and every 100 hours for the engines. Spares are reported to be both inexpensive and easy to obtain.

1. Polish-built LIM-6 ground-attack version with enlarged wing root housing twin-wheel main undercarriage and extra fuel.
2. Cannon-armed MiG-17PF Fresco D limited all-weather fighter.
3. Now obsolete, the MiG-17PFU Fresco E was armed with the primitive AA-1 Alkali missile.
4. Non-afterburning Fresco A.
5. MiG-17F Fresco C.
6. LIM-6 with braking parachute.

Below: The MiG-17F played a major role in North Vietnam's air defences during the mid-1960s.

Below: Syrian MiG-19SF with uprated R-9BF engines.

1. MiG-19PM with radar in intake lip and centrebody.
2. MiG-19SF with cannon in wing root and forward fuselage.
3. MiG-19UTI two-seat trainer.
4. Slim centrebody on some Shenyang J-6 fighters.

5. Reconnaissance version of Shenyang J-6.
6. Shenyang-built J-6 two-seat trainer. The cockpit transparencies are larger than those on the Soviet MiG-19UTI trainer, and there are no wing-root cannon.

Mikoyan MiG-21 Fishbed

Data for MiG-21MF
Type: multi-role fighter.
Dimensions: 51ft 9in (15.8m); span, 23ft 6in (7.2m); height, 13ft 6in (4.1m); weight (max. T.O.) 20,700lb (9,400kg).
Max speed: Mach 2.1
Service ceiling: 59,000ft (18,000m).
Range: (combat radius) 250nm: (460km).
Armament: one 23mm cannon plus up to 3,500lb of external ordnance on five hardpoints.
Powerplant: one Tumanski R-13 turbojet rated at 11,200lb (5,100kg) dry thrust, 14,500lb (9,800kg) with afterburner.

In developing the MiG-21, Soviet designers faced the same problem of producing a wing thin enough for supersonic flight using the production technology of the time as the French team which created the Mirage III. (The problem, and the merits of the French pure-delta solution, are explained in the Mirage III entry.) The Soviet solution, adopted after flight tests had shown its superiority over a conventional swept wing, was ingenious—a tailed delta layout combining the easy-to-fabricate delta wing with conventional Fowler rear-edge flaps and a conventional tailplane.

When deployed for take-off and landing, flaps increase wing lift, allowing the use of a wing small enough to operate in conjunction with a tailplane and elevators. These in turn eliminate the need for the lift-destroying trailing edge control surfaces associated with tailless deltas. When matched with a simple nose intake and the then-new Tumanski R-11 turbojet, this development settled the basic configuration of the MiG-21.

First version to enter operational service was the MiG-21F Fishbed C. This was a simple aircraft with good handling characteristics although somewhat lacking in thrust, being powered by the R-11, developing 12,600lb (5,750kg) with full afterburner. Internal fuel capacity was limited, giving short endurance—a problem which has been suffered by all types.

The limitations of such a basic fighter without radar and armed only by a single slow-firing 30mm NR-30 cannon and two AA-2 Atoll guided missiles soon became apparent. Early-production MiG-21PF Fishbed D aircraft introduced a degree of limited all-weather capability with its intake-mounted 100kW I-band R1L Spin Scan radar but was soon replaced on the production line by the definitive (Fishbed E?) model which introduced a new pattern of broad-chord vertical fin intended to improve directional stability at high speed.

Not all the differences could be deemed improvements. The revised canopy, intended to reduce drag, has a poorer rear view, while thrust-to-weight ratio had deteriorated.

The R1L Spin Scan radar was replaced by the more advanced R2L version in later production MiG-21PF aircraft, while the uprated R-11-F2S engine offered 8,600lb (3,900kg) of dry thrust and 13,700lb (6,200kg) with afterburning. Late-model PF aircraft also carried a twin-barrelled GSh-23 23mm cannon mounted in an

external pack, rather than the traditional NR-30 weapon. The new gun offered a much improved rate of fire of 3,000 rounds per minute.

Evolution of the basic design continued during the 1960s. The MiG-21PFS introduced a flap-blowing system intended to reduce landing speed, but this proved to be an interim model and was replaced by the MiG-21PFMA Fishbed J with an enlarged dorsal fairing for additional avionics and two additional wing pylons, allowing drop tanks as well as missiles to be carried.

The wing structure was also improved allowing the aircraft to stand up better to the stresses of low-level flight. These features gave the Fishbed a limited ground-attack capability with payloads of 2,500lb (1,000kg) or more. Another feature relevant to low-altitude operations was the provision for the first time of a zero-zero ejection seat. Late-series PMAs introduced an internally-mounted version of the GSh-23 gun. By now the R2L Spin Scan radar was somewhat dated, so it was replaced in the Fishbed J by the J-band (12-18 GHz) Jay Bird set with a useful range of around 12 miles but no look-down capability.

Thrust-to-weight ratio had sunk to an all-time low, so the succeeding MiG-21MF introduced the new Tumanski R-13 powerplant with 11,200lb (5,100kg) of dry thrust and 14,500lb (9,800kg) with afterburner. Unlike earlier variants, the MF could fly supersonically at low altitude, being red-lined at Mach 1.06. Next major model was the MiG-21SMT Fishbed K with an extended dorsal spine reported to house both avionics and fuel.

By this time, much of the fine handling qualities of the original aircraft had deteriorated. The MF carries some 2,600 litres of internal fuel, but the last 800 litres—30 per cent of the total—are virtually unusable due to a rearward drift of aircraft c.g. as fuel is used up. If the c.g. moves too far aft, all remains well at high speed, but a low-speed pitch-up prevents the aircraft

being brought in to land. Brochure figures for the MF seem unattainable in practice. Practical top speed of mid-1970s aircraft was reported to be Mach 1.9, while the useful ceiling of 46,000ft (14,000m) is well below the published 59,000ft (18,000m).

Ultimate development to date has been the MiG-21bis Fishbed N. This introduced yet another new engine—the Tumanski R-25, offering 16,500lb (7,500kg) of afterburning thrust—and an even deeper dorsal spine which may contain fuel as well as avionics. Indian plans to develop an indigenous radar for licence-built MiG-21bis aircraft suggests that if the Soviets have produced a better radar than Jay Bird, it is not being fitted to export aircraft. Although not in the American F-16 category, these third-generation Fishbeds would pose a significant threat to NATO strike aircraft and even to high-performance fighters, but it remains to be seen whether the handling qualities have been improved by the re-engining and development.

For the moment, the MiG-2bis can still be counted a good air-superiority fighter, but its ground-attack capability remains limited. Low-level turbulence poses severe strains on any airframe, and the Fishbed is not really built to withstand this kind of punishment. According to one report published in the mid-1970s, the fatigue life of the wing is limited to what would by Western standards count as only two years of operational flying.

Workmanship on early MiG-21s was poor, little better than that seen on the subsonic MiG-15 and MiG-17. Physical inspection of aircraft has shown gaps of several millimetres between badly fitting skin panels, making the finished aircraft look more like the product of blacksmith's shop than an aerospace factory, but the finish on second and third-generation Fishbeds is much better.

Like many Soviet types the MiG-21 requires minimal front-line servicing, making it suitable for air arms having limited servicing facilities. Such customers will have to return the aircraft to the Soviet Union for regular major overhauls, so only a portion of the "paper" front-line strength will be operational at any one time.

Below: MiG-21PMFA Fishbed-J of the North Vietnamese Air Force. This was the first model to be fitted with the deeper pattern of dorsal spine.

Above: MiG-21 with Jay Bird radar in intake centrebody.

Below: MiG-21bis Fishbed-N multi-role fighter.

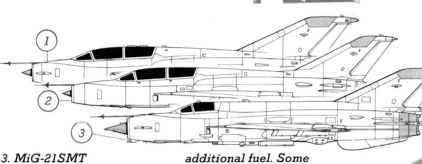

Left: MiG-21 trainers:
1. *MiG-21UM Mongol-B with broad-chord fin.*
2. *MiG-21U Mongol-A with MiG-21F-style narrow-chord and earlier R-11 turbojet.*

3. *MiG-21SMT Fishbed-K with extended dorsal spine housing*

additional fuel. Some aircraft carry wingtip ECM pods.

Left: The shallow spines and narrow chord fins indicate these East German MiGs to be of the MiG-21PF Fishbed-D type. Spin Scan A all-weather radar fitted.

Above: The Mig-21PFMA is the most advanced Fishbed version in Jugoslav service.

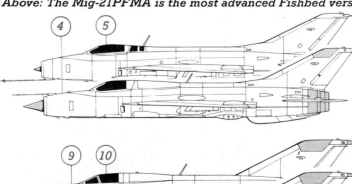

Above right: Early MiG-21 versions:
4. *MiG-21PF Fishbed-E introduced a broad-chord fin. The earlier Fishbed-D version of the PF was the first to have R1L radar in the intake centrebody, but retained the original narrow-chord fin.*
5. *MiG-21F Fishbed-C was the first major production version.*

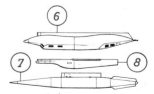

Above: Belly-mounted stores:
6. *Reconnaissance pack.*
7. *GSh-23 gun pack.*
8. *Ventral fuel tank.*
Left:
9. *MiG 21PFMA was the first multi-role version.*
10. *MiG-21PFM Fishbed-F was the first to have a sideways opening canopy and the R2L radar.*

Mikoyan MiG-23 Flogger

Data for MiG-23MF
Type: tactical fighter.
Specifications: length, 55ft 1in (16.8m); span, swept—26ft 9in (8.17m), unswept—46ft 9in (14.25m); height, 14ft 4in (4.35m); weight, (maximum take-off), 33,000lb (15,000kg).
Max speed: Mach 2.3.
Service ceiling: 61,000ft (18,600m).
Range: (tactical radius): 500-750 nm (900-1,200km).
Armament: one GSh-23 gun pack plus up to 6,600lb (3,000kg) of ordnance on five hardpoints.
Powerplant: one Tumanski R29B rated at up to 27,500lb (12,500kg) with afterburning.

The MiG-23 series seems to have been conceived in the early 1960s, perhaps in the form of a requirement for a USAF-style 'tactical fighter' capable of carrying substantial weapon loads on strike missions but still able to defend itself in air combat with the opposing fighters. The US forces already possessed such an aircraft in the form of the F-4 Phantom, but Soviet designers were forced to start with a clean sheet of paper. At least two designs were test flown in the mid-1960s. Flogger tested the concept of variable-geometry wings, while the experimental Faithless tailed delta explored the use of fuselage-mounted lift engines to reduce take-off and landing runs.

The swing-wing design was selected for service but subjected to an extensive re-design before large-scale production was initiated. Small numbers of Flogger-A fighters entered service in 1970 to prepare the way for the definitive version.

Flogger-A seems to have suffered from stability problems, perhaps associated with changes of trim with varying angles of sweepback. Evidence for this can be seen in the modifications applied to the basic design. The tail surfaces of the production aircraft were moved rearwards and the dorsal fin was increased in size. Despite this modification, fuselage length was decreased by a shortening of the jet pipe as a result of the installation of a more modern engine.

The wing planform was also modified, its new and extended leading edge creating a dog-tooth notch at the junction between the fixed and moveable sections. The contemporary swing-wing Sukhoi-17/20/22

series have a prominent wing fence in this location, but the Flogger dog-tooth probably serves a similar function in controlling the airflow at this critical location.

Flogger-A was probably powered by a single Lyulka AL-7 afterburning turbojet, but production aircraft use Tumanski twin-shaft engines of more modern design. Details of these are contradictory. According to 'Jane's All the World's Aircraft', these engines are turbojets, but some other sources claim these engines to be turbofans.

The available evidence suggests that three powerplants are used by the Flogger series. The engine carried by Soviet AF MiG-23s is reported to be the Tumanski R29B rated at up to 27,500lb (12,500kg) with afterburner. This engine is optimised for flight at Mach 2. The powerplant fitted to early production and export aircraft is thought to be the R27, rated at 15,400lb (7,000kg) dry thrust and 22,500lb (11,200kg) with full afterburner.

No designation has been reported for the engine fitted to the MiG-27 strike aircraft. Optimised for low-altitude use, this is thought to have a dry thrust of 17,600lb (8,000kg), rising to 25,300lb.

Main combat version of Flogger in current service is the MiG-23MF Flogger-B. This aircraft is the main Soviet Air Force type which NATO pilots would face in Central Front air-to-air combat. It lacks the manoeuvrability of the earlier MiG-23 and is thus much less of a 'pilot's aircraft', but its high thrust:weight ratio and clean lines give it a fast acceleration exceeded only by the latest generation of Western types.

In air-to-air combat this aircraft carries the new AA-7 Apex and AA-8 Aphid missiles plus a GSh-23 gun pack, while its High Lark radar offers some degree of look-down shoot-down performance. A laser ranger is mounted beneath the fuselage and just below the cockpit, while the antenna for a Doppler navigation radar is mounted in a dorsal location just aft of the radome.

For training purposes, the broadly similar MiG-23U Flogger-C is used. This has a second seat mounted above and behind the pupil's position and fitted with a retractable periscopic sight. The dorsal fairing is deepened and the lower rated R27 powerplant is used. The smaller nose radome indicates that the normal radar is replaced in this version by the Jay Bird set carried by third-generation MiG-21s.

This reduced equipment standard has also been adopted for

the Flogger-E export model, which also lacks other items of operational avionics such as the laser rangefinder and Doppler radar. Libya has used the aircraft in its border clash with Egypt in the late 1970s, Iraq used the type in air strikes during the protracted war against Iran, while several Syrian Floggers have fallen in combat against Israeli aircraft. Egyptian MiG-23s are no longer operational, some may remain in storage, but several were passed to the USAF and China. Several are maintained in flying condition in the USA.

Arrival of six Flogger-G intercepters in Finland during a good-will visit in the summer of 1978 seems to have surprised Western Intelligence. This version has a smaller pattern of dorsal fin, probably to improve manoeuvrability, and may rely on an active flight-control system to maintain stability.

The aircraft seen on this occasion and during a visit to France later the same year had deliberately been stripped of all operational equipment, leading some pundits to postulate that Flogger-G was a specialised version created in small numbers purely for aerobatic displays. This theory soon collapsed when operation versions were seen carrying improved sensors in an under-nose pod.

Left: Soviet Air Force MiG-23 Flogger-B taxies out to begin a training sortie. Note the intake blow-in doors.

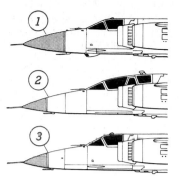

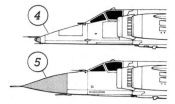

1. MiG-23MF Flogger-B.
2. MiG-23U Flogger-C trainer.
3. Flogger-E export version with Jay Bird radar.
4. MiG-23BN Flogger-F simplified strike version.
5. "Stripped" version of Flogger-C with enlarged nosewheel doors.

Above: Libyan-operated MiG-23 Flogger-E armed with Advanced Atoll AAMs but less complicated avionics.

Above: Unwilling to export the High Lark radar fitted to Soviet Air Force MiG-23MF interceptors, the Soviet Union installs the smaller and less powerful Jay Bird set in aircraft such as this Libyan Flogger-E.

Left: The avionics of this Soviet Air Force MiG-23MF Flogger-B are broadly comparable to those on the US F-4 Phantom, while the high acceleration of the Soviet fighter was one factor which influenced the design of the Northrop F-5G Tigershark.

Above: East Germany was the first member of the Warsaw Pact outside the Soviet Union to receive the MiG-23MF.

Left: MiG-23 Flogger-G all-weather fighters visiting Finland in 1978. Note the short dorsal fin on this version.

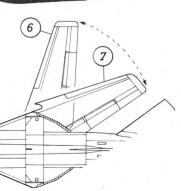

6. Wing at fully-forward (16°) position.
7. Maximum sweep angle is 72°. An intermediate position of 45° may also be selected.
8. Vertical fin on most current Flogger versions, including MiG-23MF, -23U and simplified export aircraft.
9. Revised fin first seen on Flogger-G.

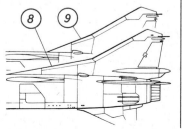

Mikoyan MiG-25 Foxbat

Data for Foxbat-A
Type: all weather interceptor; also available in reconnaissance versions.
Specifications: length, 78ft 2in (23.82m); span, 45ft 9in (13.95m); height, 20ft 0in (6.1m); weight (maximum take-off), approx. 80,000lb (36,500kg).
Max speed: Mach 2.8.
Service ceiling: 75,000ft (23,000m).
Range: (tactical radius) approx. 500nm (900km).
Armament: see text.
Powerplant: two Tumanski R-31 turbojets, each rated at 16,750lb (7,600kg) dry thrust, 24,500lb (11,100kg) with afterburner.

Faced with the need to develop an interceptor capable of dealing with the planned US B-70 bomber, the Mikoyan team was forced to tackle the problems of Mach 3 flight using the technology of the late 1950s and early 1960s. Western reactions to the resulting aircraft have run the gamut from "Soviet wonderplane" to "crude botch-up".

In practice, the MiG-25 Foxbat is an effective solution to a military requirement which should have been abandoned in the early 1960s once it became known that B-70 would never see service. The Soviet Air Force persisted with the project, deploying more than 300 Mach 3 interceptors by late 1970s.

Wherever possible, the Soviet design team opted for the simplest solution. Steel rather than titanium was used in the construction of the airframe, and observers who see this as evidence of the backwardness of Soviet aerospace technology overlook the fact that in its own abortive attempt to create a high-speed research aircraft the UK also opted to use steel.

The basic configuration of the aircraft broke no new ground, being similar to that adopted in the mid-1950s for the North American A-5 Vigilante and complete with the twin vertical tail surfaces originally planned for the US aircraft. This resemblance in no way implies a connection between the two projects, but illustrates how two widely separated design teams can come up with similar technical solutions. One problem the Mikoyan team solved in a bold manner was that of fuel-tank sealing. Both the US Mach 3 aircraft had problems with fuel-tank integrity, but the Soviet team simply welded their wing tanks into place in the structure.

None of the available range of Soviet aircraft powerplants was suitable for the new project, so the Tumanski bureau offered the massive R-31, a single-shaft engine of simple construction,

having only five compressor stages and a modest pressure ratio. At high speeds it acts more like a ramjet than a turbojet. Some sources even claim that the design was not new, but developed from the powerplant of a supersonic RPV. For Mach 3 operations Soviet engineers devised T-6 fuel, which features a low freezing point and high flash point.

For armament, early production Foxbats probably carried the AA-3 Anab or AA-5 Ash missile, but these were later replaced by the larger AA-6 Acrid. The nose radome of Foxbat contains the Fox Fire air-interception radar, a powerful 600kW equipment. This is used only in the final stages of flight, since Foxbat is virtually a manned missile, spending most of its flight time under strict ground control.

The Foxbat-A interceptor probably flew for the first time in 1964 and entered front-line service in 1970. A dedicated two-seat Foxbat-C training version became operational in 1973, development effort having apparently been concentrated on the Foxbat-B reconnaissance version rather than the trainer. A year later the Foxbat-D Elint version completed the quartet, but any hopes that the designers may have entertained of being allowed to rest on their laurels were shattered two years later when a Foxbat-A fell into Western hands, thanks to a defecting pilot.

According to some reports the Soviet Air Force hastily modified its existing Foxbat-A fleet to improve the now-compromised radar and fire-control system, but the most important effect of the

defection was probably the urgency injected into the development of a more advanced interceptor version.

Production of Foxbat-A declined during the next two years, most deliveries being made to export customers such as Algeria, Libya and Syria. At least one of the Syrian aircraft has been shot down, the first combat loss being reported on 29 July 1980, following an Israeli intrusion into Syrian airspace.

By the mid-1970s a modified Foxbat designated Ye-266M was setting time-to-altitude and absolute height records, using the new R-31M engine of 30,100lb (13,680kg) thrust, and this engine is likely to be the powerplant of the revised aircraft variously described as MiG-25MP, or "Foxhound". Foxbat-A had

virtually no look-down shoot-down ability, but the MP version has already been observed engaging low-flying target drones with the new AA-9 radar-guided missile.

Flying at 20,000ft (6,100m), one test aircraft despatched a target drone which was cruising at a height of only 200ft (60m). Intelligence sources are not yet agreed on whether such snap-down attacks can be carried out over all types of terrain, but it seems likely that three or four targets can be

engaged simultaneously by utilising the "fire-and-forget" performance resulting from the use of active-radar terminal seekers on the new AA-9 missile.

According to US reports, the new aircraft has a second seat for a weapon systems operator, but claims that the intake ramps have been redesigned to move in the horizontal plane should be treated with reserve.

Below: MiG-25 Foxbat-B camera and radar-equipped reconnaissance aircraft (right) and Foxbat-D radar-only version (left). Note the fairing on intake of -B.

Left: Despite its huge size, and heavy weight, the AA-6 Acrid air-to-air missile arming this MiG-25 cannot match the performance of the Hughes Phoenix, the most potent weapon carried by Western fighters. Radar and infra-red guided versions are available.

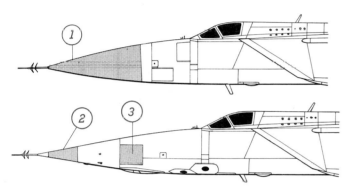

1. MiG-25 Foxbat-A with Fox Fire 600kW radar in nose radome.
2. MiG-25R Foxbat-B with Jay Bird radar in extreme nose.
3. Unidentified sideways-looking sensor (radar?) on MiG-25R.

Above: Libya was one of the first export customers for the basic MiG-25 interceptor and its AA-6 missile. Of no close-range combat value, the aircraft does have some stand-off kill capability.

Left: Following the unofficial "export" of a Foxbat-A to Japan, the aircraft was made available to selected Soviet client states. This AA-6 Acrid-armed interceptor is in Libyan markings.

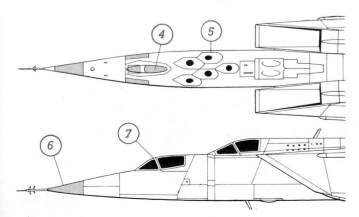

Above: Official designation of the Foxbat-A, seen here in Soviet PVO Strany markings, is reported to be MiG-25P.

4. Unidentified sensor fairing on MiG-25R. Some sources suggest that this may be a navigation radar.
5. Camera ports on MiG-25R.
6. Jay Bird radar fitted to MiG-25U Foxbat-C trainer.
7. Two cockpits on MiG-25U.

Right: Nozzles of the R-31 engines; maximum area of the variable nozzles is greater than that of the variable inlets.

Mikoyan MiG-23BN and MiG-27 Flogger

Data for Mig-23BM
Type: single-seat tactical attack aircraft.
Specifications: length, 59ft (18m); span (unswept), 46ft 10in (14.3m); span (fully-swept), 27ft 3in (8.3m); height, 14ft 4in (4.4m); weight (max T.O.), 44,300lb (20,100kg).
Max speed: Mach 2.3.
Service ceiling: 50,000ft (16,500m).
Range: 510nm (950km) hi-lo-hi tactical radius.
Armament: twin-barrel GSh-23L 23mm cannon plus up to 10,000lb (4,600kg) of ordnance on five hardpoints.
Powerplant: one Tumanski R-29B turbofan with 17,600lb (8,000kg) dry thrust, 23,350lb (11,500kg) with afterburner.

The first ground-attack Flogger to enter service was probably the MiG-23BF Flogger F which combined a revised front fuselage with the intakes, powerplant and jet nozzle of the standard interceptor. At first this was thought to be a special "export-only" variant, a ground-attack equivalent of the reduced standard Flogger E, but it is now known to be in Soviet service.

In producing the definitive MiG-27 Flogger D version, the Mikoyan design bureau optimised the aircraft for medium and low-altitude use, replacing the normal Tumanski R-29B turbofan powerplant with the more recent development, and fitting the redesigned fuselage with larger fixed-geometry inlets, a shorter and simplified afterburner, a new

gun installation and an under-carriage with wider low-pressure tyres. The latter feature dictated a local widening of the lower fuselage and the fitting of bulged undercarriage doors.

The new nose section and revised canopy give the pilot a better view of the terrain ahead to improve his chances of locating targets. It also houses the avionics required to conduct all-weather strikes against ground targets. This equipment includes a laser rangefinder (probably incorporating a marked-target seeker) mounted behind a window in the extreme tip of the nose, a simple terrain-avoidance radar and a Doppler navigation system. Small radomes mounted on the wing glove leading edges house avionics antennas, probably for

the command links of the AS-7 Kerry air-to-surface missile and "smart" bombs.

Flogger F has an internal fuel capacity of 1,260 Imperial gallons. Fuel capacity of the MiG-27 is understood to be similar, but the lower fuel consumption of the new engine—a result of the higher bypass ratio and lower thrust—

should provide an increase in range.

At low level, the MiG-23BM has a top speed of Mach 1.1, rising to Mach 2.3 at altitude. The higher bypass ratio of the MiG-27 powerplant also allows Mach 1.1 at sea level but cuts the top speed down to around Mach 1.5 and

Mikoyan MiG-29 Fulcrum (RAM-L)

Data: no reliable specifications available.

Reports of a new air-superiority fighter capable of replacing the MiG-21 have been current since the early 1970s, but details of the MiG-29 were slow to emerge. US intelligence sources report that a twin-engined design similar in configuration and performance to the Northrop F-18L has been under flight test since at least 1979.

Following its detection at the Ramenskoye flight test centre, the type has been dubbed RAM-L. Operational deployment is not expected until the mid-1980s.

Attempts to ascribe design bureaux for this new generation of Soviet aircraft have proved confusing. Most sources state that RAM-L is a Mikoyan design, but some claim it to be from the Sukhoi bureau.

Relatively little is known about the aircraft, despite the publication of one detailed "description" which even solemnly speculates on the number of combustion chambers in the cannular section of the powerplant. Maximum

take-off weight is probably in the 25,000lb (11,000kg) class, and the reported thrust to weight ratio of 1.2:1 suggests engines rated at roughly 12,000lb (5,500kg) each in full afterburner. Maximum speed is thought to be at least Mach

2—perhaps as high as Mach 2.3—at altitude, and Mach 1.2 at low level.

The radar may have a maximum search range of at least

Mil Mi-4 Hound

Type: utility and ASW helicopter.
Specifications: fuselage length, 55ft 1in (16.8m); height, 17ft 0in (5.18m); rotor diameter, 68ft 11in (21.0m); weight (maximum take-off), 17,200lb (7,800kg).
Max cruising speed: 113kt (210km/hr).
Range: 215nm (400km).
Max payload: 3,500lb (1,600kg).
Powerplant: one Shvetsov ASh-82V radial rated at 1,700hpp (1,270kW).

At least three versions of this piston-engined helicopter remain in Warsaw Pact service, although largely relegated to the support role. It has also been widely exported to the Third World.

The prototype flew in 1951 and production began in the following year. Approximately 3,500 aircraft were built during a production run which probably ended in 1969.

Basic version was the Hound-A transport capable of carrying

up to 14 fully-equipped troops. Variants of this basic transport were used as medevac aircraft and as assault helicopters. To suit the aircraft to the latter role, a flexible machine gun was fitted in an under-fuselage gondola, while pods for unguided rockets could be fitted on either side of the main cabin.

Although similar in configuration to the Sikorsky S-55, the Mi-4 is a significantly larger aircraft closer in size to the Sikorsky S-58. As an alternative to the troop load mentioned above, Hound can carry up to 3,500lb (1,600kg) of freight, a light vehicle such as the GAZ-69 four-wheeler or an anti-tank gun and crew.

For the ASW role, the Hound-B was developed as a replacement for the earlier Ka-15. This carried a search radar whose antenna was located in a chin radome of bulbous profile. This model also retained the ventral gondola. Sensors included a towed MAD detector, a dipping sonar

and externally carried sonobuoys.

For EW duties, the Hound-C was fielded in the late 1970s. This is easily recognisable by the array of Yagi antennas fitted to the fuselage, and is used as a mobile communications jammer.

For high-altitude operations, the Mi-4V was developed. Powered by a Ash-82FN engine—a derivative of the standard powerplant fitted with a cooling fan and two-stage supercharger, this became a standard production variant.

At least 1,000 Hounds were built in China at the Harbin aircraft plant. Not all were used by the military but some 400 remain in service in the transport and ASW roles with the People's Liberation Army and People's Navy under the designation Z-5. China also built at least one Hound powered by the Pratt & Whitney Canada PT6T-6 Turbo Twin Pac powerplant. This flew in 1979, but there are no reports of the revised aircraft entering production.

Above: Hound-B may be recognised by its chin-mounted search radar. It carries a towed MAD sensor and externally-mounted sonobuoys.

Right: This Czechoslovakian Hound-A lacks the ventral gondola used to carry a heavy machine gun on assault versions of the aircraft.

the combat ceiling to 45,000ft (14,000m).

Both aircraft have five external hardpoints capable of carrying munitions—one under each wing-root glove and three beneath the fuselage. Frontal Aviation Floggers have been seen operating with tandem ordnance racks on the glove hardpoints.

Each wing has a single hardpoint "plumbed" to carry 800-litre external tanks, but these do not swivel as the wing moves through a sweepback range of from 17 to 72 degrees. Tanks can only be carried in these locations if the wings are in the forward position. Aircraft manoeuvrability is reported to be severely restricted when the wings are fully forward, so these hardpoints cannot use fully be used to deliver ordnance.

Above: Most obvious recognition points of the MiG-27 Flogger are the new front fuselage with Jaguar-style nose and flat armoured sides, the simpler pattern of air intakes and the shorter and simpler afterburner.

20nm (37km), although some sources claim up to 60nm (111km). It will certainly offer "look-down" capability, overcoming a serious weakness of all current Soviet fighter radars.

A new pattern of IR-homing dogfight missile known to be under development is probably destined for this aircraft, but the current AA-8 Aphid will probably be used on early production aircraft. An internally mounted cannon is likely, probably in 30mm calibre.

Below: Artist's impression of the new MiG-29 (formerly RAM-L), with next-generation radar-guided missile.

Right: Mi-4 Hound-A transport helicopter, complete with starter trolley, awaits its crew.

Mil Mi-6 Hook and Mi-10 Harke

Type: heavy transport helicopter.
Specifications: fuselage length
108ft 10in (33.18m); height, 32ft
4in (9.86m); rotor diameter,
114ft 10in (35.0m); weight, (max.
take-off), 93,700lb (42,500kg).
Max cruising speed: 135kt
(250km/hr).
Range: (with 8-tonne payload)
330nm (620km).
Max payload: see text.
Powerplant: two Soloviev
D-25V turboshafts each rated at
5,500shp (4,100kW).

Soviet aircraft designers have
never been afraid of tackling large
aircraft. When the Mil bureau
developed the Mi-6 in the mid-
1950s, the specification called for
an aircraft capable of carrying
items of cargo which would be
flown to forward bases by the An-
12 Cub.

The resulting aircraft probably
flew for the first time early in 1957
and was unveiled later that year
during the celebrations for the
40th anniversary of the October
Revolution. Everything about the
Mi-6 was impressive by the standards of the late 1950s. Two
Soloviev turboshafts each having
around three times the output of
the Mi-4 powerplant drove a
massive five-bladed rotor almost

115ft (35m) in diameter via an R-7
gearbox weighing more than the
twin engines. The fuselage was
almost as wide as that of the An-
12 and could accommodate up
to 90 personnel and bulky items
of cargo weighing up to 26,500lb
(12,000kg).

Loads too large for the cabin
could be carried as under-fuselage slung payloads, while two
stub wings of 50ft 2in (15.3m)
span provide around 20 per cent
of the lift in normal cruising flight,
easing the strain on the rotor
assembly. If the aircraft is being
used at low airspeeds as a "flying
crane", these stub wings may be
removed. Maximum external payload is 17,600lb (8,000kg).

It might be expected that such
a large and specialised aircraft
would be built only in small numbers, but approximately 850 civil
and military examples were to be
delivered. Around half serve with
military operators, and small numbers have been exported to the
Third World. Soviet Hooks played
a major role in the war between
Ethiopia and Somalia in 1979. By
airlifting light tanks over mountainous terrain, a small number of
Mi-6s helped the Ethiopian army
to outflank Somali forces operating
in the disputed Ogaden region.

Most recent version to be reported is a dedicated airborne
command post. These operate in
the territory of the Soviet Union's
Warsaw Pact allies, and com-

municate with Moscow by radio.
From the basic Mi-6 design,
the Mil bureau also created the
Mi-10 and -10K "flying cranes"
which first flew in 1960 and
around 1964 respectively. These
use the same engine, transmission
and dynamic components as the
Mi-6 mated to a modified fuselage

of greatly-reduced depth, and a
four-point undercarriage. The Mi-
10 undercarriage legs are tall
enough to allow the aircraft to
straddle large payloads, but the

Mi-10K has shorter undercarriage
legs and a ventral gondola to
house the winch operator. The
latter model may be in civil service
only. Neither is fitted with stub
wings. Production of "flying cranes"
probably began in the early 1960s
and continues at a low rate. More
than 55 have been built.

Mil Mi-8 Hip and Mi-17

Type: transport helicopter.
Specifications: fuselage length,
59ft 7in (18.17m); height, 18ft 6in
(5.65m); rotor diameter,
69ft 10in (21.29m) weight (max
take-off) 26,500lb (12,000kg).
Max cruising speed: 122kt
(255kmhr).
Range: 240nm (445km).
Max payload (internal):
8,800lb (4,000kg).
Powerplants: two Isotov TV-2
117A turboshafts each rated
at 1,700shp (1,270kW).

Although similar is overall dimensions to the piston-engined Mi-4
Hound, the Mi-8 can carry up to
28 passengers in four-abreast
seating. Clamshell doors at the
rear of the cabin allow substantial
freight loads such as the BRDM
armoured car to be carried within
the cabin. It has been produced
in lavish quantities for civil and
military operators, and widely
exported to Eastern Europe and
the Third World. With more than
8,000 built, it is already the biggest
success story in Soviet helicopter
design.

The Hip-A prototpye which flew
in 1960 or thereabouts had a
four-bladed rotor driven by a
single 2,700shp Soloviev engine,
but was later fitted with the definitive five-bladed design, and was
re-designated Hip-B by NATO
Twin 1,700shp Isotov TV2-117A
turboshafts were introduced on
the second prototype, which flew
in 1962. When this version entered civil and military service in

the mid-1960s, it was designated
Hip-C.

Used primarily as an assault
transport, it was often armed,
carrying up to 128 57mm unguided rockets on a total of four
boom-mounted hardpoints on
the fuselage sides. Other weapons
have been reported, including
anti-tank missiles. Military Mi-8
helicopters can be distinguished
from their civil counterparts by
the presence of circular rather
than rectangular fuselage windows.
These allow the troops being
carried to fire their personal weapons against ground targets.

Even heavier armament is carried by the Hip-E, whose six
hard-points can handle up to 192

rockets in 32-round pods, plus
four AT-2 Swatter anti-tank missiles mounted above the fuselage
booms. A single 12.7mm machine
gun is fitted in a flexible mounting
in the aircraft nose. The AT-2
Swatter has never been exported
outside the Warsaw Pact, so the
Hip-E model substitutes the more
widely-available AT-3 Sagger wire-
guided anti-tank missile.

Hip-D is a specialised EW aircraft which carries equipment
canisters on its outer stores positions, plus an array of antennas
on the fuselage. Like the Mi-4
Hound-C, it is probably intended
for communications jamming.

Some operators report disap-

pointment with the Mi-8 performance. Finnish experience with
the type led the Ilmavoimat to
reject the type in the late 1970s
when a SAR helicopter was required. The aircraft had insufficient weight-lifting ability if one
engine failed, its critics claimed. In
practice however, political considerations outweighed technical
factors, and the service eventually
received a further five Hips.

More power is available from
the uprated 1,900shp (1,420kW)
Isotov TV3-117 powerplant first
installed on the Mi-14 Haze ASW
helicopter and now fitted to the
Mi-17. This is closely based on the
Mi-8, as can be recognised by the

Below: Most of the early production Mi-6 Hooks were delivered to the Soviet Army. After quarter of a century of service, these will now be replaced by Mi-26 Haloes.

Right: For most missions, the Mi-6 is fitted with stub wings, but these may be removed for flying-crane operations.

Left: Mi-8 prepares to land marines on a beach during a Warsaw Pact exercise. Up to 28 personnel may be carried in the cabin.

shorter engine nacelles above the fuselage and by the relocation of the tail rotor on the port side of the tail boom instead of the starboard location used on Hip. Both engines run at less than full rating, and should one fail, the output of the other is automatically raised to a contingency rating of 2,200shp (1,640kW).

Above: Egypt's Mi-8 fleet was originally supplied without weaponry as shown here, but some were later fitted with externally-mounted rocket pods.

Left: Able to carry two AT-2 Swatter anti-tank missiles and up to six rocket pods, Hip-E is currently the world's most heavily-armed helicopter.

Above: Note the chin-mounted radar on this Finnish Hip-C transport.

1. AT-2 Swatter missiles on Hip-E (Hip-F has AT-3 Sagger in same location).
2. Triple stores pylon on Hip-E and Hip-F.
3. Intake filter (optional fitting on some aircraft).
4. Equipment containers on Hip-D EW aircraft. These probably contain jamming and/or monitoring equipment.

145

Mil Mi-14 Haze

Type: land-based ASW helicopter.
Specifications: fuselage length, 60ft (18.3m); height, not yet known; rotor diameter, 69ft 10in (21.3m); weight (max take-off), 26,500lb (12,000kg).
Max cruising speed: probably 122kt (255km/hr).
Range: approx. 270nm (500km).
Armament: no details available.
Powerplant: two Isotov TV3-117 turboshafts each rated at 1,900shp (1,420kW).

In creating a new ASW helicopter for the Soviet navy, the Mil bureau adopted the basic and well-proven configuration of the Mi-8. The fuselage was remodelled to create a boat-hull bottom which, in conjunction with two sponsons on either side of the rear fuselage, gave a degree of amphibious capability. The landing gear is of tricycle configuration like that of the Mi-8, but all elements are retractable and probably have twin wheels.

The basic rotor and transmission of the Mi-8 were retained, but the tail rotor was moved from the starboard side of the tail boom to the port side. In place of the earlier Isotov TV2-117A turbo-shafts, the ASW aircraft uses the more powerful Isotov TV3-117.

Most conspicuous sensor system is a 360 degree search radar, whose antenna is located in a chin-mounted radome. The latter will come in for some rough treatment during landings on water, suggesting that the amphibious capability may be for emergency use rather than normal anti-submarine operations.

A towed MAD detector is normally stowed at the rear of the fuselage, but the only other evidence of sensor systems is a fitting beneath the tail boom which some observers interpret as a Doppler radar, others as an electrical battery whose bulk can no longer be accomodated in the redesigned engine housings. A small pod-like object mounted beneath the tail boom is probably a float intended to prevent the rotor blades from striking the water. Scrutiny of the available photographs shows no sign of racks for sonobuoys or weaponry, so it seems likely that these are carried in a small internal weapons bay.

Haze always operates from land bases. First export customer is Bulgaria, which is reported to have received 12 aircraft in 1979. Bulgaria normally is low on the Warsaw Pact priority list for receiving new weaponry, but in this case the potential usefulness to the Soviet navy of having another Mi-14 operator on the Black Sea seems to have resulted in the delivery of modern hardware.

A helicopter designated Mi-18 is known to be under development. This could be an amphibious transport aircraft based on the Mi-14.

Mil Mi-26 Halo

Type: heavy transport helicopter.
Specifications: Fuselage length, 110ft 8in (33.73m); height, 26ft 5in (8.05m); rotor diameter, 105ft (35m); weight (max take-off), 123,500lb (56,000kg).
Cruising speed: 137kt (255km/hr).
Range: 430nm (800km).
Max payload: 44,000lb (20,00kg).
Powerplants: two Lotarev D-136 turboshafts each rated at 11,400shp (8,500kW).

Development of this heavy transport helicopter began in the early 1970s and the type had its public debut at the 1981 Paris Air Show. At that time the aircraft was said by the Soviets to be ready for production, having undergone two years of flight trials. First flight may have been in early 1979, but there is evidence that an experimental aircraft may have been flying even earlier.

Halo is virtually a Vtol C-130, able to carry payloads of up to 44,000lb (20,000kg) in a freight hold some 10ft 6in (3.2m) wide and 50ft (15m) long, although it obviously cannot match the range of the US fixed-wing aircraft. Maximum external payload is some 1.5 times that carried by the Sikorsky CH-53E. The cabin is fitted with overhead cranes. Some observers think that it may be sealed and slightly pressurised for use in an NBC environment.

Two Lotarev D-136 turboshaft engines—derivatives of the D-36 three-shaft turbofan—drive a massive rotor 105ft (32m) in diameter via a VR-26 gearbox designed by the Mil team and similar in weight to the lower rated unit on the Mi-6.

The rotor has an unprecedented total of eight blades, a configuration thought impractical by most Western observers, but which allowed the designers to dispense with stub wings used on the earlier Mi-6. According to the Mil bureau's chief test pilot, the use of eight blades markedly reduces vibration levels in the cabin. The main rotor blades are built up from steel spars and glass-fibre skins, while the five-bladed tail rotor is made entirely from glass fibre. The main rotor hub is made from titanium in order to save weight.

Normal crew is five—pilot, co-pilot, flight engineer and navigator on the flight deck, plus a load master in the hold. Four "blister" windows on the flight deck give a degree of rearward and downward vision, and these are supplemented by a closed-circuit TV system capable of monitoring the undercarriage, and slung payload, and the terrain immediately below the aircraft.

Avionics systems include weather and Doppler radars, a moving-map display with a drift rate of 2-3 per cent/hr, and an automatic hover-control system capable of bringing the aircraft down to within 5ft of touchdown. The aircraft is fitted with an APU able to provide ground hydraulic and electrical power as well as air-conditioning. All ground checks on the electrical and hydraulic systems can be carried out under APU power before the main engines are started.

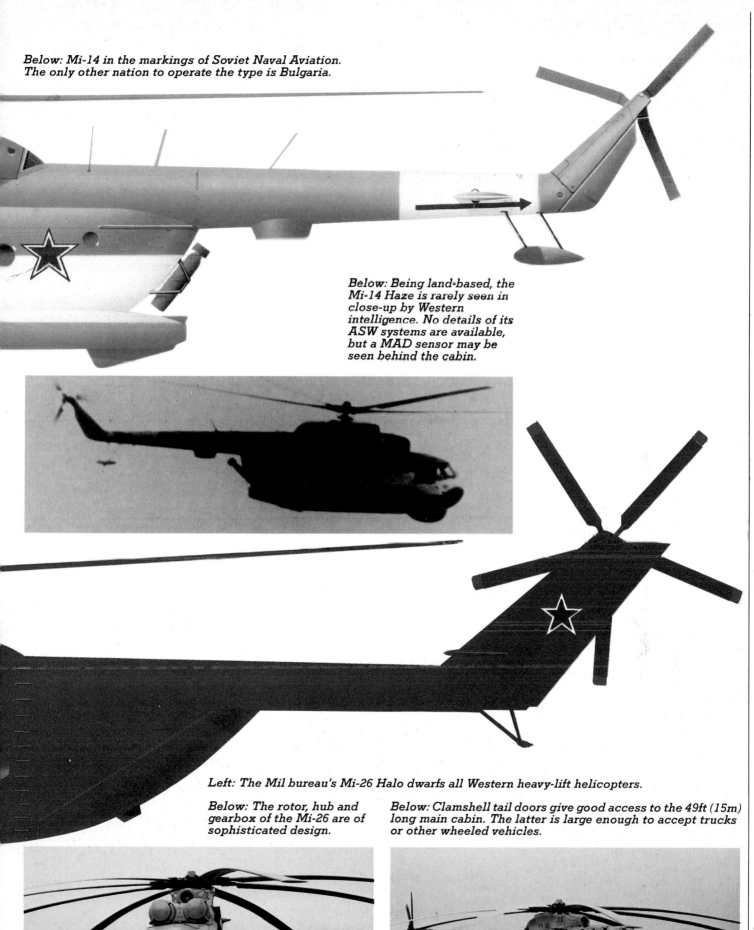

Below: Mi-14 in the markings of Soviet Naval Aviation. The only other nation to operate the type is Bulgaria.

Below: Being land-based, the Mi-14 Haze is rarely seen in close-up by Western intelligence. No details of its ASW systems are available, but a MAD sensor may be seen behind the cabin.

Left: The Mil bureau's Mi-26 Halo dwarfs all Western heavy-lift helicopters.

Below: The rotor, hub and gearbox of the Mi-26 are of sophisticated design.

Below: Clamshell tail doors give good access to the 49ft (15m) long main cabin. The latter is large enough to accept trucks or other wheeled vehicles.

Mil Mi-24 Hind

Data for Hind-A
Type: heavy assault helicopter
Specifications: length overall, 55ft 9in (170m); height, 14ft (4.25m); rotor diameter, 55ft 9in (17.0m);
weight (max take-off), 25,400lb (11,500kg).
Max cruising speed: not yet known).
Range: not yet known.
Armament: see text.
Powerplants: two Isotov TV3-117 turboshafts each rated at 1,900shp (1,420kW).

This massive helicopter has become something of a "bogeyman" to the NATO Allies, and for good reason. No other helicopter developed by the East or West is so effective in so many roles. In many cases it is easy to think of helicopters which out-perform the Mi-24 in any one area, but none offers the same range of capability.

Development of the Mi-24 began in 1968; the type was first reported by Western intelligence in 1972. Rather than develop a direct equivalent to US anti-tank helicopters such as the AH-1, the Soviet Union decided to create a multi-role aircraft capable of attacking tanks, providing fire-support, conducting reconnaissance missions, or evacuating casualties.

Early Hind-A and Hind-B models were armed assault helicopters capable of carrying eight fully-equipped troops in the main cabin as well as its regular crew of four—two pilots seated side by side, plus a gunner/navigator and an observer. Offensive weaponry consisted of a single 12.7mm nose-mounted machine gun, AT-2 Swatter anti-tank missiles carried on launch rails mounted at the tips of the auxiliary wings, plus various items of ordnance such as pods for unguided rockets carried on four underwing hardpoints.

The first version to be built was not initially detected by the West, and thus received the designation Hind-B despite entering service ahead of Hind-A. It was built only in modest numbers, some of which have since been delivered to export customers. Others were rebuilt to later standards. The Mi-24 was originally thought to use the engines, rotor and transmission of the Mi-8, but it soon became obvious, although based on the Mi-8 components, the rotor and transmission were modified for the new role. The main rotor of the Mi-24 is smaller than that of the Mi-8, for example.

Definitive assault version was the Hind-B, immediately recognisable by the anhedral of its stub wings and by the fact that the latter each have three hardpoints instead of the two on Hind-B. The tail rotor was also moved from the starboard side of the tail boom to the port.

Hind-C seems to have been another short-lived model. Generally similar to the Hind-A, it lacked the 12.7mm nose gun of the latter, as well as the wingtip missile rails and a chin-mounted fairing which form part of the missile guidance system.

In creating the anti-tank Hind-D version, the Mil bureau abandoned the side-by-side cockpit layout in favour of tandem seating. Instead of adopting a two-man tandem cockpit, the designers chose to fit two stepped tandem cockpits for the pilot (rear) and co-pilot/gunner (front). The cockpit area was given titanium armour, and similar protection was applied to vital components.

The nose-mounted machine gun was replaced by a four-barrelled rotary weapon of the same calibre mounted in a chin turret, behind which are located two smaller turrets containing sensors for target detection and missile tracking. An electro-optical sensor mounted on the inboard pylon of the port wing on earlier Hinds was moved to a new wingtip location.

Hind-E is further improved, and carries AT-6 Spiral laser-homing tube-launched missiles used instead of the earlier AT-2 Swatter. The structure is strengthened, with steel and titanium components replacing some assemblies previously made from aluminium alloy. The rotor blades are more damage-resistant, being glass-fibre skinned. New equipment associated with the AT-6 missile is mounted beneath the aircraft nose.

Soviet operations in Afghanistan gave Hind its "baptism of fire".

A number of aircraft were lost in the early stages due to pilot error at low altitudes. Soviet aircrew found themselves flying "nap-of-the-earth" sorties—tactics for which they had not been trained—and several Mi-24s were lost when the main rotor struck the tail boom during high-g manoeuvres. Reports also suggested that Hind was vulnerable to attack from the rear, and that guerillas had learned to hold their fire until the aircraft had passed, then aim for the rear of the cabin. Some Hinds were reported to be flying with locally-devised rear gun positions—part of the same process of experimenting with helicopter armament which the US forces had gone through during the Vietnam War. Hinds tended to work in pairs, often guided to their targets by elderly An-2 biplane operating in the FAC role by marking targets with smoke rockets.

Main disadvantages of the type for Central European use are its sheer size, which will make it a good target for anti-aircraft weapons in the class of the US DIVADS self-propelled gun or the British Rapier missile. On the ground, it will be difficult to conceal between sorties. The main rotor is of conventional design, and is not thought capable of negative or zero-g operations.

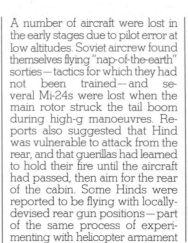

Left: Soviet FA Mil Mi-24s of the later Hind-E variant. Main features of this type are the "H"-shaped AT-6 Spiral tube-launched missile carriers on the outboard pylons and the offset missile guidance pod under the left side of the nose.

3. AT-2 Swatter on Hind-D.
4. Pods for 57mm unguided rockets (carried by all versions).
5. Optional intake shields.
6. Electro-optical sensor on most aircraft.
7. Hind-E is armed with tube-launched AT-6 Spiral anti-tank missiles.
8. Target illuminator for use with AT-6 Spiral missile. Fitted to Hind-E in place of item (9).
9. Command link antenna for AT-2 missile?
10. Electro-optical sight.

Left: Soviet Air Force Mil Mi-24 Hind-D firing a Swatter anti-tank missile. The later Hind-E variant carries four longer-range tube-launched AT-6 Spiral missiles.

Below:
1. *On Hind-A, the tail rotor was located on the starboard side of the tail boom.*
2. *On Hind-B and subsequent versions the rotor is on the port side.*

Above: Hind-D with undercarriage lowered and a warload of unguided rocket launchers and AT-2 Swatter radio/IR-guided missiles on the external pylons.

Below: With undercarriage raised, Hind-D presents a cleaner appearance. Despite built-in armour, the aircraft is vulnerable to AAA fire.

Right: Hind-A was the first full-scale production version of the Mi-24. Essentially an assault helicopter, it is heavily-armed with rockets, missiles and a nose gun. Early version had tail rotor on the right side of pylon.

11. *Early stub wing (Hind-B only)*
12. *Hind-C had no launch rails for anti-tank missiles.*
13. *Large canopy on Hind-A, -B and -C.*
14. *Command link antenna for AT-2 anti-tank missile.*
15. *12.7mm machine gun on Hind-A, -B and -C.*

149

Mitsubishi F-1 and T-2

Data for F-1
Type: close-support fighter.
Specifications: length 56ft 9in (17.31m); span, 25ft 10in (7.88m); height 14ft 4in (4.38m); weight (max take-off); 30,150lb (13,700kg).
Max speed: Mach 1.6.
Service ceiling: 50,000ft (15,250m).
Range: (hi-lo-hi tactical radius with two ASM-1 and external fuel), 300nm (556km).
Armament: one 20mm cannon plus two ASM-1 missiles or up to 6,000lb (2,700kg) of ordnance.
Powerplants: two licence-built Rolls-Royce/Turboméca Adour turbofans each rated at 4,710lb (2,140kg) dry thrust, 7,070lb (3,210kg) with afterburning

Less than a decade after receiving its first F-86 Sabres, the Japan Air Self-defence Force began design work on a supersonic replacement. The service also saw a requirement for an advanced trainer capable of bridging the gap between the aging Lockheed T-33 and the planned F-104 force,
so studies concentrated on a dual-role design which would initially serve as a supersonic trainer.

The programme was formally launched in 1965 under the designation T-X (Trainer Experimental), the specification calling for Mach 1.6 performance at altitude. The resulting Mitsubishi T-2 was Japan's first indigenous supersonic aircraft, so it was hardly surprising that costs escalated far beyond the original estimates. Despite this, construction work on two prototypes plus a static test aircraft continued during the late 1960s, and the first was flown on 20 July, 1971.

In general appearance the T-2 bears a close resemblance to the Sepecat Jaguar, and even uses the same Adour engines as the Anglo/French fighter. Ishikawajima Harima builds the Adour under licence under the designation TF40-IHI-80IA. Compared to Jaguar, the Japanese aircraft has a longer fuselage, shorter wing span and weighs around 13,900lb (6,300kg) — some 10 per cent less.

Following trials with the two prototypes and two development aircraft flown in 1972, Mitsubishi
was to build and deliver 81 T-2 trainers from 1975 onwards. Thirty-one are T-2 advanced trainers, while a further 48 are T-2A combat trainers armed with a 20mm JM-61 Vulcan cannon.

The remaining two examples were rebuilt as prototypes of the F-1 close air-support fighter. In the early 1970s it had seemed unlikely that the planned SF-X (Strike Fighter Experimental) would ever be built, since the end product would be not only too late to match the planned date of F-86 phase-out, but also too expensive for Japan's planned defence budget.

The first objection was overcome when examination of the F-86 fleet showed that sufficient airframe hours remained to allow the planned retirement to be delayed five years. The second was
overcome by the need to maintain employment in the Japanese aerospace industry following the cancellation in 1972 of the planned P-XL maritime-patrol aircraft.

Contracts for two fighter prototypes were signed in 1973, and two T-2 trainers were earmarked for conversion to fighters. Wherever possible, changes were kept to a minimum to reduce cost. Plans for a forward fuselage of revised profile were dropped in favour of the simple expedient of fairing over the rear cockpit and maintaining the same external shape. The space created by deleting the rear cockpit was used to house much of the new avionics, including a Ferranti INS, and computers for the radar warning and homing system and weapons release system. Like the T-2A combat trainer, the F-1 is

Myasischev M-4 Bison

Data for Bison-A
Type: strategic bomber and tanker.
Specifications: length, 154ft 10in (47.2m); span, 165ft 7in (50.48m); height, 46ft 0in (14.4m); weight (maximum take-off), 350,000lb (158,750kg).
Max speed: 485kt (900km/hr).
Service ceiling: 45,000ft (13,700m).
Range: (with 10-ton bombload) 4,300nm (8,000km).
Armament: up to 33,000lb (15,000kg) of bombs, tail gun position and two barbettes all with twin 23mm cannon.
Powerplant: four Soloviev D-15, each rated at 28,700lb (13,000kg) dry thrust.

More than 40 M-4 bombers remain in service with the Long Range Aviation arm of the Soviet
Air Force, supplementing the main strategic bomber force of more than 100 Tu-95 Bears. A further 30 have been converted into tanker aircraft by the addition of a fuselage-mounted hose and reel installation, and used to support this offensive force. Dedicated Bison-B and Bison-C maritime reconnaissance aircraft have mostly been withdrawn from active service.

As originally delivered, the aircraft did not meet its range requirements, but the fleet has been rebuilt with Soloviev D-15 engines in place of the original Mikulin AM-3 turbojets. The former engine is probably of turbofan type, and forerunner of the current generation of Soloviev civil powerplants.

Other modification incorporated under the rebuild programme include the deletion of two of the

original five gun barbettes (rear upper and rear lower), and the fitting of a flight refuelling probe. Despite the extensive nature of these modifications, the type apparently still carries the NATO reporting name "Bison-A" originally assigned to the basic aircraft.

Unlike the Tu-95 Bear, it has never been armed with stand-off air-to-surface missiles. The bicycle-configuration undercarriage gives insufficient ground clearance for a belly installation, but underwing carriage could have been adopted, since the
technique has been successfully applied to the smaller Tu-16.

There have been no reports of the M-4 being flown at low level. This may be due to the unsuitability of a long-span wing and wing-root engine locations for the higher stresses imposed at low altitude. A total of around 200 were originally built, and the survivors are likely to be scrapped during the 1980s as the new RAM-P variable-geometry bomber enters service, along with tanker versions of the Il-76 Candid or Il-86 Camber wide-bodied airliner.

armed with a single 20mm Vulcan cannon.

Both prototypes of what was then designated FS-T-2-Kai were flown in June 1975, then handed over in the following month to the Air Self-defence Force Proving Wing for trials. In March 1976, the first production order was placed for a batch of 18 F-1 aircraft. A year later the first was rolled out, and the first 18-aircraft squadron was fully equipped by March 1978. A total of 70 are due to be ordered. This should have been sufficient to equip three 18-aircraft squadrons, but with the switch to 25-strong squadrons in the JASDF, the planned fleet will only be sufficent for two units.

In addition to the cannon, the F-1 has four underwing hard points and one beneath the fuselage. Up to 6,000lb (2,700kg) of ordnance may be carried plus two heat-seeking missiles for air-to-air use. The latter weapons will probably be AIM-9 Sidewinders, but the indigenous AA-1 or AA-2 could presumably also be carried.

One of the major roles of the F-1 is maritime strike, and for this Mitsubishi has developed the ASM-1 anti-ship missile. Each F-2 can carry two of these 1,345lb (610kg) weapons, releasing them up to 10nm (18km) from the target. Deployment of this missile required the existing F-1 fire-control system to be replaced by the Mitsubishi Electric J/AWG-12.

The main criticism of the aircraft to emerge from initial operating experience is that the Mitsubishi Electric air-to-ground/air-to-air radar lacks range performance, but this unit is unlikely to be replaced in the near future.

Production of the T-2 trainer is due to end in 1983. As part of a research programme into CCV technology, Mitsubishi is fitting horizontal and vertical canard control surfaces, manoeuvring flaps and slats and a fly-by-wire control system to a single T-2 testbed. The contract for this work was placed by the Technical Research and Development Institute, and the modified aircraft is expected to fly before the end of 1982.

Below left: The T-2 trainer was Japan's first indigenous supersonic design, paving the way for the latter F-1 fighter derivative.

Below: The F-1 has a fairing in place of the rear canopy and a radar warning receiver antenna on top of the fin.

Above: M-4 Bison-C maritime reconnaissance bomber with extended nose section.

Below: Ceremonial parade at a Soviet Long Range Aviation base equipped with Bison-A strategic bombers.

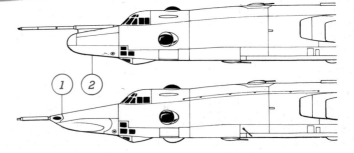

1. M-4 Bison-C with extended nose, "duckbill" radome and refuelling probe.
2. M-4 Bison-B was the first Soviet type to carry a refuelling probe. The type served as an interim-standard maritime-reconnaissance aircraft with Soviet Naval Aviation.

Nancheng Q-5

Type: light strike fighter.
Specifications: length, 50ft (15.25m); span, 33ft 5in (10.2m); height, 11ft (3.35m); weight (maximum take-off), 23,600lb (10,700kg).
Max speed: Mach 1.35.
Service ceiling: 52,500ft (16,000m).
Range: (hi-lo-hi tactical radius): 350nm (650km).
Armament: two 30mm NR-30 cannon plus up to 4,400lb (2,000kg) ordnance on external hardpoints and in the weapons bay.
Powerplants: two afterburning turbojets (see text).

First reports of this MiG-19 development appeared in the mid-1970s, and claimed that a radar-equipped "F-9" was under development as an all-weather interceptor. In practice, the new aircraft finally made its public debut not only with a "hard" nose totally lacking any form of radome but also with an internal weapons bay. The "interceptor" was in fact a strike fighter.

For a long time, China avoided releasing any photographs which might give a true indication of the exact configuration of the new aircraft, which was given the reporting name Fantan-A by NATO. Working from a single clandestine colour photograph, the staff of the journal *Flight International* prepared the first detailed analysis of the type in 1979. Far from being a revamped MiG-19, the Q-5 is a much more extensive modification of the original Soviet design that had

been suspected until that time.

The view—still held in some quarters—that the aft section of the Q-5 is basically that of the MiG-19 overlooks the fact that the new aircraft has a much greater mass ahead of the wing than the MiG-19. To compensate for this, the Chinese design team had to extend the rear fuselage in order to maintain the lateral balance of the aircraft. These changes obviously increased the weight of the aircraft, but the wing span and area were also increased by the simple expedient of adding a new inboard section with an unswept leading edge.

The main section of the wings are similar to those of the J-6, complete with original wing fences, but a significant amount of redesign was necessary. The undercarriage pivot points have been moved to a more inboard location, so that the wheels are partly stowed in the new wing root section, while the latter also houses the twin 30mm cannon.

A new vertical fin of greater height maintains directional stability,

although the shallow ventral strake on the J-6 has been replaced by two shorter strakes. Horizontal tail surfaces are based on those of the J-6. The twin powerplants are WP-6 turbojets similar to those of the J-6, but probably an uprated model based on the Soviet R-9B-811 engine and developing 5,730lb

(2,600kg) of dry thrust and 8,270lb (3,760kg) with afterburning. The logic behind the internal weapons bay is difficult to understand, since this can house only four 250kg bombs, and cuts into the fuselage volume available for internal fuel.

Using J-6 technology and components was obviously easier than

North American F-100 Super Sabre

Data for F-100D.
Type: fighter/bomber and weapons trainer.
Specifications: length, excluding boom, 49ft 6in (15.09m); span, 38ft 9in (11.81m); height, 15ft 0in (4.57m); weight (maximum take-off), 34,832lb (15.8t).
Max speed: 864 mph (1,390km/h, Mach 1.3).
Service ceiling: 50,000ft (15.24km).
Range: max combat radius with tanks, 530 miles (853km).
Armament: Four 20mm Pontiac M-39E cannon each with 200 rounds; maximum of 7,500lb (3.4t) of external stores carried on six underwing pylons including six 1,000lb (454kg) bombs, Bullpup or Maverick ASMs (or Paveway or Hobos "smart" weapons), rocket or gun pods, ECM payloads or tanks.
Powerplant: One 17,000lb (7,711kg) Pratt & Whitney J57-P-21A augmented turbojet.

Apart from the contemporary MiG-19 the F-100 was the world's first supersonic combat aircraft. Planned as an air-superiority

fighter it became more and more a bomber, and in the 940 of the D model the avionics were augmented by an autopilot and air/ground sighting, while the wing was redesigned to have outboard (instead of inboard) ailerons, flaps and six weapon stations. The result was an aircraft which, though still austerely equipped by later standards, proved so useful in Vietnam that three wings flew considerably more hours than all the P-51s of World War 2, serving in the low attack, high top cover and fast FAC roles, and proving adequate in all three.

From the start the F-100 was a "hot" aircraft, landings being called "controlled crashes", though the flaps of the D helped somewhat and overruns were reduced by

fitting sprung arrester hooks. As a basic fighter the F-100 did a fair job for no less than 25 years (1955-80), though by modern standards it is outclassed in thrust/weight ratio, aerodynamics and avionics. Popularly called The Hun, from "hundred", the basic ability to fly both air/air and air/ground missions kept it in front-line units even in the USAF until the end of the Vietnam war in 1973, and it served in the ANG for five further years.

Today a few are left in Taiwan, but the main user is Turkey where over 50 F-100Cs, Ds and two-seat Fs are in storage and a very

small number of Ds and Fs remain in the active inventory (they never had the reported 260). Here a combination of good airbases and fine weather have enabled this venerable tactical machine to survive far beyond its allotted span. Fatigue problems have been average, although the USAF funded a major wing modification programme following inflight failure during a Thunderbirds display in 1967. Today the few aircraft still flying are not subject to any particular limitations but are normally flown as weapon trainers and rarely pull more than 3g on attacks on surface targets.

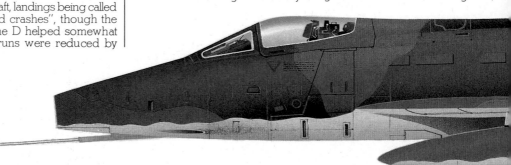

Left: A new nose, side intakes and an internal bomb bay were the main changes when China re-engineered the MiG-19 to make the Fantan.

3417

Above: First Q-5s to be seen by the West were in bare metal finish. The type's internal weapons bay makes little sense in conventional terms but might perhaps be intended to house a Chinese tactical nuclear weapon.

Below: Q-5 in the camouflage scheme used during the 1979 war between China and Vietnam. The type probably saw only limited action in what was largely an infantryman's war.

starting from scratch, but the amount of engineering required to create the Q-5 must not be under-estimated. The prototype probably flew around 1970 and several hundred are now in service. Reports of an interceptor version have never been confirmed, but the Chinese Navy is reported to operate Fantan as an air-defence fighter.

Despite Pakistani denials than an order has been placed for the Q-5, a batch of up to 50 aircraft are expected to enter service with the Pakistan Air Force some time in 1982 and to serve alongside the Shenyang J-6 (MiG-19).

Above: Denmark is phasing out its last Super Sabres. The finish used on these aircraft was not successful, giving a "worn" appearance.

Below: There is little prospect of Turkey being able to replace its Super Sabres in the near future. This F-100C is in the markings of 111 Sqn at Eskisehir.

O-41798

Below: Nose avionics bay open, side gun panels off, an F-100 Super Sabre undergoes routine maintenance.

Northrop F-5

Data for F-5E Tiger II
Type: light fighter/bomber.
Specifications: length, including probe, 48ft 2in (14.68m); span, excluding AAMs, 26ft 8in (8.13m); height, 13ft 4in (4.01m); weight (maximum take-off), 24,676lb (11,193kg).
Max speed: clean, high altitude, Mach 1.63 (about 1,080mph, 1,735km/h).
Service ceiling: 51,800ft (15.79km).
Range: max fuel, tanks dropped when empty, 1,779 miles (2,863km).
Armament: two 20mm Pontiac M-39A2 guns with 280 rounds each; maximum of up to 7,000lb (3,175kg) of external ordnance and tanks on one centreline and four underwing pylons, plus AAMs on wingtip rails, precision missiles including Maverick and laser-guided bombs of Paveway or Hobos series.
Powerplant: two 5,000lb (2,268kg) General Electric J85-GE-21 augmented turbojets.

The Northrop F-5 family is by a wide margin, even in terms of numbers of aircraft sold, quite apart from dollar value, by far the most successful military aircraft never bought by its own country, except for one evaluation squadron and a handful of other aircraft used for special combat training. It proved too limited in capability for the US Air Force, and the Navy turned down an attractive carrier version at the very start of the programme, yet the number sold to air forces all over the world exceeded 1,100 by 1972 with the F-5A, two-seat F-5B and variants, and continued with the F-5E and two-seat F-5F which have so far added a further 1,300-plus. With the brilliant F-5G Tigershark now on test the total for all F-5s is bound to reach the 3,000 mark within two or three years.

Like all the small Northrops with twin J85 engines, which as far as production machines are concerned began with the T-38A Talon supersonic trainer, the F-5 in all its versions is neat, attractive, and extremely pleasant and rewarding to fly. The original F-5A was a blend of good 1950s technology, with area rule for minimum transonic drag, afterburning engines, a low-mounted slab tailplane for good control and stability up to high AOA, the air-to-air punch of two rapid-fire guns and two of the new Sidewinder missiles, and not least the ability to carry a total warload (bombs, missiles, or other ordnance, plus external fuel) of no less than 6,000lb (2,710kg). As an option a camera nose could be fitted, resulting in the RF-5A, which retained its nose guns. This was sufficient for very wide acceptance by customers who would never have bought a British fighter that had not been adopted by the RAF. They found it ideally matched their own limited capabilities and budgets, and in countries enjoying prolonged clear weather the F-5A actually conferred considerable defensive and offensive capability. In the course of production in 1965-72 numerous improvements were brought in, including a flight-refuelling probe, assisted-takeoff rockets, arrester hook, birdproof windshield, improved gunsight, auxiliary engine inlets, more powerful engine, manoeuvre flaps, extensible nose gear and large drop tanks.

Back in 1954 Welko Gasich had started the Northrop baby fighter family in competition with the F-104, but lost. It is ironic that the Northrops were unquestionably much better fighters than any F-104, though they lacked power. Throughout the 1960s the F-104 sold in large numbers largely because of its adoption by Germany—in the low attack role, in which a small wing is a positive asset. What was obviously needed

Above: An Aggressor looking for trouble in his F-5E.

was a Northrop with a lot more "poke", but the next generation added only 16 per cent, up to 5,000lb compared with 4,300. The F-5E Tiger II was developed to meet a 1969 competition for a new export fighter, and apart from the slightly greater power introduced a wider fuselage housing more fuel, improved inlets extended forward with wing LEX (leading-edge extensions) alongside, APQ-153 small multi-mode radar, and many of the F-5A family improvements. Some recent F-5Es, such as those for Saudi Arabia, have an avionic fit that leaves little to be desired, including inertial navigation system, radar warning system and chaff/flare dispensers, as well as Maverick EO-guided missiles.

Though most F-5s have sold to minor air forces, where they provide limited day air-combat and ground-attack capability at appreciably lower cost than the Mirage, small numbers have been delivered to the US Air Force and Navy, where they have built up a remarkable reputation in the Aggressor role, as mounts for

fighter pilots in DACT (dissimilar air combat training). Their roles include pilot training, investigation of tactics, evaluation of visiting pilots flying their own aircraft, and assistance in development of new hardware such as the TCS (TV camera system) and similar long-range magnifying opto-electronic sensors. In many respects the F-5E resembles the MiG-21, and though it has appreciably less power it can dogfight as well as the Soviet fighter. Its all-round performance in close air combat has been astonishing, and though it ought in theory to be destroyed long before it could reach Sidewinder or gun distance from a larger fighter such as the F-14 or F-15 the DACT record shows that the kill ratio of these over the F-5 is considerably exceeded by the ratio of their costs.

During the period 1968-72 the F-5 was developed into the P.530 Cobra, from which stemmed the YF-17 and F/A-18A. Today the wheel has turned full circle, and the F/A-18A's F404 engine is being put into the F-5 to yield the F-5G Tigershark. Without question this will be a smash hit, giving the "more poke" that the family has always lacked. With greater internal fuel, a fine pulse-doppler radar matched to Sparrow or Sky Flash missiles, a modern cockpit with HUD and electronic displays, and flight performances typically increased by 30 to 50 per cent (and rate of climb and specific excess power are up by 100 per cent) the F-5G is a brilliant performer at a competitive price.

Northrop T-38 Talon

Type: advanced pilot trainer.
Specifications: length, 46ft 4½in (14.14m); span, 25ft 3in (7.7m); height, 12ft 10½in (3.92m); weight (maximum take-off), 11,820lb (5,361kg).
Max speed: 858mph (1,381km/h).
Service ceiling: 53,600ft (16.34km).
Range: normal (no external fuel), 860 miles (1,384km).
Armament: none.
Powerplant: two 3,850lb (1,746kg) General Electric J85-GE-5A augmented turbojets.

Though Welko Gasich's lightweight Fang fighter was never built, the N-156T trainer version did succeed in attracting USAF interest in late 1956, and eventually a prototype flew as the YT-38 on 10 April 1959. The aircraft was painted all white, and so was every T-38 that followed, a total of 1,189 being completed by 1972. The T-38A Talon entered service at Randolph AFB in March 1961, and ever since the type has flown intensively as the final stage of USAF undergraduate pilot training. The production total includes 46 in USAF markings which were supplied for the Luftwaffe pilot training programme in the United States, and also 24 supplied to NASA for use as Astronaut flight-readiness and pilot proficiency trainers.

From the outset the T-38 has set high standards for trouble-free operation, low maintenance burden, popularity with instructors and students and the lowest attrition rate of any known supersonic aircraft (typically one major accident per 100,000 hours). This quashed the notion, prevalent at the start, that the small-winged supersonic trainer would prove a dangerous mistake, feared by pupils. At all times its handling has proved exemplary, and a perfect introduction to the smooth and attractive qualities of the best operational machines. Features include a thin unswept wing, area-ruled fuselage of curving profile, low-mounted slab tailplane, inboard ailerons, rocket-assisted seats with the instructor seated appreciably higher (then a new idea), powered controls with two-axis stability augmentation, and extensive honeycomb structure especially in the wing.

The number of Talons supplied to the USAF was 1,139, in blocks up to T-38A-85-NO, though differences between blocks were small. The only big question mark concerned the validity of the supersonic trainer as a concept. Though most things about the T-38 are on a small scale, acquisition

1. F-5A with flight-refuelling probe.
2. F-5B two-seat trainer.
3. F-5E Tiger II fighter.
4. F-5G Tigershark with "bubble" canopy.
5. F-5G planform with large leading-edge extensions (LEXs).
6. F-5E planform.
7. Broad nose on F-5G and some F-5E.
8. F-5A planform with wingtip tank.

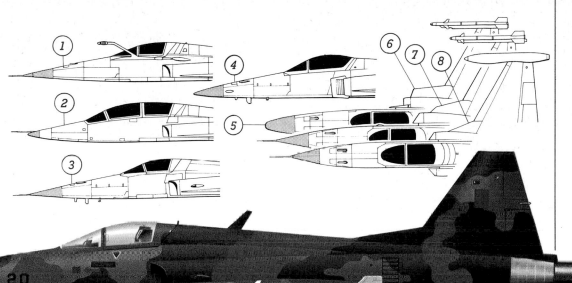

Right: Some F-5Es, including this Brazilian aircraft, have a fin extension housing an ADF antenna.

9. F-5A, complete with wingtip tanks.
10. The F-5E introduced larger air intakes to handle the airflow demands of uprated engines, plus a small radome nose.
11. The F-5G has even larger intakes with splitter plates to feed the single F404 turbofan, and an air inlet at the base of the fin.
12. F-5E two-seat trainer.
13. RF-5E recon version with nose-mounted sensors.

Below: F-5E of the US Navy's "Top Gun" training scheme at Miramar NAS, Calif. Note the nose radome which houses the Emerson APQ-159 radar.

and operating costs were still several times higher than for sub-sonic trainers, and the benefits have been closely questioned in the USAF. Fortunately the T-38 airframes have proved to have an excellent life and resistance to damage, but when they have to be replaced it is doubtful if the concept will be repeated.

The Anglo-French Jaguar was wisely kept for front-line use, and only the Japanese followed the T-38 philosophy with the T-2. In recent years a few surplus T-38s have been passed to Portugal and Turkey, while conversions include several with different avionics in the US Navy (including four rebuilt as DT-38 drone directors) and a single AT-38 evaluated as an attack trainer with special avionics for the air-to-ground mission.

Below: T-38A of 64th Fighter Weapons School. Although it is supersonic, students rarely exceed Mach 1.

Panavia Tornado

Data for Tornado IDS
Type: interdiction strike aircraft.
Dimensions: length, 54ft 10in (16.7m); span (unswept), 5ft 7in (13.9m); span (swept), 28ft 3in (8.6m); height, 18ft 8in (5.7m); weight (max. T.O.), 58,000lb (26,300kg +).
Max speed: Mach 2 +.
Service ceiling: 50,000ft + (15,000m +).
Range: 750nm (1,400km) typical tactical radius.
Armament: two 27mm cannon plus up to more than 16,000lb (7,250kg) of ordnance.
Powerplant: two Turbo-Union RB.199 turbofans with more than 8,000lb 93,600 kg) dry thrust, plus more than 15,000lb (6,800kg) with afterburner.

Probably no aircraft packs so much punch in so small an airframe as Panavia Tornado. Certainly none will play a greater part in ensuring NATO strike effectiveness in the 1980s and 1990s. The aircraft may be later in timescale than originally planned, and more expensive than anticipated, but it lacks nothing in effectiveness.

A high degree of automation has been provided. For most of the flight, Tornado may be automatically flown by its avionics. During a blind low-level mission, the autopilot and terrain-following radar may be engaged and the attack "flown" by the navigator in the rear cockpit. As the flight proceeds, he can adjust and update the navigation system, select, arm and release the ordnance without much assistance from the pilot who under such circumstances acts more as a monitor of the terrain-following radar and other aircraft systems than as a traditional "jet jockey". At least one Tornado navigator claims that given an automatic take-off and landing system, Tornado could make the term "single-seat aircraft" take on a new meaning.

The Command and Stability Augmentation System and triplex fly-by-wire controls effectively isolates the pilot from most of the effects of wing sweep position, ordnance load, altitude and speed. Describing the handling characteristics in an article published in *Flight International*, British Aero-space chief test pilot David Eagles wrote: "Stick forces are light to moderate—perhaps slightly lighter than American fashion—and harmony between pitch and roll is excellent... There is no trim change during sweeping and very little change in handling qualities... Ride comfort in low-level turbulence is unequaled by any aircraft flying".

Should the fly-by-wire system be put out of action, perhaps by electro-magnetic pulses from nuclear explosions, a mechanical back-up control system may be used to get the aircraft home.

One of the technical advances which made Tornado possible was the adoption of the Turbo-Union RB.199 three-spool turbofan. So compact is this engine compared with contemporary powerplants of similar thrust, that Panavia decided to break the old rule of "never put an all-new engine in an all-new airframe". Despite some problems with afterburner ignition in the mid-1970s, the gamble paid off and the esngine entered service with fewer problems than some contemporary US military turbofans have exhibited. On each flight the engines can be run at a "combat rating" for up to five minutes, giving extra thrust to cope with the demands of combat or take-off with heavy weapon loads.

Development of a low-level strike aircraft is something of a compromise. The lower the aircraft flies to the terrain, the more difficult it is to detect. Flying close to the ground does impose a risk of crashing, particularly in mountainous terrain under bad weather conditions. Optimum survivability is obtained at the point where the combined risk is lowest, and this sets the optimum cruise height for terrain-following flight. Tornado can cruise comfortably at up to Mach 0.92 at a height of 200ft (60m).

Texas Instruments developed both of the forward-looking radars carried by Tornado. One provides terrain-following data, while the other is used for ground mapping. Data from the radar and navigation systems are presented to the pilot via a head-up display (HUD), terrain-following head-down display and moving-map display, while the rear cockpit contains two TV displays and a combined radar and projected-map display. The latter shows a moving-map display at one of three scales with radar data superimposed, while the TV units can operate in modes displaying information such as a plan of the route to be flown, navigation data needed during the sortie and information required in order to fix the aircraft position or aim the weaponry.

During an attack, the crew will select the desired attack mode and weapons to be used, then carry out a final navigation update some 20 miles from the target, locating the target on the radar display and positioning a marker over it. If the target does not show up well, the marker may be placed on a suitable offset point.

Final run in and weapon release may be completely automatic. Targets of opportunity may also be engaged either visually or automatically. In the latter case, the navigator selects the type of attack to be flown and the weaponry to be used, then marks the target on the radar display.

The Air Defence Variant is a dedicated interceptor intended for service only with the Royal Air Force. Production of the first batch of 18 was authorised during 1981 and a total of 165 are planned. The first prototype flew on 27 October 1979 and production deliveries will be from 1983 onwards to replace the current Lightning and Phantom squadrons. Service designation will be Tornado F.2.

The aircraft is not intended to be an F-15 style "dogfighter" but an interceptor able to carry out autonomous patrols at long range. It can operate at ranges of 350nm (650km) or more from its home airfield under adverse weather conditions by day or night, and can operate out of runways shortened by enemy attack.

A 4ft 5in (1.36m) fuselage stretch allows four missiles to be carried beneath the fuselage in Phantom-style semi-flush mount-

Above: The extended radome and nose section and belly-mounted Sky Flash missiles identify this aircraft as a Tornado F.2 of the Royal Air Force.

ings, and provides space for an additional 200 Imperial gallons (909 litres) of internal fuel. The fixed glove section of the wing has a 68° sweep angle instead of the standard 60°, and a new elongated nose radome gives the aircraft a more fighter-like appearance.

Heart of the revised avionics suite is the Foxhunter pulse-Doppler radar developed by Marconi Avionics and Ferranti. This track-while-scan equipment is highly resistant to ECM, and offers good look-up and look-down capability. For target identification at long range, an LLTV system is carried. Prime long-range armament is the BAe Dynamics Sky Flash missile, backed up at shorter ranges by AIM-9L Sidewinder and a single 27mm Mauser cannon.

Left: Prototype of Tornado F.2, with Sky Flash missiles.

1. Interdictor/strike version.
2. Interceptor version (Air-Defence Variant) for UK.
3. Wing fully forward (25°).
4. Wing fully swept (68°).
5. Stores on swivelling pylons.
6. Sidewinder missile (ADV).
7. 27mm cannon (IDS has two).
8. Sky Flash missiles (ADV).
9. Extended wing-root glove.

Left: Daul-control training Tornado IDS of the West German Luftwaffe.

Left: Tornado IDS version with Ajax ECM pods (outboard) and drop tanks (inboard) on swivelling pylons, plus eight 1,000lb bombs on fuselage racks.

Above: The "TTE" marking on the tail fin of this RAF Tornado IDS indicates that the aircraft is assigned to the Tri-national Training Establishment.

Above left: Prototype P-02 in Marineflieger markings with Kormoran missiles.

Republic F-105 Thunderchief

Data for F-105D
Type: single-seat attack aircraft; F-105G, two-seat ECM and defence-suppression platform.
Specifications: length, 64ft 0in (19.51m); span, 34ft 11¼in (10.65m); height, 19ft. 8in (5.99m); weight (maximum take-off), 52,838lb (23,967kg).
Max speed: clean, high altitude, 1,387mph (2,232km/h).
Service ceiling: 52,000ft (15.85km).
Range: tactical radius, 900 miles (1,448km); ferry range, 2,200 miles (3,540m).
Armament: one 20mm M61A-1 gun with 1,029 rounds; internal weapon bay for various nuclear weapons or up to 8,000lb (3,630kg) of other stores (later usually locked shut and used to house additional 325 gal (1,477-lit) fuel tank), and maximum external load of 14,000lb (6,350kg) of very wide range of stores on five pylons including all normal bombs, rocket/gun pods, ECM payloads, air/surface missiles and Sidewinder AAMs.
Powerplant: one 26,500lb (12t) Pratt & Whitney J75-P-19W augmented turbojet (thrust is with max afterburner plus water injection).

One of the most well-liked aircraft in the USAF, the F-105 was known by such names as Ultra Hog, Thud and Lead Sled, none of these being used in a derogatory sense. Pilots posted to fly the F-105 in its early career, which began with the F-105B in May 1958, were disheartened to find it was really a bomber, and one so large that even a tall man found it difficult to leap up, grab the sharp-edged inverse-swept engine inlet and haul himself up to preflight the duct for absence of foreign bodies. Again, it was possible for most pilots to walk under the weapon bay door without stooping. In the air there was a great deal of new technology to assimilate, and it often took weeks to get used to the idea of opening the airbrakes when full speed was selected by going into afterburner. In fact the powerful airbrakes formed the secondary nozzle, as well as the complete tail of the very large fuselage, and selecting afterburner only opened them enough to obtain the required wide-open primary nozzle.

Only 71 of the B version were built, the main model (610 aircraft) being the F-105D with the General Electric FC-5 radar fire control system with Nasarr radar and integrated autopilot, doppler, toss-bomb computer, air-data computer, missile computer and advanced sight. The D was probably the first single-seater, and one of the first aircraft of any type, to offer air/air and air/ground semi-automated weapon delivery, including air search, contour mapping, terrain following and auto-tracking in blind conditions. With weapons internally attacks could be made at just over Mach 1, but in Vietnam heavy loads of conventional external stores were the rule. Republic also built 143 stretched F-105F dual two-seaters, 54 of which were rebuilt as F-105G Wild Weasel defence-suppression platforms with special avionics and Shrike and Standard ARM anti-radar missiles.

Surviving F-105Ds were often updated with Thunderstick II mission avionics in a saddleback spine giving further augmented all-weather attack capability. By the 1980s very few remained in ANG squadrons, and the last survivors were rather tired and certainly unable to reach Mach 2.

Rockwell International B-1B

Type: strategic bomber and ALCM carrier.
Specifications: length, including probe, 150ft 2½in (45.78m); span, 15° sweep, 136ft 8½in (41.67m), max (probably 60°) sweep, about 84ft (25.6m); height, 33ft 7¼in (10.24m); weight (maximum take-off), 477,954lb (216,800kg).

Max speed: 1,290km/h (800mph, Mach 1.2) above 25,000ft (7,620m).
Service ceiling: about 48,000ft (14.6km).
Range: 7,460 miles (12,000km).
Armament: conventional, 128Mk 82 bombs (84 internal) or 38 Mk84 (24 internal); nuclear, 20 B-28 (12 internal), 26 B-43 (12 internal), or 38 B-61 or B-83 (24 internal); missiles, 38 SRAM (24 internal) or 22 ALCM (8 internal).
Powerplant: four 30,000lb (13.6t) General Electric F101-GE-102 turbofans, each rated at 30,000lb (13,600kg) with afterburner.

By far the most costly aircraft of all time, if the whole programme proceeds to completion, the B-1B looks very much like the B-1 bomber cancelled by the Carter administration in June 1977. But, in fact much of the detail design, and most of the more crucial systems, are new. The whole viability of the new aircraft, which was resurrected in August 1980 as the LRCA (long-range combat aircraft), rests on its ability to penetrate defended airspace. With the original B-1 this capability had involved flight at Mach 2.2 at 50,000ft (15km) or Mach 0.85 at 200ft (90m). The B-1B is only half as fast, and recognises the undisputed fact that speed makes virtually no difference to bomber survivability. Instead it is almost invisible on hostile radars, and has much more advanced defensive avionics even than the unprecedented installation created for the B-1.

President Reagan announced his support for LRCA in October 1981, announcing a programme of 100 aircraft, costing at least $20 billion and possibly $28 billion, to provide a continued recallable global deterrent between the time when the ALCM-armed B-52G can no longer effectively penetrate (put at the mid-1980s by the DoD, though some sources, such as the CIA, are optimistically suggesting 1990) and the entry to service in numbers of the ATB "stealth bomber". The latter will not be before 1990.

Compared with the B-1 it has a stronger airframe and landing gear which enables it to use all its available fuel volume, including when necessary a tank in the 22ft (6.73m) forward weapon bay (while still leaving room for ALCMs). Maximum gross weight is increased by 82,121lb (37.25t), almost all of which is fuel; indeed thanks to a weight-reduction programme empty weight is virtually unchanged. A flight-refuelling receptacle is retained, but without it the range is sufficient for almost all likely missions, which was not the case with growth versions of the FB-111. Another important reason for the B-1B is its very large payload, the only possible weakness being the need to carry the ninth and subsequent ALCMs externally, adding drag.

Apart from its effect on range, drag is not a crucial problem. The engine inlets have been redesigned as simpler fixed snake ducts, each with two heated guide vanes, the outer wings will seldom need to go to full sweep (the full 67°30' will be available) and the large fixed glove fairings are redesigned to reduce drag. The main external weapon (or other load) pylons, numbering eight, are disposed along the underside of the fuselage; the maximum number of external ALCMs is 14, but the number of external Mk 82 bombs is 44. The internal bay is new, with three major compartments of which the front two can be opened into one for ALCMs by removing the bulkhead.

Almost all parts of structure and powerplant have been refined to reduce weight, improve life and reduce costs. The tailplanes, for example, which work with the spoilers to give roll control, will be composite and have the pivot moved aft for reduced hinge-moment with greater control autho-

Left: F-105G Wild Weasel defense-suppression fighter. Note the antenna-capped fairing on the fuselage side.

Left: After a spectacular combat career in the skies over North Vietnam, the F-105 now serves only with the US ANG.

Right: B-1 VG wing . . .
1. Full forward position (15° sweep).
2. Maximum sweep for high-speed dash (c. 67°).

Above: The antennas faired into the fuselage sides of this two-seater identify it as an F-105G Wild Weasel.

Below: The fourth B-1 prototype was tested against simulated air defences to prove the viability of the B-1B.

rity. But the most vital changes concern diminution of radar signature, using extensive RAM (radar-absorbent materials), changed structure (for example a tuned nose radome and a sloping metal bulkhead behind it) and such details as adding conductive flashing over the cockpit windscreens. As a result, while the radar cross-section of a typical B-52 is a horrific 100m², that for the B-1 was about 10m², that for the B-1B will be 1m². This small remaining signature is expected to be masked by the very large, powerful and computer-controlled ALQ-161 defensive avionic system, which in theory can instantly detect and counter every likely emission from (current) Soviet radars.

As this book went to press the decision had been taken to build the B-1B but neither Rockwell nor GE had received contracts. The present estimate is that, measured from the full go-ahead, the first aircraft (the rebuilt No 2 B-1) could fly in 21 months, the first production B-1B in 38 months, and the last of the 15-aircraft initial batch in 57 months. By the latter date, say March 1988 if go-ahead was authorised in June 1982, the IOC (initial operational capability) would just have been reached, though these first 15 are intended mainly for training. The 100th aircraft could be delivered 22 months later, say January 1990. But by this time the ability of the B-1B is expected to be questionable.

Above: Rockwell B-1A prototype. The definitive B-1B, will have revised inlets of simpler type, and no dorsal spine.

Rockwell International OV-10 Bronco

Data for OV-10A
Type: multi-role Co-In and utility aircraft.
Specifications: length, 41ft 7in (12.67m); span, 40ft 0in (12.19m); height, 15ft 2in (4.62m); weight (maximum take-off), 14,444lb (6,552kg); normal take-off, 9,908lb (4,494kg).
Max speed: clean at sea level, 281mph (452km/h).
Service ceiling: 24,000ft (7,315m).
Range: combat radius, max weapons, 228 miles (367km); ferry range, 1,382 miles (2,224km).
Armament: two 7.62mm M60C machine guns firing ahead; maximum of 3,600lb (1,633kg) of stores carried on centreline (max 1,200lb) and four pylons under short sponsons (600lb each)
Powerplant: two 715ehp Garrett T76-G-416/417 turboprops.

The OV-10 was the result of numerous studies in the 1960-62 era into aircraft designed for Co-In (counter-insurgency) missions, fighting either limited wars or police actions against terrorist groups. Objectives were a low-cost platform with versatile air/ground firepower, outstanding visibility, protection against close-range small-arms fire, the ability to use short unprepared airstrips and if possible the ability to fly casevac and local transport missions including air-dropping. The main impetus came from the US Marine Corps, which had previously been a partner in the Army OV-1 programme. The eventual requirement was called a LARA (light armed recon aircraft), and the industry competition was won by NAA's

NA-300 design in August 1964. The first of seven prototype YOV-10As for tri-service evaluation flew on 16 July 1965.

Outstandingly compact, eager and popular with its two-man crews, the OV-10A was nevertheless a limited programme with 114 delivered to the Marines and 157 to the USAF. Almost all were immediately taken to Vietnam where they were intensively used in the FAC role, the USAF additionally using them for urgent close support of friendly ground troops and the Marines as helicopter escorts and offensive reconnaissance vehicles. At all times the OV-10 operated at very low level, and proved easy to keep serviceable in austere environments and well able to survive typical infantry fire. Pilot and observer sit in ejection seats with an almost perfect view except to the rear, dual controls being optional, and the rear of the nacelle is a payload compartment for up to 3,200lb (1,452kg) of cargo, two litter (stretcher) casualties or five paratroops, though this space has seldom been used.

By far the main emphasis has been on exploiting the very good rate of roll and generally high agility in the lightly loaded condition by adding avionics for all-weather operation. Following extensive testing of two YOV-10D NOG (night observation gunship) conversions, the Marines received 17 OV-17D Broncos with a FLIR ventral turret, laser designator in a ball turret on an extended nose, ventral GE M97 20mm gun in a powered barbette and various other new features, with performance maintained or enhanced by fitting T76-420/421 engines of 1,040shp. These are

capable aircraft but major powers still seem uncertain of their value. Other air forces, however, have purchased appreciable numbers, recipients including Venezuela, Indonesia, Morocco, Thailand and the Philippines. West Germany uses a jet-boosted target-towing model.

Below: The twin-booms of the OV-10 were intended to allow good access to a small payload compartment in the rear fuselage. This would have allowed the aircraft to carry cargo or personnel. In practice, OV-10 is largely employed in the FAC role.

Rockwell International T-2 Buckeye

Data for T-2C
Type: basic pilot training with weapon options.
Specifications: length, 38ft 3½in (11.67m); span, including tanks, 38ft 1½in (11.62m); height, 14ft 9½in (4.51m); weight (maximum take-off), 13,191lb (5,983kg).
Max speed: 530mph (853km/h).
Service ceiling: 40,400ft (12,315m).
Range: 1,047 miles (1,685km).
Armament: normally provided with two underwing hardpoints for total of 640lb (290kg) of practice bombs, rockets, gun pods, target-towing gear or other stores. No inbuilt armament.
Powerplant: two 2,950lb (1,338kg) General Electric J85-GE-4 turbojets.

The Buckeye was designed in the mid-1950s to meet the need of the US Navy for a low-cost jet basic

trainer. The original T2J-1, which was redesignated T-2A in 1962, served from 1958 until 1973 but the twin-engined T-2B and C models have already had a much longer life and will not be replaced by a new type until the second half of the 1980s. On most counts the T-2 has been an outstanding success, and particularly since the switch to twin GE engines (replacing the single obsolescent Westinghouse J34) the flight performance has been exceptionally good for a basic trainer of 1950s design.

Features include tandem cockpits, with the instructor seated 10in (0.25m) higher than the pupil to give him a good forward view (today common but a new feature in the 1950s), rocket-powered ejection seats, a large internal fuel capacity in the mid fuselage supplemented by tanks on the wingtips, hydraulically boosted ailerons and elevators, a sting-type arrester

hook and a long upwards-hinged clamshell canopy. The Naval Air Training Command does not normally use the T-2 for weapons training (that is the task of the TA-4J) but it has been found useful by such export customers as Venezuela and Morocco, whose T-2Ds do not have carrier equipment. The Greek Air Force received 40 of an updated model designated T-2E which has major attack capability, with six wing pylons carrying a load of up to 3,500lb (1,587kg) of weapons or other stores, and various forms of protection against light ground fire. The T-2E thus figures in the Greek order of battle as a combat type, 363 Squadron at Kalamata having a secondary combat role, unlike 362 which is a pure training unit. These aircraft retain their arrester hook, though of course are not equipped for carrier operation as are the Navy T-2C force.

Right: T-2E Buckeyes of the Greek Air Force Training Command. Before being assigned to fly the type, students must pass through 125hrs of basic training on the Cessna T-37B. In wartime, Greek T-2Es would serve in the light strike role.

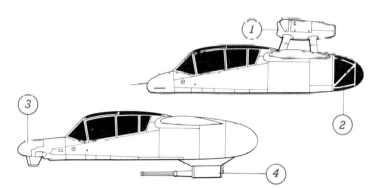

Below: The basic OV-10A—seen here in a low infra-red finish—is a simple and uncluttered aircraft suitable for FAC and light-attack duties.

1. Overwing pod with single General Electric J85-GE-4 turbojet booster as fitted to West German OV-10(Z) target tugs.
2. Glazed rear section for OV-10B(Z) target winch operator.
3. Steerable chin turret with Texas Instruments AAS 37 FLIR sensor and laser target designator (on OV-10D only).
4. Turret mounted General Electric M197 cannon on OV-10D. This three-barrelled 20mm Gatling-type weapon can be directed by the chin-mounted sensor systems.

Above: Bronco plays a major anti-guerrilla role with the Royal Thai Air Force. Additional aircraft were purchased during the late 1970s to make up for the attrition inevitable during counter-insurgency warfare.

Left: T-2E Buckeye of 350 Sqn Hellenic Air Force. Similar to the T-2C trainer, these aircraft have six underwing hard points and fuel tanks able to withstand small arms fire.

Saab-Scania 2105 Jakt/Attack/Spaning (JAS 39)

Data: no reliable specifications available.

Swedish industry is currently working on a lightweight multirole fighter designated Jakt/Attack/Spaning (Fighter/Attack/Reconnaissance), and normally referred to by the initials 'JAS'. This is a lightweight canard design for service from around 1990 onwards as a replacement for the Viggen family. Project definition began in 1980. Goal of the project is to create an aircraft about half the weight and 60 per cent of the cost of Viggen.

The work is being handled by a consortium known as Industri Gruppen JAS, and is the first time that the Swedish aerospace industry has jointly tendered for a complete aircraft system. Formed in 1980, this group consists of Saab-Scania, Volvo Flygmotor, L.M. Ericsson, SRA Communications and FFV. Saab-Scania will be prime contractor on the airframe, and has signed techno-logy-exchange agreements with MBB and Rockwell.

Some 30 per cent by weight of the structure will be made from composite materials, so that the aircraft maximum take-off weight can be kept down to around eight tonnes, allowing the use of a single General Electric F404J turbofan engine which will be assembled in Sweden by Volvo Flygmotor. This engine is an uprated and improved version of the US powerplant rated at 18,000lb (8,180kg) with full after-burner, plus increased redundancy and other modifications intended to improve safety.

L.M. Ericsson is developing the target-acquisition avionics including a multi-mode pulse-Doppler radar and a pod-mounted FLIR system. The new radar will be software-controlled and occupy some 60 per cent of the space required for the current PS-46/A set carried by Viggen.

Cockpit displays are the respon-sibility of SRA Communications. The pilot will have a wide-angle holographic HUD and three CRT displays. Few conventional instruments will be fitted, mainly as back-ups for the CRTs. The left-hand CRT will display data normally presented on instruments, the central unit will be used to display a moving map image, while the right-hand unit will present data from radar and FLIR sensors.

Data processing will be handled by means of an SDS80 on-board computer, development of which has been under way by L.M. Ericsson, SRA and DataSaab since 1978.

Air-to-air missiles will be carried on wingtip launch rails and ordnance loads of bombs, missiles or reconnaissance equipment on underwing hardpoints. An internal cannon will be fitted, almost certainly a version of the 30mm Oerlikon KCA carried by Viggen.

Like earlier Swedish military aircraft, JAS will be operated by an air force made up largely of conscripts. Front-line servicing must therefore be simple, and FFV is responsible for the planning and design of central workshop maintenance.

Saab-Scania 105

Data for Sk60

Type: basic trainer and light attack aircraft.
Specifications: Length, 34ft 5in (10.5m); span, 31ft 2in (9.5m); height, 8ft 10in (2.7m); weight (maximum take-off), 8,930lb (4,050kg).
Max speed: 388kt (720km/hr).
Service ceiling: 39,400ft (12,000m).
Range: 960nm (1,780km).
Armament: up to 1,500lb (700kg) of ordnance.
Powerplants: two Turboméca Aubisque turbofans each rated at 1,640lb (740kg) dry thrust.

Like many Swedish aircraft, this trainer and light strike design was never to see its qualities matched by export sales. It was originally developed as a private venture, flying for the first time in 1963. In 1964 it was adopted as a trainer by the Swedish Air Force, which gave it the service designation Sk60A.

At first the type was used as a simple trainer, its side-by-side seating offering both pupil and instructor a good forward view. Most were later given gunsights and underwing hardpoints to allow weapons training. These aircraft were later supplemented by the Sk60B attack/weapons training version and the Sk60C reconnaissance variant which carried a camera in the nose.

Maximum payload of all these versions was a mere 1,500lb (700kg) of underwing stores, but Saab created a more pugnacious version in the mid-1960s. The 105XT has more powerful Gene-ral Electric J85-17B turbojets of 2,850lb (1,295kg) thrust in place of the standard Turboméca Aubisque, additional internal fuel, and a strengthened wing whose four hardpoints could carry a total of 4,400lb (2,000kg) of ordnance. These changes turned the Saab trainer into a useful attack aircraft, but the sole customer to place an order used the aircraft as an interceptor!

Austria's armed forces are limited by treaty in the sophistication of the equipment they may deploy, and the 105XT's modest performance was guaranteed to raise no political problems. Forty were procured under the designation 105O, and nine still serve with the Surveillance Wing of Fliegerregiment 2 at Graz. A further 14 are operational as fighter-bombers with Fliegerregiment 3. After a long evaluation of possible replacements ranging in sophistication from the F-5E to the Viggen, the Mirage 50 was finally selected in the early 1980s, but the planned order for 24 has been delayed by funding problems. The 105O is likely to be the sole guardian of Austrian skies for many years.

Final version was the 105G, which first flew in 1972. This was equipped with nav-attack and weapon-aiming systems and could carry up to 5,180lb (2,350kg) of ordnance, but failed to attract an order.

Saab-Scania J35 Draken

Data for J35F

Type: all-weather interceptor.
Specifications: Length, 50ft 4in (15.4m); span, 30ft 10in (9.4m); height, 12ft 9in (3.9m); weight (maximum take-off), 27,050lb (12,270kg).
Max speed: Mach 2.0.
Service ceiling: approx. 65,000ft (20,000m).
Range: approx. 700nm (1,300km).
Armament: two RB27 and two RB28 missiles plus ADEN cannon situated in wings.
Powerplant: one Svenska Flygmotor RM6C turbojet rated at 17,110lb (7,760kg) with afterburner.

Many of the older models have been phased out, but the J35 Draken still plays a significant role with the Swedish and Danish Air Forces. Most Swedish examples are J35F interceptors, although small numbers of the earlier J35D still served with F4 Wing as this text was in preparation.

Draken gradually evolved from the early and somewhat austere F35A which first entered service in the 1960s to the final J35F all-weather interceptor. This ultimate Draken entered operational service in 1966/7 and is equipped with an advanced L. M. Ericsson PS-01 pulse-Doppler radar, Hughes infra-red passive sensor mounted in an F-4 style chin position, S7B fire-control system and Hughes Falcon missiles. The latter are the SAR-guided RB27 and the smaller infra-red homing RB28 versions of the Hughes weapon. Specialised avionics link the aircraft with Sweden's STRIL automatic air-surveillance and operations-control system.

Earlier Drakens had been fitted with two 30mm ADEN cannon in the leading edge of the inner wing sections, but the Saab designers had to make do with one in the J35F in order to make room for additional avionics. All Drakens currently in service (apart from a small number of Swedish Air Force J35C two-seat trainers) are powered by the Svenska Flygmotor RM6C engine —a development of the Rolls-Royce Avon fitted with a Swedish-developed afterburner. This develops 17,100lb (7,760kg) of thrust, almost eight per cent more than the most powerful Avon version in RAF service.

Denmark ordered 46 Drakens in 1968, a mixture of fighters, reconnaissance aircraft and two-seat trainers, and added five more trainers in 1973. Danish interceptors were the model designated J35XD. These have extra internal fuel, two 30mm ADEN cannon and the ability to carry an even heavier weapons load. Denmark is currently modifying its surviving Drakens for the ground-

For a nation the size of Sweden, JAS is a major undertaking. At least 200 are likely to be built, the project absorbing approximately eight per cent of the average annual Swedish defence budget between now and the end of the century—reaching a total of around 25 billion Kroner (£2,250 million).

Below: Jakt/Attack/Spaning will be the principal Royal Swedish Air Force combat type in the 1990s. JAS is expected to be about half the weight of the Viggen.

Right: Saab 105s or SK 60s of the Swedish Air Force. In the foreground are SK 60C light strike versions fitted with nose cameras for recce.

Below: Saab 105 (Sk60) trainer of F5 Wing Flight Training School at Ljungbyhed.

Above: Finnish J-35BS Draken (ex-Swedish J-35B).

1. Draken's unique double-delta planform in which the wing blends smoothly into the fuselage was an ingenious mid-1950s solution to the problem of creating a supersonic wing.
2. TF-35 two-seat trainer.
3. Camera nose of RF-35.

Below: The camera nose of the Danish AF Draken identifies it as an RF-35.

attack role, adding a laser ranger, HUD and other avionics.

Finland was the final export customer, ordering twelve J-35XS interceptors in 1970. These were assembled in country by Valmet.

Saab-Scania 37 Viggen

Data for JA37
Type: all weather interceptor.
Specifications: length, 51ft 1in (15.58m); span, 34ft 9in (10.60m); height, 19ft 4in (5.90m); weight (loaded), 37,500lb (17,000kg).
Max speed: Mach 2.0+.
Service ceiling: not available.
Armament: one 30mm KCA cannon plus up to 15,000lb (7,000kg) of external ordnance.
Powerplant: one Volvo Flygmotor RM8B turbofan rated at 16,200lb (7,360kg) of dry thrust 16,200lb (7,360kg) of dry thrust and 28,100lb (12,770kg) with after-burner.

If any object lesson in how to run an advanced combat aircraft programme is required, Viggen shows how it should be done. Working together, the Royal Swedish Air Force and the local aerospace industry identified a firm requirement, then designed, developed flew, built and deployed the hardware with a single mindedness all too rare in combat aircraft procurement. Early plans for a fleet of 500 Viggens may have been over-optimistic, but by the time that deliveries of the final version come to an end, Saab-Scania will have delivered a total of more than 300 aircraft.

The only sad note in the Viggen story is the repeated failure of this superb warplane to gain export orders. Given the appalling levels to which European weather may sink, it is tempting to suggest that this is the aircraft which deserved to win NATO's mid-1970s. fly-off between the F.1E, F-16, YF-17 and Viggen. Attempts to sell the aircraft to India came to naught when the USA vetoed the export of the RM.8 powerplant on the grounds that the latter is based on a US engine. Although the type was a serious candidate in Austria's evaluation of potential Saab 105O replacements, Viggen more than a flying police force.

The design team came up with an ingenious solution to the problems of operating a heavy supersonic fighter from short runways, creating a canard configuration which is virtually a supersonic biplane. The aircraft is highly manoeuvrable and can operate out of 1,600ft (500m) airstrips. Getting airborne from such modest runways is a problem solved by a combination of high lift and a good thrust:weight ratio. Canards have an advantage here—ie, conventional elevators control aircraft pitch by pressing down the tail, but on canards the forward-mounted elevators control pitch by applying nose lift.

Landing on short strips is a more difficult operation. Viggen is flown on to the ground in the type of flareless approach normally reserved for carrier-based aircraft. The pilot keeps the aircraft on the glideslope by movements of the control column, while the aircraft's autothrottle controls speed and attitude. Reverse thrust is used after touchdown, being initiated automatically as soon as the nose wheel strut is compressed.

The basic layout was devised in 1961, and a contract for the development of Viggen was signed in October 1962. Previous generations of Swedish military aircraft had been powered by engines based on Rolls-Royce originals but further developed by what was then Svenska Flygmotor. For Viggen, Sweden turned to the USA, selecting the civil JT8D turbofan as the basis for the RM8 military powerplant. This embodies an afterburner of Swedish design.

The Viggen prototype flew for the first time in February 1967 and the initial AJ37 attack version was operational by 1971. This soon earned the respect of its pilots. It is reported to be near-viceless in handling, but must not be flown at angles of attack greater than 15 degrees. Gust response is low, reducing the stress on the pilot during low-altitude flight at high speeds. Viggen was briefly grounded in 1976 following several in-flight wing failures, but the cause was swiftly determined and modifications devised.

An entire family of customised Viggen variants was to follow, starting with the SK37 two-seat trainer. This carries the full range of armament normally toted by the AJ37 but has a taller tail fin to offset the effects of the bulged hood of the second cockpit.

Two specialised reconnaissance versions were created for land (SF37) and maritime (SH37) use. The nose of the former is filled with cameras operating in the visible light and infra red portions of the spectrum, but the maritime aircraft is fitted with a nose radar.

Penultimate Viggen is the JA37 interceptor which first flew in June 1974. Development was protracted and service deliveries did not begin until 1980. JA37 has a strengthened structure better suited to stresses generated by low-altitude interception missions, a slightly-lengthened fuselage made necessary by the installation of an uprated RM8B turbofan, and a taller tail fin. It is armed with a mixture of Sidewinder and Sky Flash missiles and fitted with a new avionics system based around an L.M. Ericsson PS—46/A pulse-Dopplor radar with a range of more than 27nm (50km). A Singer-Kerfott computer replaces the Saab unit carried by earlier Viggens and the same company provides the INS. JA37's digital flight-control system was the first to be adopted for a production military aircraft.

Left: Viggen SH37 maritime reconnaissance aircraft with ventral fuel tank on the fuselage centre line and a long-range camera in a fairing beneath the intake.

Left: By shooting from the open tail ramp of a Swedish AFC-130 Hercules, a photographer was able to capture this spectacular view of a JA37 interceptor. Note the tall tail fin, and Sidewinder (outboard) and Sky Flash (inboard) missiles on the underwing pylons. The large pod carries test instrumentation.

Below: The nose section of the SF37 reconnaissance aircraft carries a total of seven cameras—four vertical or oblique units for low-level work, two vertically-mounted for high-altitude use, plus a single infra-red camera. By the addition of external pods, the aircraft may be given further day or night reconnaissance facilities such as cameras or a Red Baron infra-red line scanner.

Above right: The unique canard-delta configuration of Viggen gives many of the advantages of variable-geometry but without the latter's cost and complexity.

Below: Sky Flash missile armament, plus a tall tail fin with a blade antenna mounted immediately behind are the features which identify the JA37 interceptor.

Left: Two-seat SK37 trainer in bare metal finish. Deletion of one of the four fuselage fuel tanks and some avionics created the space needed for the rear cockpit.

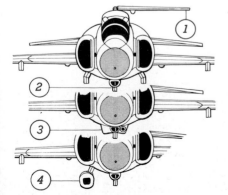

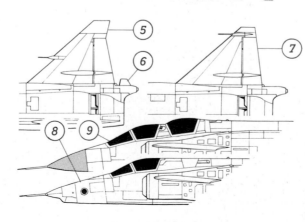

1. Folding fin for use in underground hangars.
2. Centreline pylon on AJ37
3. Fairing for 30mm KCA cannon on JA37 interceptor.
4. SH37 maritime-reconnaissance aircraft sensor pod.
5. Taller fin of modified profile on SK37 and JA37.
6. Blade antenna for communications.
7. Standard pattern of fin.
8. SF37 recon version.
9. SK37 two-seat trainer.

SEPECAT Jaguar

Data for Jaguar S
Type: tactical-support aircraft.
Specifications: length 55ft 11in (15.52m); span, 28ft 6in (8.69m); height, 16ft 0in (4.89m); weight (max take-off); 34,600lb (15,700kg).
Max speed: Mach 1.6.
Service ceiling: 45,000ft (14,000m).
Range: (hi-lo-hi tactical radius with internal fuel), 460nm (852km).
Armament: two 30mm ADEN cannons plus up to 10,500lb (4,700kg) of ordnance on five hardpoints.
Powerplants: two Rolls-Royce/Turboméca Adour Mk 104 each rated at 5,320lb (2,420kg) of dry thrust, 8,040lb (3,655kg) with afterburner.

When the Jaguar project was launched in mid-1960s, none of those involved could have had any idea of just how effective the end product would become. Britain needed a new trainer (and in the era of pre-1973 fuel prices the concept of a supersonic trainer still seemed realistic), while France needed an inexpensive strike aircraft. At a time when European collaboration seemed, at least to the UK Government, to be the best way of developing and procuring combat aircraft, the prospects for a joint Anglo-French project looked good.

In practice, France received a strike aircraft somewhat higher in performance than a purely national project would have created, while the UK switched its aircraft from the training role, deploying instead a strike version equipped with a comprehensive navigation/attack system. In developed form, this UK-standard aircraft was offered on the export market as Jaguar International, winning orders from Ecuador, India and Oman.

Breguet, the original French partner in the program, was amalgamated with Dassault in the 1970s. The Dassault-Breguet company tends to see Jaguar as a rival to the all-French Mirage series, so most of the development and marketing effort on the former is carried out by the UK. In 1980, the British Aerospace formally took over the responsibility for future Jaguar development, although the French company will continue to share the manufacturing workload.

The original program envisaged five variants. Jaguar A was the first to enter service and is operational with the French Air Force. It was also the first to see combat action, being flown against guerrilla forces operating in Mauritania during the winter of 1977. The basic avionics suite is fairly simple by current standards, the main units in the nav/attack system being a SFIM 153-6 twin-gyro inertial platform, an EMD/Decca RDN 72 Doppler radar, a CSF laser rangefinder and Crouzet Type 90 navigation computer. The final 30 aircraft to be delivered have been equipped with Thomson-CSF/Martin Marietta Atlis II target-acquisition and laser-designation pods.

Jaguar B (designated Jaguar T.Mk.2 by the RAF) is a two seat trainer used only for conversion training. Less than 40 were built. French Air Force equivalent is the Jaguar E.

It had been intended that Jaguar would serve with Aéronavale units aboard the carriers *Clemenceau* and *Foch*. A single Jaguar M was built and tested from carriers, but was rejected in favour of the subsonic but all-French Super Etendard. There were technical problems with the afterburning system on the engines of early Jaguars which might have caused the Aeronavale to be nervous but these were soon solved. It is hard to avoid the conclusion that such minor problems were the excuse rather than the reason for the cancellation of the Jaguar M. The end result was that that the French Navy had to wait until 1979 to begin replacing the Etendard IV.

Most combat-effective of the original five variants was the Jaguar S—known to the Royal Air Force as Jaguar GR.Mk 1. This carries a sophisticated Marconi Avionics nav/attack system whose main components include an E3R three-gyro inertial platform, MCS 920M digital computer, Ferranti Type 105 laser ranger and Type 106 marked-target seeker, plus moving-map and head-up displays. This equipment fit is currently being updated, a Ferranti FIN 1064 digital INS and weapon-aiming system replacing a major portion of the original nav/attack system. The newer equipment is smaller in size, leaving more space for a planned internal ECM system.

Jaguar International is the basic designation of export versions of the aircraft. Avionics fit is specified by the individual customers, but is broadly similar to that of the Jaguar S. Indian aircraft are fitted with a HUD and weapon-aiming system similar to those of Sea Harrier, plus a Ferranti COMED combined map and CRT display. Eight of the Indian aircraft will be maritime-strike version. This has a Thomson-CSF Agave radar (the set used in Super Etendard) in a nose radome, and a Ferranti laser ranger in a chin-mounted fairing.

The original production powerplant was the Rolls-Royce/Turboméca Adour Mk 102 rated at 7,300lb (3,320kg) of after-burning thrust. This is still used in French Air Force Jaguars, but British pilots considered Jaguar to be somewhat underpowered for the very low-level tactics which the service uses. RAF aircraft have therefore been retrofitted with the 8,040lb (3,655kg) Adour Mk 104. First Jaguar International versions used the similarly-rated Adour Mk 804, but the demands of high-temperature operations resulted in Indian aircraft receiving the 8,400lb (3,820kg) Adour Mk 811. The same engine will also be fitted to the second batch of aircraft for Oman.

The Indian order is the most significant so far received for Jaguar International. Forty aircraft were supplied from British and French production lines and 45 more are being assembled in country by Hindustan Aeronautics India had planned to build a further 65 aircraft under licence but the future of this phase of the

programme seems uncertain in the light of Indian plans to build the Mirage 2000 and the purchase in 1980 of 70 MiG-23BN Flogger strike aircraft.

British Aerospace is using a single Jaguar as a testbed for a quadruplex fly-by-wire system.

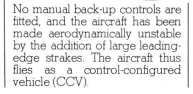

No manual back-up controls are fitted, and the aircraft has been made aerodynamically unstable by the addition of large leading-edge strakes. The aircraft thus flies as a control-configured vehicle (CCV).

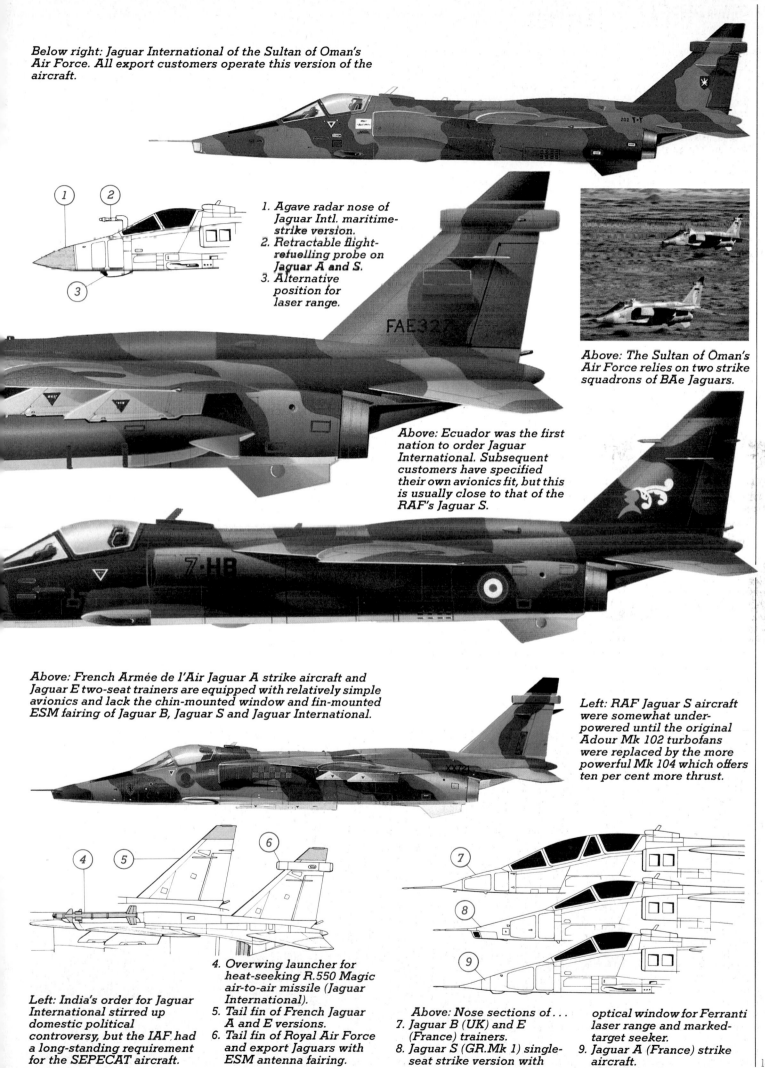

Below right: Jaguar International of the Sultan of Oman's Air Force. All export customers operate this version of the aircraft.

1. Agave radar nose of Jaguar Intl. maritime-strike version.
2. Retractable flight-refuelling probe on Jaguar A and S.
3. Alternative position for laser range.

Above: The Sultan of Oman's Air Force relies on two strike squadrons of BAe Jaguars.

Above: Ecuador was the first nation to order Jaguar International. Subsequent customers have specified their own avionics fit, but this is usually close to that of the RAF's Jaguar S.

Above: French Armée de l'Air Jaguar A strike aircraft and Jaguar E two-seat trainers are equipped with relatively simple avionics and lack the chin-mounted window and fin-mounted ESM fairing of Jaguar B, Jaguar S and Jaguar International.

Left: RAF Jaguar S aircraft were somewhat under-powered until the original Adour Mk 102 turbofans were replaced by the more powerful Mk 104 which offers ten per cent more thrust.

Left: India's order for Jaguar International stirred up domestic political controversy, but the IAF had a long-standing requirement for the SEPECAT aircraft.

4. Overwing launcher for heat-seeking R.550 Magic air-to-air missile (Jaguar International).
5. Tail fin of French Jaguar A and E versions.
6. Tail fin of Royal Air Force and export Jaguars with ESM antenna fairing.

Above: Nose sections of . . .
7. Jaguar B (UK) and E (France) trainers.
8. Jaguar S (GR.Mk 1) single-seat strike version with optical window for Ferranti laser range and marked-target seeker.
9. Jaguar A (France) strike aircraft.

167

Shenyang J-8 Finback and J-12

Data: no reliable specifications available.

At least two Mach 2 fighters have been developed by Chinese industry, but detailed descriptions of these are not yet available. Designations "J-8" and J-12" have been applied to these designs. The former is understood to be a variable-geometry aircraft powered by two Chinese-built copies of the Tumanski R-11 turbojet, and the latter a heavier Spey-engined design.

China has had at least two injections of foreign technology which must have played some role in the design process. In exchange for Shenyang J-6 fighters and spare parts, Egypt handed over at least one MiG-23 Flogger to China. Technology from this aircraft has probably been used in the J-8, which has been assigned the reporting name Finback. US sources describe it as having a nose intake with a MiG-21-style centre-body radome.

Development of the aircraft probably began in the early 1970s. Taiwanese sources claim that several hundred are already in service, but it is more likely that only a few squadrons were in operational service by 1982.

China entered into a technological agreement with Rolls-Royce in 1975 covering licence-production of the Spey turbofan. A batch of 25 afterburning Speys was supplied from the UK, along with components for four engines which were built and run at Sian. The first of the latter began testing in July 1979. More than 500 Chinese personnel were trained in the UK and some components for future production were supplied, but any further work on this programme is being carried out entirely in China. Some observers see the entire Chinese Spey programme as being a method of increasing local design and manufacturing expertise, rather than a project intended to provide operational hardware — effectively an elaborate training exercise, but most think that the engine already powers, or is intended to power, at least one of the new Chinese designs.

The designation J-12 is thought to refer to an aircraft powered by one or two afterburning Speys and weighing around 45,000lb (20,000kg) some reports of the J-12 design suggest a smaller single-engined aircraft, as shown in the plan view). A reported maximum speed of Mach 2.4 seems at first sight unlikely, since RAF Phantoms are limited to a top speed of Mach 2 by their Spey engines. In practice, Spey could be made capable of Mach 2.4 operation if suitable alloys were used in the compressor stages.

Both aircraft will be able to carry Chinese-built copies of the Soviet AA-2 Atoll, but a new pattern of radar-guided air-to-air missile is also under development, probably for the J-12.

Shin Meiwa PS-1 and US-1

Data for US-1
Type: search and rescue amphibian.
Specifications: length, 109ft 9in (33.46m); span, 108ft 9in (33.15m); height, 32ft 3in (9.82m); weight (max take-off), 99,200lb (45,000kg).
Max speed: 268kt (496 km/hr).
Service ceiling: 27,000ft (8,200m).
Range: 2,270nm (4,200km).
Powerplants: four licence-built General Electric T64-IHI-10 turboprops each rated at 3,060ehp (2,280kW).

When Shin Meiwa delivers the eighth and last US-1 search and rescue flying boat to the Japan Air Self-Defence Force in 1983, the handover will mark the end of this expensive and controversial programme. These SAR aircraft serve alongside 19 examples of the earlier PS-1 ASW flying boat, but no further procurement of either variant is planned. The PS-1 force will be supplemented by land-based P-3C Orions currently being built under licence by Kawasaki.

The 1966 decision to proceed with the development of a new ASW flying boat was a brave one based on experience gained with the experimental UF-XS flying scale model built in the early 1960s. In theory, a flying boat is a near-ideal ASW platform in view of its ability to alight on the water to conduct sonar searches. In practice however, land-based ASW aircraft are usually a more cost-effective solution.

The first of two prototypes was flown on 5 October 1967, and both were extensively flight tested by the JASDF. Trials confirmed the aircraft's sea-worthiness, so contracts were awarded for two pre-production aircraft and a first production batch. Like many Japanese aircraft projects, the PS-1 was hit by spiralling costs, so a total of only 23 were built. Several have been lost in accidents, 19 currently remaining in JASDF service. Although such losses may seem alarming in a small force, they represent a not unreasonable attrition rate for seven years of operational service.

Most flying boats require a reasonably smooth water surface from which to operate, but the PS-1 can cope with wave heights of up to 14ft (4.3m), allowing operations in Pacific waters for up to 80 per cent of the time. A compressor mounted in the upper fuselage provides air for boundary-layer control. The wing trailing edge flaps are blown, generating sufficient lift to give a take-off speed of less than 50kt (90km/hr).

The crew consists of two pilots, navigator, flight engineer, radio operator, radar operator, MAD operator, two sonar operators and a tactical co-ordinator. Sono-buoys, smoke bombs and depth charges are carried in an internal weapons bay, while pods located under the wing each contain two homing torpedoes. Launchers for unguided rockets may be fitted to the wingtips.

The US-1 SAR aircraft is basically similar to the PS-1 but has additional internal fuel and lacks the weaponry and ASW systems. Blister transparencies for observers were added along with a large hatch for the launching and recovery of a rubber rescue boat.

The PS-1 was fitted with a tricycle undercarriage intended for use when beaching the aircraft, but the US-1 required a normal undercarriage suitable for land use on conventional runways. This has twin-wheel main legs which retract into sponsons on the sides of the hull.

The first US-1 was flown in November 1974 and entered service the following spring. Uprated engines offering 10 per cent more take-off thrust will be fitted to the final two production aircraft, but will be retrofitted to the US-1 fleet.

Right: US-1 prototype (in foreground) flies with the original PS-1 flying boat. The US-1 is the only fixed-wing air/sea search and rescue aircraft in production, eight being funded by 1982. US-1s serve with the 71st Koku-tai of the JMSDF.

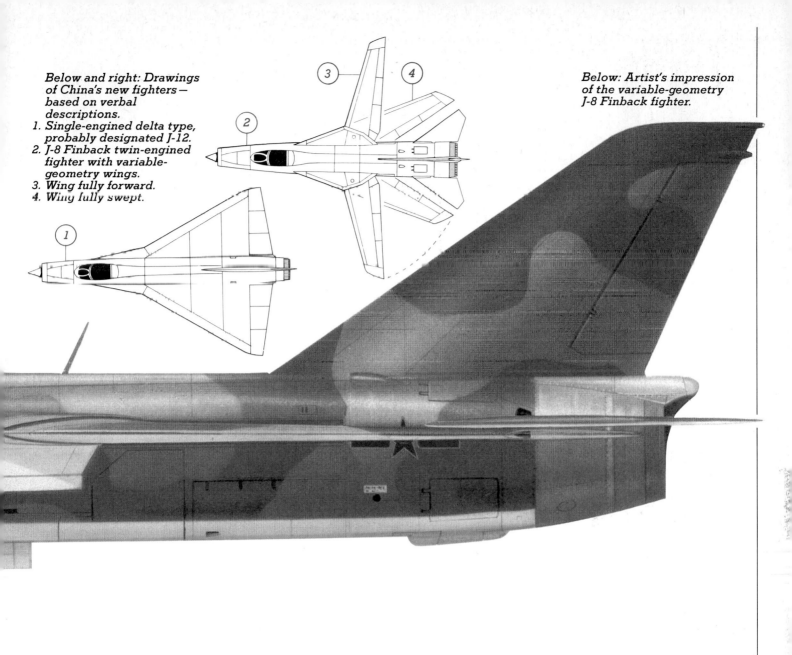

Below and right: Drawings of China's new fighters — based on verbal descriptions.
1. *Single-engined delta type, probably designated J-12.*
2. *J-8 Finback twin-engined fighter with variable-geometry wings.*
3. *Wing fully forward.*
4. *Wing fully swept.*

Below: Artist's impression of the variable-geometry J-8 Finback fighter.

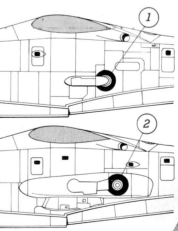

1. *Single-wheel main undercarriage unit of PS-1. This was designed for use when beaching the flying boat, rather than to give amphibious capability.*
2. *Twin-wheel main undercarriage unit of US-1. This retracts into a fairing on the hull.*

Above: Shin Meiwa PS-1 maritime-patrol flying boat of the JMSDF.

Short Skyvan

Data for Skyvan 3M
Type: Stol transport.
Specifications: length, 40ft 1in (12.21m); span, 64ft 11in (19.79m); height, 15ft 1in (4.60m); weight (maximum take-off), 14,500lb (6,575kg).
Max cruising speed: 176kt (327km/hr).
Range: 580nm (1.075km).
Max payload: 5,200lb (2,360kg).
Powerplant: two Garrett TPE331-201 turboprops, each rated at 715shp (533kW).

Never was an aircraft more aptly named than the Skyvan. A simple rectangular-section unpressurised fuselage, fixed undercarriage, high-mounted braced wing, and twin Garrett TPE331-201 turbo-prop engines result in an aircraft which could never be described as pleasing to the eye, but which allows loads of up to 22 fully equipped soldiers or 5,200lb (2,400kg) of freight to be lifted out of rough airstrips. Normal take-off run of the military Skyvan 3M version is 780ft (240m), while the landing run is even shorter at just under 700ft (210m).

This level of performance makes the aircraft suitable for use as a light transport, VIP transport or even as an assault transport. The full-width rear door may be lowered in flight for the airdropping of freight, and the cabin can house up to 16 paratroops.

Skyvan started life as an airliner and first flew in 1963. The Skyvan 3M military version was developed in the late 1960s, the prototype flying in 1970. This was similar to the airliner, but was fitted with a wide door, lightweight loading ramps, roller conveyors for cargo handling, and a blister window on the port side which allowed the dispatcher to monitor airdropping operations.

More than 50 have been sold to 11 nations, along with several for coastguard (Argentina) and police (Malawi and Thailand)

use. Largest military operator is the Sultan of Oman's Air Force, whose 15 aircrft have been used to support anti-querilla operations in Dhofar province. Part of the credit for suppressing the rebellion in the early 1970s must go to the hard-working Skyvans of 2 and 5 Sqns SOAF, which operated a scheduled service around a network of military airstrips. Pilots learned how to dodge ground fire during take-off and landing, while turn-around times were kept to 15 minutes or less at airstrips likely to come under fire.

Three of Singapore's six Skyvans are equipped for search and rescue operations, operating alongside the transports from Changi air base.

SIAI-Marchetti S.211

Type: basic trainer.
Specifications: length, 30ft 5in (9.28m); span: 26ft 3in (8.0m); height, 12ft 3in (3.73m); weight (maximum take-off): 6,170lb (2,800kg).
Max speed: 390kt (723km/hr).
Service ceiling: 42,000ft (12,800m).
Range: (hi-lo-hi tactical radius with light armament) 350nm (650km).
Armament: up to 1,320lb (600kg) of ordnance.
Powerplant: one Pratt & Whitney Canada JT15D rated at 2,500lb (1,140kg) dry thrust.

Most nations having an aeronautical industry offer a basic jet trainer, but Italy currently has two entrants in the sales stakes. Traditionally a supplier of piston-engined types, SIAI-Marchetti started work on a jet-powered S.211 design in the mid-1970s. In order to keep cost down, the design was made as small and light as possible, with an empty weight of 3,180lb (1,445kg) and a maximum take-off weight of less than 3 tonnes.

As a result, the company hopes to sell the aircraft to air forces which currently use the SF.260 piston-engined trainer. According to SIAI-Marchetti, it makes economic sense to train a pilot through the elementary and basic stages on the S.211, then move him directly on to an advanced trainer. Company studies suggest potential savings of up to 40 per cent compared with the conventional primary/basic/advanced training sequence using three aircraft types.

Transfusions of North American technology came in the form of assistance with the design of the super-critical wing section from the universities of New York and Kansas, and from Pratt & Whitney Canada's JT15D turbo-fan in the engine bay. Martin-Baker seats are fitted in the cockpit—Mk8 seats were selected as a standard, but zero-zero seats from the same manufacturer may be installed.

Techniques used to keep weight and cost down include use of simple sheet-metal structures fabricated by means of large-scale bonding techniques based on those used during sub-contract work on the CH-47 helicopter. Wherever possible, glass fibre is used for secondary structures. The aircraft is made up around 2,000 component parts—which is 1,000 fewer than are used on more conventional designs, according to company claims.

Go-ahead for the project was given in 1977, and the prototype flew on 10 June 1981. Production tooling was used from the start, so that deliveries could begin by the end of 1982. Plans have been drawn up for a production rate of 50 per year from 1983 onwards.

Given such a small airframe, payload is obviously limited, but four underwing hardpoints have been provided. The inboard locations are stressed to accept loads of up to 660lb (300kg), the outboard to take up to 330lb (150kg) each.

Below: Development of the jet-powered S.211 basic trainer was a bold step for a company which specialises in high-performance piston-engined training types.

Left: Workhorse of the Sultan's Air Force in Oman is the Skyvan 3M. One of 15 in use is pictured over typical scenery. The Skyvans are based at Seeb and Salalah.

Right: One of the Sultan of Oman's Air Force's hard-working Skyvan 3M transports. A total of 15 serve with 2 Sqn and 5 Sqn .

Above: Two Skyvan 3Ms serving with the transport squadron of Fliegerregiment 1 based at Tulln are the heaviest fixed-wing aircraft in Austria's small air force.

Left: Despite its diminutive size, the SIAI Marchetti S.211 offers the raised rear cockpit regarded as an essential feature by most potential operators. The low running costs of such a simple aircraft may make "all-jet" training feasible.

Sian J-7 Fishbed

Type: air-superiority fighter.
Specifications: Length, 44ft 2in (13.46m); span, 23ft 5in (7.15m); height, 14ft 9in (4.5m); weight (loaded), 17,000lb (7,750kg).
Max speed: Mach 1.9-2.0.
Service ceiling: approx. 50,000ft (15,000km).
Range: tactical radius) approx. 200nm (375km).
Armament: one 30mm cannon plus two AA-2 Atoll heat-seeking missiles.
Powerplant: one Shenyang-built R-11 copy rated at 9,500lb (4,300kg) dry thrust and 12,700lb (5,750kg) with afterburning.

Shortly before the 1960 split in Sino/Soviet relations, the Soviet Union supplied a small number of MiG-21F day fighters to the Chinese Air Force. These were promptly studied by Chinese engineers and plans drawn up for unlicenced production of the type at the Sian aircraft plant. Despite the problems inherent in tackling this work without Soviet assistance, the first Chinese-built aircraft flew in December 1964, production deliveries beginning the following year.

Production seems to have run at around three aircraft per month, but was suspended in 1966 after less than 100 had been delivered. Some aircraft were supplied to the Chinese Air Force while a few number were exported to Albania.

In the late 1970s production restarted, but the aircraft now being produced are thought to be an improved model, perhaps embodying some technology from the second-generation MiG-21s which China was able to borrow in the late 1960s while the latter were in transit through China by surface transport on the way to North Vietnam. Photographs released by the Chinese show aircraft externally similar to the Mig-21F, suggesting that an all-weather version is not yet available. Current production rate is reported to be around 30 per month, and at least two regiments

Sikorsky CH-53 Sea Stallion

Data for CH-53E
Type: heavy transport helicopter.
Specifications:
length, 73ft 4in (22.35m); height (including tail rotor), 28ft 5in (8.66m); rotor diameter, 79ft. 0in (24.08m); weight (max. take-off), 73,500lb (33,340kg).
Max speed: 170kt (315km/hr).
Range: 1,120nm (2,075km).
Max payload: (external) 32,000lb (14,500 kg).
Powerplants: three General Electric T64-GE-416 turboshafts each rated at 3,700shp (2,760kW).

Rather than adopt the US Army's CH-47 Chinook, the US Marine Corps decided in 1960 to procure its own design of heavy-lift helicopter suitable for shipboard use. In creating the S-65, Sikorsky was able to take advantage of work carried out under the US Army's CH-64 Tarhe flying-crane programme, mating that aircraft's dynamic system with a new fuselage incorporating a large cargo cabin and rear-loading doors. Rotor blades of the new aircraft were made from titanium and arranged to fold for on-board storage.

The first S-65 flew on 14 October 1964, and the first of a total of 139 production aircraft—now designated CH-53A Sea Stallion were delivered to the USMC in September 1967.

The basic design was soon to spawn a series of variants. For minesweeping, the US Navy devised the RH-53A version by converting 15 ex-USMC CH-53A aircraft. Next major development was the USAF search and rescue HH-53B Super · Jolly, which packed three miniguns or cannon for supressing ground fire during sorties to rescue downed US aircrew in the Vietnam War. Such operations were often hazardous, particularly over North Vietnam, so the HH-53B was armoured and given flight-was armoured and given flight-refuelling equipment to stretch its range and endurance. The CH-53C was a broadly similar transport version.

HH-53C is another USAF SAR version and is fitted with more powerful 3,925shp (2930kW) T64-GE-7 engines. This variant entered service in 1968, and eight were modified to the HH-53H standard in the late 1970s in order to provide the service with a night and adverse-weather rescue capability. These reworked aircraft received a stabilised Texas Instruments AAQ-10 FLIR and APQ-158 terrain-avoidance radar, Litton INS and other items of avionics.

With the development of the CH-53D, the potential of the basic twin-engined design was stretched almost to the limit. Two T64-GE-413 engines each rated at 3,925shp (2,930kW) provided the power needed to lift 55 fully-equipped infantrymen. Most CH-53Ds were also equipped for minesweeping operations, but the design was eventually modified to create the dedicated RH-53D minesweeper, which entered service in 1973.

Development of the three-engined CH-53E began in 1973, but despite a successful flight-test programme the award of a production contract did not follow until 1978. Three T64-GE-416 engines, each delivering up to 3,696shp (2,756kW) of continuous power or up to 4,380shp (3,270kW) for up to ten minutes, give the CH-53E 50 per cent more power and twice the lifting capacity of the earlier CH-53D. As a result, the aircraft can carry more than 90 per cent of the items of equipment which serve with the USMC, including most aircraft. Deliveries began in June 1981. More than 100 are likely to be built, and some may be the proposed MH-53E minesweeper. Main USAF transport model is the T58-GE-5-powered CH-3E. The earlier CH-3C was fitted with the less powerful T58-GE-1, but all have been rebuilt as CH-3Es. Fifty CH-3Es were fitted with armament, armour and self-sealing fuel tanks and retractable flight-refuelling equipment, entering service as the HH-3E Jolly Green Giant. These latter aircraft saw much combat service in Southeast Asia, flying missions into North Vietnamese airspace to rescue downed US aircrew. HH-3F Pelican serves with the US Coast Guard. This SAR aircraft lacks the armour and armament of the -3E, but carries extra avionics.

Below: HH-53H Super Jolly ASAR version is a rebuild of the earlier HH-53C with the nose-mounted Pave Low night/adverse-weather sensor.

of the Chinese Air Force now fly the type. The Soviet AA-2 Atoll heat-seeking missile is also built in China to arm the J-7.

Egypt plans to operate the aircraft, and claims that it has better engines and avionics than the Soviet versions currently in Egyptian service. A batch of 100 have been ordered for service as advanced trainers. Unit cost is reported to be $1.0 million, a price which might attract other Third World customers.

The only known variant is a reconnaissance version, but China plans further updates. In 1980, assistance from US industry was requested in improving the radar and engine, to help the aircraft cope with more modern Soviet types. Production will probably continue until newer designs enter large-scale service.

Below: The Sian J-7 is an unlicenced copy of the Mikoyan MiG-21, but may have been internally modified by the Chinese.

Left: The "top-hat" fairing above the rotor head, broad vertical tail-boom section and exhaust for a third engine identify this USMC helicopter as a CH-53E.

MARINES

1. Towing equipment for sweep on HH-53D minesweeper version.

MARINES

Left: CH-53A Sea Stallion assault helicopter of the USMC in low-visibility markings. The later CH-53D has more power and auto-folding main rotor blades.

Below Two of the US Marine RH-53Ds devoid of markings, being prepared for the abortive 1980 Iranian rescue mission.

2. HH-53H Pave Low night and adverse-weather search and rescue helicopter fitted with . . .
3. Texas Instruments stabilised FLIR sensor.
4. Flight-refuelling probe and cover on USAF and some USN and USMC aircraft.

5. Rear-view mirror on HH-53D minesweeper and some transports.
6. Enlarged dorsal fairing on CH-53E.
7. Broad-chord fin of the CH-53E is canted 20° to port.
8. Narrow-chord fin on earlier models.

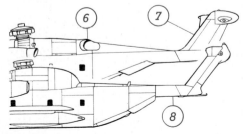

Sikorsky UH-60 Blackhawk and SH-60 Seahawk

Data for UH-60A
Type: combat assault
helicopter.
Specifications: length, 50ft 1in
(15.26m); height, 12ft 4in
(3.76m); rotor diameter, 53ft 8in
(16.36m); weight (mission take-
off), 16,260lb (7,375kg).
Maximum speed: 160kg
(296km/hr).
Range: (at max. take-off wt.)
324nm (600km).
Maximum payload: 8,000lb
(3,600kg) external load.
Powerplants: two General
Electric T700-GE-700
turboshafts each rated at
1,560shp (1,150kW).

Development of the UH-60/SH-
60 series of helicopters began a
decade ago under the US
Army's Utility Tactical Transport
Aircraft System (UTTAS) programme. Prototypes were
ordered from Sikorsky and

Boeing Vertol, then test-flown
against each other in the mid-
1970s. Sikorsky's YUH-60A was
selected in December 1976, and
production deliveries began in
June 1979.

UH-60A Blackhawk is the
basic transport version, and can
carry eleven soldiers within the
cabin or up to 8,000lb (3,600kg)
of cargo as a slung load. It is
scheduled to become the main
US Army assault helicopter, a
total of 1,100 being planned by
the mid-1980s. Add-on kits have
been devised to allow the basic
aircraft to carry out medical
evacuation missions.

Two GE T700 turboshafts
drive a four-bladed main and tail
rotors. The main rotor has
leading edge droop and a
trailing edge tab to minimise the
aerodynamic effects to the pre-
ceding blade. Manufactured with
a titanium spar and composite

body, these blades are able to
withstand small-arms fire. Their
hollow interiors are pressurised,
so that the presence of cracks,
combat damage or similar de-
fects may be detected and
signalled to the crew.

The transmission may run for
up to 30 minutes without lubrication, and the main fuel tanks are
bulletproof and crashworthy.
Tests have shown that the
aircraft can survive a landing at a
forward speed of 63kt (117km/hr)
and descent rate of 11.5ft/sec
(3.5m/sec).

Development of an external
stores support system (ESSS)
began in 1981 to give the aircraft
the ability to carry a variety of
weapons including Hellfire air-
to-surface missiles and dispensers for anti-tank mines.

EH-60A is an ECM variant
intended for communications
jamming, and carries 1,800lb

(810kg) of Quick Fix II electronic
systems. The US Army plans to
deploy a total of 36 examples.
EH-60B is intended to have a
more offensive role, and carries
Stand-Off Target Acquisition
System (SOTAS) electronics
including a moving-target indi-
cating radar with a belly-mounted
antenna. The latter rotates in
flight, so the normal pattern of
fixed undercarriage is replaced
by retractable units which will
not obscure the antenna. The
EH-60B is designed to detect
hostile ground forces and to
pass their position back to a
ground station using a data link.

SH-60B Seahawk was the
winner of a 1977 competition to
select a LAMPS III (Light
Airborne Multi-purpose System
III) helicopter for the US Navy.
Primary LAMPS mission is ASW,
and the aircraft carries an
extensive avionics suite de-

*Above: SH-60A Seahawk, seen here operating from the Perry-
class frigate* **McInerny,** *carries a complex suite of mission
avionics and sensors.*

veloped by an industrial team headed by IBM. Main sensors are a Texas Instruments APS-124 search radar in the forward section of the fuselage and ASQ-81 towed MAD system, IBM UYS-1 acoustic processor and Raytheon ALQ-142 ESM system. Two Mk 46 lightweight torpedoes may be carried on pylons, while a 25-tube sonobuoy launcher is fitted in the port side of the fuselage.

Secondary LAMPS missions include anti-ship surveillance and targeting, vertical replenishment, medical evacuation and search and rescue.

The US Navy plans to buy around 200 Seahawks for service aboard guided-missile frigates such as the Perry-class, Aegis-armed guided-missile destroyers, and Spruance-class anti-submarine warfare destroyers.

Left: Unlikely to become as mass produced as the UH-1, the UK-60 Blackhawk is steadily joining US Army units in ever increasing numbers. Design features include a low-slung body, canted tail rotor and a large, very distinctive slab tailplane. A number of variants are planned including an ECM EH-60A.

Above: Compared with the SH-60B Seahawk shown below, the US Army's UH-60A Blackhawk has an uncluttered appearance. Note the additional cabin windows.

NAVY

SH-58B
1611691

DANGER
KEEP AWAY

Left: Instantly-recognisable naval features of the SH-60B Seahawk include a chin-mounted equipment fairing, torpedo armament, sonobuoy launch tubes in the fuselage sides, small ventral radome, revised undercarriage and a folding tail.

Sikorsky S-61 Sea King

Data for SH-3D
Type: ASW helicopter.
Specifications: length, 54ft 9in (16.69m); height, 156ft 6in (4.72m); rotor diameter, 62ft 0in (18.9m); weight (maximum take-off), 18,620lb (8,450kg).
Max speed: 144kt (267 km/hr).
Range: 542nm (1,005km).
Armament: see text.
Powerplants: two General Electric T58-GE-10 turboshafts each rated at 1,400shp (1,045kW).

More than two decades after its first flight the S-61 Sea King is still in production, more than 770 having been built by Sikorsky and a further 400 built under licence by Agusta (Italy), Mitsubishi (Japan) and Westland (UK). (Since the UK-built aircraft are much modified from the original design, these are described in a separate entry as the Westland Sea King.)

The type started life as the HSS-2 anti-submarine warfare helicopter, but was to enter service with the US Navy in the early 1960s as the SH-3A. Examples borrowed by the US Air Force for use as transports soon resulted in the first of a series of variants for that service.

Standard USN ASW helicopter is the T58-GE-10-powered SH-3D. This is fitted with a Bendix AQS-13 dunking sonar and can carry sonobuoys and armament such as homing torpedoes and depth bombs.

This version is also built by Agusta. Some of the Agusta-built

SH-3D aircraft have been fitted with a Sistel APQ-706 search and attack radar and armed with Marte anti-ship missiles. From 1971 onwards, earlier USN SH-3A and -3D models were updated to the improved SH-3H standard for ASW duties. Mitsubishi currently builds an ASW version known in Japan as the SH-3B.

By stripping the ASW gear out of obsolescent SH-3As, the USN has created the SH-3G utility helicopter. Several have been fitted out as armed search and rescue aircraft.

Below: Agusta-built Italian Navy SH-3D, with nose-mounted Sistel APQ-706 search and attack radome, but without the Marte anti-ship missile.

SOKO Galeb and Jastreb

Data for Galeb
Specifications: length, 33ft 11in (10.34m); span, 34ft 4in (10.50m); height, 10ft 9in (3.28m); weight (max take-off for weapons training), 8,790lb (3,990kg).
Max speed: 438kt (812km/hr).
Service ceiling: 39,400ft (12,000m).
Range: 669nm (1,240km).
Armament: two 12.7mm machine guns plus up to 660lb (300kg) of ordnance.
Powerplant: one Rolls-Royce Viper II Mk 22-6 turbojet rated at 2,500lb (1,130kg) dry thrust.

Development of the Galeb (Seagull) trainer began in 1957 and the first aircraft flew in May 1961. Production began in 1963 to meet the requirements of the Jugoslavian Air Force. In appearance, Jastreb bears some similarity to the Aermacchi MB.326. It is a simple design, powered by a Rolls-Royce Viper turbojet. The wing is unswept and carries a jettisonable tank of 375lb (170kg) capacity at each tip. The cockpit is unpressurised, but air-

conditioning may be fitted if required.

Two 12.7mm machine guns are mounted in the nose, and underwing hardpoints can carry light ordnance such as 110lb (50kg) or 220lb (100kg) bombs, 57mm or 127mm unguided rockets, or clusters of practice

Above: A formation of Jugoslav Air Force single-seat Jastréb strike aircraft, developed from the two-seat Galeb, showing faired-in rear canopy section in metal.

bombs. A hook for target towing is provided beneath the fuselage.

Some 60 Galebs currently serve with the Jugoslavian Air Force at Pula, while a small number serve as reconnaissance aircraft along with the veteran Lockheed T-33 which they will probably replace.

Using the same basic airframe and systems, Soko created the Jastreb (Hawk) close-support aircraft. This is powered by a Rolls-Royce Viper Mk 531 of 3,000lb (1,360kg) thrust instead of the 2,500lb (1,130kg) Mk 22-6. The second cockpit was deleted and the rear section of the canopy replaced by a metal fairing. The structure was strengthened for the low-altitude role, a third machine gun was fitted in the nose, and a total of eight underwing hardpoints were provided. Jastreb still forms a major component of Jugoslavian air strength, 150 being currently operational along with several RJ-1 reconnaissance versions. A two-seat version designated TJ-1 was developed for operational conversion. This first flew in

1975 and entered service in the following year.

It seems suprising that any air force in the market for a jet trainer or light strike aircraft would turn to an almost unknown supplier, but in 1971 Zambia ordered two Galebs and four Jastrebs. Six MB.326 trainers were already in service, but the Jugoslavian aircraft were used to form the Zam-

bian Air Force's first combat squadron.

An export version of Galeb designated G-2AE flew in 1974. This features unspecified improvements, probably to the avionics, and a total of 50 were delivered to Libya between 1976 and 1980. (Some sources claim that only 20 were delivered.) Galeb is still in production.

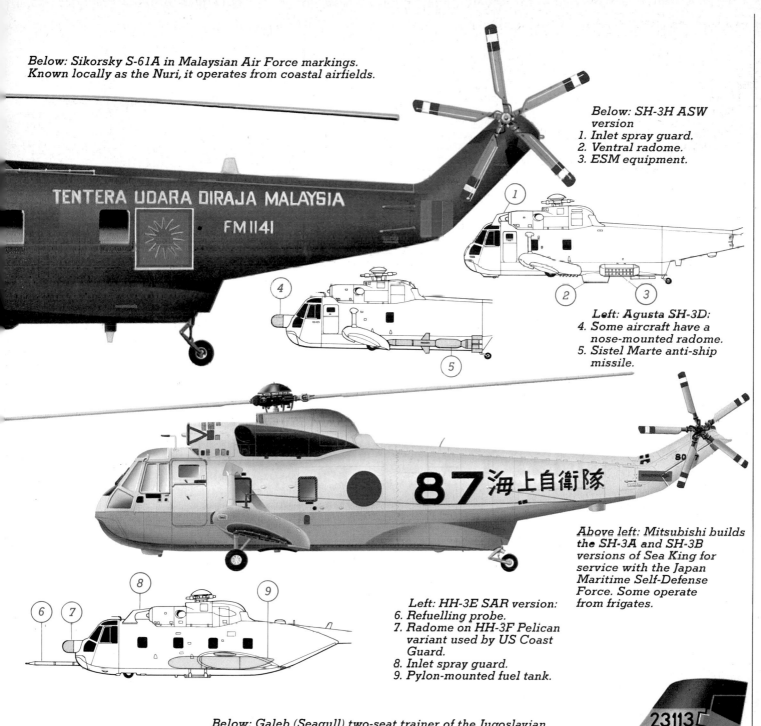

*Below: Sikorsky S-61A in Malaysian Air Force markings.
Known locally as the Nuri, it operates from coastal airfields.*

TENTERA UDARA DIRAJA MALAYSIA
FM 1141

*Below: SH-3H ASW
version*
1. *Inlet spray guard.*
2. *Ventral radome.*
3. *ESM equipment.*

Left: Agusta SH-3D:
4. *Some aircraft have a
nose-mounted radome.*
5. *Sistel Marte anti-ship
missile.*

87 海上自衛隊

*Above left: Mitsubishi builds
the SH-3A and SH-3B
versions of Sea King for
service with the Japan
Maritime Self-Defense
Force. Some operate
from frigates.*

Left: HH-3E SAR version:
6. *Refuelling probe.*
7. *Radome on HH-3F Pelican
variant used by US Coast
Guard.*
8. *Inlet spray guard.*
9. *Pylon-mounted fuel tank.*

*Below: Galeb (Seagull) two-seat trainer of the Jugoslavian
Air Force Flying Training Headquarters at Mostar. Normal
armament is a pair of 0.5in (12.7mm) nose-mounted guns plus
light stores on underwing pylons.*

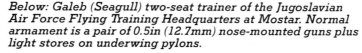

23113

*Left: Single-seat Jastreb
(Hawk) strike version. Three
machine guns are carried in
the nose, while a total of
eight hardpoints are provided
beneath the wings.*

24002

002

Sukhoi Su-7 Fitter

Data for Su-7BMK
Type: ground-attack fighter.
Specifications: length,, 57ft 0in (17.37m); span, 29ft 3in (8.93m); height, 15ft 0in (4.57m); weight (maximum take-off), 29,750lb (13,500kg).
Max speed: Mach 1.6—917kt (1,700km/hr).
Service ceiling: 49,700ft (15,100m).
Range: (combat radius) 170—260nm (320—480km).
Armament: up to 2,200lb (1,000kg) of ordnance, plus two 30mm cannon.
Powerplant: one Lyulka AL-7F-1 turbojet rated at 15,400lb (7,000kg) dry thrust, 22,000lb (10,000kg) with afterburner.

In some respects the Su-7 Fitter is a good example of how not to design a supersonic fighter. Like several other first-generation Soviet supersonic types, the Su-7 substitutes brute force for sophistication, relying on the power of a single engine of ten tonnes thrust to provide the required level of performance. The penalty paid is that of short range and limited payload.

Maximum internal fuel capacity is only 7,000lb (3,200kg) but the massive Lyulka AL-7 single-shaft turbojet swallows more than 200lb (90kg) of fuel per minute at maximum dry thrust. With the afterburner lit, fuel consumption hits more than 800lb/minute (360kg/minute), at which rate the entire 7,000lb (3,200kg) of internal fuel can be used up in around 8 minutes. Indian Air Force pilots who made liberal use of the afterburner during the 1971 Indo/Pakistan war sometimes ran out of fuel and were forced to abandon their aircraft.

In theory, late-series Su-7s can carry up to 5,500lb (2,500kg) of ordnance on underwing hard points. In practice, two under-fuselage hardpoints are normally used to carry external tanks which give the aircraft an extra 2,100lb (950kg) of fuel, but when these are fitted, the armament load must be reduced to a mere 2,200lb (1,000kg).

The original Su-7B had only two underwing pylons, so offered little in the way of offensive capability. Discussing this point with the author several years ago, one Fitter pilot remarked that the need to assign the limited pylon capacity to external tanks was no problem, because "You still have the

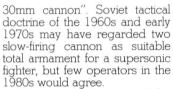

30mm cannon". Soviet tactical doctrine of the 1960s and early 1970s may have regarded two slow-firing cannon as suitable total armament for a supersonic fighter, but few operators in the 1980s would agree.

With the deployment of the improved Su-7BKL and BM versions, four underwing hardpoints were fitted, while the latter also had an uprated engine and twin braking parachutes. The demand for better rough-field performance led to the Su-7BMK with a low-pressure nosewheel, fittings beneath the rear fuselage for JATO bottles and provision for three hardpoints beneath each wing.

If used at ranges short enough

for high fuel consumption not to be an embarrassment, Fitter is an effective attack aircraft. During operations over Israeli-occupied Sinai, the Egyptian Air Force found the Su-7 to be a reliable and steady platform for low-altitude weapons delivery.

Other positive features of the design are its rugged construction and simple maintenance procedures, as well as its general suitability for use from second-class airfields. The Nudelmann-Richter NR-30 cannon may be slow-firing, but it throws a heavy projectile whose destructive effect on target is better than that of the

US 20mm Vulcan or the widely deployed 30mm ADEN/DEFA.

On the debit side, modest range, limited payload, unsophisticated navigation and attack systems, plus vulnerability to ground fire have led to the aircraft being largely phased out of Warsaw Pact service. Like the US F-100 Super Sabre, the Su-7 was an acceptable fighter-bomber in its day, but is now largely obsolete. At low altitudes the ALF-7 afterburner must make the aircraft an easy target for such man-portable SAMs as the SA-7 Grail, Redeye or Stinger.

Below: Sukhoi Su-7 Fitter-A ground-attack aircraft of the Soviet Air Force.

Sukhoi Su-9/11 Fishpot

Type: all-weather interceptor.
Specifications: length, 56ft 0in (17.0m): span, 27ft 8in (8.43m); height, 16ft 0in (4.88m); weight (maximum take-off), 30,000lb (13,600kg).
Max speed: Mach 1.8.
Service ceiling: 55,700ft (17,000m).
Armament: four AA-3 Anab missiles.
Powerplant: one Lyulka AL-7F-1 turbojet rated at 14,200lb (6,455kg) dry thrust, 22,000lb (10,000kg) with afterburning.

Despite its age and obsolescence, this all-weather interceptor is still deployed in significant numbers with the Soviet Air Defence Forces. Unlike the smaller MiG-21, which it resembles in aerodynamic configuration, it was never exported, but serves only in the Soviet Union.

The original Su-9 Fishpot-B en-

tered service in the late 1950s, armed with the Sidewinder-derived AA-2 Atoll heat-seeking missile and carrying in the inlet centrebody the same R1L Spin Scan radar as was fitted to the MiG-21. Although some remain operational, many have been expended as target drones.

Definitive version was the Su-11 Fitter-C, which flew in 1960 or early 1961, and had the larger intake necessary to house the longer-range Skip Spin radar. The latter could be used to guide SAR-homing missiles, so the AA-3 Anab was carried in place of Atoll. No attempt was made to give the type the ability to serve as an air-superiority fighter. Like the Su-9, the Su-11 had no cannon armament but was designed for the task of intercepting bombers under all weather conditions by means of IR or SAR versions of Anab.

Like the swept-wing Su-7 Fitter,

Below: Soviet Air Force Su-11 with AA-3 Anab missiles.

the Su-11 was of simple but robust construction, and used the same fuel-hungry Lyulka AL-7F-1 turbojet. (Powerplant of the Su-9 had been the less powerful AL-7F developing 19,840lb (9,020kg) with afterburner.) This approach resulted in an effective interceptor which was broadly comparable with the BAC Lightning, but which has a top speed of only Mach 1.8 despite having ten tonnes of thrust. Many Soviet interceptor squadrons have

retired their Su-11s in favour of the twin-engined Su-15 Flagon, but several hundred are still in service, the number diminishing as units are converted to the newer aircraft. At least 300 were still operational in the early 1980s. No trainer version of the Su-11 was created, pilots converting to the type being trained on the two-seat Su-9U Maiden.

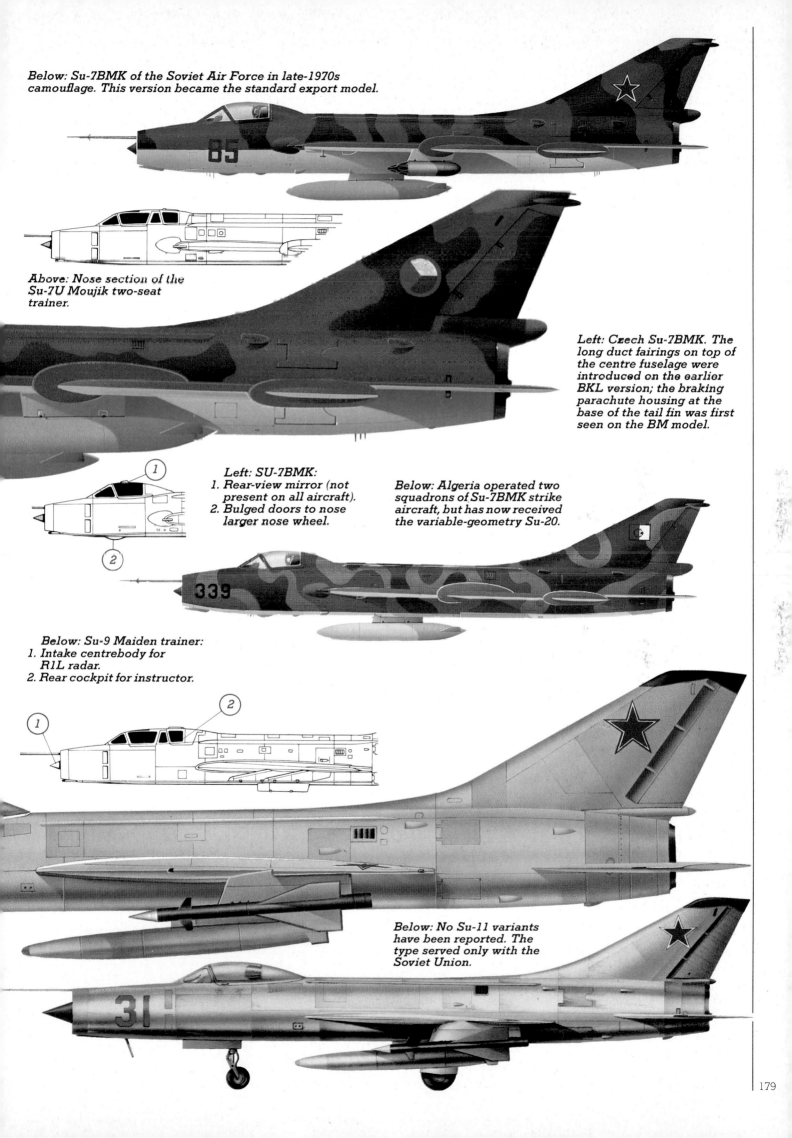

Below: Su-7BMK of the Soviet Air Force in late-1970s camouflage. This version became the standard export model.

Above: Nose section of the Su-7U Moujik two-seat trainer.

Left: Czech Su-7BMK. The long duct fairings on top of the centre fuselage were introduced on the earlier BKL version; the braking parachute housing at the base of the tail fin was first seen on the BM model.

Left: SU-7BMK:
1. Rear-view mirror (not present on all aircraft).
2. Bulged doors to nose larger nose wheel.

Below: Algeria operated two squadrons of Su-7BMK strike aircraft, but has now received the variable-geometry Su-20.

Below: Su-9 Maiden trainer:
1. Intake centrebody for R1L radar.
2. Rear cockpit for instructor.

Below: No Su-11 variants have been reported. The type served only with the Soviet Union.

Sukhoi Su-15 Flagon

Data for Flagon-F
Type: all-weather interceptor.
Specifications: length 68ft 0in (20.5m); span, 34ft 6in (10.53m); height, 16ft 6in (5.0m); weight (maximum take-off), 35,300lb (16,000kg).
Max speed: Mach 2.3-2.5.
Service ceiling: 65,000ft (20,000m).
Range: (combat radius) 390nm (725km).
Armament: up to four AA-3 or AA-3-3 Advanced Anab.
Powerplant: two Tumanski turbojets (see text).

Created to meet a late-1950s requirement for a heavy interceptor to replace the Su-9/11 Fishpot series, the Su-15 Flagon is still a major component of the PVO Strany interceptor force. Like earlier Sukhoi interceptors, it has never been exported, but serves only with the Soviet Air Force. None are currently deployed outside Soviet territory, but NATO planners expect that some would be brought forward to East European bases in wartime.

In general concept Flagon resembles the earlier Su-9 and -11, and probably uses many sub-assemblies from the latter aircraft. The Soviet Union did not have a 25,000-30,000lb (11,360-13,640kg) turbojet in existence by the early 1960s when the aircraft was designed and flown, so two engines were installed side-by-side in the rear fuselage. The intakes were tailored according to the area rule.

In the early 1970s analysts of Soviet aircraft generally assumed that the Lyulka AL-7 was used, an assumption whose absurdity should have been obvious to anyone comparing the rear fuselage section of the Su-11 and Su-15. There simply is not enough room for an engine of such diameter. Early production aircraft were almost certainly powered by Tumanski R-11 turbojets—the powerplant of the early MiG-21 series.

Most Western sources identify the nose radar as the I/J-band set known to NATO as Skip Spin. This seems unlikely at first sight, since Skip Spin was used in the Su-11, and the latter has a much smaller nose radome. If the radar in early-series Flagons is Skip Spin, this was probably a revised version of the basic equipment with a larger antenna and perhaps a more powerful transmitter.

The early Flagon-A seems to have been used to gain early squadron experience before committing the type to large-scale production. It obviously exhibited shortcomings in performance, since the definitive Flagon-D production model which entered service in the late 1960s had revised wings of greater span and compound sweep. The increased wing area almost certainly improved the turning performance, while the short mid-span unswept section of the leading edge acted in the same way as a leading-edge slot. Despite the latter effect, the Flagon-D wing still retained at mid-span the traditional wing fence preferred by Soviet designers.

The improved E model entered service in 1973, aerodynammically resembling the earlier aircraft but much modified beneath the skin. The R-13 turbojet fitted to second-generation MiG-21s replaced the earlier R-11, offering a six per cent thrust increase, while the avionics installation was completely revised. No radar type has been publicly identified with this version, but the 35nm (65km) range radar known to NATO as Twin Scan seems a likely candidate.

Latest model to enter service is the Flagon-F. Despite the new pattern of ogival nose radome, this variant probably uses the same avionics as Flagon-E, but the engines have again been uprated—probably by replacing the R-13 with the latest Tumanski R-25 turbojet used by third-generation MiG-21s.

Despite the repeated upgrading, Flagon remains a relatively primitive interceptor by Western standards. There is, for example, no sign of a HUD in the cockpit, so the interception is presumably flown by means of head-down displays. At first sight it is surprising that the opportunity was not taken to add a second cockpit for a radar operator, since the two-seat Flagon-C trainer shows that this would have been possible. Extensive Soviet reliance on GCI techniques allows the use of single-seat interceptors and the aircraft is a Soviet equivalent to the US F-106.

Normal warload consists of two AA-3 Anab or AA-3-3 Advanced Anab missiles on underwing pylons. Two more can be fitted on the under-fuselage pylons normally used to carry external fuel tanks. A mixture of infra-red and SAR-guided rounds are carried. Although the latest models have been reported as carrying AA-6 Acrid, a more likely armament might be the newer AA-7 Apex. Some sources claim that Flagon is fitted with an internal cannon, but there are no signs of such an installation.

Sukhoi Su-17/20/22 Fitter

Data for Su-17
Specifications: length, 61ft 6in (18.75m); span, (swept) 34ft 9in (10.6m), (unswept) 45ft 11in (14.0m); height, 15ft 7in (4.75m); weight (maximum take-off), 39,000lb (17,700kg).
Max speed: Mach 2.17.
Service ceiling: 59,000ft (18,000m).
Range: (hi-lo-hi tactical radius) 340nm (630km).
Armament: see text.
Powerplant: one Lyulka AL-21F-3 turbojet rated at 17,200lb (7,800kg) dry thrust, 24,700lb (11,200kg) with afterburner.

In order to create the first of what has now become a long series of VG Fitter variants, the Sukhoi designers started by replacing the Lyulka AL-7F-1 single-shaft turbojet of the Su-7 with the newer AL-21F-3. This engine is based on the earlier powerplant and may even be directly interchangeable. Various components, such as the compressor, have been redesigned, and this has given the unit more than 16 per cent more dry thrust and an 11 per cent improvement in after-burning thrust.

Given the low internal fuel capacity and resulting short range of the original Su-7, these increased thrust levels might have reduced endurance still further, but the new engine had significantly better sfc performance, while an additional 1,200lb (550kg) of internal fuel was provided by fitting a shallow dorsal spine, first used on the two-seat Su-7U Moujik trainer, in order to house the internal fuel displaced by the addition of a rear cockpit.

Long-overdue improvements were also made to the avionics installation. The SRD-5M radar (known to NATO as High Fix) was retained in the intake centre-body, but the latter was modified to alter its position automatically with changing airspeed and altitude. The simple pitot boom of the Su-7 was replaced by two probes containing the new air-data sensors. Passive radar-warning facilities were upgraded by substituting the 360-degree coverage Sirena III RWR for the earlier Sirena II, which covered only the rear sector.

Four pylons for fuel tanks or ordnance are located under the non-swivelling centre section of the wing. Two are located directly beneath the large fences mounted at the outboard edges of the centre section, and the other two project forwards from the fixed-section leading edge. Stores may also be mounted on four under-fuselage locations. Up to 11,000lb (5,000kg) of ordnance may be carried.

The resulting Su-17 aircraft was designated Fitter-C by NATO when the first operational deployments were detected in 1972. The new type could carry about twice the load of the Su-7 over about a third greater range, while requiring half the runway length.

Next model to appear was dubbed "Fitter-D" by NATO. This had an extended forward fuselage, a chin-mounted radome housing the antenna of a terrain-

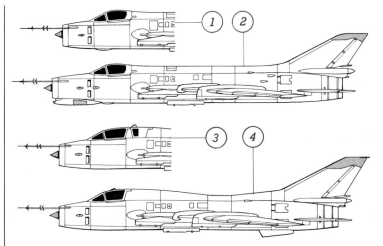

1. **Flagon-D interceptor with conical nose radome.**
2. **Flagon-C two-seat trainer, probably designated Su-15U.**
3. **Low-drag ogival radome introduced on Flagon-F.**
4. **Simple delta wing flown on Flagon-A.**
5. **Compound-sweep tested on Flagon-B STOL prototype.**
6. **Definitive wing used on Flagon-C, -D, -E and -F.**

Above: The fitting above the rear canopy of this Flagon-C trainer is a periscope to give the instructor a forward view.

Below: Flagon-F interceptor of the Soviet PVO air-defence forces.

Below: Su-20 Fitter-C is the limited-standard export version of the Soviet Air Force's Su-17. This example is Polish.

Left: Fitter variants:
1. *Su-17 Fitter-C with short forward fuselage.*
2. *Fitter-D with elongated nose and chin-mounted equipment fairing.*
3. *Latest two-seat model.*
4. *Fitter-J with Tumanski engine and revised tail fin.*

Right: Su-17 Fitter-C:
5. *Wing fully forward (28°).*
6. *Wing fully swept (62°).*

avoidance radar, and a small optical port in the lower part of the intake centrebody behind which was mounted a laser marked-target seeker.

Having created these versions, the Sukhoi bureau then broke from tradition by assigning new type numbers to a further series of export variants with simplified avionics. First export version was the Su-20, which was basically a simplified Su-17 Fitter-C. When

Peru announced the acquisition of a version designated Su-22 in 1977, utter chaos descended on the designations of the Fitter series, most of the subsequent versions being known only by their NATO reporting names at present, rather than by Su-designations.

The Peruvian Su-22s turned out to have a heavily bulged rear fuselage housing not the AL-21 powerplant but the Tumanski R-29B engine originally developed for the MiG-27. Some sources report this as being a turbofan, some a turbojet. The Su-22 wing pylons were wired for AA-2 Atoll missiles in order to give a limited air-to-air capability, but in most other respects the aircraft was very much "stripped-down" to an avionics standard similar to that of the Su-7. This is probably the

version known to NATO as Fitter-F.

The first two-seat trainer was the Fitter-C, with a drooped nose section to improve the view from the rear seat, and only one cannon. The revised forward fuselage seems to have created problems with directional stability, since this version was followed by the Fitter-G, which introduced a taller pattern of vertical fin and a shallow ventral fin, in addition to

receiving a deeper dorsal spine plus the centrebody-mounted marked-target seeker.

Next single-seat version for the Soviet Air Force was the Lyulka-engined Fitter-H, with the new tail fins and deeper spine. Fitter-J has the Tumanski engine and a more angular pattern of vertical fin. The latest two-seat model combines the Fitter-E nose section with a Fitter-F-standard rear fuselage and Tumanski engine.

Sukhoi Su-24 Fencer

Type: all-weather strike aircraft.
Specifications: length, 69ft 10in (21.29m); span, (swept) 31ft 3in (9.53m), (unswept) 56ft 3in (17.15m); height, 18ft 0in (5.5m); weight (maximum take-off), 87,000lb (39,500kg).
Max speed: Mach 2.0+.
Service ceiling: 57,500ft (17,500m).
Range: (hi-lo-hi tactical radius with external fuel and 4,400lb (2,000kg) warload) approx. 900nm (1,700km).
Armament: see text.
Powerplant: see text.

With the entry into service in 1974 of the Sukhoi Su-24 Fencer, the capabilities of Frontal Aviation units of the Soviet Air Force experienced a significant improvement. For the first time regiments were receiving an aircraft which was custom-designed for the deep-penetration/strike role instead of having to make do with off-the-shelf equipment. Fencer is virtually a "mini-F-111", capable of ranging over most of Western Europe and delivering its payload within 180ft (55m) of the target in all weathers. The aircraft was first reported as the Su-19, a designation which may have been applied to the prototypes. Production aircraft are designated Su-24.

For a long time Fencer was a mystery aircraft never seen by Western eyes. As numerical strength built up, the aircraft was assigned only to units operating within the Soviet Union. Only in 1979 was one regiment briefly deployed to Templin air base in East Germany in what may have been a deliberate ploy to allow the West its first glimpse of the type.

From nose to tail the aircraft is packed with "firsts" for the Soviet aerospace industry. The nose radome houses a multi-mode pulse-Doppler radar. No simple re-hash of existing technology, this all-new set represents a major step forward for the Soviet avionics industry, offering terrain-avoidance and other modes. The same radome probably contains a second radar for the navigation/attack function. Also in the nose section is a laser ranger and marked-target seeker, while existence of other sensors such as FLIR and LLTV is likely.

The two-man crew sit side-by-side in an F-111-style cockpit. One is a weapon system operator to handle the avionics suite, which undoubtedly includes a HUD for a low-level navigation/attack data, plus a comprehensive internally mounted ECM system.

The aircraft seems remarkably "clean", lacking many of the conspicuous antenna arrays easily indentifiable on most Soviet types. This suggests that great care has been taken to minimise drag by means of flush-mounted patterns of antenna. Some protrusions can be seen, particularly under the nose. Navigation is almost certainly via an INS, but the antenna for a Doppler radar is located immediately behind the nosewheel doors.

Soviet designers tend to use platforms laid down by a central research authority, and the wing-tailplane combination of the Su-24 is broadly similar to that on the MiG-23/27 series. There are significant differences, however. Although the fixed section of the wing may superficially resemble that of Flogger, the moveable section is wider in chord and lacks the distinctive leading-edge "dog-tooth" of the Mikoyan aircraft. Like the Mikoyan aircraft, Fencer uses differential spoilers

for roll control, but the trailing-edge flaps are thought to be double slotted rather than the single-slotted configuration used on Flogger.

Each wing moving section is fitted with the first example of a swivelling pylon to be seen on a Soviet aircraft. Large external tanks have been seen on two pylons located under the fixed section, while a further four hardpoints are available beneath the fuselage. Total weapon load is estimated at 17,500lb (8,000kg), and can consist of free-falling "iron" or "smart" bombs, fuel-air explosives, or specialised anti-tank or anti-runway weapons. Missiles available for use include the AS-7 Kerry command-guided missile, the AS-9 anti-radar weapon or the new AS-10 electro-optical or AS-11 TV-guided missile. Some sources claim that AA-2 Atoll or AA-8 Aphid missiles can be carried, but, like the F-111, Fencer is

Sukhoi Su-25 Frogfoot (RAM-J)

Data: no reliable specifications available.

First evidence that the Soviet Union was developing an equivalent to the Fairchild A-10 came in 1978. USAF reconaissance satellites have photographed prototypes of the aircraft, thought to a product of the Sukhoi design bureau, during tests at the Soviet Air Force experimental centre at Ramenskoye. When first identified, the type was given the designation RAM-J by the US. Some reports have also used the designation "T-58", but this does not fit any known Soviet, US or NATO system of designations. The aircraft has been assigned the reporting name Frogfoot.

In appearance RAM-J is smaller than the US aircraft, and has a maximum take-off weight of around 35,000lb (16,000kg). Reports suggest that the aircraft has

an unswept wing, engines located in the wing roots and an armament of one multi-barrel rotary cannon of heavy calibre and up to ten hardpoints capable of carrying "iron" or "smart" bombs up to 1,100lb (500kg) in weight, and air-to-surface missiles or pod launchers for unguided rockets.

The twin powerplants are probably non-afterburning versions of the Tumanski R-13 turbojet. The degree to which the aircraft has been armoured against hostile fire and fitted with redundant

systems is impossible to judge at this stage, but clues may be gleaned once photographs become available. Deliveries of production aircraft are expected to begin in 1983 or 1984.

In the past, Soviet Air Force tactical thinking did not favour

US-style close-support operations, emphasising pre-planned "set-piece" attacks, but there are already signs that tactical doctrine is being updated to allow the more flexible style of operations needed to make best use of the RAM-J.

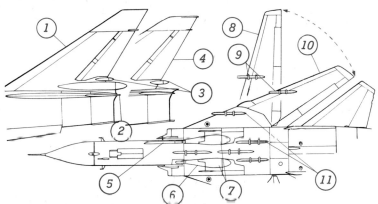

Left: Su-24 details:
1. Later pattern of tail fin.
2. Braking parachute fairing.
3. Antenna for radar-warning receiver (Sirena III?).
4. Early pattern of tail fin with lower height, rounded tip and no braking parachute.
5. Fairing for 30mm cannon.

6. Fairing for 23mm cannon?
7. Air brakes.
8. Wing in fully-forward (16°) position.
9. Swivelling stores pylon on wing.
10. Wing at maximum sweep (68°). Intermediate position is 45°.
11. Fixed hard points.

Left: Su-24A carrying large auxiliary fuel tanks, with small nose fins, on wing glove pylons. Note swivelling pylons on moving wing section.

Below: Su-24A with early-model tail fin, braking parachute and large fuel tank on the glove pylon. The small fins on the tank nose help ensure clean separation.

essentially a bomber, lacking the wing loading and thrust-to-weight ratio for air-to-air combat.

Two fairings may be seen below the fuselage, that on the port side being clearly a cannon, thought to be of 30mm calibre. The smaller fairing to starboard is more controversial. It is similar in shape to the port installation, leading some observers to suggest that it contains a second cannon of 23mm calibre. Such a mixture of calibres would complicate weapon aiming, and no convincing hypothesis to explain the usefulness of such dual-calibre armament has been advanced.

The dorsally mounted air-brakes are mounted at the same location as the port and starboard fairings. They must conform to the same shape, therefore, and may even form part of the fairing skin.

In the past the twin powerplants of the Su-24 have been reported as being ALF-7 turbojets, but this was a throwback to the days when analysts were prone to quote this engine as being the powerplant of such diverse types as the MiG-23 and Su-15. Current opinion favours the Tumanski R-29B turbojet used in the MiG-23.

NATO expects the operational role of Fencer to be deep strike in the rear areas, tactics which could severely disrupt the Alliance's reinforcement plans. It will probably be based well back from the front line in an attempt to keep its bases relatively safe from NATO air strikes, and to provide the extensive maintenance facilities which this complex aircraft requires.

Given the need to intercept USAF cruise-missile carriers at long distances from the Soviet borders, the Sukhoi team may produce an interceptor variant to replace the ageing Tu-128 Blinder.

Below: Artist's impression of the Su-25 ground-attack aircraft (formerly known as RAM-J). Service trials have included combat use in Afghanistan against guerilla positions. If the engines are non-afterburning Tumanski R-13 turbojets as suggested by US Intelligence, intake air may be mixed with the hot efflux to reduce the infra-red signature.

Sukhoi Su-27 (RAM-K)

Data: no reliable specifications available.

This two-seat heavy interceptor is reported to be in the same performance class as the Grumman F-14. It is armed with six or eight missiles, and possesses a track-while-scan radar having a maximum search range of at least 60nm (111km) and ability to track at 45nm (83km). Offering look-down shoot-down performance, the new fighter is designed to cope with low-altitude intruders. Most sources describe this aircraft as being a Sukhoi design

with a radar search range of up to 130nm (240km) and the ability to track targets at 100nm (185km). It is possible that two aircraft are under development, but more likely that the current attributions are not completely clear. Similar confusion existed with the smaller RAM-L fighter.

Combat thrust-to-weight ratio is expected to be at least 1.2:1, and top speeds of Mach 2.3 at

altitude and 1.1-1.2 at sea level are reported. Combat radius is likely to be around 500nm (925km). RAM-K is reported to be twin-engined but no details of the powerplant have emerged. The new interceptor is expected to enter service around 1985 and is probably intended to replace

the Sukhoi Su-15 Flagon.

Primary armament of the new interceptor is likely to be the latest AA-9 missile, a radar-guided weapon of 25nm (46km) range. In the longer term, it may carry two

Transall C-160

Type: tactical transport.
Specifications: length, 106ft 3in (32.40m); span, 131ft 3in (40.00m); height, 38ft 3in (11.65m); weight (maximum take-off), 112,430lb (51,000kg).
Max speed: 277kt (513km/hr).
Service ceiling: 28,000ft (8,500m).
Range: (with 16-tonne payload), 1,000nm (1,850km).
Max payload: 35,300lb (16,000kg).
Powerplants: four Rolls-Royce Tyne turboprops; each rated at 6,100ehp (4,550kW).

On 2 December 1980 Aérospatiale rolled out the first production Transall of a batch of 25 being built for the French Air Force. This aircraft took to the air on 9 April 1981, almost two decades after the first flight of the prototype C.160 and eight years after the last example of the original production run had been delivered. The Franco-German transport is thus one of the few aircraft to have completed its production run only to be resurrected as a much later date. Some of the original jigs had been retained, but others had been broken up and had to be replaced.

The basic aircraft was developed as a replacement for the piston-engined Noratlas, and a total of 179 examples were delivered to the air forces of France (60), West Germany (110) and South Africa (9). The Luftwaffe later transferred 20 aircraft to the Turkish Air Force and placed others in storage. Less than 30 are currently operational with the Luftwaffe.

In theory France might have been able to obtain additional aircraft from West German stocks but the decision taken in 1976 to restart production seems to have owed more to the desire to maintain employment than to any urgent Armée de l'Air requirement. The French Air Force re-order is for 25 aircraft.

Some modifications have been made to the basic design. The wing centre-section contains

integral fuel tanks of 1,980 Imperial gallons (9,000l), and a refuelling probe is fitted over the cockpit to extend the aircraft's range. Total fuel capacity is 6,170 Imperial gallons (28,000 l), almost twice that of the original version. The wing has also been reinforced, new avionics fitted and the rarely used forward port-side fuselage door has been deleted. Some updating of the avionics has been carried out, but the French Air Force has insisted that the new aircraft be compatible with the old, so that crews can be easily assigned to either version.

West Germany had planned a life-extension programme for its C.160 fleet, but this was cancelled in 1981 as part of a programme of measures intended to reduce defence spending.

Several specialised versions have been proposed. The first is the C.160S maritime-patrol aircraft, equipped with an Omera ORB.32 or Thomson-CSF Varan search radar, Crouzet Nadir Doppler navigation system, fuselage observation blisters and fuselage-mounted Omera cameras. The

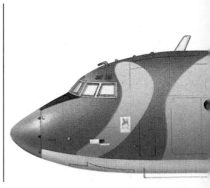

C.160ASF is similar in configuration, but armed with anti-ship missiles or other stores on hardpoints located under the wings or on the main under-carriage fairings.

Aérospatiale and Marconi Avionics have studied a possible AEW version which would use avionics based on the systems of the Nimrod AEW.3, but it is unlikely that this will be ordered. France's requirement for an AEW aircraft will probably be met by the Grumman E-2C Hawkeye.

newer weapons—the medium-range AA-XP-1 and the longer-range AA-XP-2. These are all-aspect missiles with maximum ranges of around 20nm (37km) and 38nm (70km) respectively.

Below: Artist's impression of the variable-geometry Sukhoi interceptor currently on trial at the Ramenskoye flight test centre. The missile shown is an AA-7 Apex medium-range weapon.

1. Flight-refuelling probe on ten of the new-production Transalls. These will provide long-range airlift capability for French rapid-deployment forces.
2. Extended nose radome on new-production aircraft.
3. Proposed maritime-patrol version with . . .
4. AM39 Exocet anti-ship missiles . . .
5. DF and ELINT antennas in wingtip pods and . . .
6. OMERA ORB-32 or Thomson-CSF Varan radar in ventral radome. Both would offer a 360° search capability against surface targets.

Left: The Transall C-160 executes a slow pass with flaps down and tail ramp lowered.

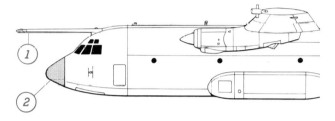

Below: Many of the Luftwaffe's C.160 fleet are currently in storage, so West Germany will not be placing follow-on order for new-build aircraft. Less than half the force is in operational service, and some have been sold to Turkey.

50 ✠ 17

61-MQ

Above: Transall C-160 of the 61e Escadre de Transport of the French Air Force.

Tupolev Tu-16/Sian H-6 Badger

Type: strategic bomber, tanker, maritime patrol and EW aircraft.
Specifications: length, 114ft 2in (34.8m); span, 108ft 0in (32.93m); height, 35ft 6in (10.8m); weight (normal take-off), 160,000lb (72,000kg).
Max speed: 535kt (992km/hr).
Service ceiling: 40,000ft (12,000m).
Range: 2,600-3,100nm (4,800-5,700km).
Armament: see text.
Powerplant: two Mikulin AM-3, turbojets each rated at 19,250lb (8,750kg) dry thrust.

Despite their age and limited performance, more than 800 Tupolev Tu-16 Badgers remain in service with the Soviet Air Force. Small numbers were exported, but only Egypt continues to operate the type, maintaining 16 of the 25 originally supplied in the late 1960s with the help of spare parts provided by China.

When the type first flew, back in 1952, its Mikulin AM-3 turbojet was one of the most powerful in existence and clearly a major step forward in Soviet engine technology, allowing a useful strategic

bomber to be created with only two engines instead of the four fitted to the British V bombers and the six powerplants of the Boeing B-47.

In all other respects, the design is conservative and offers limited performance. Even by the standards of the mid-1950s a cruising speed of 535kt (992km/hr) and a service ceiling of only 40,000ft (12,000m) offered few challenges to defending interceptors, but the aircraft is equipped with a heavy battery of defensive armament — twin 23mm cannon in remotely controlled dorsal and ventral barbettes and in a manned tail position.

Many of the older versions have been phased out. Badger-D is still used for maritime reconnaissance, and has a large "duck-bill" nose radome plus additional dorsal radomes. The missile-armed Badger-G started life with the AS-5 Kelt missile, but some have been modified to carry the new AS-6 Kingfish.

Four variants are used for EW duties. Badger-F carries Elint systems in two underwing pods, while the -K has been fitted out with under-fuselage Elint radomes.

Badger-H is a "chaff-bomber" intended to screen attacking formations, while Badger-J carries jamming systems in a canoe-shaped ventral fairing beneath the weapons bay.

The original Badger-A bomber version, complete with the traditional Soviet-style glazed nose, is still deployed in small numbers by the Soviet Air Force as a tanker aircraft. Badger-A received

a new lease of life in 1968 when the first Chinese-built examples left the Sian production line. Construction of this aircraft as the Sian H-6 was a major project for Chinese industry, which may capitalise on the experience gained by developing reconnaissance, tanker or EW variants. A missile-armed equivalent of the Badger-G is also possible. A total of 80 aircraft have been built so far.

Tupolev Tu-95/142 Bear

Data for Bear-F
Type: maritime reconnaissance bomber.
Specifications: length, 162ft 5in (49.5m); span, 167ft 8in (51.1m); height, 39ft 9in (12.12m); weight (maximum take-off), 415,000lb (188,000kg).
Maximum speed: see text.
Service ceiling: 44,300ft (13,500m).
Range: 6,770nm (12,550km).
Armament: ordnance in fuselage bay, plus tail-mounted 23mm cannons.
Powerplants: four Kuznetsov NK-12MV turboprops each rated at 14,800ehp (11,000ekW).

In creating an intercontinental bomber Soviet designers selected the unlikely combination of turbo-

ched by current service aircraft, which have a top speed of no more than 470kt (870km/hr) at best, and likely to be around 435kt (805km/hr) in practice. Normal cruising speed is around 405kt (750km/hr).

It is just possible that at the time when the Bear wing planform was developed, plans called for the new bomber to be jet-powered. Once the decision to use turboprops had been taken, the need to minimise development time might have resulted in the existing planform being retained.

Some 100 Bears still serve as bombers with the Long Range Aviation arm of the Soviet Air Force. Their usefulness in this role is probably more due to the negligible strength of the US air

type in their own right, with the designation Tu-142. First subtype for this role was the Bear-C, which seems to have been a simple adaptation of Bear-B. Main task of the later Bear-D is thought to be over-the-horizon targeting of anti-ship missiles such as the SS-N-3 Shaddock and SS-N-12. Bear E is thought to be an Elint aircraft, but carries an array of camera ports in the weapons bay.

Many aircraft are being upgraded to the Bear-F standard, which now makes up half Naval Aviation's Bear fleet, and features extended nacelles on the inboard engines (probably to reduce drag), an extended front fuselage, repositioned ventral radome, and additional storage bays in the rear fuselage replacing the normal

Above: USAF F-4 Phantom escorts a prowling Bear away from US-controlled airspace.

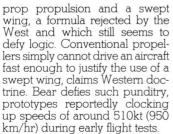

prop propulsion and a swept wing, a formula rejected by the West and which still seems to defy logic. Conventional propellers simply cannot drive an aircraft fast enough to justify the use of a swept wing, claims Western doctrine. Bear defies such punditry, prototypes reportedly clocking up speeds of around 510kt (950 km/hr) during early flight tests. This figure could not be mat-

defences than to any virtues of the original design. These aircraft are probably Bear-B missile carriers converted to accept the AS-4 Kitchen instead of the original AS-3 Kangaroo missile.

At least 70 Bears are used for maritime reconnaissance by Soviet Naval Aviation, a task for which the type's long range makes it well suited. The Soviet Union regards such aircraft as a separate

dorsal gun barbette. Bulged nose-wheel doors suggest that the undercarriage has been revised, perhaps to make the aircraft more suitable for use from poor airfields while on detachment to overseas air bases.

Minor variations on these basic types are common. Some Bear-D aircraft have a cropped tail cone

fitted in place of the normal rear-gunner's position. This may house a trailing VLF antenna for strategic communications with submarines, making the type a Soviet equivalent to the US Navy's C-130 TACAMO aircraft. Some Bear-Fs have what may be an antenna fairing projecting from the rear of the vertical fin.

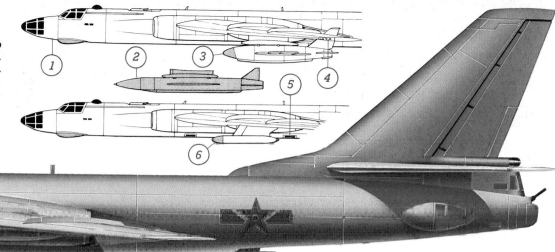

Left: Tu-16 Badger-G anti-shipping bomber of the Arab Republic of Egypt Air Force. Underwing are Kelt missiles.

Below: China's Sian H-5 bomber is based on the Tupolev Badger-A. It is currently the only effective Chinese long-range bomber.

Top and left:
1. Badger-A bomber.
2. AS-6 Kingfish air-to-surface missile carried by some Badger-Gs.
3. Most Badger-Gs carry the AS-5 Kelt.
4. Wingtip flight-refuelling connector on some aircraft.
5. Bomb bay camera pack on Badger-E bomber.
6. ESM pod on Badger-F.
7. Badger-C with . . .
8. AS-2 Kipper missile.
9. Badger-D maritime ESM version with ventral radomes.

Below: A small number of obsolescent Kelt-armed Badger-G aircraft still serve with the Egyptian Air Force.

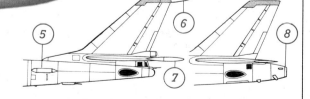

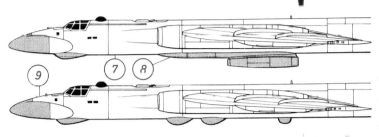

1. Bear-B (missile-armed) and Bear-C (maritime patrol) versions share a common nose section with a large "duck-bill" radome.
2. AS-3 Kangaroo missile (on Bear-B only).
3. Bear-A nose section with small chin-mounted radome.
4. Camera ports on Bear-E.

Left: Bear-D maritime-patrol and missile-targetting aircraft with large belly radome. The tail cone seen here is not widely-fitted to Bear-D, and may house a trailing VLF antenna.

5. Blister fairing on Bear-B, -C and -D.
6. Fairing on late Bear-F.
7. Fin-tip ESM antennas on Bear-D.
8. Tail cone on some Bear-D.

9. Bear-D maritime-patrol and missile-targetting version with enlarged chin radar and large ventral radome.
10. Fuselage stretch on Bear-F. Note smaller ventral radome.

Tupolev Tu-22 Blinder

Data for Blinder-A
Type: supersonic tactical bomber.
Specifications: length, 132ft 11in (40.53m); span, 90ft 10in (27.7m); height, 35ft 0in (10.67m); weight (maximum take-off), 185,000lb (83,900kg).
Max speed: Mach 1.4.
Service ceiling: 60,000ft (18,300m).
Range: (tactical radius) 1,670nm (3,100km).
Armament: up to 17,500lb (8,000kg) of bombs plus a single 23mm tail gun.
Powerplants: see text.

In the same way that the West continued to pour defence funding into improved high-altitude bomber projects during the late 1950s and early 1960s, the Soviet Air Force clung stubbornly to this obsolete method of weapon delivery. The prototype Tu-22 probably flew in 1959, at a time when Western Europe had already flown supersonic interceptors such as the Mirage III and Lightning. The type should logically have been scrapped, since it lacked the Mach 2 performance necessary to make interception difficult. A small number of the Blinder-A version were built as long-range bombers, but thereafter production was quickly switched to the missile-armed Blinder-B and maritime-reconnaissance Blinder C.

All Blinder-A bombers and Blinder-B missile-carriers have now been retired from Soviet service, but small batches of the former have been exported to favoured client states. Iraq operates 12 examples, which have seen action against Kurdish guerrillas. Libya operates 24, and despatched several to Uganda to combat the invasion which toppled the Amin regime.

The aircraft is much less technically advanced than such Western first-generation supersonic bombers as the Convair B-58 Hustler, Rockwell A-5 Vigilante and Dassault Mirage IV, and has a lower performance. The area-ruled fuselage and highly swept wing were low-risk technical solutions, but the traditional Tupolev undercarriage fairings look odd on a supersonic type. The engines are thought to be Koliesov VD-7 afterburning turbojets rated at 31,000lb (14,00kg) maximum thrust and the tail mountings represent a novel but probably unsuccessful method of reducing drag.

For conversion training, a small number of Blinder-D were built, complete with a second canon for the instructor above and behind the flight deck.

At least one variable-geometry Blinder is reported to have flown, but the project was presumable shelved in favour of the custom-designed Backfire, although the latter is referred to by the Soviet authorities as the "Tu-22M"—the logical designation for a swing-wing Blinder. The existence of a long-range interceptor version has not yet been confirmed.

Tupolev Tu-22M (Tu-26) Backfire

Data for Backfire-B
Type: long-range medium bomber.
Specifications: length, 132ft (40.2m); span, swept 86ft (26.2m), unswept 113ft (34.4m); height, 33ft (10.1m).
Max speed: Mach 1.8-2.0.
Service ceiling: 62,000ft (19,000m).
Range: see text.
Armament: see text.
Powerplants: two Kuznetsov turbofans each rated at 45,000lb (20,500kg) with afterburner.

Ever since the first prototypes were reported to be on trial back in 1971, Backfire has been a source of political controversy. Many assessments of the aircraft's capability reflected the bomber's perceived role rather than aerodynamic and engineering reality, with some sources still claiming an unrealistic Mach 2.25 dash capability and intercontinental range.

For a long time Backfire was assumed to have a maximum take-off weight of around 285,000lb (129,545kg) and to carry sufficient fuel to allow strategic bombing operations against Continental USA. These figures, if correct, would give Backfire an unusually high wing loading of around 160lb/sq.ft (783kg/m²), and imply unacceptable engine-out performance.

In practice, maximum take-off weight is likely to be no more than 245,000lb (110,000kg)—a value which gives more acceptable wing loading and thrust-to-weight ratio figures. As the Soviet Union has long insisted, the aircraft is intended for "Eurostrategic" missions rather than as an intercontinental bomber. Hi-lo-hi combat radius is likely to be around 1,400nm (2,600km). Should the defences in the target area be penetrable at high altitude, Backfire could probably manage a tactical radius of 2,500nm (4,600 km), including a 200nm supersonic dash at top speed. The latter figure is probably no more than Mach 1.8 to 2.0.

For the purposes of Salt II, the US Government stated that it assessed Backfire to have an intercontinental capability "under certain flight conditions". This probably reflects a one-way sortie with in-flight refuelling in mid-ocean and a subsequent landing in Cuba. The military realism of such a flight profile is questionable, since the USAF would certainly attack any airfield offering sanctuary to bombers which had attacked US territory.

Backfire is fitted with an airborne refuelling probe. During the protracted Salt II negotiations in the late 1970s, some aircraft

Above: The massive tail fin is believed to house a fuel tank.

were seen to have this fitting removed, but until more evidence is available it must be assumed to be a standard fixture.

In most respects the design is conservative, drawing upon experience gained on the earlier Tu-22 and Tu-28 programmes. The engines are almost certainly militarised versions of the Kuznetsov NK-144 reheated turbofans which power the Tu-144 supersonic transport. The wing planform uses the outboard pivot points

Tupolev Tu-? Blackjack (RAM-P)

Data: no reliable specifications available.

First evidence for the existence of a new Soviet variable-geometry bomber came in the late 1970s, when the aircraft was reported to be almost ready for roll-out. Flight trials at Ramenskoye test centre gave US Intelligence its first detailed look at the new aircraft. Far from being a derivative of Backfire, it is a new design significantly larger than the Rockwell B-1, and the long-awaited replacement for Long Range Aviation's obsolete Tu-95 Bear and Mya-4 Bison bombers.

Given the interim designation RAM-P by US Intelligence, the new aircraft has a full variable-geometry wing and four powerplants clustered two on either side of the fuselage in a B-1-like configuration. It is tempting to speculate that these engines may be the variable bypass-ratio units developed by the Koliesov bureau and used to power the latest version of the Tu-144 Charger supersonic transport. RAM-P has been photographed on the same flight line as several Chargers, lending credence to earlier reports that a reconnaissance bomber version of this delta-winged airliner is being developed.

Earliest reports of the new bomber suggested that the aircraft might be operational by 1982,

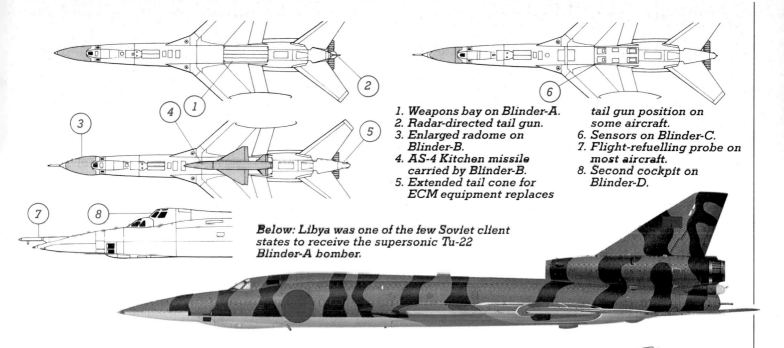

1. Weapons bay on Blinder-A.
2. Radar-directed tail gun.
3. Enlarged radome on Blinder-B.
4. AS-4 Kitchen missile carried by Blinder-B.
5. Extended tail cone for ECM equipment replaces

tail gun position on some aircraft.
6. Sensors on Blinder-C.
7. Flight-refuelling probe on most aircraft.
8. Second cockpit on Blinder-D.

Below: Libya was one of the few Soviet client states to receive the supersonic Tu-22 Blinder-A bomber.

pioneered by the Su-17 Fitter. This scheme reduces trim changes resulting from wing movement, but aerodynamic penalties are created by the relatively large fixed section. The wing is effectively of semi-variable configuration, and Backfire sports a prominent wing fence, intended to control the local air-flow at the wing-glove junction.

The early Backfire-A version, believed to equip only a single squadron, used the traditional Tupolev trailing-edge pods to house the rearward-retracting undercarriage. The drag penalties associated with this installation on the earlier Tu-22 were obviously not sufficient to warn the design team against using these on a Mach 2 design.

Flight testing soon showed that Backfire-A fell short of range targets, so a redesign was undertaken. The undercarriage was

changed to an inward-retracting design in which the wheels are stowed within the fuselage. At the same time, according to some sources, the outer wing panels were redesigned with increased taper on the trailing edge in order to reduce the loads on the wing carry-through box. These changes resulted in the current Backfire-B, which began service trials in 1975.

Maximum weapons load has been estimated as up to 26,500lb (12,000kg), and can consist of free-falling bombs carried in the weapons bay or externally mounted air-to-surface missiles such as the AS-4 Kitchen. Fittings mounted beneath the inlet trunking of some aircraft have been interpreted as weapons racks, but such installations would impose a severe drag.

1. Tu-22M's external racks, perhaps for missiles, decoy RPVs, add-on ECM equipment, chaff rockets or other penetration aids.
2. AS-4 Kitchen rocket-propelled stand-off missile.
3. Wing in fully-formed (20°) position.
4. Wing fully-swept (55°) for high-speed dash.

Below: Backfire-B with refuelling probe and AS-4 Kitchen missile.

44

but this time scale always seemed optimistic. Like most Soviet next-generation types, it will probably not enter service with regular squadrons until 1985 or later. First estimates suggest that the

aircraft is some 190ft (58m) long with an unswept wingspan of 170ft (52m). Maximum range has been estimated as 7,300nm (13,528km) but a reported Mach 2.3 dash speed seems optimistic.

Below: Artist's impression of the RAM-P swing-wing bomber.

Tupolev Tu-28 Fiddler

Type: long-range interceptor
Specifications: length 85ft (26m); span 65ft (20m); height 23ft (7m); weight (maximum take-off) 100,000lb (45,000kg).
Max speed: Mach 1.75.
Service ceiling: 65,600ft (20,000m).
Range: 2,700nm (4,990km).
Armament: four AA-5 Ash missiles.
Powerplants: two after-burning turbojets, each rated at around 27,000lb (12,300kg) maximum thrust.

Development by the West of long-range stand-off weapons such as the British Blue Steel and US Hound Dog required the Soviet Air Force to field a long-range interceptor capable of engaging the parent aircraft before it released its missiles. This requirement was met by the huge Tu-28 Blinder, a 35-tonne interceptor which owes its origin to the experimental Tu-98 Backfin bomber flown in the 1950s.

The prototype probably flew in 1960, and production deliveries began at a low rate in 1963-4.

These early aircraft carried a large dorsal fairing which may have been the radome for a PPI radar offering 360 degrees of search for use in regions where coverage by ground radars was poor or even non-existent. Strakes fitted beneath the rear fuselage of this version may have been needed to overcome the aerodynamic effects of this large excrescence.

Full-scale production followed in the late 1960s, and the resulting aircraft are deployed at the Soviet Union's northern air bases, where its long range allows interceptor coverage to be provided from the smallest possible number of airfields. Maximum range on internal fuel is around 2,700nm (5,000km), giving a combat radius of anything from 810 to 1,080nm (1,500-2,000km).

This definitive version lacks the dorsal fairing and stabilising strakes of the early models. The semi-autonomous role of this aircraft required a long-range air interceptor radar and missiles to match. The I/J-band radar installed is known to NATO as Big Nose, which, when it first entered service, was almost certainly the most complex airborne radar in Soviet service as well as being the highest powered. Big Nose operates in conjunction with the AA-5 Ash, a weapon available in IR and SAR-guided forms, and having a maximum range of 16nm, (30km).

Less than 100 remain in service, but they are likely to remain operational for some time. The eventual replacement will probably be either the new RAM-K (see Sukhoi Su-25), now under flight test, or else an interceptor version of the Su-24 Fencer.

Tupolev Tu-126 Moss

Type: airborne early-warning aircraft.
Specifications: length, 181ft 1in (55.2m); span, 168ft 0in (51.20m); height, 52ft 8in (16.05m); weight (maximum take-off), 375,000lb (170,000kg).
Max speed: 460kt (850km/hr).
Range: 6,770nm (12,550km).
Armament: none.
Powerplants: four Kuznetsov NK-12MV, each rated at 14,800ehp (11,000ekW).

When the existence of the airborne early warning aircraft was first revealed in 1968 by a Soviet documentary film, alarm was created in some Western defence circles, since the equivalent US aircraft was still on the drawing board and not due to enter service until the mid-1970s.

Moss is an adaption of the Tu-114 transport, rather than the Tu-95/142 bomber, since the civil aircraft had a fuselage of greater diameter, and was thus more able to house the new avionics. Only about ten examples were built, and they may have been created from airframes originally built for Aeroflot. This small number gives the first clue to the type's limited performance, since an effective aircraft would almost certainly have been procured in larger numbers.

Known to NATO as "Flat Jack", the equipment is mounted in a radome some 36ft (9m) in diameter. The Boeing E-3 Sentry has two antenna installations mounted back-to-back in a single radome, but the Soviet system has only one—examination of photographs shows that half the rotating "saucer" assembly is built of metal. Moss carries a crew of 12, five fewer than that of the US E-3A, and almost certainly a reflection of the Soviet aircraft's simpler avionics. Britain's Nimrod AEW manages to make do with a 12-man crew, but its avionics were not designed in the mid-1960s and therefore they make extensive use of advanced technology automatic data-processing.

Extraction of target returns from ground clutter is the biggest technical problem to be faced in designing a "look-down" radar. Limited signal-processing is the Achilles heel of Moss, giving it some capability over water but almost none over land.

Published reports originating from Pakistan credit Moss with having directed Indian Air Force strikes during the 1971 Indo-Pakistan War, a single Tu-126 having allegedly been deployed temporarily to India. According to Indian authorities, a high-flying aircraft observed by Pakistani radar was indeed helping with Indian air strikes, but was a signals-relay aircraft handling communications with the strike formations. Unless fresh evidence is forthcoming, the reported Indian deployment must be regarded as unproven.

Left: Although similar to the E-3A in appearance, the Tu-126 is no rival to the Boeing aircraft in the performance stakes, claim intelligence sources.

Left: Tu-28 "Fiddler" interceptors with canopies shut and dark sheets over cockpits, inlets and engine bays, and blanking caps in engine nozzles.

Below: No variants of Fiddler have been reported. It remains in service but the current radar has virtually no capability against low-level targets.

Below: The configuration of Moss has been virtually unchanged since the type first entered service. Normal cruising speed is around 350kt (650km/hr).

Below: The tall undercarriage is required in order to give adequate ground clearance to the 18ft 4in (5.6m) diameter propellers.

Vickers VC10

Type: flight-refuelling tanker.
Specifications: length, Mk2—158ft 8in (48.36m), Mk3—171ft (52.32m); span, 146ft 2in (44.55m); height, 39ft 6in (12.04); weight (maximum take-off), approx. 320,000lb (146,500kg).
Max speed: 493kt (914km/hr).
Range: (basic airline configuration) 3,390nm. (6,275km).
Powerplant: four Rolls-Royce Conway Mk 550B turbofans, each rated at 21,800lb (9,900kg) dry thrust.

Nine ex-airline VC10 transports are being rebuilt by British Aerospace for use as flight-refuelling tankers for the Royal Air Force. Five are VC10s formerly operated by British Airways, while the remaining four are Super VC10s supplied to East African Airways. Modifications to both versions are broadly similar and the resulting configurations will be designated K Mk2 and K Mk3 respectively.

An aperture is being cut in the rear fuselage to house the standard Flight Refuelling Mk17 remotely controlled hose and drogue system fitted in a similar location aboard RAF Victor tankers, while Mk32 refuelling pods will be mounted beneath each wing. A non-retractable refuelling probe is being added on the nose.

Basic fuel capacity of the standard VC10 is 17,900 Imperial gallons (81,500l), while the Super can carry almost 19,400 Imperial gallons (88,000l). On both types this is being supplemented by five tanks within the fuselage. Other modifications include the fitting of floodlighting in the wings and rear fuselage for night-refuelling operations, and the installation of an APU in the tail cone. The latter provides ground electrical power and a supply of compressed air for engine starting. Both versions will be powered by Rolls-Royce Conway Mk 550B turbofans, thrust reversers being fitted on the outboard engines.

The RAF already operates the VC10, ten C Mk1 aircraft serving as long-range transports. This version was custom-designed for the RAF, and, broadly speaking, combines the shorter fuselage of the standard VC10 with the increased fuel capacity and wing of the Super. The C Mk1 is currently the only version fitted with the tail-mounted APU, and its Conway 301 engines are physically interchangeable with the Mk 550B on the new tankers.

These transports have flown fewer hours that the youngest ex-airline examples and it is possible that they too will be converted into tankers, and ex-British Airways aircraft used to replace them (especially if a decision is taken to scrap the Victor tankers).

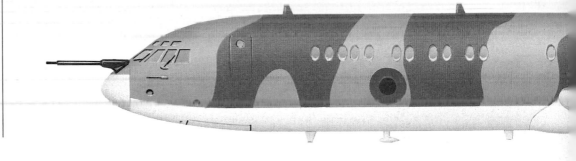

Vought F-8 Crusader

Data for F-8J
Type: single-seat carrier-based fighter/attack aircraft.
Specifications: length, 54ft 6in (16.61m); span, 35ft 2in (10.72m); height, 15ft 9in (4.8m); weight (maximum take-off), 34,000lb (15.4t).
Max speed: 1,188mph (1,912km/h, Mach 1.88).
Service ceiling: 58,000ft (17.7km).
Range: 1,100 miles (1,770km).
Armament: four 20mm Colt-Browning Mk 12 guns; fuselage side pylons for four Sidewinder AAMs, wing triple ejector racks for two 2,000lb (907kg) bombs or Bullpup ASMs, rocket packs or other stores to maximum of 5,000lb (2,268kg).
Popwerplant: one 19,600lb (8,890kg) Pratt & Whitney TF30-P-420 augmented turbofan or 18,000lb (8,164kg) Pratt and Whitney J57-P420A augmented turbojet.

Unique among production fighters in being designed with a variable-incidence wing, so that the pilot could retain a good view over the down-sloping nose during the approach to a carrier, the F-8 was from March 1957 the top fighter in the US Navy and Marine Corps, and even after arrival of the F-4 in 1961 successively improved versions kept it in the front line, and in full production until 1965. It played a major role in Vietnam, not least in its unarmed RF-8A model with large recon cameras in place of the guns, and since 1966 Vought has completed a major remanufacturing programme, converting 61

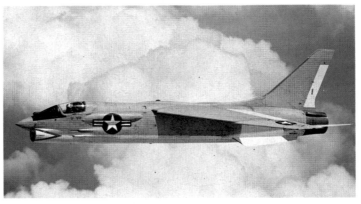

Left: With the phasing out of the RF-8G, the US Navy may find itself deficient in reconnaissance capability.

old F-8Bs into zero-time F-8Ls. 87 Cs into Ks, 89 Ds into Hs, 136 Es into Js and 73 RF-8As into RF-8Gs.

The J remains the most effective version, based on the F-8E in which heavy weapons load was combined with APQ-94 search and fire-control radar. The same basic E model was the starting point for 42 F-8E (FN) aircraft for the French Aéronavale with special high-lift features to permit operations from the small carriers *Foch* and *Clémenceau*. These aircraft operate both in the attack role and also in air-defence roles carrying two Matra R 530 missiles. Like the surviving American F-8s the French aircraft have been remanufactured to zero the airframe life and update the systems and avionics and Flotille 12F is expected to remain operational with these aircraft until at least 1985. No successor has been publicly discussed.

At all times the handling of the F-8 has been very good, and its high regard is shown by the US Navy slogan of the late 1960s (when the remanufacturing programme hardly kept pace with the demand for front-line aircraft), "When you're out of F-8s, you're out of fighters". The fact that about 100 of the 136 F-8Js were re-engined within Navy establishments with the much later and more fuel-efficient TF30 turbofan is not widely known, and it combined with the rebuilt structure to restore flight performance to an even higher level than when new.

Several countries showed interest in acquiring secondhand F-8s, one recipient being the Philippines which for only $11.7 million secured 35 F-8H Crusaders, ten of which were used as spares and the other 25 completely overhauled by Vought and used to equip the 7th Tactical Fighter Squadron of the Philippine Air Force operating from a land base. With over 10,000 hours available on each airframe they are effective multi-role aircraft in the Philippines environment, and must be an all-time record in terms of cost/effective procurement.

Left: A new role for the VC10 airliner is that of airborne tanker. ZA141 is the first of nine K.2/K.3 three-point refuellers for the Royal Air Force.

Below left: This VC10 K.Mk 2 is a rebuilt ex-airline Model 1101. The VC10 K.Mk 3 is based on the Model 1154 Super VC10 airliner and has a longer fuselage.

Left: French Aéronavale F-8E(FN) Crusader at moment of launch from the port catapult of the carrier Foch. Note the angle of wing incidence needed for take-off.

Above left: Light Reconnaissance Squadron 63 (VFP-63) was the last USN regular unit to operate the RF-8G reconnaissance variant. This version is still operational with Reserves.

Below: Rebuilt F-8H Crusader of the Phillipines Air Force. The small fairing immediately ahead of the canopy is an infra-red sensor used to supplement the nose-mounted radar set.

Vought A-7 Corsair II

Data for A-7E
Type: attack fighter.
Specifications: length, 46ft 1in (14.06m); span, 38ft 9in (11.8m); height, 16ft 1in (4.9m); weight (maximum take-off), 42,000lb (19,000kg).
Max speed: 595kt (1,100km/hr).
Service ceiling: 42,000ft (13,000m).
Range: (hi-lo-hi tactical radius with 6,000lb (2,730kg) warload) 450nm (835km).
Armament: up to 15,000lb (6,800kg) of ordnance plus one 20mm cannon.
Powerplant: one Allison TF41 turbofan rated at 15,000lb (6,800kg) dry thrust.

Developed to meet a mid-1960s US Navy requirement for an A-4 replacement, the Vought A-7 Corsair II not only successfully replaced the navy bomber but also emulated the earlier A-3D Skywarrior and F-4 Phantom in being selected for USAF service. The aircraft was not a large-scale export success, but this may have been more a result of US Government policies than any short-comings in the design.

The USN requirement called for an aircraft capable of lifting twice the warload of an A-4 or of carrying the payload of the latter for twice the range. The aircraft was urgently required and had to be both small and cheap, preferably an adaption of an existing type. No speed require-ment was set, but great emphasis was placed by the USN on the need for minimal maintenance. Penalty clauses in the contract would have been invoked had the number of maintenance manhours per flight hour exceeded 11.5.

Vought's winning submission was at first sight a subsonic short-fuselage version of the F-8 Crusader, equipped with a non-afterburning Pratt & Whitney TF30-P-6 turbofan engine of 11,350lb (5,160kg) thrust. In practice, of course, the aircraft grew into a new type in its own right, with a new wing of thicker section and additional fuel capacity but lacking the variable-incidence feature of the F-8. Vought's design team stayed with established technology in order to minimise development time and maintenance require-ments. More than half the fuselage skin area is made of access panels—a total of 35.

By current standards the avionics installation seems very basic, but the APQ-116 radar, roller map display, navigation computer and other components offered a weapon delivery accuracy far in advance of that available from the A-4. Critical systems aboard the aircraft were duplicated or triplicated, and steel and aluminium armour plate was used to protect the pilot from hostile fire.

The first prototype flew on 27 September 1965, less than 18 months after the R&D contract was awarded, and deliveries to operational units began just over a year later in October 1966.

Service reaction to the initial A-7A was favourable, but the type was clearly underpowered. By switching to the TF30-P-8 engine, Vought was able to provide an extra 850lb (385kg) of thrust for the A-7B, which later received the directly interchange-able -P-408 engine, rated at 13,400lb (6,080kg).

In combat the A-7 aquired a good reputation as a long-range "bomb truck" capable of toting payloads of up to 15,000lb (6,800kg) of ordnance and of being able to absorb combat damage. The modest fuel demand of the TF30 engine gave the type such a long range that training missions were often flown with a partial fuel load, but in combat the resulting lack of forward "urge" was criticised.

The first response to these shortcomings was the suggestion that a limited degree of after-burning be used on future versions of the aircraft, but a better solution was available from the UK in the form of the Rolls-Royce Spey engine, built in the US as the 14,500lb (6,600kg) thrust Allison TF41-A-1. In its search for a replacement for the F-100 fighter-bomber the USAF turned to the A-7, and Vought flew the first prototype of the TF41-engined A-7D in 1968. A US Navy TF41 version desig-nated A-7E flew two months later, and production figures for these second-generation variants were eventually to run to more than 1,000 aircraft.

Both had greatly improved avionics. The A-7D featured a new APQ-126 radar, ASN-190 Doppler radar, digital computer, moving-map display and HUD, and carried the 20mm M61A1 rotary cannon in place of the earlier pair of Mk12 weapons. The resulting aircraft may have lacked the simplicity envisaged in the original requirement, but made up for this in increased weapon-delivery accuracy. The avionics of the USN A-7E were broadly similar but biased towards carrier operations. The Navy also opted to use the more powerful 15,000lb (6,800kg) thrust TF41-A-2. USN A-7Es can be fitted with FLIR pods capable of projecting an infra-image into the HUD during night attacks.

The A-7D had a short career in the USAF front line, entering service with the US Air National Guard from 1977 onwards. ANG units received some new-build aircraft from the Vought line as well as ex-USAF examples. These new aircraft include two-seat A-7K trainers. USN training version is the TA-7C, a two-seat variant produced by rebuilding 60 existing A-7B and A-7C single-seaters to add a second cockpit and A-7E avionics.

Despite a successful series of

trials in Switzerland, the A-7G with an uprated TF41-A-3 engine was not adopted by that nation. First export customer was Greece, which ordered 60 A-7Hs. Like the USN A-7E, the Greek aircraft had self-sealing protection on critical fuel lines and on some tanks, as well as fire-suppressing foam in the engine sump tank.

A batch of 20 A-7A ex-USN aircraft was rebuilt with new avionics to meet an order from Portugal. Vought refurbished the airframes, fitted the TF41-P-408 engine used by the A-7B and installed A-7E-standard avionics. The resulting A-7P configuration flew for the first time in 1981.

Above: Snakeye retarded bombs tumble away from a USAF A-7D Corsair II of the 23rd Tactical Fighter Wing based at England AFB. Note TAC badge on fin and unit badge on nose.

Above: Two-seat A-7K Corsair of the 162nd Tactical Fighter Group, Air National Guard, based at Tucson Airport, Arizona.

Below: The A-7H is a land-based version of the TF41-powered A-7E naval aircraft. It retains the wing-folding mechanism and is operated by the Greek Air Force.

1. TA-7C two-seat trainer (rebuilt A-7A or A-7C).
2. A-7K new-build two-seat trainer for US ANG.
3. Universal air-refuelling receptacle on TA-7K.
4. Pave Penny laser marked-target seeker on some USAF aircraft.
5. "Stretched" sections of TA-7K.
6. Air-refuelling receptacle on A-7D.
7. Retractable flight-refuelling probe on A-7E.
8. Single 20mm M61 cannon (A-7D).
9. Two 20mm cannon (A-7A and -P).

Above: Seen prior to delivery is one of the 60 A-7H Corsair IIs acquired by the Greek Air Force in the early '70s. They were the first export customers.

Above: The USAF's A-7D has a dorsal-mounted flight-refuelling receptacle and carries an internally-mounted 20mm Vulcan cannon.

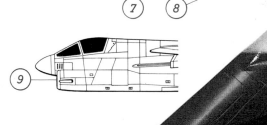

Above: A-7E was the final US Navy attack version, with a TF-41 turbofan engine and avionics broadly similar to those of the land-based A-7D.

Westland Lynx and WG.30

Data for HAS.2 naval version
Type: shipboard ASW and utility/helicopter.
Specifications: fuselage length, 39ft 1in (11.92m); height, 11ft 5in (3.48m); rotor diameter, 42ft (12.8m); weight (maximum take-off), 10,500lb (4,760kg).
Max speed: 125kt (232km/hr).
Range: 320nm (593km).
Armament: see text.
Powerplant: two Rolls-Royce Gem 2, each rated at 750shp (560kW).

Lynx has virtually become the standard West European naval helicopter of the NATO alliance, being in service with the navies of Britain, France, Denmark, the Netherlands, Norway, and West Germany. Along with Puma and Gazelle, it formed part of the 1968 Anglo/French helicopter agreement, and more than 300 have been ordered to date.

Most customers have adopted the type as shipboard helicopter, and the Bendix AQS-18 or Alcatel DUAV 4 "dunking" sonar may be fitted as required by individual operators. A towed ASQ-81 MAD sensor may also be carried. Armament of naval versions can include Mk 44 or Mk 46 light-weight homing torpedoes, carried on pylons on either side of the fuselage, or two Mk 11 depth charges. Royal Navy Lynxs are fitted with a nose-mounted Ferranti Sea Spray search radar and two British Aerospace Dynamics Sea Skua SAR-guided

anti-ship missiles. Aircraft and missile had their combat debut in May 1982. During the British reoccupation of South Georgia, RN Lynxes badly damaged the Argentinian submarine *Santa Fe* with unguided rockets and wire-guided missiles, forcing it to beach and surrender. Sea Skuas saw action a few days later, when RN helicopters sank one Argentinian patrol vessel while operating near Britain's South Atlantic Battle Group, and badly damaged another.

The British Army is the only large-scale user of land-based Lynx aircraft, having more than 100 in service. Up to 100 of these will be fitted to carry eight TOW anti-tank missiles and the associated roof-mounted sighting system. The latter is based on the US Army's chin-mounted sight, but allows the helicopter to expose less of itself while launching and guiding missiles. Britain has ordered 8,400 rounds. Assuming that half of these are earmarked for training purposes, war stocks

should be sufficient to allow each helicopter to reload five or six times.

Early in 1976 Westland began private-venture studies of a heavier twin-engined version with a larger cabin. The resulting WG.30 Lynx is powered by two Rolls-Royce Gem 41-1 turboshafts, each developing 900shp (671kW) of continuous power and up to 1,120shp (835kW) in an emergency. The fixed under-carriage of the standard Lynx is replaced by retractable units; a

Westland Scout and Wasp

Data for Wasp HAS.1.
Type: shipboard utility and ASW helicopter.
Specifications: fuselage length, 30ft 4in (9.24m); height, 11ft 8in (3.56m); rotor diameter, 32ft 3in 99.83m); weight (maximum take-off), 5,500lb (2,500kg).
Max cruising speed: 106kg (196km/hr).
Range: 235nm (435km)
Armament: two Mk 44 homing torpedoes.
Powerplant: one Rolls-Royce Nimbus 503 turboshaft-rated at 710shp (530kW).

Between 1961 and 1974 Westland delivered a total of more than 250 Scout and Wasp helicopters. Scout is a light tactical helicopter for army use, while the navalised Wasp is for general utility and ASW tasks. Most production aircraft were Scouts, but more than 100 Wasps were delivered to the navies of Britain, Australia, Brazil, the Netherlands, New Zealand and South Africa, making the Wasp the most widely exported version.

Scout is of simple design and powered by a single 685shp (511kW) Rolls-Royce Nimbus 102

turboshaft. The cabin can carry a crew of two plus three passengers. The landing gear is of simple skid construction, and the aircraft can carry a wide range of armament, including machine-guns or 20mm cannon on flexible mountings, fixed 7.62mm machine-guns, unguided rockets or even SS.11 anti-tank missiles. Aircraft fitted with the latter carried sighting equipment mounted oin the roof of the cabin.

In order to suit the basic design for shipboard use, Lynx has a four-element landing gear which enables it to straddle bulky ordnance loads such as two Mk 44 homing torpedoes. Other weaponry, including AS.11 or AS.12 wire-guided missiles, can be carried on pylons located on either side of the fuselage. Each undercarriage leg has a single castoring wheel, lockable by sprag brakes. Powerplant of Wasp is the more powerful Nimbus 503 rated at 710shp (530kW).

Although a valuable ASW weapon in its day, Wasp carried no sensors, but was used to deliver homing torpedoes to the location of a hostile "contact" as

determined by the parent vessel from sonar or data from other aircraft or vessels. Most operated from smaller surface ships such as frigates and destroyers, as

well as auxiliary vessels such as the Royal Navy ice-patrol ship *Endurance*.

Most operators are now replacing Wasp with the more

Below: The use of a roof-mounted sight on British Army TOW-equipped Lynx requires the aircraft to expose less of itself when firing and guiding missiles than would have been the case with a US Army-style chin sight.

ARMY XZ647

Left: WG.30 Lynx has a longer fuselage, more powerful engines and a retractable undercarriage.

new fuselage can house up to 14 troops with full equipment, four more than the standard aircraft. The main rotor is increased in size to 43ft 8in (13.31m) diameter, and the size of the tail rotor will also be increased on production aircraft. Wherever possible, the transmission system uses components already proven in Lynx, the WG.30 dynamic system having 85 per cent commonality with the earlier aircraft. The prototype— at that time designated simply "WG.30"—flew on 10 April 1979, but at the time of writing the only sales announced were for the civil Westland 30 version.

Below: Wasp has a wheeled undercarriage instead of the twin skids fitted to land-based Scouts.

ROYAL NAVY DANGER

433

powerful Lynx. The last to remain in front-line service will probably be the small number serving with 22 Sqn of the South African Air Force.

Left: Originally known by its maker's designation P.531, the Scout (seen here) and the Wasp were developed by Saunders-Roe Ltd., later Westland Helicopters. The Scout was designed for the Army and uses a skid undercarriage. The Wasp, ordered by a number of countries for shipboard use, features a castoring four-legged undercarriage for better control on ship decks and a folding tail.

Westland Sea King and Commando

Data for HAS.2
Type: ASW helicopter.
Specifications: fuselage length, 55ft 10in (17.01m); height 15ft 11in (4.85m); rotor diameter, 62ft (18.9m); weight (maximum take-off), 21,000lb (9,525kg).
Max cruising speed: 112kt (208km/hr).
Range: 664nm (1,230km).
Armament: four homing torpedoes or four depth charges (see text).
Powerplants: two Rolls-Royce Gnome H.1400 turboshafts, each rated at 1,660shp (1,240kW).

Latest in a long line of Sikorsky types to be built by Westland, the Sea King is based on the airframe of the US Navy's S-61 Sea King but "under the skin" is a very different aircraft, intended to operate independently of surface vessels when hunting submarines. This requirement led Westland to fit the aircraft with a complete tactical centre and a full range of sensors. All Westland Sea Kings are powered by two Rolls-Royce Gnome turboshafts, engines based on the General Electric T58 used in the S-61.

The original Sea King HAS.1 ordered for the Royal Navy flew on 7 May 1969, and 56 had been delivered by mid-1972. These were later modified to the HAS.2 standard decribed below. Twenty-one of the latter version were built from 1976 onwards, and the entire RN fleet is now being updated to the HAS.5 standard. Search radar of the HAS.2 and HAS.5 is the AW.391, whose dorsal radome gives the cabin a

recognisable "hump". This will later be replaced by the MEL Sea Searcher, whose antenna requires a larger radome. The Plessey Type 195 "dunking" sonar is supplemented by Ultra Electronics miniature sonobuoys. In the HAS.5 the resulting sonic data will be handled by an advanced Marconi Avionics LAPADS acoustic-processing and display system.

Armament includes up to four homing torpedoes—either the US Mk 46 or the new Marconi Space and Defence Sting Ray "smart" homing torpedo—or four Mk 11 depth charges. It is also possible that RN aircraft can carry nuclear depth bombs, but this has never been officially announced. Export aircraft carry simpler avionics, as selected by the customer—usually similar to the RN HAS.1 or HAS.2 standard.

Other versions in UK service are the HAR.3 search and rescue helicopter flown by the RAF and the HC.4 commando transport used by the Royal Marines. The latter is a version of the Westland Commando, a troop-carrying aircraft based on Sea King and capable of lifting 28 fully equipped soldiers. Small numbers of the latter version have been supplied to Egypt and Qatar.

There can be little doubt that the Royal Navy Sea King is the most advanced ASW helicopter in the world, particularly the latest HAS.5 version. The opportunity to prove this came when they were used to protect the British fleet from submarine attack during operations around the Falkland Islands in 1982.

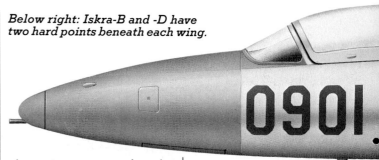

Above: Two of the initial batch of four Commando 2A/C for the Qatar Emiri Air Force. Engine-inlet sand filters are fitted.

WSK Mielec TS-11 Iskra

Data for Iskra-B
Type: basic trainer.
Specifications: length, 36ft 7in (11.15m); span, 33ft 0in (10.06m); height, 11ft 5in (3.50m); weight (max take-off), 8,400lb (3,800kg).
Max speed: 388kt (720km/hr).
Service ceiling: 36,500ft (11,100m).
Range: 626nm (1,160km).
Armament: one 23mm cannon plus light ordnance on two underwing hardpoints.

Despite pressures within the Warsaw Pact for equipment standardisation, Poland decided to adopt the TS-11 Iskra as its basic jet trainer after the design lost in the competition to choose a standard trainer for all Pact air arms.

First studies of a successor to the piston-engined TS-8 Bies trainer started in the mid-1950s, around the time that the Warsaw Pact laid down the requirements for the planned standard trainer. This specification was modest in some respects, calling for a top

speed of only some 350kt (650km/hr), but demanded that the aircraft be easy to maintain and able to operate from grass airfields.

The Polish design team accordingly drew up an unswept mid-wing design powered by a single turbojet engine of indigenous design. In order to keep the jet pipe short, consideration was given to a twin-boom layout, but the final design mounted the tail surfaces at the end of a single tail boom.

The first prototype was used for static tests, but the second flew in February 1960. Two more followed, the latter of which was entered in the Warsaw Pact "fly-off" in 1961. Delays with the SO-1 turbojet resulted in the production rate being held down. First deliveries to the Polish Air Force were of aircraft fitted with the interim H-01 engine.

Iskra A was the basic trainer version, but this was soon joined by the Iskra B (also known as the Iskra 100). This had two hard points under each wing capable

Below right: Iskra-B and -D have two hard points beneath each wing.

of carrying a gun pod, rocket launcher or small bomb.

The improved versions which followed were designated Iskra 200 for the purposes of export promotion. Iskra-C was a single-seat reconnaissance version carrying a camera in the lower fuselage aft of the cockpit. Iskra-D was a two-seater with stronger under-wing hardpoints, and was intended for the light-strike role. Iskra-DF was a hybrid version with the camera payload of the "C" plus the four hardpoints of the "D" version.

Only export customer to order Iskra was India, which bought a batch of 50 in 1975 to act as stop-

gap aircraft until the indigenous Kiran became available in large numbers. More than 40 are still in service. Some attempts were made in the late 1970s to find further customers, but the aircraft, although well made, was by then completely dated. Forward view from the aft cockit is very poor, and can in no way compare with that from modern "stepped-tandem" cockpits. Development of an uprated version powered by an Ivchenko AI-25 turbofan was reported in the late 1970s, but this never entered service.

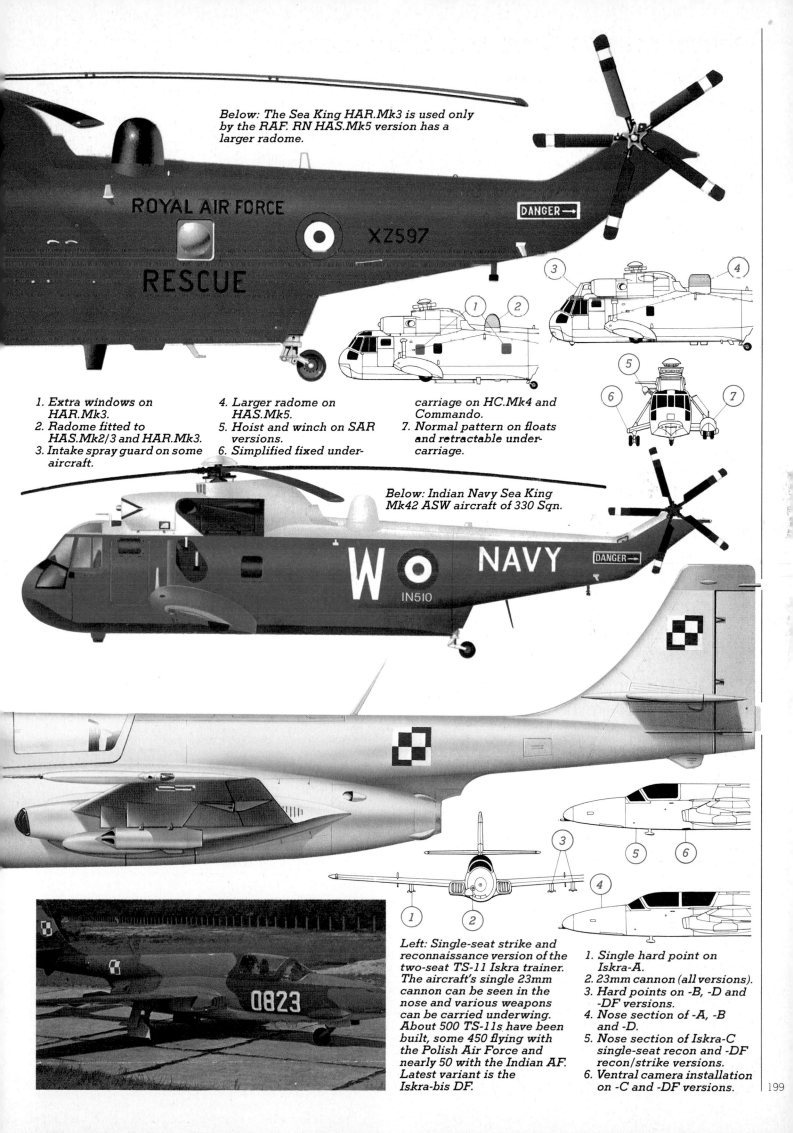

Below: The Sea King HAR.Mk3 is used only by the RAF. RN HAS.Mk5 version has a larger radome.

ROYAL AIR FORCE

XZ597

RESCUE

DANGER →

1. Extra windows on HAR.Mk3.
2. Radome fitted to HAS.Mk2/3 and HAR.Mk3.
3. Intake spray guard on some aircraft.
4. Larger radome on HAS.Mk5.
5. Hoist and winch on SAR versions.
6. Simplified fixed under-carriage on HC.Mk4 and Commando.
7. Normal pattern on floats and retractable under-carriage.

Below: Indian Navy Sea King Mk42 ASW aircraft of 330 Sqn.

W NAVY

1N510

DANGER →

Left: Single-seat strike and reconnaissance version of the two-seat TS-11 Iskra trainer. The aircraft's single 23mm cannon can be seen in the nose and various weapons can be carried underwing. About 500 TS-11s have been built, some 450 flying with the Polish Air Force and nearly 50 with the Indian AF. Latest variant is the Iskra-bis DF.

1. Single hard point on Iskra-A.
2. 23mm cannon (all versions).
3. Hard points on -B, -D and -DF versions.
4. Nose section of -A, -B and -D.
5. Nose section of Iskra-C single-seat recon and -DF recon/strike versions.
6. Ventral camera installation on -C and -DF versions.

0823

Yakovlev Yak-28 Brewer and Firebar

Data for Yak-28P Firebar
Type: all-weather interceptor.
Specifications: length 71ft (21.65m); span 42ft 6in (12.95m); height, 12ft 11in (3.95m); weight (maximum take-off), 35,000lb (15,875kg).
Max speed: Mach 1.1.
Service ceiling: 55,000ft (16,750km).
Range: (tactical radius at high altitude) approx. 500nm (925km).
Armament: two AA-3 Anab missiles.
Powerplants: two Tumanski R-11 turbojets, each rated at 8,600lb (3,910kg) dry thrust, 13,120lb (5,960kg) with afterburning.

Brewer is probably the Soviet aircraft that many export customers wanted, but were not allowed to order. Like the British Buccaneer, bomber versions of the Yak-28 were deemed sufficiently "offensive" for their export to be viewed with disfavour by the Government which had originally ordered the type.

The prototype Yak-28 flew in 1960, and service deliveries began in 1963-4. Brewer-A, -B and -C were light bombers fitted with a ventral radome and a small weapons bay capable of carrying a pair of 500kg bombs or a nuclear weapon. Brewer-C was developed in parallel with the Yak-28P interceptor, and, like the latter, has a stretched fuselage and longer engine nacelles.

By the early 1980s Brewer-A, -B and -C were being rapidly phased out as the numbers of Su-24 Fencer strike aircraft continued to rise. Some 50 or so may be retained by the Soviet Air Force for use in secondary areas where the capabilities of the Su-24 are not yet required or could create political problems. As a front-line strike aircraft, Brewer's career is over. Brewer-D remains in Soviet service in the tactical reconnaissance role, but may eventually be supplanted by a dedicated version of the Su-24.

Although only 20-40 Brewer-E were in service in early 1982, the importance of this sub-type should not be underestimated. These aircraft are configured for ECM escort, having a active jamming system built into the bomb bay, and no ventral radar installation. In a Central Front conflict these aircraft would accompany Warsaw Pact strike formations, screening the latter by means of active jamming and the use of chaff rockets fired from pod launchers mounted under the outer section of the wing.

Firebar is the Yak-28P interceptor version of the basic design, and is similar in general configuration to the Brewer-C strike version. A large radome containing an I/J band Skip Spin radar replaces the glazed nose of the earlier versions, and an armament of two AA-3 Anab missiles is carried. The Yak-28P entered service in the mid-1960s. Late production aircraft have a longer

pattern of radome, which has been retrofitted to most of the fleet of around 200 examples. This was probably fitted to reduce drag and improve radome resistance to rain erosion. These interceptors are probably being phased out.

For training purposes, the Yak-28U Maestro was devised. This has a solid nose incorporating a second cockpit in place of the normal glazed section.

Yakovlev Yak-36 Forger

Data for Forger-A
Type: ship-based Vtol fighter.
Specifications: 50ft (15.3m); span, 24ft (7.3m); height, 14ft 4in (4.37m); weight (maximum take-off), 25,500lb (11,500kg).
Max speed: Mach 1.1.
Service ceiling: 39,000ft (12,000m).
Range: (hi-lo-hi tactical radius) 200nm (370km).
Armament: four underwing hardpoints capable of carrying a total of 3,000lb (1,300kg) of stores.
Powerplants: see text.

There has been little sign of evolution in the design of this first operational Soviet Vtol aircraft since the first examples went to sea aboard the carrier *Kiev* in 1976. Only one variant has been reported—the two-seat Forger-B trainer—and it is hard to escape the conclusion that the Yak-36 is an interim design intended to give Soviet Naval Aviation pilots "hands-on" experience of Vtol operations while more advanced designs are being developed and cleared for service. Evidence for the semi-experimental nature of the Yak-36 came in the late 1970s, when the Soviet Union made no attempt to offer the aircraft to India to meet the Indian Navy's requirement for a Sea Hawk replacement.

The avionics systems seem relatively simple. There are no signs of a sophisticated fire-control system, and US intelligence sources report having seen only cannon and unguided-rocket firings. Like Harrier, Forger may be fitted with heat-seeking missiles for air-to-air use.

Unlike Harrier and AV-8B, it cannot use its vectored-thrust powerplant for "viffing" (Vectoring in forward flight) operations, so will lack the high manoeuvrability of the Western V/Stol designs.

Like the 1960s VFW 1262, Forger uses a mixture of vertically-mounted lift and vectored-thrust cruise engines. It differs from the German design in having much less sophisticated powerplants and a less satisfactory configuration. The main engine is thought to be a single-shaft unreheated turbojet of around 18,000lb (8,200kg) thrust. This may even be a version of the Lyulka AL-21 afterburning turbojet fitted to the Su-17, -20 and -22. Two lift jets installed ahead of the wing are products of the Koliesov bureau, with a thrust of around 9,000lb (4,100kg) each.

The Pegasus engine used by Harrier and the Av-8B are two-shaft designs in which the high and low-pressure sections rotate in opposite directions, minimising gyroscopic effects. Having only a single shaft, and thus a single rotating mass, the Soviet engine has significant effects on low-speed handling, so take-off and landing manoeuvres are carried out under the rigid control of a fully-automatic system.

Like Harrier and the AV-8B, Forger uses "puffer" jets for attitude control, the wingtips having been thickened to house the roll-control nozzles. Unlike the Western aircraft, the Yakovlev design uses reaction controls only for yaw and roll. Control in pitch is obtained by selective throttling of the engines. Conventional elevators are fitted to the horizontal tailplane to improve the latter's low-speed effectiveness.

The basic configuration selected for Forger has one serious weakness. The use of forward-mounted lift jets coupled with single rearward set of vectoring nozzles rules out the use of a short take-off run. Stability and safety in this mode would be unacceptable, so the Soviet Navy has effectively denied itself the increase in take-off weight and thus payload weight which results from Stol operation.

Transition from vertical to horizontal flight and back again are lengthy procedures. More than one and half minutes can elapse between the aircraft leaving the deck and the nozzles being pointed fully rearwards. This long period of operation at full or near-full engine thrust must make inroads on the internal fuel capacity.

Right: Yak-36 features:
1. *Strakes fitted after initial deployment, probably to reduce re-ingestion of hot gas from the main nozzles by the lift engines.*
2. *GSh-23 gun pods.*
3. *Door for lift engine intakes.*
4. *Efflux from angled (10° aft) lift engines.*
5. *Range of travel on nozzles of main engine.*
6. *Folding wingtips.*
7. *Forger on the lift of a Kiev-class carrier.*

Left: Forger-B must be one of the ugliest trainers ever devised, but plays a vital role aboard Kiev-class carriers.

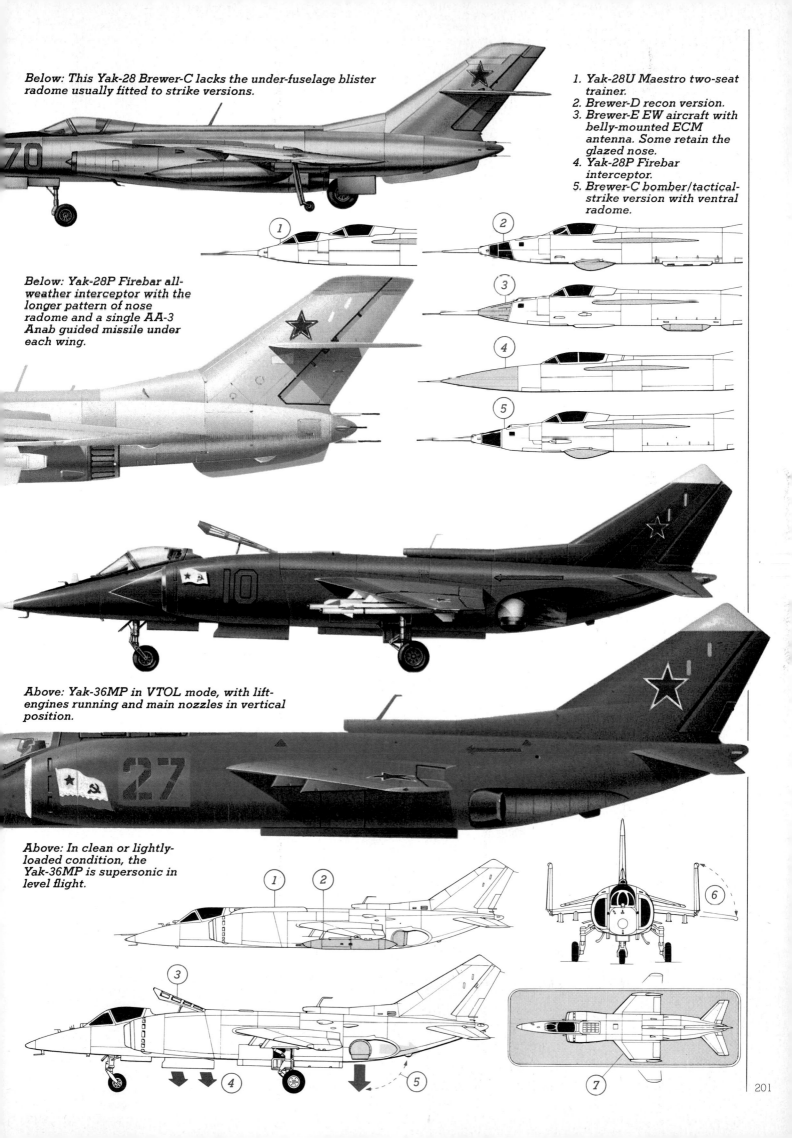

Below: This Yak-28 Brewer-C lacks the under-fuselage blister radome usually fitted to strike versions.

1. Yak-28U Maestro two-seat trainer.
2. Brewer-D recon version.
3. Brewer-E EW aircraft with belly-mounted ECM antenna. Some retain the glazed nose.
4. Yak-28P Firebar interceptor.
5. Brewer-C bomber/tactical-strike version with ventral radome.

Below: Yak-28P Firebar all-weather interceptor with the longer pattern of nose radome and a single AA-3 Anab guided missile under each wing.

Above: Yak-36MP in VTOL mode, with lift-engines running and main nozzles in vertical position.

Above: In clean or lightly-loaded condition, the Yak-36MP is supersonic in level flight.

Glossary

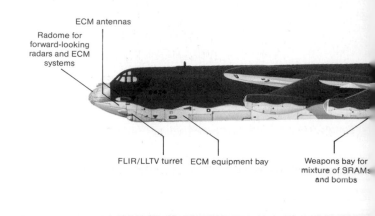

Radome for forward-looking radars and ECM systems

ECM antennas

FLIR/LLTV turret ECM equipment bay ECM equipment bay

Weapons bay for mixture of SRAMs and bombs

AA—	US designation for Soviet air-to-air missiles.
AAA	Anti-aircraft artillery.
Active	Weapon or sensor which emits radio, radar, laser or other energy.
AGM—	US designation for air-to ground missiles.
AIM—	US designation for air-to-air missiles.
AFB	Air Force Base.
Afterburner	Device for boosting the thrust of turbojet or turbofan engines by burning additional fuel in the engine efflux.
ALE—	US designation for airborne chaff/flare dispensers. Equipment of this type is used to launch packages of radar-reflecting chaff, high-intensity flares capable of decoying heat-seeking missiles, or even tiny active jammers.
ALQ—	US designation for airborne active ECM equipment.
ALR—	One of the standard US designations for airborne ESM receivers.
Anhedral	Downward slope of a wing from root to tip.
APG—	US designation for airborne fire-control radar.
APQ—	US designation for airborne multipurpose or special-purpose radar.
APR	One of the standard US designations for airborne ESM receivers.
APS—	US designation for airborne surveillance radar.
APU—	Auxiliary power unit—used to supply electrical and hydraulic power before the aircraft's engines are running, to supplement the output of the normal engine-driven generators.
AQS—	US designation for airborne sonar equipment.
ARC—	US designation for airborne sonar equipment.
ASM—	US designation for Soviet air-to-surface missiles
ASQ—	US designation for MAD sensor equipment.
ASW	Anti-submarine warfare.
AWG—	US designation for airborne fire-control radar
Canard	Fixed or movable foreplane located ahead of the main wing
CCV	Control-configured vehicle
Chaff	Thin strips of aluminium foil or aluminised fibres. If matched in length to the wavelength of the hostile radar, and scattered in large numbers, these will return a powerful echo tending to swamp the return from the aircraft being protected.
CAS	Close air support—operations in support of front-line ground forces

COD	Carrier on-board delivery. The term is usually applied to fixed-wing cargo-carrying aircraft capable of landing on an aircraft carrier.
COIN	Counter-insurgency—for use against lightly-armed or unsophisticated opposition.
CRT	Cathode-ray tube—an electronic screen similar to that of the TV set and used to display alpha-numeric characters and/or imagery
CW	Continuous wave; radio-radar term describing a transmission which is not pulsed.
Derated	Deliberately limited to less than maximum potential output—a term often applied to engines.
Dihedral	Upward slope of a wing from root to tip
DME	Distance-Measuring Equipment (radio-navigation aid which operates in conjunction with VOR).
ECM	Electronic countermeasures—technology used to confuse or counteract hostile radars or communications systems.
EHP	Equivalent horsepower. Power rating of a turboprop which takes into account the residual thrust of the exhaust.
ELINT	Electronic intelligence-gathering, the technique of sampling and recording radio, radar and other signals from hostile weapons systems and communications equipment.

IR suppressor

Low radar-signature tail rotor

"Anti'glint" canopy

Steerable FLIR/LLTV turret

Steerable cannon

Armoured cockpit Hellfire missile

Stub wing

VHF/UHF antennas

Radar warning receiver antenna

VOR antenna

Radar warning rec antenna

Head-up display

VHF antenna

IFF antenna

Wing fence

Fuel jettison pipe

Pitot probe

Optical ports for laser ranger and marked-target seeker

Trough for cannon muzzle Blow-in doors Fuel drop tank

TACAN antenna buried in wingtip

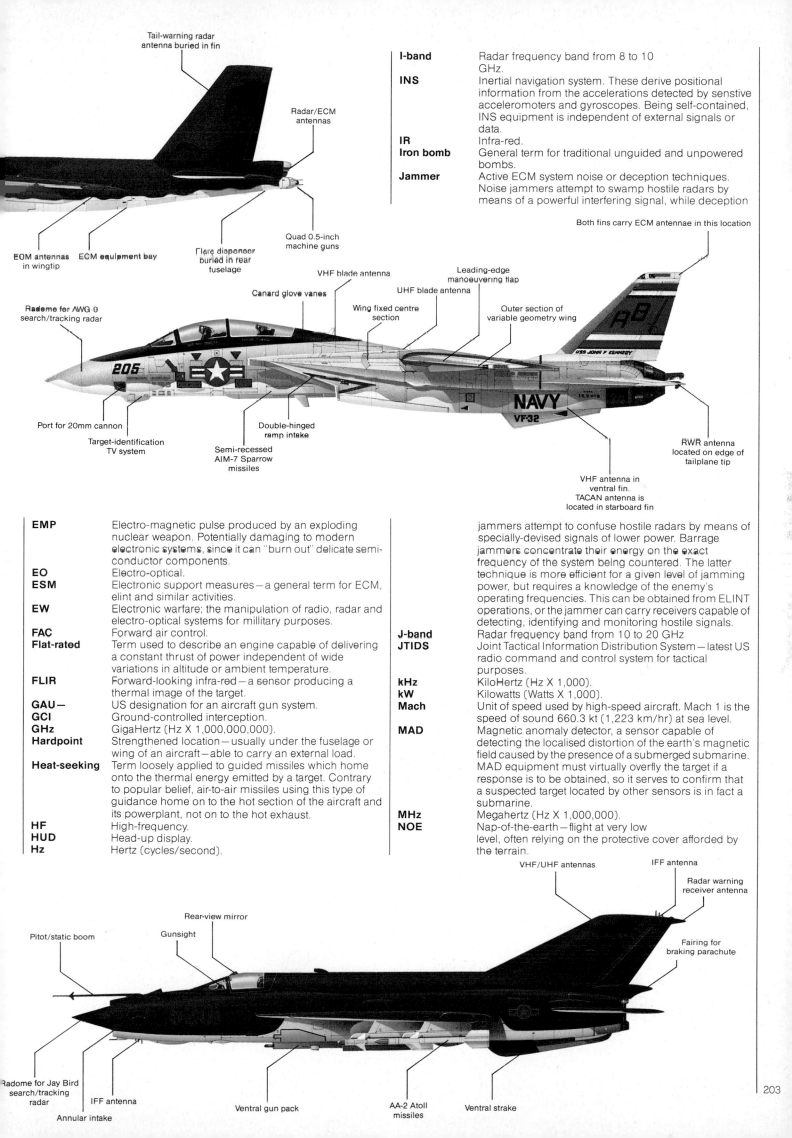

Tail-warning radar antenna buried in fin

Radar/ECM antennas

EOM antennas in wingtip

ECM equipment bay

Flare dispenser buried in rear fuselage

Quad 0.5-inch machine guns

I-band — Radar frequency band from 8 to 10 GHz.

INS — Inertial navigation system. These derive positional information from the accelerations detected by senstive accelerometers and gyroscopes. Being self-contained, INS equipment is independent of external signals or data.

IR — Infra-red.

Iron bomb — General term for traditional unguided and unpowered bombs.

Jammer — Active ECM system noise or deception techniques. Noise jammers attempt to swamp hostile radars by means of a powerful interfering signal, while deception

Both fins carry ECM antennae in this location

VHF blade antenna

Canard glove vanes

Radome for AWG-9 search/tracking radar

Leading-edge manoeuvering flap

UHF blade antenna

Wing fixed centre section

Outer section of variable geometry wing

Port for 20mm cannon

Target-identification TV system

Double-hinged ramp intake

Semi-recessed AIM-7 Sparrow missiles

RWR antenna located on edge of tailplane tip

VHF antenna in ventral fin. TACAN antenna is located in starboard fin

USS JOHN F KENNEDY

NAVY VF-32

EMP — Electro-magnetic pulse produced by an exploding nuclear weapon. Potentially damaging to modern electronic systems, since it can "burn out" delicate semi-conductor components.

EO — Electro-optical.

ESM — Electronic support measures — a general term for ECM, elint and similar activities.

EW — Electronic warfare; the manipulation of radio, radar and electro-optical systems for millitary purposes.

FAC — Forward air control.

Flat-rated — Term used to describe an engine capable of delivering a constant thrust of power independent of wide variations in altitude or ambient temperature.

FLIR — Forward-looking infra-red — a sensor producing a thermal image of the target.

GAU— — US designation for an aircraft gun system.

GCI — Ground-controlled interception.

GHz — GigaHertz (Hz X 1,000,000,000).

Hardpoint — Strengthened location — usually under the fuselage or wing of an aircraft — able to carry an external load.

Heat-seeking — Term loosely applied to guided missiles which home onto the thermal energy emitted by a target. Contrary to popular belief, air-to-air missiles using this type of guidance home on to the hot section of the aircraft and its powerplant, not on to the hot exhaust.

HF — High-frequency.

HUD — Head-up display.

Hz — Hertz (cycles/second).

jammers attempt to confuse hostile radars by means of specially-devised signals of lower power. Barrage jammers concentrate their energy on the exact frequency of the system being countered. The latter technique is more efficient for a given level of jamming power, but requires a knowledge of the enemy's operating frequencies. This can be obtained from ELINT operations, or the jammer can carry receivers capable of detecting, identifying and monitoring hostile signals.

J-band — Radar frequency band from 10 to 20 GHz

JTIDS — Joint Tactical Information Distribution System — latest US radio command and control system for tactical purposes.

kHz — KiloHertz (Hz X 1,000).

kW — Kilowatts (Watts X 1,000).

Mach — Unit of speed used by high-speed aircraft. Mach 1 is the speed of sound 660.3 kt (1,223 km/hr) at sea level.

MAD — Magnetic anomaly detector, a sensor capable of detecting the localised distortion of the earth's magnetic field caused by the presence of a submerged submarine. MAD equipment must virtually overfly the target if a response is to be obtained, so it serves to confirm that a suspected target located by other sensors is in fact a submarine.

MHz — Megahertz (Hz X 1,000,000).

NOE — Nap-of-the-earth — flight at very low level, often relying on the protective cover afforded by the terrain.

VHF/UHF antennas

IFF antenna

Radar warning receiver antenna

Rear-view mirror

Pitot/static boom

Gunsight

Fairing for braking parachute

Radome for Jay Bird search/tracking radar

IFF antenna

Annular intake

Ventral gun pack

AA-2 Atoll missiles

Ventral strake

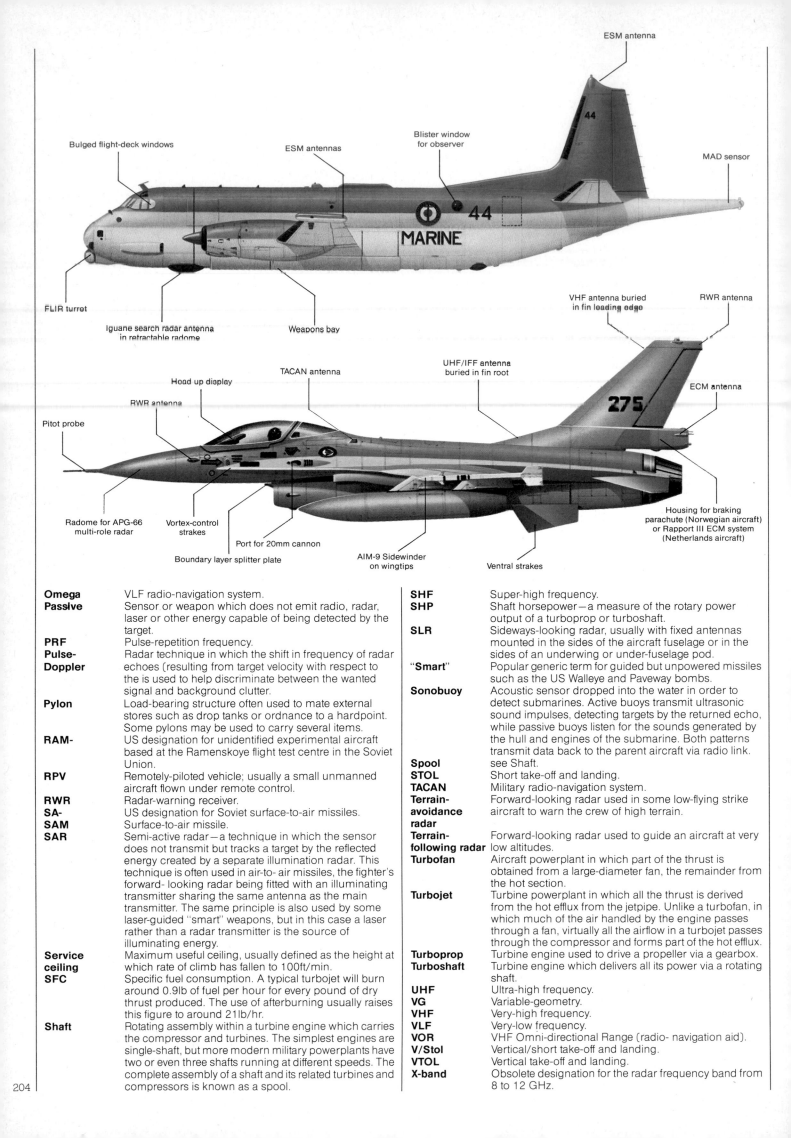

Bulged flight-deck windows

ESM antennas

Blister window
for observer

ESM antenna

44

MAD sensor

MARINE

FLIR turret

Iguane search radar antenna
in retractable radome

Weapons bay

VHF antenna buried
in fin loading edge

RWR antenna

TACAN antenna

Head up display

RWR antenna

UHF/IFF antenna
buried in fin root

ECM antenna

275

Pitot probe

Radome for APG-66
multi-role radar

Vortex-control
strakes

Port for 20mm cannon

Boundary layer splitter plate

AIM-9 Sidewinder
on wingtips

Ventral strakes

Housing for braking
parachute (Norwegian aircraft)
or Rapport III ECM system
(Netherlands aircraft)

Omega	VLF radio-navigation system.
Passive	Sensor or weapon which does not emit radio, radar, laser or other energy capable of being detected by the target.
PRF	Pulse-repetition frequency.
Pulse-Doppler	Radar technique in which the shift in frequency of radar echoes (resulting from target velocity with respect to the is used to help discriminate between the wanted signal and background clutter.
Pylon	Load-bearing structure often used to mate external stores such as drop tanks or ordnance to a hardpoint. Some pylons may be used to carry several items.
RAM-	US designation for unidentified experimental aircraft based at the Ramenskoye flight test centre in the Soviet Union.
RPV	Remotely-piloted vehicle; usually a small unmanned aircraft flown under remote control.
RWR	Radar-warning receiver.
SA-	US designation for Soviet surface-to-air missiles.
SAM	Surface-to-air missile.
SAR	Semi-active radar—a technique in which the sensor does not transmit but tracks a target by the reflected energy created by a separate illumination radar. This technique is often used in air-to- air missiles, the fighter's forward- looking radar being fitted with an illuminating transmitter sharing the same antenna as the main transmitter. The same principle is also used by some laser-guided ''smart'' weapons, but in this case a laser rather than a radar transmitter is the source of illuminating energy.
Service ceiling	Maximum useful ceiling, usually defined as the height at which rate of climb has fallen to 100ft/min.
SFC	Specific fuel consumption. A typical turbojet will burn around 0.9lb of fuel per hour for every pound of dry thrust produced. The use of afterburning usually raises this figure to around 21lb/hr.
Shaft	Rotating assembly within a turbine engine which carries the compressor and turbines. The simplest engines are single-shaft, but more modern military powerplants have two or even three shafts running at different speeds. The complete assembly of a shaft and its related turbines and compressors is known as a spool.
SHF	Super-high frequency.
SHP	Shaft horsepower—a measure of the rotary power output of a turboprop or turboshaft.
SLR	Sideways-looking radar, usually with fixed antennas mounted in the sides of the aircraft fuselage or in the sides of an underwing or under-fuselage pod.
''Smart''	Popular generic term for guided but unpowered missiles such as the US Walleye and Paveway bombs.
Sonobuoy	Acoustic sensor dropped into the water in order to detect submarines. Active buoys transmit ultrasonic sound impulses, detecting targets by the returned echo, while passive buoys listen for the sounds generated by the hull and engines of the submarine. Both patterns transmit data back to the parent aircraft via radio link.
Spool	see Shaft.
STOL	Short take-off and landing.
TACAN	Military radio-navigation system.
Terrain-avoidance radar	Forward-looking radar used in some low-flying strike aircraft to warn the crew of high terrain.
Terrain-following radar	Forward-looking radar used to guide an aircraft at very low altitudes.
Turbofan	Aircraft powerplant in which part of the thrust is obtained from a large-diameter fan, the remainder from the hot section.
Turbojet	Turbine powerplant in which all the thrust is derived from the hot efflux from the jetpipe. Unlike a turbofan, in which much of the air handled by the engine passes through a fan, virtually all the airflow in a turbojet passes through the compressor and forms part of the hot efflux.
Turboprop	Turbine engine used to drive a propeller via a gearbox.
Turboshaft	Turbine engine which delivers all its power via a rotating shaft.
UHF	Ultra-high frequency.
VG	Variable-geometry.
VHF	Very-high frequency.
VLF	Very-low frequency.
VOR	VHF Omni-directional Range (radio- navigation aid).
V/Stol	Vertical/short take-off and landing.
VTOL	Vertical take-off and landing.
X-band	Obsolete designation for the radar frequency band from 8 to 12 GHz.

Index

207

Picture Credits

The publishers wish to thank the following organisations and individuals who have supplied photographs for this book. Photographs have been credited by page number.
Page 10: Top, Italian Air Force; bottom, Aeritalia. **12:** Aermacchi. **14:** British MoD. **15:** Aermacchi. **16:** Aérospatiale. **23:** Aérospatiale. **24:** US Navy. **25:** Agusta. **26:** Tass. **29:** Top, Tass; bottom, Bell Helicopters. **3** Bell Helicopters. **32:** Bell Helicopters. **35:** Top, left and right: Bell Helicopters; bottom, Tass. **36:** Boeing. **37:** Boeing. **39:** Top, US DoD; Bottom, Boeing. **40:** Top two, USAF; centre, AMD-BA; bottom, USAF. **41:** USAF. **42:** Top and bottom, Boeing Vertol. **44:** British Aerospace. **45:** AMD-BA. **46:** Top, British Aerospace; bottom, Royal Naval Air Station, Yeovilton. **47:** NATO HQ. **48:** British Aerospace. **54:** CASA. **55:** Cessna. **56:** USAF. **57:** Breguet Aviation. **59:** SIRPA Air. **60:** Top, SIRPA Air; bottom, BIAF. **61:** Dassault-Breguet. **62:** SIRPA Air. **63:** AMD—BA. **65:** Armée de L'Air. **67:** Dassault-Breguet. **68:** USAF. **69:** Top, Royal Australian Air Force; bottom, De Havilland Canada. **70:** British Aerospace. **73:** USAF. **74:** FMA. **75:** FMA. **78:** General Dynamics. **80:** USAF. **82:** Grumman. **83:** Grumman. **84:** Top, Grumman; bottom, US Navy. **84:** Grumman. **85:** US Navy. **88:** Grumman. **89:** Grumman. **90:** British MoD. **91:** Top, British MoD; bottom, British Aerospace. **92:** Royal Naval Air Station, Yeovilton. **93:** British Aerospace. **102:** Top and bottom, US Navy. **103:** US DoD. **105:** BIAF. **108:** Tass. **109:** Top and bottom, US Navy. **112:** Italian Air Force. **114:** US Navy. **117:** Lockheed. **119:** USAF. **120:** USAF. **121:** USAF. **122:** Messerschmitt Bolkow Blohm. **123:** Messerschmitt Bolkow Blohm. **126:** USAF. **130:** McDonnell Douglas. **136:** British MoD. **137:** Tass. **138:** Top, Tass; bottom, P. Heinemann. **139:** US DoD. **140:** Top, US DoD; bottom, Tass. **141:** Top and bottom, British MoD. **145:** Top and bottom, British MoD. **147:** Top, US Navy; bottom (two), Mike Jerram. **151:** US Navy. **152:** PRC Defence Ministry. **153:** Chinese Embassy, USA. **154:** USAF. **156:** British Aerospace. **157:** British Aerospace. **159:** Top and bottom, USAF. **160:** USAF. **161:** Rockwell International. **163:** Saab-Scania. **164:** Saab—Scania. **166:** British Aerospace. **167:** British Aerospace. **169:** Shin Meiwa. **170:** Short Bros. **171:** SIAI Marchetti (via Flight International). **172:** US DoD. **173:** US DoD. **174:** Sikorsky. **175:** US DoD. **176:** Top, Sikorsky; bottom, British MoD. **178:** British MoD. **182:** via Pilot Press. **184:** Rolls Royce. **186:** Top, Interinfo; bottom, US Navy. **188:** Royal Swedish Air Force. **190:** US Navy. **191:** E and TV Films. **192:** Vought. **193:** Top, British Aerospace; bottom, Aéronautics. **194:** USAF. **195:** Top and bottom, Vought. **197:** Westland. **198:** Westland. **199:** British MoD. **200:** US DoD.

PRINTED IN BELGIUM BY
proost
INTERNATIONAL BOOK PRODUCTION